A HANDBOOK OF CONTEMPORARY THEOLOGY

A
BRIDGEPOINT
BOOK

BridgePoint,
the academic
imprint of
Victor Books, is
your connection
for the best in
serious reading
that integrates
the passion of
the heart with
the scholarship
of the mind.

A
HANDBOOK
C OF ONTEMPORARY
THEOLOGY

A
BRIDGEPOINT
BOOK

Copyediting: Robert N. Hosack
Cover Design: Scott Rattray

Library of Congress Cataloging-in-Publication Data

Smith, David L. (David Lorne)
    A handbook of contemporary theology / by David L. Smith.
      p.   cm.
    Includes bibliographical references and index.
    ISBN 0-89693-699-6
    1. Theology—20th century—Handbooks, manuals, etc. I. Title.
    BT28.S55   1992
    230'.09'04—dc20   91-46801
                                          CIP

BridgePoint is the academic imprint of Victor Books.
© *1992 by SP Publications, Inc. All rights reserved. Printed in the United States of America.*

1 2 3 4 5 6 7 8 9 10 Printing/Year 96 95 94 93 92

CONTENTS

To Gail
"He who finds a wife finds what is good
and receives favor from the Lord" (Prov. 18:22).

Preface

"Of making many books there is no end," says the Preacher (Ecc. 12:12), and rightly so. But he never envisioned how quickly they could go out of print, or become outdated. This is especially so when one is talking about contemporary theology. "Contemporary" does not last a very long time.

The making of this book arose from necessity. I was asked to teach a class on contemporary theological trends, and so I began to cast about for a text that would provide an overview of the varying modern theologies today from an evangelical perspective. I could find nothing in print that would do the job. There were some excellent materials from the 1970s, such as Harvey Conn's *Contemporary World Theology: A Layman's Guidebook* (Presbyterian and Reformed Publishing, 1973) and Gundry and Johnson's *Tensions in Contemporary Theology*, second edition (Baker Book House, 1976), but they had already gone out of print. And they were missing some of the more recent theologies, those that have come on the scene in the 1980s. Necessity being the mother of invention, you find the work before you.

I have attempted to keep the work truly contemporary and, as a result, some of the materials which may have appeared in earlier works of a similar nature have been either dropped completely or relegated to a historical section of a chapter as the forebear of a more recent movement (e.g., "God is dead" theology in relation to secular theology). Some of the more recent theologies have been included, and I have tried to keep current to the time of writing; you will accordingly find New Age theology and creation spirituality. If any modern theology has been omitted, it is entirely my fault and no one else's.

The book is divided into three sections. The first consists of the foundational theologies in vogue today, those on which the overwhelming bulk of our Christian denominations are founded. In the second section, one will find the more esoteric theologies, which are praised by some and damned by others; some will be lasting, while others are a "flash in the pan." The final section is a brief appendix of Third World theological directions. I have confined this section to Asia and Africa, omitting South America because the main direction of that continent is liberationism, which is extensively covered in its own chapter.

Each chapter consists of a basic definition or description of the theology under examination, its historical basis or background, a description (from primary sources as much as possible) of its doctrinal tenets, and an evaluation of those tenets from an evangelical viewpoint. A brief bibliography of works in print for further study is found at the end of the book. I recognize that this text provides a basic overview of these theologies and the reader is encouraged to use it as an introduction, going further to individual works of detail.

I have to thank my Contemporary Theological Trends class (Winter 1991) at Winnipeg (now Providence) Theological Seminary, whose research and papers on various aspects of contemporary theologies have proved very helpful in writing this text. They include: Daryl Arendt, Phil Bonk, Roy Dearing, Rhoda Dueck, Bonnie Friesen, Cindy Giesbrecht, Roland Grenier, Kerri Klassen, Judy Loewen, Wesley Penner, Clara Schnupp, Laurel Shram, Glen Siemens, and Roger Stoesz. The Seminary has also been gracious in its provision of time and technological help in the production of the manuscript and in encouragement, as have my wife and family. In the final analysis, however, *soli Deo gloria.*

DAVID L. SMITH,
August 1991.

PART ONE

Basic Contemporary Theologies

One. Fundamentalism

Fundamentalism originated in early twentieth-century North America as a movement to preserve and promote conservative, biblical Christian orthodoxy. It was a militant reaction against challenges from liberal theology, the theory of evolution, and higher critical methodology in biblical studies.

The Early Days

The term "fundamentalist" (generally credited to Curtis Laws in 1920 in the Baptist *Watchman-Examiner*) probably came as the result of the publication of a series of twelve pamphlets (1910-15) entitled *The Fundamentals*. The project was underwritten by two Los Angeles laymen, Lyman and Milton Stewart, who wanted to ensure that "every pastor, evangelist, minister, theological professor, theological student, Sunday School superintendent, YMCA and YWCA secretary in the English-speaking world" might receive these booklets in which were discussed the essential theological topics of the day.[1] Writers included noted conservative scholars and preachers such as G. Campbell Morgan (Westminster Chapel, London), Edgar Y. Mullins (Southern Baptist Seminary), James Orr (United Free Church College, Glasgow), and Benjamin B. Warfield (Princeton Seminary) to name a few. Their essays addressed what these writers saw as enemies of the Christian faith: socialism, cultic heresies, higher criticism, evolution, spiritism, and so forth. Positively, they affirmed the Virgin Birth, deity and substitutionary atonement of Christ, and the unity and plenary inspiration of Scripture. Their work was scholarly, systematic, and biblical without rancor of any sort.

Presbyterian fundamentalism. During the first quarter of the twentieth century, defenders of the Christian fundamentals became well organized and mounted an offensive against the foes of orthodoxy. They were especially aggressive within the Presbyterian and

Baptist denominations. Under their influence the General Assembly of the northern Presbyterian Church in 1910 issued a five-point doctrinal summary declaring as essential beliefs the inerrancy of the Bible, Christ's virgin birth, His substitutionary atonement on Calvary, His physical resurrection, and the sharing of His love and power through literal miracles. This declaration was reaffirmed in 1916 and in 1923.

In 1922, Harry Emerson Fosdick, a Baptist liberal theologian on the Union Seminary faculty—and an outstanding preacher—who was acting minister of New York's Old First Presbyterian Church, reacted by preaching a sermon entitled, "Shall the Fundamentalists Win?" Although the sermon was a plea for peace and toleration, it was not received in such a spirit by fundamentalists, who used the Five-Point Declaration to demand that Fosdick either become a Presbyterian and accept Presbyterian doctrine or else leave the church. After a protracted controversy, Fosdick resigned and returned to the Baptists.

The liberal Presbyterian wing was not long in effecting a counterattack. Their battlefield was the seminaries, where teaching became increasingly liberal. In 1929, for example, they were successful in ousting J. Gresham Machen from the faculty of Princeton Seminary. He, in turn, helped to found Westminster Seminary as a conservative alternative. In 1936, the increasing liberalization of the northern Presbyterian Church resulted in his departure from that denomination and the founding of a new Orthodox Presbyterian Church.

Baptist fundamentalism. The struggle was equally virulent among the major Baptist groups in North America. In 1919, William B. Riley of the Northern Baptists, Frank Norris of the Southern Baptists, and Thomas T. Shields of the Canadian Baptists, founded the World's Christian Fundamentals Association in Philadelphia. Its goal was to recapture for biblical Christianity the primary place in American religious life through literature, debates with liberals, and Bible conferences. It was joined in its endeavor by other organizations, such as the Anti-evolution League and the Bible Crusaders of America.[2] In 1923, Riley, Norris, and Shields circulated a "Call and Manifesto" to their Baptist colleagues and, as a result, the Baptist Bible Union of North America was born in Kansas in

May of 1923. Its purpose was "to give the people the fullest information respecting the ravages of Modernism in all departments of . . . denominational life."[3]

Southern Baptists, while not untouched, were the least bothered by liberalism. They had long seen themselves as the protectors and sustainers of orthodoxy. Their denomination was in the hands of a conservative leadership and they were (at this point) untroubled, for the most part, by questions of higher criticism and modern science. Consequently, they did not react very sympathetically to the carping of hyper-fundamentalists, especially those like Norris, who had an unsavory reputation for fear-mongering and divisiveness. At Memphis in 1925, the Southern Baptist Convention adopted a Confession of Faith (based on the New Hampshire Confession) which restated historic Baptist principles, along with a statement on "Science and Religion" (written by E.Y. Mullins) which promoted "free research," but railed against the dissemination of theory as scientific fact. The following year at Houston, the Convention adopted a statement by its president, George McDaniel, which accepted the Genesis account of creation and rejected "every theory, evolution or other, which teaches that man originated in, or came by way of, a lower animal ancestry."[4] These steps seemed to bring peace and harmony to Southern Baptists at large.

For Northern Baptists, it was a different story. Pluralism was exacting a frightful toll. Again, the battlegrounds were the institutions of higher learning. Newton, Crozer, and Chicago were Northern Baptist hotbeds of modernism. Some fundamentalists made efforts to secure control of the schools and the denominational bureaucracy. When they failed in their attempts, many decided to maintain purity of doctrine by separating in 1932 to form the General Association of Regular Baptist Churches (GARBC). Others stayed within the denomination, but countered by founding new, conservative colleges and seminaries such as Gordon College in Massachusetts, Eastern College and Seminary in Pennsylvania, and Northern Seminary in Illinois.

In Canada, T.T. Shields, celebrated pastor of Toronto's Jarvis Street Baptist Church, attacked modernist teaching at McMaster University, the school of the Baptist Convention of Ontario and Quebec. The result was his censure by that denomination in 1926.

Two years later, he and a large number of other dissident Baptist churches withdrew to form the Union of Regular Baptist Churches, with Toronto Baptist Seminary as their school. During this same period, a number of churches in the West also broke ranks with the Baptist Union of Western Canada over modernist teaching at their denominational school, Brandon College (in Manitoba). Many of these churches held strongly to dispensational premillennialism as promoted by Moody Bible Institute. Shields was much opposed to such eschatology and, when he roundly denounced it, many of his followers left him to found the Independent Baptist Fellowship, which held to the premillenial stance they espoused.

The advent of the Great Depression found fundamentalism in decline. The forces of theological liberalism were firmly in control of most of the major denominations. It may well be said that, by 1930, the modernist-fundamentalist controversy was over, with modernists clearly the winners.

The Emergence of Neo-Fundamentalism: The 1930s

Initially, fundamentalism was an alliance of many diverse groups all of whom were determined to preserve biblical Christianity. There were Calvinists and Arminians, those who were amillennial in their eschatology and those who were dispensational, those who were episcopal in their polity and those who were congregational. But these varied elements soon seemed predestined to fracture as a result of self-interest and intolerance of one another.

Those who had separated themselves from their denominations gradually began to look upon those who had chosen to stay and fight as "compromisers." Increasingly, they drew apart from them, seeing complete spiritual separation as essential to the maintenance of all they held precious.

There was also a crystallization in theological focus. These separatist fundamentalists[5] began to identify themselves more and more with the dispensationalism of *The Scofield Reference Bible* (1909). Included was a strong adherence to a Calvinistic, deterministic "security of the believer" which, in some cases, went to the extreme of making a public decision followed by baptism a saving sacrament which ensured one's place in heaven for eternity.

Once again, a basic area of activity was in higher education. A major contributor to the expansion of neo-fundamentalism was the development of the Bible institute. Initiated by A.B. Simpson (Missionary Training Institute, 1882) and D.L. Moody (Moody Bible Institute, 1886) some years earlier, these institutions were used by fundamentalists as an alternative to denominational colleges and seminaries. By 1930, there were more than fifty of these schools in existence. In addition to the two noted above, some of the more noteworthy were: Providence (Rhode Island) Bible Institute, Bible Institute of Los Angeles, Denver Bible Institute, Prairie Bible Institute (Alberta), and Winnipeg Bible Institute.

On the heels of the Bible schools came Christian liberal arts colleges. The major ones included Wheaton in Illinois (founded in 1857, but greatly expanded under the presidency of J. O. Buswell from 1926–40), Gordon (Mass.), and Bob Jones (first in Cleveland, Tenn. and, since 1947, in Greenville, S.C.).

The formation of the GARBC. It was largely during the 1930s that the movement developed its own denominational groupings. The General Association of Regular Baptist Churches, already mentioned, was an outgrowth of the Bible Baptist Union which became defunct in 1932. At its founding meeting, five key goals were identified:

1. An association of churches, not a convention.
2. Complete separation from and no association whatsoever with any Northern Baptist work.
3. Conformity to the London and New Hampshire Confessions of Faith.
4. The fostering of a spirit of missions among pastors.
5. Aiding churches in finding sound pastors.[6]

The GARBC constitution prevented any school or organization from having direct contact with the denomination. Each would have to make annual application for approval. In this way the GARBC could withdraw approval from any school or organization which drifted from its principles. In its early years five mission boards were approved: Baptist Mid Missions; the Association of Baptists for World Evangelism; the Fellowship of Baptists for Home Missions; Evangelical Baptist Missions; and Hiawatha Independent Baptist Missions. Two seminaries—Los Angeles and

Grand Rapids—were approved along with five colleges: Western Baptist Bible College in Oregon; Los Angeles Baptist College in California; Faith Baptist Bible College in Michigan; Cedarville College in Ohio; and Baptist Bible College in Pennsylvania.

The founding of the IFCA. In 1930, the Independent Fundamental Churches of America (IFCA) was organized out of the American Conference of Undenominational Churches. At the organizational meeting were twelve Congregationalists, three Presbyterians, one Baptist, nineteen Independents, and four nondenominational persons. The IFCA closely matched the GARBC in growth, with thirty-eight churches in 1935 and seventy-five in 1940. Among the early leaders were M.R. DeHaan, John F. Walvoord, and J.O. Buswell, Jr.

The American Baptist Association. The American Baptist Association was organized in 1925 and was based on the thought of Southern Baptist preacher J.R. Graves (1820–93). His teaching was known as "Landmarkism," for it commended a return of churches to the "old landmarks." The true church, Graves believed, is one which affirms the local church and excludes any notion of a church universal. Baptism is valid only when performed by the duly ordained pastor of a local Baptist church (by immersion, of course!); and the ordinance of the Lord's Supper must be restricted to the members of that specific local Baptist church where the ordinance is being observed. Graves also taught "the trail of blood," a succession of true churches from the New Testament church to the present day, usually a martyrs' church—always a believer's church—and, despite what name it bore, always Baptist in doctrine.[7] The American Baptist Association differs from all other Baptists in its insistence that the baptism of John the Baptist was really Christian.[8]

The Grace Brethren. The Grace Brethren was another major group, founded in 1937 as an alternative to liberalism among the Brethren as modeled in the Ashland Theological Seminary. Its key institution was Grace Theological Seminary at Winona Lake, Indiana, founded under the influence of men such as Alva McClain, Herman Hoyt and L.S. Bauman.

Fundamentalists and mass media. Fundamentalists were among the first religious practitioners to understand the importance of the mass media to church growth. In 1925, Charles E. Fuller began the "Old-Fashioned Revival Hour" on radio. It was a weekly program and, by 1942, was heard on 456 stations in Canada and the United States. His program became a model for other fundamentalist radio shows such as DeHaan's "Radio Bible Class" and Barnhouse's "Bible Study Hour." Over the years, fundamentalist schools purchased radio stations over which to air their beliefs: WMBI (Moody), Chicago; WMUU (Bob Jones), Greenville, South Carolina; and KBBI (Biola), Los Angeles, were a few of these.

In 1934, John R. Rice launched a weekly newspaper, *The Sword of the Lord*, as an adjunct to his evangelistic work. Its purpose, according to its masthead, was to be "an independent religious weekly, standing for the verbal inspiration of the Bible, the deity of Christ, His blood atonement, salvation by faith, New Testament soul winning, and the premillennial faith." Each issue further declared its opposition to "modernism, worldliness, and formalism." By 1944, it had more than 30,000 subscribers and, by 1956, a circulation of more than 100,000.

The American Council of Christian Churches. In September of 1941, the American Council of Christian Churches (ACCC) was founded through the efforts of the Bible Presbyterian and the Bible Protestant Churches. It was led by Carl McIntire, pastor of the Bible Presbyterian Church in Collingswood, New Jersey. Its purpose was to counter the Federal Council of Churches' claim to speak on behalf of all Protestants; no church with ties of any sort to the Federal Council was eligible for membership.[9]

Seven years later, McIntire founded the International Council of Christian Churches (ICCC) to oppose the World Council of Churches. That same year, after the First Assembly of the World Council, and after the First Plenary Congress of the ICCC, he wrote a diatribe against the former entitled *The Modern Tower of Babel* and, after its Second Assembly in 1954, *Servants of Apostasy*. His deep-seated and loudly proclaimed conviction was that its "blatant and blasphemous unbelief should be known in all the churches of the world."[10]

Initially, the ACCC and ICCC were supported by both the

GARBC and the IFCA. Interestingly, both saw fit to withdraw their support because of McIntire's pugnacious leadership style and, in 1970, the ACCC rejected his leadership amidst a debacle of charges and countercharges.

The Conservative Baptist Association. In spite of the departure of many fundamentalists to form the GARBC, the Northern Baptist Convention had remained plagued by fighting between conservatives and modernists. In 1943, Northern Baptist fundamentalists organized the Conservative Baptist Foreign Missions Society to provide an avenue for the sending and support of conservative missionaries overseas. Requests were made to the Convention to recognize the society as an official Northern Baptist agency. When it became apparent that the Convention would not do so, a large number of churches split away in 1947 to form the Conservative Baptist Association of America. In 1950, the new denomination was made complete with the addition of the Conservative Baptist Home Missions Society.[11]

Bible Baptist Fellowship. The birth of the Bible Baptist Fellowship (BBF) on May 22, 1950 has been termed "one of the most important events in the history of fundamentalism."[12] It was formed as the result of a split in Frank Norris' World Baptist Fellowship under the leadership of men such as G. Beauchamp Vick, John Rawlings, Wendell Zimmerman, and W.E. Dowell. That same year also saw the founding of the *Baptist Bible Tribune* as the official publication of the BBF and of the Baptist Bible College in Springfield, Missouri, as its official school.

The BBF explained its purposes as follows:

Our faith and practice is the historic Baptist faith and practice. We believe in an infallible Bible, in the virgin birth, in the substitutionary death of the Savior, in His physical resurrection, in His physical ascension, in His literal, premillennial return to the earth. We believe that the fundamental basis for the fellowship of apostolic churches was not educational but missionary. We believe in every kind and form of evangelism which is effective in bringing men and women to Christ. We are in every practical way against the Modernism now rampant in the Northern and Southern Baptist Conventions. For that we have no apology.[13]

The BBF grew rapidly. It has been noted especially for the planting and development of numerous aggressive and evangelistic "mega-churches," such as Akron Baptist Temple (Ohio); Temple Baptist Church (Detroit); Landmark Baptist Temple (Cincinnati); Indianapolis Baptist Temple (Indiana); and Thomas Road Baptist Church (Lynchburg, Virginia). There are presently close to 4,000 churches in the BBF, and it has become the largest fundamentalist denomination on the continent.

Contemporary fundamentalism. During the 1970s and 1980s, the fundamentalist movement grew rapidly as some of its leadership became caught up in the principles of church planting and church growth. Under the leadership of John R. Rice and the *Sword of the Lord*, and Christian administrators and educators like Elmer Towns who wrote extensively on the "mega-churches" and isolated the principles used by their founders, large numbers of pastors were motivated to put these principles into operation. They worked well for many, and every major city in the United States soon had one or more of these churches which were aggressively evangelistic in their thrust and whose membership numbered in the thousands. Although fundamentalists have not been alone in this endeavor (Southern Baptists, Pentecostals, and charismatics were also active), they generally hold an overwhelming number of the 100 largest churches in an annual poll conducted by *Christian Life* magazine.

One of the methods used in spreading their doctrinal views and life-style has been continued use of media. Fundamentalist publishing houses, magazines, and papers abound. They have continued to make excellent use of radio, and recommend to those wishing to build a large church that a daily radio program is almost a "must."[14] Even more important, fundamentalists were quick to recognize the impact of television and to utilize it for evangelism and publicity purposes. During the last two decades, Falwell's "Old-Time Gospel Hour" has been his chief vehicle for spreading his philosophy outside of the Lynchburg (Va.) area, and was critical to his development of the "Moral Majority," a conservative political lobby.

Cultural Aspects of Fundamentalism

Because fundamentalism involves well over ten million persons in North America, it is a social movement of some consequence. As such, it has certain aspects which are common to most of its members. It may be helpful to examine some of fundamentalism's peculiarities.

Cultural isolation. The term "fundamentalist," while quickly identified with a secondary religious separation (that is, separation from other Christians who did not see their faith in the same absolute terms), soon became identified with cultural separation as well. Fundamentalists were often caricatured for their objections to smoking, drinking, chewing (tobacco), movies, card-playing, dancing, lodges, and coed swimming. By the 1950s, they tended to identify their biblical, moral, and cultural values as the historic American cultural values. In fact, they saw themselves as the preservers and restorers of these values in American society. Consequently, they were continually battling new trends and styles in culture such as short hair, slacks, and cosmetics for women, along with modern ministry trends, such as women preachers and deacons.[15]

During the 1960s and 1970s, in fact, dress for many fundamentalists became a virtual test of faith. "In their reaction to the hippie culture, some pastors preached constantly on long hair, sideburns, beards, flare-bottomed pants, high-heeled boots, wire-rimmed glasses, silk shirts, and so on."[16]

Much of this cultural isolation is rooted in the desire for personal holiness, which has frequently led fundamentalists to a highly individualized faith. Unlike traditional Christians through the ages, (ontological) community has a very minor (if any) role in fundamentalist life. Fundamentalists are very much aware that "God has no grandchildren." "So it comes down to an individual search and a personal reception of grace."[17] One participates in the body of Christ through regeneration, as one separates from the world. As one progresses in the faith, an additional separation takes place both from sin and from those apostates who term themselves Christians, but who are not firm on the fundamentals of the faith.[18]

This secondary separation may be seen in the development of separate, voluntary church associations which have tough standards excluding those with "modernist" tendencies. Another evidence is the development of independent, private Christian schools for the children of fundamentalists. These schools foster education from kindergarten all the way to postgraduate levels of the university.

Political aggressiveness. Just as they have been conservative and narrowly focused in their theology, so fundamentalists have tended to be conservative and narrowly focused politically. The turbulent sixties and early seventies led many fundamentalists to put minor differences aside in order to face common enemies such as secularism, sexual perversion, political liberalism, socialism, communism, and the like. They majored on a return to biblical practice and traditional patriotic Americanism (which were virtually identical in their eyes!). They decided that the best way to achieve their agenda was through political activism. Thus was born what is now known in the United States as the "Christian Right."

Unlike the early decades of the century, fundamentalists who were politically active were willing to become bedfellows with anyone who espoused similar goals. Thus, Jerry Falwell, pastor of the Thomas Road Baptist Church and founder of Liberty University, both in Lynchburg, Virginia, founded the Moral Majority in the 1970s, a political action group which included evangelicals, Mormons, Roman Catholics, and anyone else who held to traditional marriage, family, and generally conservative social values.[19]

This conservative coalition campaigned for politicians who met (and usually catered to) their list of moral, political, and social criteria. As a rule, these were Republicans (although, in the deep South, there were a few conservative Democrats) at the federal level of government. They were also extremely active in registering voters who would be inclined to their views. Fundamentalists were very active (and pleased with their success) in campaigning for Ronald Reagan in 1980 and 1984, and (albeit somewhat less so) for George Bush in 1988. They saw the Republican presidency as a vindication of their striving for righteousness in the United States. Following the Reagan presidency, there was a lessening of political fervor, but—in spite of the demise of the Moral Majority in 1989—many fundamentalists are still proactive in equating their political conservatism with biblical Christianity.

Conclusions. Fundamentalism is still very much with us socially and probably always will be. During the last two decades, the movement has become more sophisticated and image conscious in publicizing its particular goals. Even though the majority of the population are not of this persuasion, there remains in them a certain nostalgic longing for "the good old days" of Christian values. In their fight to turn the United States to the right (politically and morally), fundamentalists have been aided by grateful politicians and have been rewarded by presidential appointments of conservative judges to the Supreme Court. Thus, fundamentalists have been able to influence society beyond their proportional size. And, for whatever small degree of reclamation of society may have taken place, the great proportion of praise must be given to fundamentalists for their unrelenting advocacy of strict biblical ethical ideals.

Theological Aspects of Fundamentalism

Fundamentalism had its beginnings as a theological movement. As such, it is reasonable to suppose that it therefore has a body of doctrine which can be summarized in a systematic and methodical fashion. It has been usual to teach that fundamentalist theology may be summed up in five basic statements:

1. the inerrancy and infallibility of the Bible;
2. the virgin birth and deity of Jesus;
3. the substitutionary Atonement;
4. the literal, physical resurrection of Jesus;
5. the literal, physical return of Christ.[20]

These points have sometimes been expanded to include others, such as the Person and work of the Holy Spirit, an historical Fall, salvation by faith, and so on. But the above five points remain the agreed bedrock of the movement.

Biblical inerrancy. Morris Ashcraft, in an evaluation of fundamentalist theology, writes:

It seems to me that fundamentalist theology is a theology of one major doctrine—the inerrancy of the biblical autographs. Whether we encounter it during the period of 1880–1925 among the older fundamentalists or in 1980 . . . the first point on which all others depend is the inerrant Bible in its original manuscripts.[21]

In this regard, fundamentalists are building on the theology of the Princeton theologians of the late nineteenth century, who crafted the statement of biblical inerrancy in reaction to the ever-encroaching modernist impulse. Charles Hodge introduced the concept of verbal inspiration in his *Systematic Theology* of 1872.[22] Benjamin Warfield added the idea of the errorlessness of the words in the original autographs, and declared that the Scriptures are absolutely inerrant in every subject on which they touch, be that biology, geology, history, psychology, philosophy, or religion.[23]

For fundamentalists, the Bible is not just the record of God's revelation; it is very revelation in and of itself. All that one knows about God and His relationship to Creation is found through Scripture. One must agree with the comment of theologian James Barr that, in fundamentalist teaching, the Bible usually is made "the supreme symbol of the faith."[24] On its inerrancy hangs the rest of one's theology, and even salvation itself: "If the Bible is not wholly true, then our assurance of salvation has no dependable and divine warrant."[25]

The deity of Christ. Many fundamentalists would argue for the deity of Christ as "the most essential fundamental of all," although its proof rests upon the acceptance of the full inspiration of Scripture.[26] The only Christ in whom one can trust is the One revealed in the pages of Holy Writ. At the same time, an ever-deepening relationship with Christ increases one's appreciation for that inerrant instrument which reveals Him.

Closely tied in here is the doctrine of the Virgin Birth of Jesus. Fundamentalists are in unanimous accord with James Orr, that "belief in the Virgin Birth of Christ is of the highest value" in substantiating Christ's deity.[27] This doctrine was particularly important because of its supernatural context, constantly under attack from liberals and modernists.

The Atonement. Fundamentalists have adopted (and heightened) the Reformation concept of Christ's death as God's punishment for human sin. While "mainline" Protestants accept a variety of theories—ransom, representative, example—fundamentalists cling to the substitutionary and penal theory (namely, that Christ took the believer's punishment on Himself).[28]

The Resurrection. An emphasis on the literal, bodily resurrection of Jesus from the tomb is an absolute essential for fundamentalists. Some Protestants may be willing to accept the idea of a spiritual resurrection, and others may see the resurrection as a mythological symbol of the triumph of good over evil, but fundamentalists hold that the literal resurrection of Jesus' body as set forth by the Gospel writers is integral to any truth claims Christianity makes. Jesus Christ is not a dead prophet like Buddha or Muhammad, but a living and present Savior.

The Second Coming. Just as a literal resurrection is fundamental, so is a literal, physical return of Jesus Christ to this earth. There are some differences of opinion as to when and how He will come. The overwhelming bulk of fundamentalists are dispensationalists (and so pretribulation rapturist and premillennial), but there are some who are posttribulation rapturist and premillennial, and a few who are postmillennial or amillennial in their eschatology. But all are agreed that Christ's return is certain.

An Evaluation of Fundamentalism
Fundamentalism has enjoyed a resurgence of vigor and popularity during the latter decades of the twentieth century. Much of the renewed vitality has without doubt been the result of a reaction against the instability and perversion of the sixties and seventies, when the "in thing" was to jettison any constants ethically and socially and "do your own thing" (as per Judges 21:25). Western society owes much to fundamentalists for promoting personal purity and for acting as somewhat of a restraining force against these excesses.

It may be said that fundamentalism has always defended the truth of Scripture. Ashcraft rightly comments:

> We are indebted to the fundamentalists . . . for keeping alive a love for the Bible and for reading it. They have preserved

many of the treasured doctrines of the faith which were often neglected. They have excelled and inspired others in evangelism and missions. They have contributed enormously in biblical scholarship. They have provided more than their proportionate share of young men and women for the ministry.[29]

Fundamentalists, further, demonstrate a fine emphasis on social outreach in the service of Christ. They have frequently done much more in the way of social ministries as a secondary concern (to the Gospel) than the "social-gospellers" have done as a primary concern. They have founded half-way houses, homes for unwed mothers, rescue missions, and so forth. Fundamentalists also have been in the forefront of the contemporary fight against abortion.

There is, unfortunately, a "downside" to fundamentalism. Since the 1920s, the movement has been rent asunder on numerous occasions; division has been—and still seems to be—the order of the day. A large part of this problem may result from its reactionary nature.

This division certainly reflects itself doctrinally. Many fundamentalists are not content with keeping separate from those who do not adhere to the five fundamentals; they tend toward elitism in all areas of belief—anyone who does not hold exactly the same position as they do is likely to be excluded as a brother or sister in Christ. One particularly factious area is eschatology. As mentioned earlier, most fundamentalists are dispensational in their theology and hold tenaciously to a premillennial, pretribulational eschatology. Anyone who holds to any other view (even other premillennial ones) is looked at with suspicion.

Nor are most fundamentalists open to fellowship with Pentecostals or charismatics. It is not unusual for the former to regard tongues as a tool of the devil and refuse any cooperation with the latter.[30]

This specter of secondary separation has kept fundamentalism from becoming all that Christ would want it to be. One must hope that those who are more moderate and tolerant will ultimately win majority leadership, thus permitting a full preoccupation with an aggressive campaign to win society for Christ instead of the frequent infighting which has tarnished the movement's name.

For Further Reading

Barr, James. *Fundamentalism*. Philadelphia: Westminster Press, 1977.

Cole, Stewart G. *The History of Fundamentalism*. Hamden, Conn.: Archon Books, 1963.

Dollar, George W. *A History of Fundamentalism in America*. Greenville, S.C.: Bob Jones University, 1973.

Falwell, Jerry. *The Fundamentalist Phenomenon*. Garden City, N.Y.: Doubleday-Galilee, 1981.

Gasper, Louis. *The Fundamentalist Movement*. The Hague, Netherlands: Mouton, 1963.

Machen, J. Gresham. *Christianity and Liberalism*. New York: Macmillan, 1923.

Marsden, George. *Fundamentalism and American Culture*. New York: Oxford University Press, 1981.

Russell, C. Allyn. *Voices of American Fundamentalism*. Philadelphia: Westminster Press, 1976.

Sandeen, Ernest R. *The Roots of Fundamentalism*. Chicago: University of Chicago Press, 1970.

Torrey, R.A. and A.C. Dixon, et al. *The Fundamentals*. 4 vols. 1917. Repr., Grand Rapids: Baker Book House, 1980.

Two. Neo-orthodoxy

The term neo-orthodox suggests a return to orthodoxy or a new orthodoxy. Whether neo-orthodoxy actually is either is debatable. It may better be said, in fact, to be a "double negative," a reaction against the liberal reaction against traditional orthodoxy. Known as neo-orthodoxy in North America, the movement in Europe was called "crisis" or "dialectical" theology.

The Beginnings of Neo-orthodoxy

Most historians view Karl Barth as the father of the neo-orthodox movement.[1] Born in Basel, Switzerland in 1886, he was the son of a conservative Reformed pastor and theologian. The first twenty years of his life were spent under conservative theological scholarship. In his early twenties, however, he embraced liberalism, albeit with some hesitation: "To the prevailing tendency of about 1910 among the younger followers of Albrecht Ritschl I attached myself with passable conviction."[2]

As a young pastor caught in the havoc of World War I, Barth found that his liberal theology had not prepared him to minister effectively to those searching for answers to the contemporary dilemma. Frustrated by this failure, he turned to the Bible and found himself overwhelmed by the message of Paul's Epistle to the Romans. It revolutionized his thinking, his preaching, and his theology. His *Romerbrief* (Epistle to the Romans) was an immediate success and led in 1921 to his appointment to the faculty at Gottingen. In 1925, he went to Munster, and in 1930 to Bonn.

In 1935 the Nazis expelled him from Germany because of his unqualified opposition to Hitler. He returned to his native Switzerland where he began a long and distinguished teaching career at the University of Basel.

Barth's theology. Barth was a prolific writer, but his magnum opus is his systematic theology, *Church Dogmatics*. Reaching some

8,000 pages at his death in 1968, it was still not completed.

Barth sought to repudiate the natural theology of liberalism. "Apart from and without Jesus Christ we can say nothing at all about God and man and their relationship one with another."[3] What is called natural theology, according to Barth, does not lead one to a knowledge of God, but to the formation of an idolatrous religion in which man himself takes God's place. "It is a feeble but defiant . . . attempt to create something which man could do, but now cannot do, or can do only because and if God Himself creates it for him: the knowledge of the truth, the knowledge of God."[4]

Even Christianity, as a religion, is pagan, seeking to remake God in the image of man. Real faith, on the other hand, is the result of God's searching for humanity. No human being may know God until He reveals Himself to that specific individual in a specific relational context, for God is "wholly Other," unknowable on the basis of human reason. Any logical postulations on the nature and Person of God can come about only "after the fact" of a personal experience with Him.

Barth operated from a "high" Christology. "Allowing for every difference in viewpoint and concept, the heavenly Father . . . and the person of Jesus of Nazareth . . . are practically and in effect identical."[5] God has revealed Himself supremely in Christ Jesus. He is the "Alpha and Omega" of theology. Through Christ the Trinity subsumed humanity into itself. Thus, Christ becomes both the revelation of the true God and of the true man.

Barth saw the supreme event of the Gospel as the election of Jesus Christ by the sovereign God. "The doctrine of election . . . is grounded in the knowledge of Jesus Christ because He is both the electing God and elected man in One."[6] As both God and man Christ becomes both the Elector and the elected. Through Him all human beings may be elected and reconciled to God. Barth's view of election and the sovereignty of God was so wide-sweeping that it tended towards universalism.

The doctrine of creation emphasized the "otherness" of God. The created order is "a proof of the mercy of God who agrees to the existence of something outside of Himself."[7]

The purpose of creation was God's desire to effect a covenant with humanity through Jesus. And He has done so, in spite of human disobedience. His means of fulfilling the covenant in view of human sin is the work of reconciliation. Jesus is the Reconciliator, the Mediator between God and man. Thus, there is a close link between reconciliation and justification. Justification is through faith alone, "the human action which makes a faithful and authentic response to the faithfulness of God."[8]

Barth termed his ideas a "theology of the Word of God." But one must not make the mistake of concluding that this term is synonymous with the Bible. Barth saw the idea of the Word of God in a three-fold sense: (1) the "Word Proclaimed"—the preaching of God's revelation; (2) the "Word Written"—the record by humans of God's revelation; and (3) the "Word Revealed"—God revealing Himself in Christ Jesus.

For Barth, the Bible was not the Word of God, but a "witness to a person, to Jesus Christ, to the whole nexus and history of reality and truth bound up in this name. . . ."[9] The human writers of the Bible "speak as fallible, erring men like ourselves."[10] How, then, does the Bible possess authority? It becomes the Word of God through the power of the Holy Spirit, which is nothing short of a miracle. Barth objected to attempts to cast the Bible as infallible and inerrant, for "every time we turn the Word of God into an infallible biblical word of man or the biblical word of man into an infallible Word of God we resist . . . the truth of the miracle that there fallible men speak the Word of God in infallible human words. . . ."[11] Barth regarded the Bible as inspired by God and completely dependable, not because it is infallible in and of itself, but because it becomes functionally infallible by allowing one to perceive the Person of Christ.

A brief evaluation of Barthian theology. Among evangelical theologians, Barth has received very mixed reviews. Some are extremely appreciative of his work, others deeply opposed to it. Part of the difficulty for evangelicals in understanding Barth's theology is that he was innovative whereas evangelicals, steeped in tradition, are generally reactive. They find it hard to comprehend why anyone would want to tamper with tradition. Barth attempted to cast the Gospel in a new language which could be understood by contemporary society.

Bernard Ramm adopts the right approach for evangelicals in suggesting that Barth should be interpreted dialectically: "The evangelical who reads Barth dialectically is just as ready to grant Barth one point as to criticize him at another. This means being very hard on Barth when he clearly drifts away from historical evangelical positions but applauding him when he scores a point."[12]

One may affirm Barth's theology for its vehement attack against liberalism, as well as his desire to emphasize the sovereignty of God and the centrality of Christ. Unfortunately, Barth's doctrine of God so stresses His transcendence as to make Him virtually inaccessible. If God is as hidden and inscrutable as he suggests, no human may know Him. Indeed, one wonders how one may know Him to the point of having any sort of faith (salvific) relationship!

Barth's doctrine of salvation is also to be faulted in that it is pointed toward universal election. At the same time, one must agree with Colin Brown, who writes, "If this line of thought brings Barth to the brink of universalism, he hesitates to take the final step."[13] While Barth refused to reject universalism outright, neither did he espouse it. The question was left open.

That Barth ascribed to the unique authority of the Scripture is unquestionable and praiseworthy. His adherence to the facticity of the Virgin Birth and the physical resurrection of Christ is commendable. But his refusal to connect the Bible directly to the Word of God is dissatisfying. His view of the Bible's becoming the Word of God through the work of the Holy Spirit and witnessing to the revelation of God within the believer is extremely subjective and deprives one of any reliable objectivity. His failure to acknowledge that revelation may be propositional in nature is also disappointing.

The Crisis Theology of Emil Brunner

Emil Brunner may be regarded as a virtual cofounder along with Barth of neo-orthodox theology. Born in Switzerland in 1889, Brunner studied at Zurich, Berlin, and Union Seminary in New York. He was appointed professor of theology at Zurich in 1924.

Brunner wrote scores of books and articles and was widely accepted in English-speaking theological circles (much more so than Barth). As a result, English-speaking people came to know neo-orthodoxy primarily through the eyes of Emil Brunner.

Brunner was first known in Anglo-American religious circles for his "crisis theology." He taught that a "crisis," or turning point, occurs when God in Christ confronts humanity. A person becomes aware of two divergent paths which may be followed—one toward God and life, and the other away from God toward death.

Brunner's theology. Like Barth, Brunner had rejected both liberalism and traditional orthodoxy, and had come to the theological task building on a Kierkegaardian foundation. His theology is clearly set out in his major work, the three-volume *Dogmatics*, completed shortly before his death in 1966.

Again, like Barth, Brunner held that God does not directly reveal Himself through Scripture, for "the reality of the revelation culminates in the 'subject' who receives it"[14] (in a "crisis" encounter). Verification of the genuineness of this subjective encounter, however, may come from the Bible and the inner witness of the Holy Spirit acting together as a dialectic unity (the Scripture as the thesis; the *testimonium spiritus internum* as the antithesis; and the united effect of the two as the synthesis).

The ultimate revelation of God is not found in books or sermons. It is not a set of truth propositions. It is a person, Jesus Christ. He is "God Himself present, acting in His own Person, ... the consummation of the revelation of God."[15] Because the Logos, or Word, has now become flesh and stands among human beings, any witness to Him can be characterized as revelation only in an indirect sense. Jesus, not the Bible, is the true Word of God. The Bible, therefore, is not authoritative because it is inerrant truth (for, to Brunner it was not), but "because Christ, whom I am convinced in my conscience is the Truth, meets me in the Scriptures. . . ."[16]

Brunner also emphasized the transcendence of God. Contrary to the teachings of Catholicism and conservative Protestantism, God cannot be known through a set of doctrinal propositions, but only in an "I-thou" relationship.[17] Since only God can reveal God, man cannot know Him until He chooses to reveal Himself. Indeed, "the true, valid knowledge of God can be gained only in His revelation, in Jesus Christ."[18]

In strong disagreement with Barth, Brunner held to a very broad concept of revelation. In his *Natur und Gnade* (Nature and Grace), Brunner proclaimed that revelation in Christ is only a part of God's total revelation to man, differing not in kind but only in degree from God's self-disclosure in nature and in history.[19] Christ is indeed the central focus of God's revelation to humanity, but all religions and all of creation contain divine self-disclosure, albeit somewhat foggy. Such revelation creates a "point of contact" for Christian revelation with other cultures and philosophies. Brunner's broader emphasis caused his approach to be labeled "missionary theology."

Because Brunner rejected the historical facticity of Genesis 3 (seeing it symbolically as mankind's universal experience), he rejected original sin in the sense of an inherited sin nature: "[Original sin] does not refer to the transgression of Adam in which all his descendants share; but it states the fact that 'Adam's' descendants are involved in death, because they themselves commit sin."[20] Human beings sin because they choose to do so. Brunner's definition of sin was self-centeredness—a rejection of fellowship with other human beings and with God. It is only through the "I-thou" encounter with God in Christ that the chains of self-centeredness may be sundered and the sinner's alienation from God may be terminated in favor of that fellowship originally rejected.

In his Christology, Brunner (again, contrary to Barth) used an "approach from below." Although subscribing to the Definition of Chalcedon in regard to the dual natures of Christ, he rejected His virginal conception, believing it to be in direct conflict with the doctrine of the Incarnation: " . . . the view which is often suggested, that the doctrine of the Virgin Birth is a special protection for the central doctrine of the New Testament, the doctrine of the Incarnation, is obviously wrong. . . . even those heresies which rejected the divinity of Christ believed in the Virgin Birth."[21]

Brunner claimed full human parentage for Jesus. How He is both fully God and fully man is beyond human comprehension: "All the questions concerning the different elements in the life of Jesus—which belong to His divine, and which to His human nature, are beside the point."[22] The important thing is that Christ was sent by God to mediate for mankind, and has brought to humanity the revelation of God from which sin had cut them off.

A brief evaluation of Brunnerian theology. One must affirm Brunner's desire to emphasize the universality and the awfulness of man's sin. Likewise, his emphasis of the centrality of Christ as God's salvation is commendable. His view of God and revelation seems more balanced than Barth's, for the Bible declares that God has spoken to human beings through the created order (e.g., Pss. 8; 19; Rom. 2:14ff).

At the same time, one must lament his rejection of Scripture as objective revelation in favor of its being only the record of revelation. The biblical deficiency, for most evangelicals, colors his views of original sin in a negative fashion. His emphasis on subjective experience, while not as heavy perhaps as Barth's, is little more helpful. It still leaves the individual without absolutes by which to measure his experience.

Other Important Neo-orthodox Figures

There are many other theologians whose contributions, while not as monumental as those of Barth and Brunner, gave added shape to neo-orthodox theology. These include Reinhold Niebuhr and Dietrich Bonhoeffer.

Niebuhr's "realistic" theology. Reinhold Niebuhr, who may be regarded as the major American neo-orthodox pioneer, was born in 1892 in Missouri, the son of a German Lutheran pastor. After graduating from Yale, he served a pastorate in Detroit where he found (in a somewhat Barthian experience) his liberal principles completely invalid and ineffective in ministering to the pain and poverty of the working classes. Consequently, he became a thorough-going social and political activist. In 1928, he was appointed professor of Christian ethics at Union Seminary in New York (teaching until 1960), where he promoted his "realistic" theology.

Niebuhr's theology was well-expressed in his two-volume *The Nature and Destiny of Man*. Though he believed the early chapters of Genesis to be myth, he saw them as pictures of "the estrangement resulting from man's rebellion against the divine will."[23] Sin is the result of the combination of man's finite animal nature and his capacity for spirituality. "He stands at the juncture of nature and spirit."[24] The spiritual nature causes him to seek perfect knowledge, freedom, and justice, but his finite nature frustrates its attainment. The result of this duality of nature is anxiety. Humanity attempts to relieve this anxiety by seeking self-sufficiency in life. Such self-sufficiency is nothing less than sinful pride.

For Niebuhr, then, pride was the real nature of sin. It shows itself in four different modes: (1) the pride of power, in which the secure assume that they are sufficient unto themselves, and the insecure seek to become self-sufficient by exploiting nature and their fellows; (2) the pride of knowledge, which is the sin of the sophisticate and the intellectual; (3) the pride of virtue, whereby some individuals consider themselves better than others; and (4) the pride of religion, "which is . . . pride and self-glorification in its inclusive and quintessential form,"[25] where some groups consider themselves alone to be chosen of God.

The Christian doctrine of grace provides alleviation for man's anxiety and the cure for his pride. When he recognizes that his security depends totally on God and not on himself, then a person may overcome his anxieties. When he realizes that his relationship with God depends upon God's grace and not upon his own righteousness, then he will be less likely to exploit his fellows, for he now knows himself to be as sinful as they are. At the same time, Niebuhr emphasized the danger to Christians of the pride of knowledge, virtue, and religion—grave threats.

Niebuhr took the death and resurrection of Christ very seriously. In them, "God takes the sinfulness of man into Himself; and overcomes in His own heart what cannot be overcome in human life. . . ."[26] What Christ has accomplished in His earthly ministry is God's final revelation to humankind, for it is the ultimate act of reconciliation between man and God. It also defines sin in the sharpest picture possible, for human beings come to realize that God Himself is a victim of their sin and pride. Indeed, Niebuhr termed the Atonement "an absolutely essential proposition for the understanding of human nature and human history."[27]

Niebuhr denied that one could ever completely follow Jesus' teaching. The Christian ethic as set forth by the Gospel is impossible to attain. But it is not therefore irrelevant. It judges our every action and calls us to seek an ever higher goal. Thus, Christians must take the Bible seriously, but not literally. Nor must they ever give up hope because of unachievable goals, for every social and spiritual victory has ultimate meaning in the time beyond history.

It is apparent that Niebuhr's theology was as much influenced by the "social gospel" as by the Christian Gospel. While his concern for and horror at sin was laudable, it was not based upon the Bible, but upon social experience. His emphasis seems to have been much more upon the wholistic transformation of society than upon the conversion of individuals who will in turn change society.

Bonhoeffer's "worldly" Christianity. Born in Breslau, Germany, in 1906 and educated at Tubingen, Berlin, and Union Seminary in New York, Dietrich Bonhoeffer was brought to theological distinction as much by his martyrdom at the hands of National Socialism in 1945 as by anything else.

When Adolf Hitler took over the leadership of Germany in 1933, Bonhoeffer aggressively and vocally resisted him, quickly making himself a target of government suspicion. He was forbidden, shortly after the outbreak of war, to speak publicly or to publish, and was forced to report regularly to the police. As a member of the German Resistance, he traveled to Sweden in 1942 and communicated to the British the Resistance's terms for the overthrow of Hitler and Germany's surrender. British rejection of this proposal led to the unsuccessful attempt to assassinate Hitler in 1944.

In 1943, Bonhoeffer was arrested and sent to the Tegel Military Prison outside Berlin. It was during this period that he wrote what later became *Letters and Papers from Prison*. After the failure of the Hitler bomb plot, evidence was found of his participation and he was sent to the Gestapo prison in Berlin, and then to Buchenwald, Schonberg, and finally, Flossenburg concentration camps. At Flossenburg in April 1945, he was executed, only a few days before the camp was liberated by Allied forces.

Bonhoeffer was a keen student of Karl Barth, but he arrived at his own independent theological conclusions. His logical extension of Barth's attack on "religion" as idolatrous—where Bonhoeffer proposed a non-religious interpretation of theological concepts—led to his views being characterized as "worldly Christianity."

Like Barth, Bonhoeffer had no use for "religion" per se. What counted was the personal, existential encounter with God in Christ. Bonhoeffer described such an encounter in terms of a call to discipleship, synonymous with faithful obedience: "Only he who is obedient believes."[28] Faith without obedience is a pious fraud, and its end is meaningless "cheap grace." Jesus is present in modern society and still confronts people, albeit not in the old traditional modes of repentance and regeneration, but in new and different ways, even using the so-called "godless" attitude of the secular world.

One thing is sure: the resurrection of Jesus Christ is a unique and miraculous event. It is no myth. In the resurrection, Christ grasps human beings and drives them, believing, out into the world arena to bring their world reconciliation to God. The Christian must serve Christ as Lord in every area of life, even to the point of actively (and violently?) opposing evil, to the death if need be. "If we are conformed to his image in his Incarnation and crucifixion, we shall also share the glory of His resurrection."[29] Such was the theme of his book, *The Cost of Discipleship*.

Letters and Papers from Prison called for radical church reform, with its return to the poverty of Christ and a sharing in the problems and burdens of everyday life without seeking to dominate.

Bonhoeffer emphasized a "religionless Christianity." Exactly what he meant by such a term is not clear and, consequently, has been much debated. Certainly, he correctly rejected the dichotomy most make between the "sacred" and "profane," seeing the need for Christ's lordship in all aspects of life.[30]

Bonhoeffer's early death prevented his creation of any kind of systematic theology. There is no question of his debt to Karl Barth and his holding of a similar view of Scripture. Since much of his work is somewhat enigmatic, how one interprets it will determine to a large degree one's opinion of his theology, but if his interpreters and students are to be believed, he properly belongs to the neo-orthodox movement.

A Summary and Evaluation of Neo-orthodox Doctrine

If we adopt Bernard Ramm's suggestion that the optimum way to evaluate (not only neo-orthodox, but all) theologians is to interact with them dialectically, then we must conclude that neo-orthodoxy has both good points and flaws.

Neo-orthodoxy may be affirmed for its thorough rejection of liberalism. The early neo-orthodox theologians (such as Barth and Brunner) were devastating in their criticism of liberal theology. And they were instrumental in a revival of interest in both biblical theology and Reformation theology. A review of their teaching will bring to light both strengths and flaws.

Doctrine of revelation. One must be grateful to neo-orthodox theology for its emphasis upon Scripture as the source of theology.

Both Barth and Brunner were effusive in their use of the Bible in teaching theology.

At the same time, when neo-orthodox theologians talk about the "Word of God," they do not necessarily (or even usually) mean the Bible. For them, the two are not synonymous. At best, the Bible is a witness to the revelation of God which is found, not in a set of verbal propositions, but in an existential encounter with Jesus Christ. Because the Bible is a book written by human beings, it cannot be absolutely inerrant.

Most neo-orthodox theologians make a biblical distinction between *geschichte* or "story," and *historie* or "history." The former has to do with the significance of events in revelation history (such as the Incarnation), and as the transcendent revelation of God is errorless and eternal. The latter term, however, is a vehicle descriptive of these salvific events and so may contain flaws. What matters is not the historical event or myth, but the truth which it sets forth. Consequently, neo-orthodox theologians, in their doctrine of inspiration, run a gamut of views ranging from a virtual full (but not absolute) inerrancy to a mere toleration of the Bible as a container of myths in which are embedded kernels of revelational truth.

Few neo-orthodox theologians would side with Barth in his acceptance of special revelation alone (i.e., revelation does not exist apart from Christ). Most would accept Brunner's view that God speaks through the created order (although, whether there is enough natural revelation to save, is debatable).

One must be sympathetic to the Brunnerian idea that revelation is an event or dialogue in which God encounters man. Unless both enter into encounter, revelation has not really taken place.[31] After all, if revelation is an unveiling of that which is hidden (*apokalupsis*), unless the person to whom it is unveiled sees it, it remains hidden (though there is certainly a difference between an inability to see and a refusal to see!).

The neo-orthodox doctrine, unfortunately, has removed all of the absolutes. Thus, there is no set standard of truth, and God becomes largely a matter of one's own subjective determinations.

Doctrine of God. God is presented by neo-orthodox theology as "wholly Other," that is, as completely transcendent. He can be known to humankind only to the extent to which He chooses to reveal Himself. Even when He does choose to do so, man can come to Him only through a monumental "leap of faith."

Many neo-orthodox theologians seem to trivialize the Holy Spirit, making Him into a force emanating from God the Father or from Christ. He does not seem to be a person in His own right. Such a view should not be surprising, for evangelicals (until the last decade or two) have not fared much better in their practical theology of the Spirit.

Christ and salvation. Jesus Christ is the focus of God's revelation to mankind. He is the perfect symbol of reconciliation between human beings and their Maker. His death and subsequent resurrection are God's guarantee that He has not abandoned humanity, but has come to dwell among them. It would be difficult to have a higher view of Christ than Barth and the neo-orthodox theologians seem to have.

Again, however, one must be aware that the significance of Jesus does not lie in His historical person, for neo-orthodox theologians question the accuracy of the biblical records of the historical Jesus.[32] Rather, the importance of Christ is the cross, which is the symbol of universal election in Christ to eternal life.

Most neo-orthodox theologians hold such a broad view of the Atonement that they border on universalism in their doctrine of salvation. Their idea of love is a kind of "I'm-ok-you're-ok" view which rejects any disciplinary aspect at all.

Doctrine of sin. Neo-orthodox theologians largely reject the historicity of the Genesis 3 account of the Fall of humankind, taking it to be a mythical picture of the reality of universal human sin. Sin is often defined as a relational flaw in humans (be it the self-centeredness view of Brunner or the perverse pride concept of Niebuhr). People are sinners because they choose to sin, not because of some weakness they have inherited from Adam.

Conclusions

Neo-orthodoxy must receive high marks for its emphatic rejection of liberalism. It may well be argued that Karl Barth did more to combat liberalism and stimulate renewed interest in a personal, supernatural God who loves and cares for His creation than any other person in the twentieth century.

Again, neo-orthodoxy may be affirmed for its desire to restate orthodox truth in contemporary language to help modern humanity better to understand the Gospel. The Good News in the language of the common people has always been the goal of sincere believers, ever since the evangelists first put it down in writing.

Unfortunately, neo-orthodoxy never followed through, as its name suggests, to reembrace biblical orthodoxy. Instead, it kept the doctrinal constructs, but filled them with a different content. The old, familiar words are still in use, but they have different meanings. As we have noted, definitions of such vitally important concepts as the Word of God, sin, and salvation are much different from those traditionally held by historical Christianity.

Neo-orthodoxy does have many commendable qualities. Because of its defective view of the plenary truth of Scripture, however, it is deficient in many of its theological emphases and, in spite of its seeming attractiveness, must be given failing grades in comparison with the Christian faith of the saints through the ages, for it lacks the necessary constant, a totally inspired and trustworthy Bible.

For Further Reading

Barth, Karl. *Evangelical Theology: An Introduction*. Grand Rapids: Wm. B. Eerdmans Pub. Co., 1963.

_____. *Church Dogmatics: A Selection*. New York: Harper and Row, 1961.

_____. *Church Dogmatics*, 4 vols. Edinburgh: T. and T. Clark, 1936.

Bonhoeffer, Dietrich. *Letters and Papers from Prison*. New York: Macmillan, 1971.

_____. *Christology*. Trans. John Bowden. London: Collins, 1966.

_____. *The Cost of Discipleship*, 2nd ed. London: SCM Press, 1959.

Bromiley, Geoffrey W. *Introduction to the Theology of Karl Barth*. Grand Rapids: Wm. B. Eerdmans Pub. Co., 1979.

Brunner, Emil. *Dogmatics*, 3 vols. Philadelphia: Westminster Press, 1961.

Dumas, Andre. *Dietrich Bonhoeffer: Theologian of Reality*. New York: Macmillan, 1968.

Kierkegaard, Sören. *Christian Discourses*. London: Oxford Univ. Press, 1940.

Niebuhr, Reinhold. *The Nature and Destiny of Man*, 2 vols. New York: Scribners, 1946.

_____. *Moral Man and Immoral Society*. New York: Scribners, 1932.

Ryrie, Charles C. *Neo-orthodoxy: What It Is and What It Does*. Chicago: Moody Press, 1956.

Three. Pentecostalism

The Pentecostal movement may be seen as an attempt to return to literal biblical Christianity as it was practiced in the New Testament church. Pentecostals believe that the hallmark of normative Christianity must be a modern experience of Pentecost, which they refer to as "the baptism in the Holy Spirit." Proof of this baptism is demonstrated by speaking in a tongue (language) unknown to the speaker.

A Brief History

Some chroniclers of Pentecostalism[1] maintain that it is a movement which actually began at Pentecost and moved down through history in varying groups which, while unconnected organically, held the same experiences and beliefs.[2] While it is true that throughout the centuries there have been groups which practiced ecstatic utterances, prophecy, faith healing, and the like (from the Montanists in the second century to the Irvingites in the nineteenth), it would be hard to connect them other than through certain common experiences, and it is doubtful that many Pentecostals would want to be thought of as bedfellows with some who were both bizarre in practice and heretical in doctrine.

It is generally agreed that Pentecostalism has its roots in an alliance of Black Christianity with the Holiness movement at the turn of the twentieth century. John Wesley had emphasized a distinction between ordinary believers and those who had been sanctified by a second, crisis experience (after conversion). His views were promoted by a number of American revivalists who were active in seeking greater rights for blacks. They were convinced that "Holy Spirit power" was needed not just to win people for Christ, but also to correct social, economic, and political problems.

The beginning of the "latter rain." In 1900, Charles Parham—a former Methodist preacher turned healer and revivalist—founded the Bethel Bible School in Topeka, Kansas to prepare prospective missionaries for Spirit-filled Christian service. Firmly believing that a "latter rain" of the Holy Spirit would soon inundate receptive believers, and that this would be followed by the premillennial return of Christ, Parham began teaching that students should study Acts 2 (the initial Christian experience of the Holy Spirit) in the expectation of their own reception of this blessing. On New Year's Day, 1901, one of his students, Agnes Ozman, received the anticipated baptism complete with a glossalalic experience. Parham described what happened:

> I laid my hands upon her and prayed. I had scarcely repeated three dozen sentences when a glory fell upon her, a halo seemed to surround her head and face, and she began speaking in the Chinese language and was unable to speak English for three days. When she tried to write in English to tell us of her experience she wrote the Chinese, copies of which we still have in newspapers printed at that time.[3]

Within a few days Parham and most of the other students had similar experiences. "The importance of these events in Topeka is that for the first time the concept of being baptized (or filled) with the Holy Spirit was linked to an outward sign—speaking in tongues."[4]

Parham believed that his group had experienced an outpouring of the "latter rain" and that the end of the age was at hand. As a consequence, he enthusiastically proclaimed this new movement of biblical Christianity. But his local area was much less prepared to receive than he was to give. The churches of Topeka and Kansas City harshly criticized his message and the newspapers followed suit. For some two years the result was failure and frustration.

In 1903, however, Parham was invited by a woman he had healed to conduct healing and revival services in Galena, Kansas. During three months of services it was reported that more than a thousand people were healed of various ailments, and some eight hundred were won to Christ.[5] Over the next few years Parham held revival meetings in surrounding communities and states and, by 1905, there were scores of Pentecostal groups in Kansas, Missouri, and Texas. "It is estimated that by the winter of 1905,

Texas alone had 25,000 Pentecostal believers and about sixty preachers—all the direct result of Parham's consecrated efforts."[6]

In 1905, Parham held a revival in Houston, Texas, and there he established a new Bible school. Much the same style of operation and teaching was used as at the now-defunct Bethel Bible School of Topeka.

One of his students was William J. Seymour, a Black Holiness revivalist. He had not spoken in tongues himself, but fervently believed Parham's teaching on the matter. Seymour was invited to preach for a call at a Holiness mission in Los Angeles. His text was Acts 2:4, and he claimed that anyone who did not speak in tongues was not Spirit-baptized. Outraged members of the church (for Holiness people denied the necessity of tongues for the "second blessing") expelled him from their midst, and he began to hold meetings in homes. On April 9, 1906, "the fire came down" and many in the meeting—including Seymour himself—received the Pentecostal blessing. "The records state that for three days and nights they shouted and praised God."[7]

The numbers in attendance grew so great that Seymour rented an old warehouse at 312 Azusa Street (regarded by most Pentecostals as the site of the birth of their movement) in the Los Angeles industrial sector. There, for three years, he held services. A Holiness evangelist described what was happening at these meetings as follows:

> ... demons are being cast out, the sick healed, many blessedly saved, restored and baptized with the Holy Spirit and power. Heroes are being developed, the weak made strong in the Lord. ... Jesus is being lifted up, the "blood" magnified, and the Holy Spirit is honored once more. There is much "slaying power" manifest. ... Strong men lie for hours under the mighty power of God, cut down like grass.[8]

In 1906, Seymour incorporated the work as the Pacific Apostolic Faith Movement.

While "virtually every ethnic group found in Los Angeles at that time worshiped together in harmony—a phenomenon in the 'Jim Crow' era"[9]—such harmony was not to last. In 1908, one of Seymour's helpers, Florence Crawford, offended when the revivalist married so close to the coming Rapture, left the group with a number of others. In 1910, a Chicago prophet, William Durham, arrived in Los Angeles, teaching a somewhat different doctrine of grace which siphoned off much of the remainder of Seymour's following. Although he continued at the Azusa Street Mission, the church gradually declined and, at Seymour's death in 1922, was a small band of blacks only.

The Spread of Pentecostalism

In spite of the ultimate decline of Seymour's work, the Azusa Street Mission served as the center for an evangelistic impetus which swept across North America and the world. By the end of 1906 there were nine Pentecostal churches in Los Angeles (albeit not all on amicable terms with one another). The movement spread quickly beyond California. People from other areas who had received "the baptism" at the Azusa Street services took their experience back to their homes across the United States and Canada.

Throughout America. Between 1906 and 1920, Pentecostalism overtook a small but significant number of Wesleyan, Reformed, and Alliance groups. In the southern United States, G.B. Cashwell, a Pentecostal Holiness evangelist from North Carolina, received the Pentecostal experience in November 1906 and took the news of his experience back home, where ministers of local Pentecostal Holiness, Fire-Baptized Holiness, and Pentecostal Free-Will Baptist churches became a part of the new movement. From there, Cashwell moved south, holding revival meetings in Georgia, South Carolina, Alabama, and Tennessee, in which whole churches frequently joined up. It was in one of these meetings that A.J. Tomlinson of the Church of God received the baptism.

Another man who became influential in the spread of Pentecostalism was Charles H. Mason, a former Baptist minister from Memphis, who had been expelled from his denomination for proclaiming a second work of grace, and had subsequently founded a new denomination, the Church of God in Christ. Visiting Seymour's services, Mason received the baptism of the Spirit and spoke in tongues. He returned to Tennessee, but his new experience received a cold shoulder from his church. A split occurred, and Mason reorganized the church and became its bishop. Growth was tremendous, and today the Church of God in Christ is the largest black denomination in America.

The major white Pentecostal denomination, the Assemblies of God, was organized in 1914 as a national vehicle for Pentecostal unity in the United States. Among the better-known founders were Eudorus Bell, Howard Goss, Daniel Opperman, A.P. Collins, and Mack Pinson. Almost immediately the new denomination was engulfed in controversy over the Trinity. In 1916, a general council in St. Louis, Missouri, expelled its Modalist elements and formulated a Statement of Fundamental Truths. "A hasty perusal of these truths reveals the Assemblies of God to be Trinitarian and Arminian; to proclaim two ordinances . . . ; to hold to a view of sanctification . . . 'progressive' rather than 'instantaneous'; and, finally, to be strongly premillennial."[10]

Into Canada. In Canada, Pentecostal churches began almost immediately after the Azusa Street event. The first Canadian recorded to have received the "latter rain" blessing was Robert E. McAlister, a Bible student from Ontario, who heard of the happenings in Los Angeles, went to California to investigate, and was baptized in the Holy Spirit. He returned to Canada with the message and began to propagate the Pentecostal message. Before long, there were groups all across Canada with heavy concentrations in Toronto and Winnipeg.

It was early recognized that some overarching organizational structure was needed, for "there followed a proliferation of views, nonsensical and worse, that led to endless arguments over such matters as the wearing of ties by men or earrings by women. One extreme group . . . dabbled with 'free love.' "[11] Attempts to create a national denomination began in 1909, with the formation of the Pentecostal Missionary Union, but it was not until 1917 that the Pentecostal Assemblies of Canada was formed in Eastern Canada. Two years later, the Pentecostals of Western Canada met at Moose Jaw, Saskatchewan and, under the influence of an evangelist from the American Assemblies of God, formed the Western Canada District Council of the Assemblies of God, U.S.A. In 1921, the (Eastern) Pentecostal Assemblies of Canada was reorganized as the Eastern Canadian District of the Assemblies of God, U.S.A. Thus, the two geographical units were united. Before long, it had become obvious that belonging to an American denomination was not practical and, in 1925, the Canadian churches were released from that group as an autonomous Pentecostal Assemblies of Canada. Today, it is the largest Pentecostal group in Canada and the fifth largest Protestant denomination.

Into Europe. Growth was not limited to North America. A Norwegian pastor, Thomas Barrett, had been at the Los Angeles revival. "[He] is regarded, by Pentecostals as well as by non-Pentecostal scholars, as the apostle of the Pentecostal movement in Europe. It is a fact that Barrett's work was fundamental in forming the movement in Europe."[12] With the exception of Holland and Italy, Europe was evangelized with the Pentecostal message from Norway. In Holland, Gerritt and Wilhelmina Polman were baptized in the Spirit in 1907 after reading a Pentecostal magazine. American-Italian Pentecostals took the message to Italy in 1908. Pentecostal activities in Europe were harmonized through the formation of the International Pentecostal Council in 1912. The council was a source of warm fellowship for its constituents but, sadly, was fractured by the start of World War I in 1914.

Into Latin America. The Pentecostal revival came to Chile quite independently of, and prior to, the Azusa Street event in Los Angeles. A Methodist missionary, William Hoover, District Superintendent for Chile, was constantly praying for a new Pentecost. In 1905 he heard of a revival in India where students in an Anglican school had experienced trances, visions, glossolalia, and other phenomena. Shortly after this, one of his own church members had a vision of Christ who told him to tell his pastor to gather the spiritual people of the congregation together for prayer, for He was going to baptize them with tongues of fire. Hoover was obedient to this vision; the group agreed to pray each day at 5 p.m. until something happened. As a result, revival began, and soon spread to other churches.

Although unprecedented growth took place in several of the Methodist churches where Spirit baptism had been received, reaction by the Methodist Missionary Society in New York was not favorable. On September 12, 1909, Hoover and thirty-seven of his fellow Pentecostals were excommunicated. They then founded the

Pentecostal Methodist Church. The Chilean Methodist church slowly decreased. The Pentecostal Methodist Church grew to become the largest Protestant group in the country.[13]

The Pentecostal revival was brought to the rest of Latin America through the efforts of missionaries from the United States, Canada, and Scandinavia. The initial recipients were Brazil, Venezuela, and the West Indies. Today, all Latin countries have a strong Pentecostal presence. In South America, Pentecostals outnumber all other Protestant groups combined.

Into Africa. It is generally accepted that the message of Pentecostalism was first introduced to the African continent by American missionaries. Two reputed disciples of John Alexander Dowie who had been converted to Pentecostal faith, John G. Lake and Thomas Hezmalhalch, began holding services in a South African native church in late 1908 or early 1909. Out of curiosity, many whites attended. A large number received Spirit baptism. Larger facilities had to be obtained, and they were filled every service. David du Plessis, in a sermon delivered in 1938, said of their mission that "it stirred the city [of Johannesburg]. Jews and Gentiles were saved."[14] About that same time, a Canadian, Charles Chawner, came to South Africa from the Hebden Mission in Toronto. He was an evangelist primarily to the Zulu people.

Probably as a result of this early penetration, South Africa has the heaviest concentration of Pentecostal churches. There, the three main groups are the Apostolic Faith Mission (mostly Afrikaaner), the Full Gospel Church of God in South Africa (fully integrated), and the Assemblies of God in South Africa (divided into white, colored, and African sections).

Work began in Central Africa about 1914, with the arrival of English Pentecostals, William F. Burton and James Salter, to found the Congo Evangelistic Association. While Pentecostals have grown fairly rapidly in some centers, such as Kenya, Tanzania, and Mozambique, numbers are not as great as in South Africa. There are many individual success stories in Central Africa, however, such as Pastor Benson Idahosa's 20,000-seat church in Benin, Nigeria, and Nigerian pastor William Kamuyi's 56,000-member congregation.[15]

Pentecostals have not done any better in seeking to evangelize the Moselm areas of Africa than have other evangelicals. While there are some small works, headway among this group is extremely difficult.

Across the Iron Curtain. Pentecostalism was brought to the Communist countries of Europe by a Russian Baptist preacher who had emigrated to the United States in 1912 to avoid persecution from the Russian Orthodox Church. Ivan Varonaev planted Russian Baptist churches in Los Angeles, San Francisco, and Seattle before accepting the pastorate of a Russian Baptist church in Manhattan. In 1919 at the urging of his wife and daughter, who had had the Pentecostal experience, he received the baptism of the Holy Spirit with accompanying glossolalia.

As the result of a prophecy in a prayer group which directed him to go to Russia, Varonaev and his family left New York for the Soviet Union in August 1920. They spent five months in Bulgaria where he established twenty Pentecostal churches before reaching Odessa in the Ukraine where he began to preach among the Baptists. When the Baptists excluded him because of his novel teachings concerning the Holy Spirit, Varonaev founded the first Soviet Pentecostal church. Between 1920 and 1929 (when the Communists ended all religious freedoms), he traveled throughout Russia, Poland, and Bulgaria, organizing more than 350 congregations.

In 1932 Varonaev was arrested as an American spy and spent six months in a labor camp. In 1936 he was arrested again when he applied for an exit visa. It is believed that he was executed in 1943 before a firing squad. But the work continued. It is estimated that there are some 600,000 Pentecostals in the Soviet Union today.[16]

Into Asia. As early as the end of 1906 Pentecostalism had reached into India as a movement of the Spirit broke out under the leadership of Pandita Ramabi. There is some question whether it was the result of the Azusa Street revival or a revival in Wales (majority opinion tends toward the latter).[17]

By 1908 Pentecostal missionaries were en route to China, Japan, and India, trusting that their glossalalic experience would allow them to proclaim Christ to the heathen in the native languages of the people they were seeking to evangelize. They were, of course, unsuccessful.[18] Among these pioneers were Robert and Aimee

Semple who, in 1907, went from Canada to Hong Kong with the backing of a few Pentecostal congregations. Their stay was short-lived, for Robert Semple died almost immediately after arrival, leaving his pregnant widow destitute. Helped by kind strangers, she was able to make her way back home. Twenty years later, as a successful evangelist, Aimee Semple McPherson returned to China to lay the cornerstone for the Shanghai branch of her own Foursquare Gospel Church.[19]

Some conversions to Pentecostalism took place among already evangelized Protestant believers. The most sizable of these occurred in 1912, when W.W. Simpson, a Christian and Missionary Alliance minister in Taochow, Kansu Province, experienced the gift of tongues. Shortly thereafter, his wife and family, together with about 100 members of their mission, received similar baptisms. The Alliance asked Simpson to resign, which he did, allying himself with the Assemblies of God (USA). Before long, some fifty churches and 3,000 adherents had been added to the Pentecostal fold.[20] Such success stories, however, were quite rare. The peoples of Asia have proved quite resistant to the work of the Holy Spirit.

Throughout this century, most Asian Pentecostal churches have remained under foreign mission support. A notable exception is South Korea, where the work has blossomed. There, Pentecostals have grown more than all other Christian groups combined. Most noteworthy is Paul Y. Cho's Full Gospel Central Church in Seoul, with over half a million members.

At the world level. Efforts at international cooperation on a global scale began in 1937 when the General Council of the (American) Assemblies of God invited Pentecostal leaders from many nations to attend its meetings. They, in turn, called for a World Conference in London in 1940, but it was forestalled by the outbreak of World War II. Following the war, leaders called a World Pentecostal Conference[21] which met at Zurich, Switzerland, in May 1947. The theme was "By one Spirit we are all baptized into one Body." The conference also established a quarterly journal, *Pentecost*, to be edited by English Pentecostal Donald Gee.

In 1949 another Pentecostal World Conference was held in Paris. It adopted a manifesto which declared that the goal and purpose of the Conference would be:

(a) to encourage fellowship and facilitate coordination of effort
among Pentecostal believers throughout the world;

(b) to demonstrate to the world the essential unity of Spirit-
baptized believers, fulfilling the prayer of the Lord Jesus
Christ that they all may be one;

(c) to cooperate in an endeavor to respond to the unchanging
commission of the Lord Jesus to carry the message to people
of all nations;

(d) to promote courtesy and mutual understanding "endeav-
oring to keep the unity of the Spirit in the bond of peace . . .
till we all come in the unity of faith" (Eph. 4:3, 13);

(e) to afford prayerful and practical assistance to any Pentecostal party in need of such;

(f) to promote and maintain the scriptural purity of fellowship
by Bible study and prayer;

(g) to uphold and maintain those Pentecostal truths "most
surely believed among us" (Luke 1:1).[22]

Although its organizers had envisioned the Conference as a fellowship for co-ordinating Pentecostal missions and evangelism
worldwide, Pentecostals were too independent and varied to asso-
ciate other than fraternally.

A Doctrinal Summary
The Pentecostal movement must not be seen as a uniform group
or denomination, but rather as a family of denominations. There
are certain homogeneous doctrinal strands holding them all
together, but there are also major doctrinal differences in some
areas which have been the source of sharp contention (often de-
pending upon their early religious heritage).

Authority. As do many conservative Protestants, Pentecostals
unanimously declare themselves to be devout biblicists, with no
creed but the Bible. "This biblicism is not combined with an historical and critical understanding of the Bible, but represents an
unreflecting fundamentalism."[23] Thus, early Pentecostalism sometimes came close to bibliolatry, holding a wariness that even the
study of the original languages of the Bible in an effort to uncover
the best meanings of terms and passages might somehow be detri-

mental to a reverence for the Scriptures. Today that view has mellowed among the major Pentecostal traditions who number in their memberships some of the foremost evangelical biblical scholars.

At the same time, in practice, many Pentecostals have a very subjective and experiential concept of authority. "The Lord told me" is a common revelatory device. And "word of faith" preachers often hold their revelations to be on a virtual par with the Scriptures. Prophecy is a highly regarded and common aspect of Pentecostal worship. It must, however, be subservient to the Bible.

Doctrine of God. Most Pentecostals hold to the traditional orthodox doctrine of the Trinity as stated by the historic confessions. Not many years after its inception, however, the movement was beset by a controversy over the Trinity, when a number of pastors influenced by the teaching of Frank Ewart and G.A. Cook, declared that baptism in the Triune Name (according to Matt. 28:19) was invalid. Legitimate baptism was seen to be in the name of Jesus only.

This teaching spread quickly throughout North America, and it seemed likely to become the majority position of Pentecostalism. Many leading pastors repudiated their former baptism and were rebaptized in the name of Jesus. "Soon most of the Pentecostal leaders, after searching the Scriptures, saw that the teaching was not supported by the Word of God, and repudiated it."[24]

There are three prominent Pentecostal groups which maintain this view today: the United Pentecostal Church (in Canada and the United States), the (Black) Pentecostal Assemblies of the World, and the Apostolic Church of Pentecost (Canada). They reject the doctrine of the Trinity, insisting that God is not three, but one — that One is Jesus Christ. God the Father and God the Holy Spirit are respectively Old Testament and contemporary alternative forms of Jesus. They believe that those who worship the Trinity are really tri-theists. Some of these groups, happily, are moving back toward Trinitarian orthodoxy.

Salvation and the Christian life. Like other orthodox Christians, Pentecostals believe in the necessity of regeneration as the result of a conversion experience received through the gift of God's grace in Christ. But regeneration is only a first step. Sanctification is vital, as well. For those Pentecostals with a Baptist or Reformed orientation, sanctification occurs simultaneously with regeneration. For those with a Holiness background, it must be sought as a second crisis experience, with tears and ardent prayer.

The ultimate step—whether a second or third—for all Pentecostals is the "baptism in the Spirit." According to their belief, traditional Christians have never moved beyond Easter to Pentecost, and so do not have true spiritual power which Christ has made available through the baptism of the Holy Spirit, the initial evidence of which must be to speak in an ecstatic tongue. This Spirit baptism is deeply emotional and unleashes the one baptized for Christian service of a full and victorious nature.

But the baptism of the Holy Spirit moves beyond simple empowerment for service. It is the sufficient validation of the practical truth of the Christian message. It empirically substantiates the Bible; Lewi Petrus, pioneer Pentecostal in Sweden, writes of his own Spirit baptism: "This appears to me as the greatest miracle of my life, ... that I have found it just as *impossible to doubt*, as at times I formerly found it *impossible to believe* the truths of the Bible."[25] Spirit baptism, furthermore, gives one absolute assurance of salvation. Thomas Barrett, the father of European Pentecostalism, notes that at his baptism in the Spirit, "... *I got the assurance of that*. God's Spirit was upon me and permeated my whole being."

Being Arminian in much of their theology because of their Holiness roots, Pentecostals also believe in apostasy. Any person in a condition of unconfessed sin is lost, and in a state of perdition until that sin is confessed. Following confession and forgiveness, a sinning Christian is once again in a state of grace. Such repositioning can happen any number of times.

Humankind and sin. Pentecostal theologians have been slow to deal extensively with anthropology and hamartiology, but there is no question that the movement believes that man was created in God's image, to walk in holiness and purity before Him, and that because of the Fall all humanity is in bondage to Satan.

Nonetheless, the doctrine of the freedom of the will predominates Pentecostal thinking. Human beings sin through choice, not necessity, for the Fall never deprived them of the freedom to choose between good and evil. Consequently, for Pentecostals, "it is not the sinful state, but the sinful act which implies guilt and justice."[27] In this regard, they follow John Wesley who distinguished involuntary transgressions from sin, the former being unconscious and the latter willful. It is the latter which brings humans under condemnation.

Spiritual gifts. Pentecostals, properly speaking, are charismatic. They believe that the gifts of 1 Corinthians 12:8-10 are in operation today. The baptism in the Holy Spirit actuates these gifts in the believers.

Speaking with tongues, of course, occupies the premier position in that it is the necessary evidential sign of Spirit baptism. Initially, no differentiation was made between tongues as a sign and tongues as a spiritual gift. The belief of the early revivalists was that Spirit baptism (demonstrated by tongues) brought a gift of power. But within a few years they were insisting that one must distinguish between tongues as the initial evidence of the baptism, as set forth in Acts 2:4, something given to all who ask for it in faith, and the spiritual gift of tongues, set out in 1 Corinthians 12:30, given only to those whom the Spirit may designate.

Interpretation of tongues often accompanies the gift of tongues, but a different person may interpret. Early Pentecostal leaders cautioned their people against accepting an interpretation as a means of divine guidance. Glossolalia for them were really prayers. Today, however, the interpretation of a tongue may be used as a word from God for the affirmation or guidance of an individual or group.

Pentecostals believe sincerely in the gift of prophecy. "From time to time Pentecostals have been used of God in giving prophetic utterances that were so startling as to be a wonder to listeners."[28] Generally, prophetic utterances are for warning, edification, exhortation or comfort, either to individuals or to groups.

From early on Pentecostals have advocated and practiced divine healing, although they have been careful to recognize that not all who seek healing receive it. Sickness is seen as one consequence of the Fall but, as the Statement of Fundamental and Essential Truths of the Pentecostal Assemblies of Canada states, "Deliverance from sickness is provided for in the atonement, and is the privilege of all believers (Isa. 53:4-5; Matt. 8:16-17)."[29]

Closely connected to illness is demon possession. It too is a result of the Fall. But the power of the resurrected Christ is as effective in the exorcism of demons as in the healing of illness. Pentecostals believe that, while the believer may get sick, one can never be possessed by demons, for he or she has been indwelt by the Holy Spirit.[30] Pentecostals have always been quick to discern and attack demons, exorcizing them "in the name of Jesus" (Mark 16:17). Some well-known Pentecostal leaders have been both healers and exorcists, including Aimee Semple McPherson and William Branham.

Eschatology. "Jesus is coming soon! This message has been heralded by Pentecostals in every decade of this century."[31] Eschatology is more strongly emphasized in Pentecostal preaching than in most other churches, particulary the Second Advent. Most Pentecostals are premillennial, looking for a pretribulational Rapture of the church out of this world.

Over the last several decades, though, there have been differences of opinion. The late 1940s saw the emergence of a Restoration movement, holding to a premillennial and posttribulation position. This view holds that the tribulation of Daniel occurred in first-century Judaism; thus, there will be no tribulation before the Second Coming. "They have an optimistic view of the role of the church in the world and believe that the church should expend its energy extending the kingdom rather than preaching a rescue-mission Rapture. . . ."[32]

Reconstructionist, or dominion, theology has also attracted some Pentecostal interest. It aims at establishing the kingdom of God on earth through human effort. When the kingdom has been instituted, Christ will return.

An Evaluation and Summary

Many Christian theologians tend to see Pentecostalism as second century Montanism reborn. Montanism spread throughout the Christian world of its day, claiming thousands of converts to its literal Pentecostal practices (including tongues and prophecy), winning even the notable church father Tertullian as an adherent. Had it not been condemned by Rome and stamped out as heresy, it might have become the major faith practice of Christianity. Like

Montanism, Pentecostalism has exploded across the Christian horizon, winning both pagans and believers. What it will become in the future one cannot say.

Just as the ecstasies and prophecies of Montanism were seen as heretical, so many orthodox Christians have seen the tongues and prophecies of the Pentecostal movement in a like fashion. Most traditional fundamentalists and some evangelicals have condemned modern glossolalia as "of the devil." Other evangelicals and many "mainline" Christians regard the phenomenon as a psychological aberration.

There are increasing numbers, however, who hold that all of the spiritual gifts of Pentecost are still functional. While Pentecostal enthusiasm is not their style, they rejoice in the Pentecostals' "joy in the Lord" and wish them all success.

Certainly, any features which deviate doctrinally from orthodox Christian standards are to be condemned. When a "word of faith" or a "word from the Lord," for example, are equated with the divine revelation in Scripture, then it is heresy and not truth. Nor can any defense be made for "Jesus only" unitarianism.

If there is one major sticking point between orthodox Christians in general and orthodox Pentecostals in particular, it is the Pentecostal insistence on speaking in tongues as the initial evidence of the baptism (or, as most Christians would say, filling) of the Holy Spirit. The biblical evidence for tongues as the premier gift is simply not there. Indeed, tongues and interpretation of tongues are lowest in order of importance (1 Cor. 12; 14). It is both interesting and significant that F.F. Bosworth, one of the pioneers of the Pentecostal movement and a founder of the Assemblies of God, taught that the gift of tongues was only one of many evidences of the baptism of the Holy Spirit. Unfortunately, his viewpoint did not carry the day and he was expelled from his denomination. It is noteworthy, however, that increasing numbers of Pentecostal clergy are moving towards Bosworth's position, admitting that while tongues is often the initial evidence, other gifts may also be evidential instead.

Whatever one may think of Pentecostalism, there can be no denying that the Pentecostal movement has brought to the Christian church universal a renewed emphasis on, and respect for, the Person and work of the Holy Spirit. Only a blind person would contradict the appraisal that God has greatly used this movement in world evangelization. Millions of people have come to know Christ, especially in South America, Asia, and Africa because of its ministry.

Less than a century old, Pentecostalism is still developing and maturing. Experience has taken precedence over doctrinal foundation. As increasing numbers of Pentecostals turn to scholarly theological and biblical pursuits, they are wrestling with the doctrinal bases of their faith which may lead to some minor, but important, shifts in dogma, and to a more maturely expressed faith which, nonetheless, retains the fire and zeal of its beginning.

For Further Reading

Atter, Gordon. *The Third Force*. Peterborough, On.: College Press, 1962.

Bloch-Hoell, Nils. *The Pentecostal Movement*. Oslo, Norway: Universitets-forlaget, 1964.

Burgess, Stanley M. and Gary B. McGee, eds. *Dictionary of Pentecostal and Charismatic Movements*. Grand Rapids: Zondervan Publishing House, 1988.

Conn, Charles W. *Like a Mighty Army*. Cleveland, Tenn.: Church of God Publishing House, 1955.

Durasoff, Steve. *Bright Wind of the Spirit, Pentecostalism Today*. Englewood Cliffs, N.J.: Prentice-Hall, 1972.

Gee, Donald. *The Pentecostal Movement*. London: Elim Publishing House, 1949.

Goff, James R., Jr. *Fields White unto Harvest: Charles F. Parham and the Missionary Origins of Pentecostalism*. Fayetteville, Ark.: University of Arkansas Press, 1988.

Hollenweger, Walter J. *The Pentecostals*. Minneapolis: Augsburg Press, 1972.

Kendrick, Klaude. *The Promise Fulfilled: A History of the Pentecostal Movement*. Springfield, Mo.: Gospel Publishing House, 1961.

Kuhlbeck, Gloria Grace. *What God Hath Wrought: A History of the Pentecostal Assemblies of Canada*. Toronto: P.A.O.C., 1958.

McClung, L. Grant, Jr., ed. *Azusa Street and Beyond: Pentecostal Missions and Church Growth in the Twentieth Century*. South Plainfield, N.J.: Bridge Publishing, 1986.

McPherson, Aimee Semple. *The Foursquare Gospel*. Los Angeles: Echo Park Evangelistic Association, 1946.

Nichol, John T. *The Pentecostals*. Plainfield, N.J.: Logos International, 1966.

Smith, Harold B., ed. *Pentecostals from the Inside Out*. Wheaton, Ill.: Victor Books, 1990.

Synan, Vinson. *Holiness-Pentecostal Movement*. Grand Rapids: William B. Eerdmans Publishing Co., 1971.

Four. Evangelicalism

Evangelicals have been termed by some as "fundamentalists with Ph.D.s." Although there is a historical connection between fundamentalism and evangelicalism (both coming from a common background in conservative Christian orthodoxy), the differences are much greater than such a simplistic definition would imply.

A Brief History of Evangelicalism

Although the term "neo-evangelicalism" was coined by Harold Ockenga during an address at Fuller Theological Seminary in 1948,[1] evangelicalism had really begun some time earlier. Between the two World Wars various groups who had been rejected by, or who had disassociated themselves from, fundamentalism started to group together.

Formation of the N.A.E. Between 1939 and 1941, J. Elwin Wright of the New England Fellowship toured the United States seeking a coalition of evangelicals of every kind whose merger would precipitate a national revival. He and his colleagues invited representatives of these groups to meet in a National Conference for United Action among evangelicals at St. Louis in early April 1942.

Four outstanding speakers urged delegates to come together in the truth. Harold J. Ockenga, pastor of Boston's Park Street Church, spoke about "The Unvoiced Multitudes"; William W. Ayer, pastor of New York's Calvary Baptist Church, examined "Evangelical Christianity"; Robert G. Lee, pastor of Memphis' Bellevue Baptist Church preached on "Jesus of Nazareth"; and Stephen W. Paine, president of Houghton College, discussed "The Possibility for United Action." The conference responded by drafting a tentative constitution and statement of faith and agreed to a constitutional convention a year later.

The tentative constitution stipulated that the National Association of Evangelicals for United Action would be a voluntary, democratically administered organization. The group must not oppose the role, rights, or privileges of its members. At the same time, membership was limited to those denominations, groups, or churches which could affirm the doctrinal beliefs of the new organization and which were evangelical in spirit and purpose.

The Association would concern itself with:

(1) evangelism,
(2) evangelicals' relation to government,
(3) national and local use of radio,
(4) public relations,
(5) the preservation of separation of church and state,
(6) Christian education and
(7) the guarantee of freedom for home and foreign missionary endeavor.[2]

In May of 1943, the Constitutional Convention of the National Association of Evangelicals met in Chicago. One thousand delegates from fifty denominations and numerous groups were in attendance. An unusual harmony prevailed as a constitution and statement of faith were approved. "From this meeting came the National Association of Evangelicals [N.A.E.], a . . . genuinely inclusive fellowship that signaled the formation of a new evangelical coalition."[3]

One of the chief reasons for the formation of the N.A.E. was the desire of many Christian groups and churches to steer a middle course between liberalism and extreme conservatism in an expression of Christian unity. The Federal Council of Churches of Christ had always been too liberal and social-gospel oriented to be popular with evangelicals. Its component churches were looked upon as modernist. But neither did evangelicals find acceptable the hyper-critical, hyper-fundamentalist American Council of Christian Churches founded by Carl McIntire.

Another major reason for the forming of the N.A.E. was the realization "that a positive witness could be given by united evangelicals and only by united evangelicals."[4]

A reaction against fundamentalism? In many respects the evangelical movement was birthed in a spirit of reaction against the fundamentalist movement by dissidents within the latter group. "Too often the issues and answers were oversimplified; one might express it, 'Get saved and everything else will take care of itself.' But too often the saved had blind spots in the matters of social injustice, racial prejudice, and moral incompetence."[5]

In the 1940s, a group of young fundamentalist scholars were emerging who were sharp critics of the movement's performance in many areas. They called themselves evangelicals because they wished to distance themselves from the social and political failures of fundamentalism, but not from its adherence to spiritual and biblical ideals.

In 1946, Gordon Clark decried the failure of fundamentalists to do scholarly work in areas such as philosophy, sociology, and politics: "fundamentalists have too long neglected their obligation."[6] Carl Henry, the following year, wrote a scathing polemic entitled *The Uneasy Conscience of Modern Fundamentalism* in which he condemned his former colleagues, not for being unfaithful to biblical truth, but for their failure to apply that truth "effectively to crucial problems confronting the modern mind."[7] Harold Ockenga attacked fundamentalists as having an unhealthy attitude of suspicion toward everyone who did not hold exactly the same viewpoint as them. He also scorned them for thinking that one can have a pure denomination or local church and accused them of endangering missions because of their failure to apply their theology to modern social dilemmas.[8] Edward John Carnell, then professor of apologetics at Fuller Theological Seminary, accused fundamentalism of being orthodoxy turned cultic. It had neglected to ground its convictions in the historical theological creeds of Christendom. It had now become more of a mentality than a movement.[9]

The evangelical agenda. Evangelicals believed that an existence in "splendid isolation" from the world and from other Christians was ill-advised, to say the least. Thus, within the evangelical framework, Baptists would cooperate with Methodists and Presbyterians with Pentecostals in evangelistic and social mission, minimizing their differences in polity and maximizing their common doctrinal beliefs. They also decided that they would engage those outside of the evangelical camp on their own ground and within their non-evangelical frames of reference and areas of interest. Accordingly, young evangelicals secured advanced degrees from liberal and neo-orthodox schools and became involved in higher critical methodology and in ethical pursuits.

Unlike the overwhelming number of fundamentalists who separated from their modernist-leaning denominations, evangelicals tended to remain. They were unwilling to abandon their heritage and church homes to modernism without a fight. Their goal was to win back to conservative Christian views and values the leadership of their denominations. For the same reasons, they also sought employment as faculty members in "mainline" denominational colleges and seminaries.

Other evangelicals, desirous of using conservative structures for influencing others, took control of many formerly fundamentalist Christian resource groups. Youth for Christ is an outstanding example. In 1945, under the guidance of Torrey Johnson, Youth for Christ International was formed and, by 1948, was working in forty-six countries. It was instrumental in the formation of the Far East Gospel Crusade, Greater Europe Mission, Trans-World Radio, and World Vision International.[10] From its ranks came most of the Billy Graham organization, which quickly moved beyond a fundamentalist outreach to a broad-based cooperation with a multitude of Christian denominations. Many Bible colleges and seminaries (e.g., Wheaton College and Gordon College) made a gradual transition to the evangelical stance. Other agencies were added at other educational levels: Fuller Theological Seminary was founded with leading educators from several evangelical schools as faculty members; the Evangelical Theological Society, for example, at the scholarly level—though adhering to inerrancy—gave wide latitude to its members in critical pursuits of biblical and theological research. And a magazine, *Christianity Today*, was founded to provide for the dissemination of evangelical doctrine, ethics, and world view.

The "new" evangelicalism. In the late 1960s, a new group of evangelical activists came to the fore who were unhappy with the failure of evangelicalism to attain any measure of reconciliation with non-evangelical Christians. Some of those involved in this "new mood" had participated in the earlier phase of the movement; others had more recently come to evangelicalism out of neo-orthodoxy or neo-liberalism. Donald Bloesch refers to them as "new" evangelicals;[11] they are "the fruit of a convergence of theological currents, though the tradition of evangelical revivalism is the dominant one."[12]

Nor is this movement limited to North America. It is seen in Europe in groups such as the "No Other Gospel" movement of Lutheranism and Reformed Protestantism, in the Church of England Evangelical Council, in the Evangelical Sisterhood of Mary in Germany, and in Operation Mobilization, to name only a few. It includes names like the late F.F. Bruce, Klaas Runia, John Stott, and Colin Brown.

These new evangelicals look for their theological inspiration to Pietism and Puritanism as well as to the more recent evangelicalism. Their heroes of older times include not only Luther, Calvin, and Wesley, but also Jonathan Edwards, Richard Baxter, John Owen, and Count Zinzendorf. Those of more modern times are Dietrich Bonhoeffer, Emil Brunner, and C.S. Lewis.

The following trends have been noted as characteristic of these new evangelicals:

(1) A reinterpretation of the concept of inerrancy (based on an acceptance of historical criticism) to the point of regarding the teaching of Scripture rather than its text as being without error.
(2) Christian practice as indispensable evidence of saving faith.
(3) A repudiation of Dispensationalism and its attendant pessimism.
(4) A reemphasis on the social dimension of the Gospel.
(5) A fresh dialogue not only with ecumenical liberalism, but also other religious traditions.[13]

The new evangelicals stress evangelism, but an evangelism which is concerned with the whole person rather than just the spiritual aspect. They recognize, however, that "the primary aim of the church is to preach the Gospel and make disciples of Jesus Christ."[14] Social service is integral to the mission and they support organizations which are activist socially as well as spiritually. For example, they support the International Fellowship of Students (of which Inter-Varsity Christian Fellowship is the North American segment) rather than Campus Crusade for Christ, because the former is more personally involved in social evangelism than the latter. Political action is a result of the mission of the church. "While not averse to political action and social change, the new evangelicals speak of the prior need for personal regeneration as the prerequisite to any lasting social benefits."[15] But they are quick to emphasize, along with Dietrich Bonhoeffer,[16] that "decisions" arising from high-powered evangelism tend to be shallow and that real conversion is a costly discipleship in social and spiritual action.

Since 1974, a group to the left of the "new" evangelicals has emerged. Richard Quebedeaux refers to them as "radical" evangelicals.[17] They have been heavily influenced by the Catholic left (for example, the Berrigans), Jacques Ellul, and the nonviolent Anabaptist tradition as typified by John Howard Yoder. Coming out of the New Left of the 1960s, they see Christianity juxtaposed against culture. They go beyond the new evangelicals in their desire to reform society, insisting on the formation of alternative communities which will model the simple life-style, a sincere concern for the poor and oppressed, "first-priority commitment to one another as sisters and brothers in Christ, and a prophetic critique of the institutional church (conservative and liberal) and the capitalist system in general."[18] Much of their thought is carried in several representative publications: *Sojourners* (Washington, D.C.), *The Other Side* (Philadelphia), and *Radix* (Berkeley, Calif.).

Quebedeaux has summed up this new evangelical movement as follows: "The present revolution in Orthodoxy is nothing more and nothing less than a conviction borne out in practice that Jesus Christ is still in total command."[19]

Evangelical Doctrinal Emphases

When the N.A.E. was founded in 1942, its Confession of Faith permitted freedom of doctrinal viewpoint in the areas of baptism, the work of the Holy Spirit, and eschatology. Nonetheless, they were united in their stand on the "fundamentals" of the faith. In many areas that position has become increasingly elastic. These areas of tension in doctrine will be examined.

The authority of Scripture. All evangelicals hold to the authority of Scripture as the only sufficient guide in matters of faith and practice. If there is one doctrine which would determine whether one is evangelical or not, it would have to be the authority of Scripture. No person rejecting biblical authority could be termed evangelical in any measure of truth.[20] At the same time, there are a number who have wandered from the early benchmark of absolute inerrancy (namely, that the Bible in its original manuscripts, or *autographa*, is absolutely inerrant in all respects). As they have increasingly interacted with critical methodology, many have moved to a "limited inerrancy" view, that the Bible is infallible and inerrant in matters concerning salvation, but that its writers were subject to the worldview of their time and so, in matters of science and history, may have made some errors.[21] James Davison Hunter notes the results of the Evangelical Academy Project which demonstrates that only 40 percent of the respondents (from evangelical colleges and seminaries) held to absolute inerrancy, while slightly more than 50 percent maintained the view that "the Bible is the inspired Word of God, is not mistaken in its teachings, but is not always to be taken literally in its statements concerning matters of science and historical reporting, etc."[22]

Donald Bloesch typifies this last viewpoint. He writes:

> As I see it, there are three basic approaches to scriptural authority: the sacramental, the scholastic, and the liberal-modernist. In the first, the Bible is a divinely-appointed channel, a mirror, or a visible sign of divine revelation. This was the general position of the church fathers, the doctors of the medieval church, and the Reformers. . . .Only the first position does justice to the dual origin of Scripture—that it is both a product of divine inspiration and a human witness to divine truth. We need to recognize the full humanity of Scripture as well as its true divinity. . . .[23]

This gap in biblical viewpoints has been a bone of contention between strong-minded evangelicals, with polemics from both camps being issued throughout the 1970s and 80s. Typical of absolutist broadsides was Harold Lindsell's *The Battle for the Bible* (1976), which accused limited inerrantists of opening the door to modernism. Representative of the limited view was Jack Rogers' (editor) *Biblical Authority* (1977), which declared that absolute inerrancy simply is not consistent with scientific fact. It is not presently meaningful or epistemologically necessary, and therefore, should not be a test of evangelical authenticity.[24] One must recognize, however, that both camps have a high regard for the authority of the Scriptures. All would undoubtedly agree with Millard Erickson that "the Bible is not an end in itself. Its value is instrumental: it is intended to bring the reader into a certain relationship with the God who stands behind it."[25]

The doctrine of God. The knowledge of God is foundational to all of the other Christian doctrines. One may go even further and say that it is fundamental to salvation.

Evangelicals follow the historic confessions of traditional orthodoxy in this area. Because of the biblical teaching in its entirety, they ascribe to the doctrine of the Trinity. "Father, Son, and Holy Spirit are each fully God. Each exists as a separate person with individual responsibilities within the Godhead."[26]

Evangelicals are not unanimous in all their views of the person and work of God. In this they tend to follow the variations of orthodox Protestant doctrine.

Natural (general) revelation is one prominent area of disagreement. Does God reveal Himself to human beings through the created order? Some evangelicals declare that God cannot be known to humankind other than through His special revelation, the Bible. A few would go in the opposite direction, that God can be known in nature and that this knowledge may even be salvific. Most, however, would feel that while God does reveal Himself in His creation so that humanity may know His presence and glory, because of their sin to their own condemnation they have rejected Him. Without special revelation they would be lost.

Another area of disagreement involves the attributes of God. Some evangelicals who are extreme Calvinists stress God's holiness to the expense of His love. "God, for His own glory, saves whom He will and damns whom He will, in rather arbitrary fashion."[27] Most do not find such imbalance, but see God's attributes as overlapping and complementary.

The doctrine of creation. While evangelicals are essentially united in their declaration that God is Creator of all that exists and that man is His unique creation, agreement does not extend to His methodology. Theistic evolutionists declare that God used evolution to accomplish His creative purposes (some include human beings in the evolutionary scheme, while others believe that man was a unique creation apart from the rest of the natural order). Other evangelicals do not accept evolution, nor do they believe that God "put the fossils in the rocks." Rather, they hold to a "day-age" interpretation of Genesis 1–2,[28] believing in a special complete creation, but over a long period of time. Still others are literalists, holding to a fiat creation in six twenty-four hour days.

In 1955, Bernard Ramm in *The Christian View of Science and Scripture*, criticized both the "pedantic hyperorthodoxy" of fundamentalists and the "theistic evolution" of modernists, seeking to posit a more balanced view which he termed "progressive creationism."[29] God began the process of creation with "a sovereign and fiat act of creation . . . at the level of vacancy or null and void."[30] After this beginning, which occurs outside of nature, God turned the process over to the Holy Spirit, who works within nature, to create according to the divine plan: "The Spirit . . . knows what is the divine blueprint and through process . . . realizes the divine form of intention in Nature."[31] How Ramm's theory differs in any substantial way from theistic evolution is not readily clear to the average person!

Just four years later (1959), Edward J. Carnell entered the debate with his own theory of "threshold evolution."[32] He insisted that "the verdict of paleontology cannot be dismissed by pious ridicule,"[33] and he sought to solve the problem of the great age of the earth and man (over against their seeming youth in biblical anthropology) by positing a pre-Adamic race who were similar but inferior to present humankind.[34]

In the mid-1960s, Henry Morris attempted to wed the literal biblical interpretation of creation to science with what came to be known as "scientific creationism."[35] He sought on scientific grounds to demonstrate the facticity of "a literal six-day creation, a young earth and a worldwide cataclysm flood in the days of Noah."[36]

A more recent trend among evangelicals is to de-scientize Genesis 1 and 2, and treat them instead as a theological apologetic. Protagonists of this view—critical of both scientific creationism and evolutionary naturalism—maintain that "Genesis presents a theology of creation that is fully aware of and challenges the nu-

merous polytheistic cosmogonic myths of . . . the other cultures surrounding Israel. . . ."[37] The opening chapters of Genesis should not
be seen as an attempt to detail scientific data, but rather as "framework which serves magnificently for presenting the totality of creation at the hand of God."[38] To treat Genesis in such a fashion is to
relieve oneself of onerous difficulties with modern scientific knowledge.

All of these more radical solutions to the problem of biblical
versus contemporary anthropology presuppose God as Creator. At
no point is any divergence made into the concept of a "chance
development" of life from eternal matter (as many scientists would
have us believe!).

What of the composition of humankind? Contemporary theological thinking emphasizes the unity of the person; evangelicals affirm such unity while noting that human nature has a spiritual
aspect which complements the physical. At death, these components are separated, to be reunited at the resurrection.

Some evangelicals are dichotomists, viewing humankind as a
duality—material and immaterial, body and spirit. Others are
trichotomists, seeing humans as composed of body, soul, and
spirit. The former appeal to James 2:26 and 1 Corinthians 7:34, the
latter to Hebrews 4:12 and 1 Thessalonians 5:23.

How has the immaterial part been implanted in humankind since
Adam and Eve? Again, evangelicals are divided into two camps.
Creationists believe that every human soul (or spirit) is individual-
ly created by God and placed in the child at some point between
conception and birth. Traducianists believe that the whole human
being—body and spirit—is procreated through the parents. "One's
view of the transmission of the immaterial in humans will have an
effect upon his or her view of abortion. Abortion is much more
defensible in creationism than in traducianism, especially if it is
held that the soul is not created until late in the pregnancy."[39]

Latter day evangelicalism has seen a trend toward "androgyny"
in a theological consideration of male and female. There has been
increasing controversy over the "submission" passages of Scripture (e.g., Eph. 5:21ff). While there is still a large proportion
of evangelicaldom who interpret these verses as requiring wifely subordination to male domination, the evangelical feminist
movement has exerted increasing influence, especially on younger

members in the ranks. Hunter notes that:

> From this [feminist] perspective, the problem is that notions
> of subordination and submission of the woman intrinsically
> imply inequality and inferiority, and this is contrary to the
> more prominent New Testament themes of justice and equal-
> ity among all of God's people. To be more specific, the prob-
> lems with traditional approaches to the subject stem in large
> part from faulty biblical exegesis.[40]

When properly interpreted, it is argued by feminism's proponents,
these texts demonstrate that—under Christ—husband and wife
exist not in a hierarchical arrangement, but in mutual submission
to each other. Wifely submission to the husband is balanced by
husbandly loving self-sacrifice to the wife (also a form of submis-
siveness in obedience to Eph. 5:21).

Eschatology. Unlike their fundamentalist brethren, who insist that
the only possible eschatological stance in light of Scripture is dispensational premillennialism, evangelicals come with a wide range
of views. They submit that strong emphasis must be placed on the
facts itself of Christ's return. Other details are biblically vague and
theologically peripheral.

Robert Clouse's *The Meaning of the Millennium*[41] is representative of the broad range of evangelical opinion. There are four
different schools of thought presented in it: George Ladd discusses
historic premillennialism; Herman Hoyt, dispensational premillennialism; Lorraine Boettner, postmillennialism; and Anthony
Hoekema, amillennialism. After each presentation there follows a
rebuttal from the other three antagonists.

Nor is there unanimity on the final state as it applies to unbelievers. More and more evangelicals have been moving away from the
Augustinian position of eternal conscious torment toward conditional
immortality and annihilationism. In 1988, the evangelical world was
set abuzz with the discovery that one of its leading lights, John
R.W. Stott, believed that God would extinguish the wicked rather
than allow them to be tortured for eternity.[42] And there are a few
evangelicals who adhere to a variety of universalism (albeit highly
qualified).[43] The overwhelming number of evangelicals, however, hold
to the eternal separation from God and punishment of the wicked

(whether that punishment be conscious or unconscious).[44]

Conclusions

If there were a single adjective which might describe the evangelical movement, it would be flexible. Evangelicals, for the most part, have placed a premium on a cooperative spirit. As Carnell wrote: "While we must be solicitous about doctrine, Scripture says that our primary business is love. . . ."[45] Such a stance, which permits a broad divergence of doctrinal viewpoints while cultivating a united front on the fundamental issues, is at once a tremendous strength and a dangerous weakness.

This broad divergence of opinion is admittedly historical. A study of early patristic history reveals a broad range of doctrinal viewpoints which coexisted in relative harmony for some time. (Although, ultimately, with the ascendancy of Roman Catholicism as *the* orthodox church, alternative views were severely persecuted.) Cooperation allows for a maximizing of common strengths to advance the Gospel. When Christian groups can speak with a united voice, they can accomplish much more than when they are attacking each other.

At the same time, "a little leaven leavens the whole lump" (1 Cor. 5:6, NASB). There is a problem in allowing such a latitude of views, namely, that those on the extreme fringe will tend to infect others with their views and draw the mainstream in their direction, thus destroying the balance. This seems to be the tendency with those who are on the more liberal side in their views of Scripture. Over the few decades since their inception, evangelicals as a group have moved somewhat toward the left in regard to their view of the Bible.

The dilemma of evangelicalism is that a line must be drawn somewhere to mark the boundaries of the movement. But where should it be drawn? There is little agreement on the answer.

The desire of evangelicals to go beyond the fundamentalists in ministering to the whole person (and not just some spiritual aspect) is commendable and biblical. A social application of the Gospel is mandatory. Robert Lightner's criticism of such an approach is *not* appropriate: ". . . the danger of this direction does not lie in what neo-evangelicalism now believes but in that which its present emphasis may very well lead it to believe and proclaim."[46] If one were to desist from mission because of the dangers of going in a wrong direction, the church would be static. The far greater danger is evangelicals who talk about the need for social involvement, but who fail to get involved.

An intellectual approach to the faith is highly commendable as well. Since God has created wisdom and the human brain to accommodate it, He must desire human beings to use their intellects to His glory. Fear of dialoguing with those who are opposed to our point of view is usually the result of an inadequate knowledge of, and an inability to present in a clear and concise way, our belief system. Trained, capable believers who are evangelistic apologists are absolutely necessary for the future of orthodoxy.

It may be apparent that the term "neo-evangelical" has been little used in favor of "evangelical." The reason is that evangelicalism is not a new approach, but simply a "re-rooting" in, and reproclamation of, historic orthodoxy. Succinctly defined, it is nothing more nor less than an attempt to apply the Gospel to society's contemporary needs.

For Further Reading

Bloesch, Donald G. *The Future of Evangelical Christianity: A Call for Unity and Diversity*. Garden City, N.Y.: Doubleday Co., 1983.

_____. *The Evangelical Renaissance*. Grand Rapids: William B. Eerdmans Publishing Co., 1973.

Carnell, Edward John. *The Case for Biblical Christianity*. Edited by Ronald H. Nash. Grand Rapids: William B. Eerdmans Publishing Co., 1969.

Coleman, Richard J. *Issues of Theological Warfare: Evangelicals and Liberals*. Grand Rapids: William B. Eerdmans Publishing Co., 1972.

Hunter, James Davison. *Evangelicalism, The Coming Generation*. Chicago: University of Chicago Press, 1987.

Lightner, Robert P. *Neo-evangelicalism*. Findlay, Ohio: Dunham, n.d.

Moberg, David O. *The Great Reversal: Evangelism Versus Social Concern*. Philadelphia: J.B. Lippincott Co., 1972.

Nash, Ronald H. *The New Evangelicalism*. Grand Rapids: Zondervan Publishing House, 1963.

Pierard, Richard V. *The Unequal Yoke: Evangelical Christianity and Political Conservatism*. Philadelphia: J.B. Lippincott Co., 1970.

Quebedeaux, Richard. *The Young Evangelicals: Revolution in Orthodoxy*. San Francisco: Harper and Row, 1974.

Ramm, Bernard L. *The Evangelical Heritage*. Waco, Texas: Word Inc., 1973.

Shelley, Bruce. *Evangelicalism in America*. Grand Rapids: William B. Eerdmans Publishing Co., 1967.

Wirt, Sherwood E. *The Social Conscience of the Evangelical*. New York: Harper and Row, 1968.

Five. Neo-liberalism

T he traditional liberalism fathered by Friedrich Schleiermacher and Enlightenment intellectuals which had proved so destructive to orthodox Christianity in the nineteenth century was alive and well at the dawn of the twentieth century. But two cataclysmic events in the early part of the century dealt it fatal blows.

The optimism with which the century had begun quickly dissipated in 1914 with the first World War, the most brutal conflict Europe had ever witnessed. William Hordern notes that "somewhere between 1914 and 1918 liberalism died in Europe."[1] Because of North America's relative isolation from the carnage, liberalism continued strongly in Canada and the United States, enjoying a number of successes in its campaign against fundamentalism. But the Great Depression which followed the stock market collapse of 1929 destroyed any hopes of continuing prosperity and—if that were not sufficient to quell liberal optimism—World War II and the Holocaust completed the burial.

The Advent of Neo-Liberalism

The shock of World War I and the Great Depression led many liberals to turn to secular humanism, repudiating both Christianity and God. But, from the ashes of this debacle, there arose almost immediately a "new" liberalism referring to itself as "evangelical," and espousing Jesus Christ as Lord. Represented by men such as Harry E. Fosdick, Henry S. Coffin, and H.P. Van Dusen, these neo-liberals called for a recognition of the uniqueness of the Bible and emphasized sin as the human predicament which could be ameliorated only with God's help.

Harry Emerson Fosdick. Fosdick was one of the main liberal contenders against fundamentalism in the United States during the controversies of the 1920s. An ordained Baptist, he was a teacher at Union Theological Seminary (from 1908-46), and was called to the pulpit of New York's First Presbyterian Church in 1918, as noted in chapter 1. There, one Sunday's sermon, "Shall the Fundamentalists Win?" brought such a scathing response that he was ultimately (in 1924) forced to leave Presbyterianism and return to the Baptists.

Fosdick accepted a call to Park Avenue Baptist Church, New York, the home congregation of John D. Rockefeller, Jr., on the condition that the church accept a non-creedal open-membership policy, and that Rockefeller build him a new church edifice. In 1926, Fosdick became pastor of the new Riverside Church, where he remained until retiring in 1946. The prestige of his church, coupled with his warm personality and pulpit oratory, made him probably the most influential cleric in the United States during that time.

Although he was considered by many fundamentalists to be their movement's archenemy, Fosdick was never an old-line doctrinaire liberal. He had a lofty view of the Bible, of God, and of Christ's passion, but he felt that modernism was necessary to rid the Christian faith of much of its superstition. Thus, he sought to incorporate into Christianity insights from biblical criticism, psychology, and science, stressing the ethical values of the faith over and above its doctrinal teachings.

Much of Fosdick's theology and approach to Christian practice are apparent in his popularly-written book, *Dear Mr. Brown: Letters to a Person Perplexed about Religion*.[2] In it, he emphasized belief in God based largely on experience (both that of oneself and the thousands of witnesses throughout history). His advice was to "believe in as much of God as you can,"[3] and he reiterated the liberal belief that "there is a spark of the Divine in each of us"[4] which leads one to faith.

As far as biblical inerrancy is concerned, "no intelligent Christian today feels under any constraint to thrust his mind back 2,000 years into a prescientific world view."[5] Nor should one be afraid to doubt some miracles, such as the virgin birth of Jesus, which many Christians consider vital to the faith: "personally I cannot believe it."[6] At the same time, Fosdick attributed to the Bible "the most influential development of religious ideas in man's history,"[7] especially the wonder of the salvation by Christ.

For Fosdick, being a Christian was more a matter of doing than believing. One does not attempt to accept "a huge creedal, ecclesiastical, sacramental bloc";[8] one simply begins to live a life which imitates Christ: "Being a follower of Jesus [is] something to be *done.*"[9]

Henry P. Van Dusen. Van Dusen was a theologian and scholar who, in 1945, became president of Union Theological Seminary in New York. One of his books, *The Vindication of Liberal Theology: A Tract for the Times,*[10] was an able apology for his viewpoint. His contention was that, despite its inadequacies, liberal theology was "the least inadequate, most credible and cogent interpretation of Christian faith in the nineteen centuries of its history."[11] The principles of this interpretation include: fidelity to the truth, affirmation of continuity in God's world, moral and social responsibility, the centrality of Jesus Christ, "but, above all and finally: the Truth and Authority of the Life of God in the life of Jesus of Nazareth."[12]

Van Dusen recognized that the two sources of liberalism—modern thought and Christian experience—form an insecure and ever-shifting foundation. He recommended purging "each legacy of its inadequacies—Modern Thought of its exaggerated aberrations, Christian Traditions of its outmoded superstitions"[13]—and so bringing in a truly evangelical liberalism which would stand the test of time.

Since Van Dusen's stress lay on the Person of Jesus Christ as the foundation of his liberal position, it is reasonable to evaluate his theology essentially on that basis. He held to the Incarnation and very much to the life, death, and resurrection of Jesus Christ as recorded in the Bible. At the same time, he quoted D.M. Baillie to the effect that the Son of God was not, at a certain time in history, "transformed into a human being for a period of about thirty years."[14] In so doing, he distanced himself somewhat from the historical creeds by suggesting that the divine aspect of Jesus was simply achieved by His human selfhood being lived out fully because it was lived in utter and complete dependence on God.[15] "This perplexity in understanding the Person of Christ is, *in principle,* no different and no more difficult than the relation of divine initiative and human response in all human action."[16]

In order to mediate Christ to contemporary society, Van Dusen moved away from abstract theological and metaphysical terminology such as "substance," "essence," and "infinity," and instead substituted personal words like "will," "self," "goodness," and "love." The terms of earlier centuries were inadequate to describe the Reality that is Jesus Christ.[17]

In changing the traditional theological terminology concerning Christ, Van Dusen also radically reconfigured Christ into a human being who differed from other human beings only in the degree of His relationship to God: "Unless God is in some measure incarnate in the life of every man, He cannot have become fully incarnate in Jesus of Nazareth."[18] In such a statement one finds a glimmer of traditional liberal panentheism, namely, that there is at least a spark of the divine in all creation.

Van Dusen confessed that such an approach is impossible under the ancient Christologies. It was only as one did away with the transcendence of God in favor of complete immanence that his incarnational approach was feasible: "Complete immanence would occur in a genuine person who shared, as fully as possible for a truly human life, the Vision and Purity and Purpose of God. That would be *the* Incarnation."[19]

Van Dusen's incarnational theology required, as well, a much greater limitation of Jesus' powers than was usual in orthodox, historical Christianity: "only as much of the Being and Purpose of God found expression in and through Him as was appropriate and possible for one of his heritage, his era, his span of experience."[20] Consequently, Jesus could not serve as a concrete model of moral authority. God's purposes for each human life differ according to that life's circumstances and "no two descriptions of the common Faith will wholly coincide."[21]

Van Dusen's Christology reduced Jesus Christ to mere mortality alone. It further diminished the Christian life to some nebulous seeking after the kingdom of God. While he claimed to have elevated the faith, Van Dusen actually created a situation where every person "did what was right in his own eyes" (Jud. 21:25, NASB).

Contemporary European Neo-Liberalism

In Europe, neo-liberalism was shaped by monumental theologians such as Rudolf Bultmann, who insisted on demythologizing the

New Testament to make it comprehensible for contemporary society; Paul Tillich, whose concern for Ultimate Reality led him to conclude that only in experience can one come to any true awareness of God; and Pierre Teilhard de Chardin, who maintained that the Gospel can gain the loyalty of modern people only if it is reconceptualized in harmony with the latest scientific knowledge.

Rudolf Bultmann. Bultmann (1884-1976) was born in Wiefelstede, Germany, into an Evangelical Lutheran clergy family. His father was a clergyman; his maternal grandfather was a pastor; and his paternal grandfather was a missionary. In 1903, Bultmann was admitted to the study of theology at the University of Tubingen. From there he went to Berlin and, finally, to Marburg (where he graduated). His professors included Hermann Gunkel, Adolf Harnack, and Johannes Weiss. Beginning in 1912, he taught at Marburg, then at Breslau, before going to Giessen as a full professor in 1920. The following year he accepted an invitation to become Professor of New Testament and Early Church History at Marburg, remaining there until his retirement in 1951.

His early work, *History of Synoptic Tradition* (1921), which emphasized the use of form criticism, transformed New Testament studies. Form criticism holds that the written documents of the Scriptures are based on oral traditions. Certain rules governed the development of these traditions, handed down from generation to generation. Stories follow a definite pattern as an aid to memory. The form critic examines the written document in an effort to discern the patterns back of them. He or she also seeks to isolate or separate varying chronological layers in an effort to uncover the original story (as against successive editions of it). A part of that task is to analyze the community which created and/or retold those traditions and served as a repository for them. For example, what context caused the New Testament church to build its tradition in the form we presently possess?

As Bultmann studied the New Testament, he concluded that it was not concerned with history as we conceive it. The evangelists were casting the history of Christ and the apostles in an evangelistic setting designed to win people to the Lord. Thus, while the Gospels are undoubtedly authentically historical, we cannot get an accurate picture of the historical Jesus, although we can clearly see how His life affected those with whom He came in contact.

The most controversial conclusions of Bultmann's form-critical work were published in 1941 in an essay entitled "New Testament and Mythology." In it, he claimed that "the world picture of the New Testament is a mythological world picture,"[22] and therefore, the content of the New Testament proclamation of salvation is couched in similar myths. He traced the source of individual motifs to "the contemporary mythology of Jewish apocalypticism and of the Gnostic myth of redemption."[23] Realistic contemporary Christians simply cannot expect modern humanity to understand or accept this ancient mythological world picture. He was especially critical of Christian attempts to teach the significance of Christ's death and resurrection in such a framework: "We can see God's act only in an occurrence that enters into the reality of our own true life, transforming us ourselves. But we cannot understand a miraculous natural event such as the resuscitation of a dead man — quite apart from its being generally incredible — as an act of God that is in this sense of concern to us."[24]

What, then, is one to do to communicate New Testament faith to twentieth-century secular humankind? The truths to which the New Testament kerygma attests must be demythologized by stripping away the mythological husk without also eliminating the pure kernel of truth. "The Christian understanding . . . [must be] interpreted mythologically, in existentialist terms."[25] As we do this, we are really remythologizing the kerygma in a contemporary mythical world picture.

Bultmann acknowledged that, while one might believe that God was at work in and through Christ, it could not be proven demonstrably. Indeed, he maintained, because God is Spirit, He does not miraculously reveal Himself in space and time, for history is a part of the closed system of the universe: "This closedness means that the continuum of historical happenings cannot be broken by the interference of supernatural powers from beyond the world and that, therefore, there is no 'wonder' in this sense of the word."[26] Individuals must decide for themselves whether or not they want to see God in (or even accept) the events described by the New Testament writers, whether they be miracles, the Resurrection, or the Ascension.

If an individual should reject this biblical testimony to God's work in the world, what other recourse is there? Vernon Grounds gives us an incisive answer: ". . . if modern man will not or cannot resort to a most unscientific voluntarism, his sole alternative is skepticism or atheism. Thus Bultmann becomes a John the Baptist for the God-is-dead movement."[27] It would seem that Bultmann's presuppositions cut him off from anything but a naive fideism, without which one is led only to meaningless despair.

Paul Tillich. Tillich (1886-1965), one of this century's most influential and controversial theologians, was born in Prussia of a Lutheran pastor. He did his doctoral work at Breslau and was ordained a Lutheran clergyman in 1912. His professional life was spent teaching theology and philosophy. In the troubled days of the German Weimar Republic, he became interested in socialism, and his outspoken opposition to Adolf Hitler's National Socialism led to his dismissal from his teaching position at Frankfurt in 1933. He sought refuge from probable imprisonment by fleeing to the United States, where he taught at Union Theological Seminary in New York, Columbia, Harvard, and the University of Chicago.

Tillich's theological method has been called the "method of correlation." It proposes that philosophy and theology should complement one another. Philosophy's task is to formulate questions of "ultimate concern" (man's ultimate concern is that which demands a total commitment of himself); theology's role is to dialogue with philosophy, understanding these questions, and coming up with satisfactory responses to them. "Therefore, the systematic theologian must be a philosopher in critical understanding even if not in creative power."[28]

Tillich's magnum opus was his three-volume *Systematic Theology* (published in a single volume in 1967). In it, he referred to God as the Ground of Being, "the answer to the question implied in man's finitude; He is the name for that which concerns man ultimately."[29] That is, God is ultimate and inexhaustible Reality, who is present to humanity not as "an Object which we may know or fail to know, but Being-itself, in which we participate by the very fact of existing."[30] As such, the term "God" is really only a symbol of the Other, the Abyss, the most universal concept. In fact, declares Tillich, "God does not exist. He is Being-itself, beyond essence and existence."[31] For one to suggest that He exists is as atheistic as to deny His existence.

Revelation, for Tillich, was the manifestation of our ultimate concern. The very word implies the unveiling of something hidden, of a "mystery." But revelation does not consist in propositional truths, for "nothing which can be discovered by a methodological approach should be called a 'mystery.' "[32] Revelation is a very subjective, inner experience in Tillichian methodology, as one ecstatically experiences the power and ground of being:

> Ecstasy is not a negation of reason; it is the state of mind in which reason is beyond itself, that is, beyond its subject-object structure. . . .[It] is the form in which that which concerns us unconditionally manifests itself within the whole of our psychological conditions.[33]

Tillich's view of revelation approaches very closely Schleiermacher's "feeling of absolute dependence." Anyone who completely involves himself in the ultimate concern of his existence will be grasped by God and will enter a transforming union with the Abyss, true Being-itself.

Tillich saw sin in terms of existential estrangement: "Man is estranged from the ground of his being, from other beings, and from himself."[34] Therefore, he is hostile to God. But for Tillich, it was this very fact of hostility that demonstrated the relationship between man and God! "Man's hostility to God proves indisputably that he belongs to him. Where there is the possibility of hate, there and there alone is the possibility of love."[35] While estrangement is not a biblical term, it is nonetheless implied in all of the narratives and symbols of the Fall.

Tillich found a literal interpretation of Genesis 3 to be an absurdity which deprived the account of its being a symbol of every human's individual act which actualizes the universal fact of estrangement. ". . . the combination of man's predicament with a completely free act by Adam is inconsistent. . . . It exempts a human individual from the universal human character by ascribing freedom to him without destiny. . . ."[36] The freedom man has to choose sin (when he exercises it) results in self-loss, "the loss of one's determining center, the disintegration of the unity of the person."[37]

It is in Jesus Christ that man's estrangement from the ground of his being may be vanquished. Christ is the symbol of "New Being," "a reality in which the self-estrangement of our existence is overcome, a reality of reconciliation and reunion, of creativity, meaning, and hope."[38] But Tillich rejected traditional theological assertions about the Person and nature of Christ; he found that "the term 'divine nature' is questionable and that it cannot be applied to the Christ in any meaningful way."[39] He eliminated the "two natures" concept in favor of a philosophical description of Christ as the "eternal God-man unity." "In his being, the New Being is real, and the New Being is the re-established unity between God and man."[40]

Nor did Tillich want anything to do with the literal biblical accounts of the Crucifixion. He found them essentially absurdity compounded into blasphemy. The Crucifixion and Resurrection are simply "historical, legendary, and mythological symbols" which "show the New Being in Jesus as the Christ as victorious over the existential estrangement to which he has subjected himself."[41]

How was one to overcome estrangement in the "New Being" of Christ? Once again, Tillich radically reinterpreted the traditional theological terms of regeneration, justification, and sanctification. "Regeneration is the state of having been drawn into the new reality manifest in Jesus the Christ."[42] The basis of regeneration is the faith which ascribes to Christ as the Bearer of the New Being. Justification is "an act of God which is in no way dependent on man, an act in which he accepts him who is unacceptable. . . . it enables man to look away from himself and his state of self-estrangement and self-destruction to the justifying act of God."[43] Sanctification is the mechanism in which the power of the New Being reconstructs personality and community, within and without the church.[44] While these may appear to be reasonably in alignment with what the Bible declares, seen in their context they bear little resemblance to orthodox Christian belief.

Tillich's views had little similarity to the traditional doctrines of classical Christian faith. He emptied them of their familiar meaning and reinvested them with new, philosophical significance. While his *Systematic Theology* is undoubtedly a monumental work of a very complex thought process, it remains a substitution of the Word of God by the ontology of a human being. Worst of all, Tillich reduced God's brightest and clearest revelation, Christ Jesus, to a mere symbol of the universal salvation of all humankind. Indeed, there is little in Tillich's theology (other than the symbol of Christ as the New Being) which would not be as workable in any of the major world religions as in Christianity.

Marie-Joseph-Pierre Teilhard de Chardin. Teilhard was born in 1881 at Sarcenat in the French province of Auvergne. His family name was Teilhard; the name de Chardin came from a paternal grandmother. A devout Catholic, Teilhard became a Jesuit novice in 1899, being ordained to the priesthood in 1911.

Teilhard's passion was geology and he studied geology and paleontology at the Sorbonne in Paris, receiving his doctorate in 1922. The following year, he was appointed to the chair of geology at the Institute Catholique of Paris. Four years later he was expelled for his aberrant views. The bulk of his remaining years were spent in the Orient in paleontological research, where he was associated with the American and Chinese scientists excavating the site where the skulls of Sinanthropus (Peking) man were discovered.

Teilhard finished his life on the lecture circuit in Europe and America. Although he was a prolific writer, the Roman Catholic church during his lifetime forbade the publication of his works.

Teilhard's magnum opus was his *The Phenomenon of Man* written in 1938, and it contains the essence of his thought. As the title suggests, the book used a phenomenological methodology, but unlike contemporary thinkers, the author rounded out his system in a spiritual vein.

Teilhard's purpose in writing this work was "to develop a *homogeneous* and *coherent* perspective of our general extended experience of man. A *whole* which unfolds."[45] He began his quest in the pre-scientific era; his basic premise was that, "in the world, nothing could ever burst forth as final across the different thresholds successively traversed by evolution . . . which has not already existed in an obscure and primordial way."[46] Indeed, all of the material creation is proceeding according to a fixed, evolutionary process, beginning with elemental particles and moving through a series of "spheres," culminating in what he termed the "Omega point," a hyper-personal Collective or Universal.[47] It is here that one finds the fulfillment of the thought of Paul and John that God will unify the world — by uniting it organically with Himself.[48] "Then, as Saint Paul tells us, God *shall be all in all*. This is indeed a superior form of 'panentheism' . . . the expectation of perfect unity, steeped in which each element will reach its consummation at the same time as the universe."[49]

The center of this whole evolutionary movement, Teilhard claimed, is Christ. "By a perennial act of communion and sublimation, he aggregates to himself the total psychism of the earth. And when he has gathered everything together and transformed everything, he will close in upon himself and his conquests, thereby rejoining, in a final gesture, the divine focus he never left."[50]

What drives this Christ-centered process, according to Teilhard, is love. Teilhard's definition of love was somewhat unorthodox; love is the affinity of being with being.

It should be apparent that Teilhard's faith was radically different from that of Christian orthodoxy. He took liberal theology to its extreme, creating a wholly immanent Being who, like His creation, is in the process of change. God certainly is not the compassionate Father who intervenes in human affairs, as Christ declared Him to be.

Nor was the Christ of Teilhard the Jesus known to and proclaimed by the apostles. Teilhard refashioned Him into a "new God," One who is completely in keeping with the brave new world evolving. In fact, He is the convergent point at which all creation will unite with Divinity.

What Christ accomplished on the cross Teilhard brushed off as of little importance. "Physical and moral evil originate from a process of becoming; everything which evolves experiences suffering and moral failure. . . . The Cross is the symbol of the pain and toil of evolution, rather than the symbol of expiation."[51]

Teilhard, one must conclude, was a man in advance of his time. He really belongs to the moderns of today who preach an entirely different Gospel from that received by the apostles, but who cloak it in Christian terminology, rationalizing it as a "radical reinterpretation" of the faith.[52]

Post-Liberal Directions
It has been said that a basic feature of liberalism is that "it does not produce a third generation — or not much of one."[53] Successive generations of liberals tend to drift away, a fact easily demonstrated in the declining memberships of liberal churches.

During the 1960s and 1970s, liberals engaged in a number of theological fads, chief of which was "God is dead" theology. Others included ecological theology, a theology of ecstasy, and a theology of play. Clark Pinnock evaluates them as "faddish and subjective, a bunch of theologians doing their own thing, out of touch with the community of faith."[54]

One should not suppose, however, that liberal theology is dead. It is still very much alive, especially in academe. Leading proponents include Schubert Ogden, Langdon Gilkey, and David Tracey.

Schubert Ogden. Ogden is a disciple of Rudolf Bultmann and one of the foremost proponents of process theology. Much as his famous teacher, Ogden insists that apart from demythologization the New Testament cannot be understood or taken seriously. Why is demythologizing necessary? It "arises with necessity from the situation of modern man and must be accepted without condition."[55]

Langdon Gilkey. Gilkey is professor of theology at the University of Chicago Divinity School. His theology has been strongly influenced by the secular philosophy of history. He seeks "to avoid a 'supernaturalist' explanation of history and yet to find a valid and significant meaning for the conception of divine providence."[56] He places a premium on modernity at the expense, if need be, of biblical interpretation.

In one breath, for example, Gilkey says that Jesus of Nazareth is the "final" divine self-manifestation. In the next, he notes that, "by 'final' here, . . . is not necessarily meant that God does not reveal himself/herself elsewhere" nor is Christian revelation the sole revelation. "Rather, it indicates that for those committed to it and participating in it, it provides the all-determining criterion and measure for the reality and nature of God,"[57] according to our cultural and historical context. Other people in other cultures will have a different revelation of equal uniqueness.

David Tracey. Another good example of liberal method is seen in David Tracey, Roman Catholic professor of philosophical theology at the University of Chicago Divinity School. His *Blessed Rage for Order*[58] is a model of "revisionist theology." A revisionist theologian, according to Tracey, cannot "allow belief in a 'supernatural' realm of ultimate significance or in a supernatural God. . . ."[59] Tracey is also firmly committed to the faith of secularity. Theology, for Tracey, has but two sources, common human experience and Christian texts, which are used in mutual "correlation." The truth claims of the Christian (or any other) faith must be validated by reference to common human experience. Whether the theologian is a Christian or not is of little importance, but he must be involved in finding "appropriate interpretations of the major motifs of the scriptures and of the relationship of those interpretations to the confessional, doctrinal, symbolic, theological, and praxis expressions of the various Christian traditions."[60]

Tracey claims that "the revisionist theologian is committed to continuing the critical task of the classical liberals and modernists in a genuinely post-liberal tradition."[61] Most of the leading American theologians, he declares, are engaged in such a task.

Post-liberal theology has really moved beyond classical liberalism, as its name suggests. The Bible has lost the importance it enjoyed with the "liberal evangelicals" and has now become subservient to the cultural and historical situation of the individual. Whether it has any relevance at all is highly questionable.

Conclusions

North American neo-liberalism began with high motives, namely, to apply the Gospel practically in everyday life, to make it what it was intended to be—not an academic exercise, but a way of life. Its proponents had from their childhood been immersed in the biblical fundamentals of the Christian faith and, even though they had because of their latter academic training turned toward a more naturalistic mode of theologizing, they could no more shake off their evangelical roots than a leopard could change his spots. Consequently, as practiced by those early thinkers such as Fosdick and Van Dusen, "evangelical liberalism" had many admirable aspects.

One must commend their emphasis on the centrality of Christ. There can be no question that they clung tenaciously to the concept of a personal salvation and to the lordship of Christ. While their theory may have been less than most conservatives would demand, their stress on praxis went far beyond the typical conservative efforts. The Christian faith for them was a way of life rather than a way of talk.

Nonetheless, inherent even in these early neo-liberals were those flaws which would turn the movement away from orthodoxy. Chief among these were a devotion to evolution and an ever-increasing tendency toward natural theology—which led to a suspicion of the Scriptures because the Bible proclaimed a supernatural God, the idea of which ran contrary to naturalistic thought. While the evangelical liberals—because of their early foundation—continued to hold to supernatural, biblical ideas (albeit with some reservations), when the neo-liberal mantle was passed to the next generation who were bereft of those conservative and orthodox foundations, the result was an escalating abandonment of traditional Christianity in favor of a religious scientism which bears scant resemblance to the original article. Evidence of a clear departure from orthodoxy may be seen in the work of the German theologians such as Bultmann, whose context was much more steeped in naturalism than were his North American counterparts.

The third generation, or post-liberals, have severed all links with orthodoxy. Their religious outlook is completely secular. They refer to Scripture only because without it they could not be called Christian theologians. Their theology is spiritually bankrupt.

What are the prospects for future generations of liberals? They are somewhat bleak, for their predecessors have destroyed the foundations on the historic faith and have left them nothing substantial on which to build. One is reminded of Jesus' lesson of the wise and foolish builders (Matt. 7:24-27; Luke 6:46-49). Neo-liberals are "like a man who built a house on the ground without a foundation. The moment the torrent struck that house, it collapsed and its destruction was complete" (Luke 6:49).

Dean Inge once remarked, "He who marries the spirit of the age will be widowed in the next." What little there is of such Christianity in the present generation will have disappeared by the next. One will no longer even rightly be able to term this liberalism theology. It will have become a complete secular philosophy. The only comforting note that can be sounded is that as the Christian content of this thought system declines, so do the number of its adherents.

For Further Reading

Bultmann, Rudolf. *New Testament Mythology and Other Basic Writings*. Trans. and ed. Schubert Ogden. Philadelphia: Fortress Press, 1984.

DeWolfe, Harold. *The Case for Theology in Liberal Perspective*. Philadelphia: Westminster Press, 1959.

Fosdick, Harry E. *Dear Mr. Brown: Letters to a Person Perplexed about Religion*. New York: Harper and Row, 1961.

———. *Rufus Jones Speaks to Our Time*. New York: Macmillan, 1951.

———. *The Man from Nazareth*. New York: Harper, 1949.

———. *As I See Religion*. New York: Harper, 1932.

Gilkey, Langdon. *Message and Existence*. New York: Seabury Press, 1979.

———. *Reaping the Whirlwind*. New York: Seabury Press, 1976.

Ogden, Schubert M. *Christ without Myth*. New York: Harper and Row, 1961.

Teilhard, Pierre. *The Phenomenon of Man*. Trans. Bernard Walls. New York: Harper, 1959.

———. *How I Believe*. Trans. Rene Hague. New York: Harper and Row, 1969.

Tillich, Paul. *Systematic Theology*. Chicago: University of Chicago Press, 1967.

Tracey, David. *Blessed Rage for Order: The New Pluralism in Theology*. New York: Seabury Press, 1975.

Van Dusen, Henry P. *The Vindication of Liberal Theology*. New York: Charles Scribner's Sons, 1963.

Six. Post-Vatican II Catholicism

For centuries Roman Catholics have followed the teachings of their two premier theologians, Augustine of Hippo and Thomas Aquinas. The magisterium of Rome has held that to go against scholastic theology is tantamount to opposing God Himself. As late as the First Vatican Council (1869-70)—and even into the first decades of the twentieth century—the church proclaimed that there was no place for the mediation of salvation in either the separated Christian denominations or in the world's major pagan faiths. The rule of the Fourth Lateran Council of 1215 firmly stipulated: "No salvation outside the Church!"

Over the last forty years or so, however, a new breed of Catholic scholar has come to the fore. Trained in the methods of Protestant higher criticism, radical theologians have increasingly challenged and reinterpreted much of the traditional dogma of Catholicism. Nowhere were these challenges more evident and effectual than at the Second Vatican Council (1962-65).

Vatican II

Called by Pope John XXIII (and continued under Paul VI), the Second Vatican Council (the twenty-first ecumenical church council by Rome's reckoning) was an intentional effort to renew the church and redefine Catholic dogma. It has been termed "the most significant assembly of the Roman Catholic church in the last 400 years."[1] An average of 2,300 delegates were present for the major votes of four annual sessions, approving sixteen major texts.

John XXIII set the tenor of the council by declaring that the world needs healing rather than condemnation. He held out an olive branch to all Christian groups, seeking a true ecumenical spirit. A great many delegates took him seriously and a battle developed between radical (liberal) prelates and scholars and those of a traditional (conservative) outlook as to the church's future orientation. The documents of the council demonstrate an attempt to be open to humanity in general, while maintaining harmony with Roman Catholic tradition.

The church. One of the focal doctrinal documents of the council was *Lumen Gentium*, "Dogmatic Constitution on the Church."[2] It reaffirmed the doctrine of papal infallibility, but added that "the infallibility promised to the Church resides also in the body of bishops when that body exercises supreme teaching authority with the successor of Peter."[3]

One important shift in emphasis occurred in this document's view of the laity. After having insisted for centuries that only the clergy constitute the church, the council reversed the traditional position by declaring that "these faithful are by baptism made one body with Christ and are established among the People of God. They are in their own way made sharers in the priestly, prophetic, and kingly functions of Christ."[4] In a similar shift away from historic tradition, the church recognized, as well, that:

> upon all the laity, therefore, rests the noble duty of working to extend the divine plan of salvation ever increasingly to all men of each epoch and in every land. Consequently, let every opportunity be given them so that, according to their abilities and the needs of the times, they may zealously participate in the saving work of the church.[5]

Previously, such missionary emphases had been the task of those in holy orders.

Revelation. Another focal point of the council was *Dei Verbum*, "Dogmatic Constitution on Divine Revelation." Although presented in a draft to the first session, it was rewritten for the second session, sent back for revision and then voted on in the third session, where it was again altered before final acceptance at the fourth session in 1965.

The influence of the radical group was clearly felt in the area of revelation. Whereas Scholastic tradition had held to two distinct sources of divine knowledge—natural and supernatural (special)—Vatican II opted for a salvation-history approach which saw revelation as a holistic unity.[6] The reason for this unitive approach was the council's desire for a universal ecumenicity, as evidenced by the statement in *Nostra Aetate*, "Declaration on the Relationship of the Church to Non-Christian Religions," that "God, His providence, His manifestations of goodness, and His saving designs extend to all men against that day when the elect will be united in that Holy City ablaze with the splendor of God, where the nations will walk in His light."[7]

Vatican II, then, was moving away from the Thomistic emphasis on a rational approach to the knowledge of God in favor of an experiential and intuitive one. This new orientation was very close to Protestant neo-orthodoxy, claiming that in Jesus Christ "the full revelation of the supreme God is brought to completion."[8] Indeed, one theologian was led to declare that *Heilsgeschichte* (salvation-history) is not at all a recent development, but "Neo-Orthodoxy is really *Vetusta Orthodoxia*."[9]

Non-Catholics. Several documents were issued which pertained to Rome's relationship to non-Catholic peoples and religions. These included *Unitatis Redintegratio*, "Decree on Ecumenism";[10] *Orientalium Ecclesiarum*, "Decree on Eastern Catholic Churches";[11] *Ad Gentes*, "Decree on the Church's Missionary Activity";[12] *Nostra Aetate*, "Declaration on the Relationship of the Church to Non-Christian Religions";[13] and *Dignitatis Humanae*, "Declaration on Religious Freedom."[14] These documents all attempted to retain the traditional concepts, while radically reinterpreting them. This they did by maintaining the church's role as sole custodian of salvation, but at the same time issuing declarations of universalism. In *Unitatis Redintegratio*, for example, the council declared that "it is through Christ's Catholic Church alone, which is the all-embracing means of salvation, that the fullness of the means of salvation can be obtained,"[15] but in that same document confessed that other (non-Catholic) Christian communions, "though we believe they suffer from defects already mentioned, have by no means been deprived of significance and importance in the mystery of salvation."[16]

A new openness was also extended to those of a non-Christian persuasion. The council acknowledged that all humankind seeks answers to the ultimate concerns of life:

From ancient times down to the present, there has existed among diverse peoples a certain perception of that hidden power which hovers over the course of things and over the events of human life; at times, indeed, recognition can be found of a Supreme Divinity and of a Supreme Father, too. Such a perception . . . instill the lives of these people with a profound religious sense. Religions bound up with cultural advancement have struggled to reply to these same questions with more refined concepts and in more highly developed language.

Thus in Hinduism men . . . seek release from the anguish of our condition through ascetical practices or deep meditation or a loving, trusting flight toward God.[17]

In the same way, all of the major world religions seek to attain moral and spiritual enlightenment. "The Catholic Church rejects nothing which is true and holy in these religions. . . . [which] often reflect a ray of that Truth which enlightens all men."[18]

Perhaps the most startling of all changes in the church's attitudes was toward those of an atheistic bent, who nonetheless live decent, moral lives. "Whatever goodness or truth is found among them is looked upon by the Church as a preparation for the Gospel. She regards such qualities as given by Him who enlightens all men so that they may finally have life."[19]

Some conclusions. Unquestionably, Vatican II represents a major shift in theological orientation from the past. No longer is Rome the sole repository of divine revelation. Salvation is attainable even by those who do not know Christ.[20] Thus, the council has set the church on a direct course towards universalism: ". . . the Church awaits that day, known to God alone, on which all peoples will address the Lord in a single voice and 'serve him with one accord.' . . ."[21]

In this universalist direction, the council has a view not dissimilar to that of Protestant liberalism. Missions becomes essentially a matter of helping non-Christians to realize that they are, indeed, saved. Missionaries are to learn the culture and religious traditions of non-Christians that they may "gladly and reverently [lay] bare the seeds of the Word which lie hidden in them."[22] As such efforts are patiently and sincerely undertaken, all humanity will ultimately attain salvation.

Since Vatican II

Several European scholars have been active in the agitation for change in the Roman Church. They have continued their theology in the light and direction of Vatican II. The major influences include Karl Rahner, Hans Kung, and Edward Schillebeeckx. They have replaced European Protestants as the leading theological thinkers of our day.

Karl Rahner. Born in Germany in 1904, Rahner joined the Jesuits in 1922 and was ordained a priest ten years later. He studied under Martin Heidegger and graduated in 1936 with his doctorate. His career was spent teaching dogmatic theology at Innsbruck, Munich, and Munster. He has been a prolific writer, his magnum opus being the sixteen-volume *Theological Investigations*, containing some 8,000 pages published between 1954 and 1984.

Rahner may be termed "neo-Thomist" in his methodology. His was a reinterpretation of Aquinas influenced by Heidegger and Marechal, a Belgian Jesuit. He debunked the idea of realistic paradigms of knowledge, the idea of truth as the correspondence between a statement and an object. In such paradigms, the known is something external which acts upon the object of knowledge.[23] Rather, in Rahner's model, "the knowing possession of knowledge as such, as distinguished from its objectified object, and the knowing possession of self are characteristics of all knowledge. In knowledge not only is something known, but the subject's knowing is always co-known."[24] Applied to God, this says that He is not known by an inference from the finite to the infinite; He is instead co-known in the act of knowing the finite, as the a priori illumination of knowledge.

It is important to understand what Rahner meant by grace. "Rahner consistently defines grace as the self-communication of God. In fact, for Rahner the essence of Christianity was summed up in those two words: God's self-communication."[25] In this grace, God bestows the very essence of His divine being upon human beings. It is the very divinization of humanity.[26]

When Rahner talked about "God's self-communication," he was not necessarily referring to the Bible. While it is the ultimate witness to God and His goodness, the Bible is nonetheless an historically conditioned book. It must therefore be interpreted in the Spirit and under the guidance of the magisterium of the church. Thus, tradition is a very important corollary to the Bible. Under the guidance of the Holy Spirit, the magisterium (or, episcopate of the church) possesses an infallible doctrinal authority. "The infallibility of Church teaching extends to all doctrines proclaimed with absolute assent by the Pope or a General Council or by the magisterium."[27] It would seem, then, that God's self-communication is not really the Bible, but the Roman Catholic tradition as mediated by its hierarchy.

Whether they are aware of it or not, all human beings are illuminated by the light of God's grace. "From this point of view, it is correct to say that in every philosophy men already engage inevitably and unthematically in theology, since no one has any choice in the matter—even when he does not know it consciously—whether he wants to be pursued by God's revealing grace or not."[28] Unfortunately, claimed Rahner, Christians are too selfish and narrow-minded to recognize that this "latent Christianity" resides in all.

Rahner explained in rather Tillichian terms how man comes into contact with God. God's grace in such a context "means the freedom of the ground of being which gives being to man, a freedom which man experiences in his finiteness and contingency."[29] It is this "freedom" which allows humans to experience eternity, for God is present unthematically as the ground of being underlying human freedom.

Rahner referred to this unthematic presence of God as "anonymous Christianity." He declared that even when a person does not know Christ explicitly, he "can nevertheless be a justified person who lives in the grace of Christ."[30] Consequently (as suggested by Vatican II), the Buddhist, Hindu, Muslim, and atheist may be partakers of the salvation of Christ, albeit unknowingly. Such a view should not be surprising, considering Rahner's definition of salvation: "[It is] the final and definitive validity of a person's true self-understanding and true self-realization in freedom before God by the fact that he accepts his own self as it is disclosed and offered to him in the choice of transcendence as interpreted in freedom."[31]

What part, then, does Jesus Christ play in God's plan for human redemption? Rahner held to the Definition of Chalcedon of Christ as the God-man who died at Calvary and has become the Mediator between God and man. But he interpreted the Christ-event in a much different manner from the traditional. While traditional theology has tended to see the Christ-event as constitutive of salvation, Rahner suggested that it is representative of it. "In Christ the self-communication of God takes place basically to all men. This is meant not in the sense that they would also have the hypostatic union as such, but rather that the hypostatic union takes place insofar as God wishes to communicate himself to all men in grace and glory."[32] Christ, then, becomes the ground of faith rather than its object. Wherever true faith exists, conscious of Christ or not, He is always and everywhere present.[33]

In this scheme, is there a role for the church and for missions? The church needs to become an ambassador for Christ, confronting the non-Christian, but as someone who "has already been given revelation in a true sense even before he has been affected by missionary preaching from without."[34] In other words, its mission is to help the member of an extra-Christian religion to realize that he has already received God's grace in Christ.

What can one say about Rahner's neo-Thomist theology? It makes a solid attempt to deal with those who have never heard the Gospel. The concept of Christ as the ground of faith for the uninformed is intriguing. On the other hand, one cannot be so charitable with atheists and pagans who do know the Gospel; Rahner's approach is too anthropocentric and philosophical and insufficiently theocentric and biblical. Scripture—not human reason—must be the standard for our knowledge of God and how He acts towards humanity. We must depend on Scripture and not on some inner feeling for divine revelation.

Nor is the church's task merely an informative one. Certainly, it must reach out to all peoples and, as it does, there is a need to be aware of the cultural and religious roots of the people it seeks to contact. But the reasons for such an awareness are to better confront them in love with the claims of Jesus Christ upon their lives. The concept of anonymous Christianity simply does not harmonize with the teaching of the Bible; the person who rejects Christ—no matter how moral such a one may be—is lost.

Hans Kung. Kung was born in Switzerland in 1928. He studied at the Sorbonne in Paris, in 1960 assumed the chair of fundamental theology at the Catholic Theological Faculty of the University of Tubingen, and later served as professor of dogmatic and ecumenical theology as well as director of the Institute for Ecumenical Studies at the same institution.

Kung's radical theology aroused much controversy among the Roman Catholic hierarchy, especially because of his blunt opposition to papal infallibility. In 1978, Pope John Paul II banned him as an accredited teacher of Roman Catholic theology.[35] Kung's best-known works are *On Being a Christian* (1976) and *Does God Exist?* (1978).

Kung sees proper theological method as beginning as much as possible "from below," that is, with those questions that arise from human experience. What is determined from human experience must then be given theological meaning in the light of the Gospel.[36] Kung's chief concern is "seeking out 'the' modern man in the place where he is actually living in order to relate the knowledge of God to the things that stir him."[37]

Kung, like Rahner, is very much open to non-Christian religions as possible avenues to salvation. While these other groups used to be regarded by Christians as demonic, "now they are recognized as ways of salvation."[38] Should a Christian object to this new view, he should remember that all of the major world religions seek answers to the same existential questions, that all seek a way of salvation from human misery and alienation, and that all regard murder, lying, theft, and adultery as sinful.[39]

In respect to Vatican II, Kung questions the concept of "anonymous Christian." "But is not the whole of good-willed humanity thus swept with an elegant gesture across the paper-thin bridge of a theological fabrication into the back door of the 'holy Roman Church,' leaving no one of good will 'outside'?"[40] He questions whether all of these pagan peoples are really entering the church or if it is all a figment of theologians' imaginations. His conclusion is that an amplification of traditional concepts like "church" and "salvation" is only a diminishment of the reality of Christianity.[41] Obviously, all the problems of the non-Christian religions need fresh analysis and reconsideration.

Much of the question of extra-Christian religions is wrapped up in the question of revelation. How does God reveal Himself to human beings? Like Tillich, Kung posits God as the ineffable, but immanent, ground of being. Humanity cannot come to know God by rational "proofs"; were such proofs possible, then God would become an object and not God at all.[42] Any knowledge of God that humans possess is the result of God's initiative. "Encounter with God, wherever and however it takes place, is God's gift."[43]

Human encounter with God is experiential. Kung uses an analogy to swimming: one can learn to swim only by swimming. Our experience of God comes only when we dare to venture forth in practical trust. "Belief in God is nourished by an ultimately substantiated basic trust. . . ."[44] Any person who has committed himself to such a basic trust may properly be termed a believer.

Because all of the world's major religions seek to connect their practitioners with the ground of existence, and because all human beings may commit themselves to a relationship of trust, therefore all may experience God. So Kung determines the reality of salvation for those outside of Catholicism. He terms this avenue of salvation as the "ordinary" path to God.

While the non-Christian religions may be legitimate accesses to salvation, Christianity remains extraordinary, for Jesus is "ultimately decisive, definitive, archetypal, for man's relations with God."[45] And Kung is unequivocal in his insistence that unless Jesus Christ is ultimately decisive for it, no community may be called Christian. "Christianity exists only where the memory of Jesus Christ is elevated in theory and practice."[46]

Being a Christian means following Christ, imitating Him, living life in the same spirit or attitude as Christ lived it. "By following Jesus Christ man in the world of today can truly humanly live, act, suffer, and die: in happiness and unhappiness, life and death, sustained by God and helpful to man."[47] The church's mission is to acquaint the "saved" of extra-Christian groups with Christ who mediates God's grace to the world. Unlike Rahner, who holds that the anonymous Christian is a part of the church, Kung believes that the "pre-Christians" (as he terms them) must unite with the church.

Though not going as far as Rahner, Kung follows the direction charted by Vatican II. By affirming Christ as the divine Logos who illumines all men, he has built an experiential theology which potentially embraces all humanity. Natural revelation has been enlarged to the point where special revelation becomes secondary rather than primary. The experiencing of Christ becomes the climax of the salvific process rather than its facilitator. Missions no longer is primarily an evangelistic endeavor, but an educational or dialogical one.

Edward Schillebeeckx. Born in Antwerp, Belgium, in 1914, Schillebeeckx joined the Dominicans in 1934 and was ordained in 1941. He earned his doctorate in theology from the Sorbonne in Paris and, in 1943, began teaching at the Dominican Studium in Louvain before moving to the Netherlands to teach dogmatic and historical theology at the University of Nijmegan. In 1979, Schillebeeckx—whose theology had a number of similarities to Kung's—was called to Rome and interrogated on his doctrinal views, but managed to avoid Kung's fate. Schillebeeckx's works include editing a multi-volume series on Catholic theology called *Concilium* and writing *The Mission of the Church* and *Jesus, An Experiment in Christology.*

Schillebeeckx, like Rahner, is somewhat of a "neo-Thomist," filling Aquinas' ideas with new content. He takes Aquinas' idea of *gratia fraterna* (the grace that establishes brotherhood) as the basis of the unity of humanity as a community of persons. "Communion among men is the reflection, immanent in mankind's history, of man's transcending communion with the living God."[48]

Schillebeeckx uses Scripture to demonstrate that, when God establishes a community among humans, He appoints a representative or vicarious mediator for either the salvation—or destruction—of the many. "In the Bible the establishment of a community through mediation implies that election and universal mission coalesce into one."[49] He cites God's promise to Abraham that in him all the nations of the earth will be blessed (Gen. 12:3; 18:18; 22:18) as proof of God's determination of universal salvation.[50]

Jesus is the supreme vicarious mediator. "Mankind, then, has received salvation through the fraternal service of one chosen from among ourselves—Jesus Christ, the Elect of God, the Son of the Father."[51] Schillebeeckx uses Irenaeus' theory of recapitulation to demonstrate that Christ stands at the beginning of a new mankind which He has formed into a community; in this one Man all men have already received salvation. Christ is the eschatological Man who, although in a dimension exceeding our experience, gives human history its ultimate immanent significance.[52]

The purpose of the (Roman) church is as the ever-present Body of Christ with mankind. "As the Body of our Lord, the Church forms the living link with Christ—horizontally, with the Jesus of history, . . . vertically, with the Lord of glory. . . . Because of Christ's fellowship with us the universal human fellowship too takes on a deepened meaning. . . ."[53]

Schillebeeckx tends more towards Kung than to Rahner in relating the church to anonymous Christianity. He feels that it would be better to reserve the appellation "church" for baptized communicants, and call anonymous Christians "pre-church."[54]

The church's mission is to love humanity as it loves God: "the working out of our Christian character must needs take shape in the ordinary daily dealings in and with the world and our fellowmen."[55]

Like Rahner and Kung, Schillebeeckx has concocted his soteriology "from below," using anthropology and philosophy as his bases rather than the Bible. He too shared with Vatican II the redirection of Catholic theology while maintaining the old Scholastic framework.

Other Theologians of Note

In addition to Rahner, Kung, and Schillebeeckx, a number of other theologians have been influential in the redirection of Roman Catholic theology since the Second Vatican Council. These include Gregory Baum, Raimundo Pannikar, and David Tracey. Since Tracey's thought is already summarized in chapter 4, we shall briefly examine only the first two.

Gregory Baum. Baum is a Canadian Roman Catholic priest and theologian. He came to prominence in the 1960s using a phenomenological approach to theology. His doctrine of God was particularly noteworthy.

Baum rejects the concept of God as "Other," arguing that "there is no human standpoint from which God is simply man's over-against. It is impossible to think of myself and other men over here and then of God, the supreme being, as over against us."[56] His argument is based on who man is and when he comes to completion as regards his nature: "If man is a finished substance, if his nature is fully determined at birth, then it does not make sense to speak of God's redemptive presence in man's becoming man. If man is such a substance, then God must be conceived of as extrinsic to him, then there is a human standpoint from which God is simply man's over-against."[57] In such a case, declares Baum, God is an "outsider" and it is impossible to ever get Him inside man.

On the other hand, "if man is not a finished substance, if man comes to be in a complex process of dialogue and sharing in which the whole human community is involved, then it is not necessary to think of God as extrinsic to man."[58] In such a case, man is seen to be more than himself and it is not difficult to understand that God becomes an integral part of who and what man is.

Baum rejects any charge of pantheism in such a formulation. To argue that God has become a part of man does not negate the fact that God remains everything and man by comparison is nothing.

Nor should one think that the transcendence of God is being denied:

> God is the more than human in human life. This "more than human" is his transcendence situated at the heart of his immanence. While God is wholly immanent to history . . . he can never be identified with any aspect of history. . . . God's presence in history is not exhausted by it. God rules history from within. God is always transcendent to human life as critique, as newness, as orientation.[59]

Such a reinterpretation, Baum admits, allows one to formulate the Christian creed without ever mentioning God at all, thus appealing to secular humanity in language it can understand. In following such a course, he confesses, he is following Karl Rahner. "The church's silence about God would enable Christians to overcome the objectification of God to which they have become accustomed and thus to remove the great obstacle for the Christian faith in the modern world."[60] Such a silence, however, cannot be total for, whenever truth is threatened, when people seem in danger of forgetting that the mystery at work in their history radically transcends it, then the name of God must be brought into practical life.

Baum calls his doctrine of God "the Good News that humanity

is possible."[61] It seems more likely, though, that this formulation of doctrine—worthy though its aims may be—will lead to a forgetting of God altogether.

Raimundo Pannikar. Pannikar is a theologian born of a Spanish Roman Catholic mother and an Indian Hindu father. Raised on both the Hindu and Christian scriptures, he has sought to integrate Roman Catholicism with Eastern religions, particularly Hinduism. Just as Aquinas endeavored to pour Christian doctrine into a paradigm of Greek philosophy, so Pannikar attempts to formulate Christianity in a context of Hindu philosophical thought.

In his book, *The Intra-Religious Dialogue*, he sets forth what he considers to be the necessary conditions for the promotion of a positive relationship between Christianity and the Eastern religions. Any fruitful dialogue, he argues, must be free of apologetics. "By apologetics I understand that part of the science of a particular religion that tends to prove the truth and value of that religion."[62]

Again, fruitful discussion holds within itself the threat of conversion to the other faith. "The religious person enters this arena without prejudices and preconceived solutions, knowing full well that he may have to lose a particular belief or particular religion altogether."[63]

Nor should such a dialogue be considered simply a philosophical symposium. Any attempt to reduce a faith stance to a set of propositions is to destroy it: ". . . no religion is satisfied to be *only* orthodoxy, ignoring orthopraxis."[64]

Neither is it mere theologizing. "Theology may furnish the tools for mutual understanding but must remember that the religious encounter imperative today is a new problem, and that the tools furnished by the theologies are not fit to master the new task unless purified, chiseled, and perhaps forged anew in the very encounter."[65]

As a necessary tool, Pannikar suggests *homology*, the idea that theological concepts may play equivalent roles in their respective societies. For example, though *Yahweh* and *Brahman* may not be exactly the same, they fulfill similar functions in their respective faiths.

Lastly, he sees such dialogue as an encounter in faith, hope, and love. Faith transcends systems and gets down to realities which may make sense to each partner in the dialogue. Hope is that attitude which allows the partners to transcend their initial difficulties and so to speak of the important realities of faith. Love is that force which "longs for a common recognition of the truth, without blotting out the differences or muting the various melodies in the single polyphonic harmony."[66]

Pannikar's views on dialogue fit in ideally with the conclusions reached by Vatican II in regard to the possession of truth by non-Christian religions in the world. And it is a step towards the Vatican's determination that Christians should dialogue with non-Christians of other faiths in an effort to bring them to a knowledge of Christ.

Conclusions

Post-Vatican II Catholicism has put a decisive end to Thomistic rationalism as an appropriate approach to God. While earlier Catholicism had called for a reasoned faith in God constructed upon the teachings of the Bible, the Fathers, and the Mother Church, in place of this logic the new Catholicism has opted for an inner, mystical, Tillichian experience of the ground of being. The old Roman Catholicism excluded all who would not receive its message and become a part of it. But the new Catholicism has reached out to embrace all humankind, for the experience of God is something inherent to every person. Post-Vatican II theology has substituted a subjective natural theology for the traditional theology based on special revelation.

Major changes have also occurred in the outworking of the doctrine of Christ. Under the system of modern Catholicism, the crucifixion of Jesus becomes representative of salvation rather than constitutive. It is no longer necessary to trust personally in Christ; it is sufficient to emulate His character. Thus, Islam, Hinduism, Buddhism, Judaism, and any other religions which seek to help humans to overcome their sense of alienation from Ultimate Reality are all valid avenues to salvation. The exclusivity of the Christian faith, the idea proclaimed by the apostles that "salvation is found in no one else, for there is no name under heaven given among men by which we must be saved" (Acts 4:12) has been broadened to such an extent that it has become almost universally inclusive.

Consequently, the program of the church is no longer to evangelize. Rather, it is now to dialogue with extra-Christian religions in an effort to help their adherents to discover Christ who is the focal point of salvation. Unfortunately, the Roman magisterium has chosen to distort the intention of John 14:6 where Jesus proclaims, "I am the way, and the truth, and the life. No one comes to the Father, except through Me." Instead, just as it was once said that all roads lead to Rome, now Rome says that all roads lead to God.

One must certainly commend the new and open spirit of Roman Catholicism when it advocates the reunion of "separated brethren" in Christ. That Christians should seek unity among themselves is a given, and the spirit of cooperation which has been evidenced since 1965 is a welcome one.

At the same time, one can go too far, and the Roman Catholic Church seems to have done so in seeking not only to cooperate with non-Christian religions, but also to recognize them as complementary roads to salvation. Such an attitude should be disparaged, for it forsakes the original message of the exclusiveness of the Christian path as proclaimed by Jesus Himself. Christianity, it must be remembered, was persecuted in its formative decades, for refusing to do the very thing that Roman Catholicism now seeks— to make the Christian faith one of many avenues to union with God. We must recognize that the exclusive nature of Christianity cannot be compromised without destroying the Christian faith itself.

For Further Reading

Abbott, Walter M., ed. *The Documents of Vatican II.* Trans. by Joseph Gallagher. Piscataway, N.J.: New Century Publications, 1966.

Baum, Gregory. *Man Becoming God in Secular Experience.* New York: Seabury Press, 1970.

Kung, Hans. *On Being a Christian.* Garden City, N.Y.: Doubleday Co. 1976.

_____. *Infallible? An Inquiry.* New York: Doubleday Co., 1971.

McCool, Gerald, ed. *A Rahner Reader.* New York: Seabury Press, 1975.

Pannikar, Raimundo. *The Intra-Religious Dialogue*. New York: Paulist Press, 1978.

Rahner, Karl. *Foundations of Christian Faith*. New York: Seabury Press, 1978.

Schillebeeckx, Edward. *The Church and Mankind, Concilium Theology in an Age of Renewal*, I. Glen Rocks, N.J.: Paulist Press, 1965.

Swidler, Leonard, ed. and trans. *Kung in Conflict*. Garden City, N.Y.: Image Books, 1981.

Wells, David. *Revolution in Rome*. Downers Grove, Ill.: InterVarsity Press, 1972.

Seven. Eastern Orthodox Theology

I f any church has a legitimate claim to stand in historical succession from the apostolic church of New Testament times, it is the Eastern Orthodox. Known also as the Greek Orthodox Church and the Greek Orthodox Catholic Church, the Eastern Orthodox tradition may be said to be the mother of both Roman Catholicism and Protestantism. And yet, this oldest tradition in which originated a huge portion of our theology is little known or understood.

A Brief Overview of Eastern Orthodoxy

In the history of the Eastern Orthodox tradition, there are four basic developmental periods. The first, the apostolic period, embraces early Christianity from its inception to the time of Constantine. The second, or medieval period, runs about ten centuries, from Constantine to the fall of Constantinople. The third period, known as the age of captivity, begins at the extinction of the Byzantine monarchy in the mid-fifteenth century, and concludes about 1830. The final developmental period is the modern one.[1]

The apostolic period. Hellenism was the cradle of Christianity. Christ was born into a world of Greek language and thought patterns. All of the major literature of the early church—including the Scriptures— were written in Greek. By the end of the first century the majority of Christians were Greek and carried the message of Christ throughout the civilized world. This period, one of recurring persecution, was the age of developing systematic theology under the church Fathers such as Irenaeus, Origen, and Tertullian. It was also an age of unity, when the church of Jesus Christ was truly one.

The year 313 was a monumental one for Christianity. In that year the Emperor Constantine converted to the faith. Not long afterward, Christianity became the official religion of the Roman Empire and the church was inundated by pagans. Because the church came to imitate the Empire, and the latter split into Eastern and Western factions, the church followed suit. "By the fourth and fifth centuries one can talk about clearly Western and Eastern churches, but they are still the one, holy, catholic and apostolic church, and will remain in unity for another five or so centuries."[2]

The medieval period. The early medieval period was the golden age of theology, of names like Basil the Great, Gregory of Nyssa, Gregory Nazianzus, John Chrysostom, Jerome, and Augustine. The major ecumenical councils were held in this period, meetings which would for all time decisively inform Christian theology on the Trinity and Person of Jesus Christ. Missionaries advanced the Gospel beyond civilization into Europe, Asia, and Africa. A number of ecclesiastical centers stood out: Jerusalem, Antioch, Alexandria, Cyprus, Constantinople, and Rome. All but the last were—and still are—centers of Eastern influence.

The medieval period was also one which saw a serious fracturing of the church. In 451, a number of Oriental churches dissented from the decision of the Council of Chalcedon on the nature of Christ and separated. The West was slowly moving away from the East as the Bishop of Rome (the Pope) assumed an increasingly monarchial posture. While the other major centers had acknowledged the pope's primacy of honor, he sought their recognition as first in power, a stance they emphatically rejected. In 863-69, the Photian schism was the occasion of sharp conflict between the Patriarch Photius of Constantinople and Pope Nicholas I. And 1054 saw mutual excommunications of the Patriarch and the Pope.

During this era the Eastern church evangelized the Bulgarians (864). Missionaries penetrated Russia in the tenth century. A Russian princess, Olga, accepted the Christian faith in 953 and influenced her grandson, Vladimir, to become a believer in 988. Russia followed the Patriarch of Constantinople.

The age of captivity. The fall of Constantinople, first to Western crusaders in 1204 and then to the Ottoman Turks in 1453, marked a transition which ended the medieval period and inaugurated the age of captivity. Because of the centuries of inter-church conflict, the Eastern church received no help from Rome. "At the beginning, the church seemed to thrive under the privileges which were granted her by the conqueror Mohammed II,"[3] but these privileges soon turned into religious intolerance. Prohibited by the Koran from exterminating the Christians because they were "people of the Book" (albeit incomplete), the Turks subjugated them by legal harassment. Further hindrances were added by making the patriarchal and other ecclesiastical high offices political as well as religious and then selling them to the highest bidder. This practice had two unhappy consequences: "It led first to a sad confusion between Orthodoxy and nationalism. . . . It became all but impossible for the Greeks to distinguish between Church and nation,"[4] and "the Church's higher administration became caught up in a degrading system of corruption and simony."[5] In matters theological, the Eastern church underwent a period of retrenchment; seeking only to survive, it was content to maintain a status quo position.

In 1480, Russia had come under the control of the Mongol Tartars. While this invasion was a cultural setback for the Russians, it helped the church, for it cut it off from Constantinople and forced it to fall back on its own native leadership. Russian nationalism and Christianity came together as Russians sought to preserve their religion and culture in the face of foreign oppression. People looked to the church for both comfort and leadership.[6]

After the fall of Constantinople, the Metropolitan of the Russian church became independent of the Patriarch. He was elected by the Russian bishops as "Metropolitan of Moscow and all Russia." In spite of this freedom, Russian Orthodox theology and liturgy changed very little.

In 1589 the Russian church became completely detached from Constantinople and its Metropolitan became a patriarch, equal with the other patriarchs in the Eastern Church. With Constantinople in captivity, Orthodox faithful began to look increasingly to Moscow for spiritual direction. "The earlier fall of Rome to the barbarians and Constantinople to the Moslems in 1453 led the Russians to think of Moscow as 'the third Rome.' "[7]

The modern period. The early nineteenth century marked the beginning of the modern period in Eastern Orthodoxy. In the 1830s, southeastern Europe was freed from Turkish domination. Those countries which had been liberated detached themselves from Turkish ecclesiastical domination, as represented by the Patriarchate of Constantinople, by organizing "autocephalous" (autonomous) national churches. The Church of Greece was organized in 1833; the Church of Romania, in 1859; the Church of Bulgaria, in 1870; and the Church of Serbia, in 1879. The loss of these groups substantially diminished the Patriarchate of Constantinople.

Peter the Great brought the Russian church directly under his own control in 1721 when he abolished the patriarchate of Moscow in favor of a Holy Synod whose chief administrator was a civil servant responsible to the Crown. The church became a department of the state until 1917 and the Bolshevik Revolution. The Communists separated the two and recreated the office of the patriarch.[8]

The Orthodox church today. The Eastern Orthodox church is in reality a family of churches. It is composed of fourteen autocephalous (literally, "self-headed") churches. These include the four ancient patriarchates of Constantinople, Alexandria, Antioch, and Jerusalem; the newer patriarchates of Moscow, Serbia, Romania, and Bulgaria; the autonomous churches of Greece, Cyprus, Georgia, Albania, Poland, and Czechoslovakia; the tiny autocephalous monastery of Saint Katherine on Mount Sinai; and the most recent autocephalous church, the Orthodox Church of America. There are sizable Orthodox churches in Europe, Canada, and Great Britain, but these are under the direction of Constantinople. While there are other churches or denominations which may refer to themselves as Orthodox (especially in the United States and Canada), they have no historical connection with the Eastern Orthodox church. "These irregular Eastern churches might be called autogenic or self-starting, but they cannot properly be called Orthodox."[9] This Orthodox family finds its unity both in doctrine and in the Ecumenical Patriarch of Constantinople, who is regarded by all Orthodox faithful as the chief among equals.

The American situation. Eastern Orthodoxy in America seems to be an exception to the rule of harmony and unity. In 1794 eight Russian Orthodox monks crossed the Bering Straits and established a mission at Kodiak, Alaska. Within two years some 12,000 people had been baptized. A chapel was built in the San Francisco area at the turn of the nineteenth century, and in 1872, the headquarters of the episcopal see were moved to that center. In 1905, with waves of immigration bringing thousands of Slavs into the eastern United States, the church's headquarters were transferred to New York City. The Russian Orthodox clergy cared, as well, for immigrants from other countries with Orthodox churches.

The North American Diocese of the Russian Orthodox Church was characterized by a greater lay participation than in any of its other dioceses, an aspect reflective of the American way of living. In 1907 the first American Sobor (convention) of clergy and laity was convened and, twelve years later, a convention of clergy and laity elected a ruling bishop in Cleveland, Ohio.

Shortly after the Russian revolution in 1917, the Soviet Communists—who were now in control of the Russian Orthodox Church—attempted "to appoint a 'loyal' clergyman as head of the American diocese so that the Church would become a tool in the hands of the Communist authorities."[10] When court action on the part of the Communist appointee was successful in gaining control of Saint Nicholas Cathedral in New York, an All American Sobor in Detroit declared the Russian Orthodox Diocese in America a "self-governing church," to be ruled by a locally elected archbishop. The then recently ousted Metropolitan Platon was invited to become the archbishop and agreed, declaring in 1933 that the Russian Orthodox Church in America was temporarily autonomous. In response, the Moscow Patriarchate declared the American Archdiocese schismatic and suspended its hierarchy until such time as they would sign an oath of loyalty toward the Soviet government.[11]

Years of negotiations followed and, in 1956, the Moscow Patriarchate announced that its demand for an oath of loyalty had long since lost its force. It was perhaps motivated in its decision because other Orthodox bodies, including the Ecumenical Patriarchate of Constantinople, had recognized the legitimacy of the Russian Orthodox Church in America and were cooperating with its clergy.

In 1970, the Russian Orthodox Church finally took action and established the Autocephalous Orthodox Church in America. "There was now a church in America, for Americans...."[12] Unfortunately, most of the other Eastern Orthodox churches did not join in this new venture, "claiming that Orthodox Americans, particularly Greek Americans, were not 'ready' or 'mature

enough' for either autoencephaly or unity."[13] Such reaction flies
in the face of official canonical Orthodox teaching which requires
local unity, and condemns as heresy "a coexistence of nationally
defined churches of the same faith, but independent from each
other, in the same city and village."[14]

Eastern Orthodox Theology

As noted, above, Orthodox theology has changed very little over
the last several decades. Thus, the key word in any examination of
its doctrinal composition is *Tradition*. "The Orthodox Christian of
today sees himself as heir and guardian to a great inheritance
received from the past, and he believes that it is his duty to
transmit this inheritance unimpaired to the future."[15] This Tradition, which includes the Bible, the major historical creeds of the
Eastern church, and the decisions of the first seven ecumenical
councils, is not static, but is animated by the Holy Spirit; "it is the
life of the Holy Spirit in the Church."[16]

The Eastern Orthodox church makes a major distinction between tradition and Tradition. The former consists of human elements, while the latter is divine. For example, items such as the
icons, candles, and crosses used in houses of worship are not a
part of Tradition, but are traditional symbols used to instruct the
faithful. Eastern Orthodox people do not regard such things as
idolatrous. "There is nothing pagan in symbolism so long as it
remains a means and not an end in itself."[17]

The doctrine of revelation. Unlike evangelicals, the Eastern Orthodox church holds that special revelation consists not only of Scripture but of Sacred Tradition as well. As Basil the Great declared
some fifteen centuries ago, "Some things we have from written
teaching, others we have received from the Apostolic Tradition
handed down to us in a mystery, and both these things have the
same force of piety."[18]

None of the above should be taken as an indication that the
Eastern church does not place a high value on the Bible. It counts
Scripture as the supreme expression of God's revelation to humanity. But Scripture cannot be divorced from the Tradition of the
church. The two together inseparably form the stream of God's
revelation to humankind. Orthodox theologians are quick to point

out that the church wrote the books of the Bible as its members were inspired by the Holy Spirit, and it was the church which—under the guidance of the Holy Spirit—decided which holy writings were canonical.[19] The Bible cannot be properly understood apart from the church. For that reason, the church claims to be the sole interpreter of Scripture.

While the Eastern Orthodox church uses the same New Testament as other Christian traditions, it uses the Septuagint (Greek) rather than the Masoretic (Hebrew) text for its Old Testament. The rationale for this is that the Greek text was the Scripture of the New Testament church and so it should be for the present church. Where the Septuagint differs from the Hebrew text, Orthodox practitioners believe the changes to have been caused by the Holy Spirit. The Septuagint also contains ten deuterocanonical writings not in the Hebrew text. While the Eastern church counts these as inspired, most present-day Orthodox theologians think of them as being on a lesser level than the others.

Just as the Bible contains the infallible pronouncements of the New Testament church, so the doctrinal statements and confessions of the early ecumenical councils are the infallible pronouncements of the early church and so are on an equal footing. Of these, the most important is the Nicene-Constantinopolitan Creed; it is recited or sung at every celebration of the Eucharist. Because they were not proclaimed by one of the councils, the Apostles' and Athanasian Creeds, while respected, are not regarded in the same light and are not used in Eastern Orthodox services of worship.

Nor does revelation cease with the Patristic era. Since the Seventh Ecumenical Council, the decisions of General Councils (e.g., the Councils of Constantinople of 1341 and 1351) have been accepted as infallible doctrine. Certain other statements and confessions, affirmed by the Eastern Orthodox church as a whole, hold the same status (as, for example, the Orthodox Confession of Peter of Moghila, as revised and ratified by the Council of Jassy in 1642). As long as the Holy Spirit is at work within the church, revelation is an open possibility.

The doctrine of God. All of Eastern Orthodox theology is predicated on the doctrine of the Trinity—God as Father, Son, and Holy Spirit. To the faithful this is no abstraction, but a practical reality on which the whole world is founded.

While Father, Son, and Spirit are of one essence, each is separated and distinguishable from the other. There is a unifying principle, namely, the Father. He is "the Source of the Godhead, born of none and proceeding from none; the Son is born of the Father from all eternity . . . ; the Spirit proceeds from the Father from all eternity."[20]

It is at this point that Western and Eastern theology have separated, on what is known as the *filioque* controversy. According to the former, the Holy Spirit proceeds from the Father and the Son; according to the latter, from the Father alone. While the Son sent the Holy Spirit on His temporal mission into the world to animate the church, Orthodox believers maintain that He has eternally proceeded from the Father. Should the Catholic (Western) argument be accepted, then the Father and Son are fused and confused into a single principle; "and what else is this but 'Sabellius reborn, or rather some semi-Sabellian monster,' as Saint Photius put it?"[21] Such a heresy emphasizes the unity of God at the expense of His diversity.

Eastern Orthodoxy stresses two important facts about God: God is the unknowable, but has made Himself known to humankind; He is unapproachable, but He has approached humankind.[22] He has done both by clothing Himself in flesh as Jesus of Nazareth. "Because Jesus Christ is a true man and true God, Christians have a true communion with God."[23]

It is impossible to fully comprehend what God has done in Christ until one realizes exactly who Jesus is. He is Emmanuel, "God with us." He is very God, Yahweh the God of Israel, who has come from heaven to earth to unite with humanity. Only in the Incarnation does the Christian faith make any sense.[24] The Nicene-Constantinopolitan Creed says it well:

> I believe . . . in one Lord Jesus Christ, the only begotten Son of God, begotten of the Father before all ages. Light of Light, True God of True God, begotten not made, consubstantial with the Father, through Whom all things were made. Who for us men and for our salvation came down from heaven and was incarnated by the Holy Spirit and of the Virgin Mary, and became Man.

While all Christians have a great respect for the cross, Western

Christianity (both Roman Catholic and Protestant) tends to emphasize the penal nature of Christ's death (Christ's suffering). Eastern Orthodox Christians stress the crucifixion in terms of Christ's victory over sin and death. As John Chrysostom writes, "I call Him king, because I see Him crucified."[25]

The doctrine of man. From the early church Fathers, Orthodox theologians have taken the Genesis creation narrative symbolically rather than literally. It indicates that God made humankind for fellowship with Himself, but humanity rejected that fellowship and has alienated itself from Him.

Eastern and Western views of post-Fall humanity differ substantially. Western theology adopts the Augustinian thesis that, as a result of the Fall, sin entered the human race and enslaved humankind to evil. Even though God had made Adam and Eve in His own image, that image was marred to the point of being destroyed, thus weakening the human will and giving humans over to inordinate lust. Eastern theology, however, acknowledges that, while Adam and Eve rebelled and fell from grace, their sin was not passed on to their descendants except in regard to temptation and mortality. Because they are made in God's image, humans retain freedom of choice and are still capable of goodness. They choose to sin. And all Christians are agreed that sin has ruptured the fellowship between God and humanity.

Salvation and the Christian life. The Orthodox concept of salvation is one of human deification. Only the "pure in heart" may see God; this purity is received only through divine grace in redemption. Those who are redeemed become "partakers of the divine nature"; they are deified, that is, "they become created, in contrast to uncreated, gods. . . . Maximus Confessor declared: 'All that God is, except for an identity in nature, one becomes when one is deified by grace.' "[26] One is not saved, then, by one's understanding of propositional truth, but by deification.

The Eastern Orthodox church is thoroughly sacramental, celebrating the same seven sacraments as Catholicism. The sacraments are not aids to the spiritual life but rather "the gift of a spiritual reality . . . attached to the sign perceptible by the senses."[27] Thus, the church is made the repository of salvation.

Through the Sacrament of Baptism, one receives salvation.[28] In the Sacrament of Holy Chrismation, the person baptized is sealed by the Holy Spirit and receives the gifts of the Spirit. The Christian life is maintained in the Sacrament of Eucharist, where the believer receives spiritual food. Since the Orthodox church holds to the theory of consubstantiation, they believe that in ingesting the elements of the Lord's Supper, one ingests the actual body and blood of the Lord. In so doing, one becomes quite literally one with Him.

When a Christian sins, forgiveness is effected through the Sacrament of Reconciliation. This sacrament has been called a "new baptism," for it enables a person to experience a change of heart, to turn away from sin and to God. This sacrament is very similar to the Roman Catholic Sacrament of Penance, especially to Confession. When the penitent has confessed his sins, the priest gives him or her advice and guidance and then lays hands on the penitent's head, signifying the forgiving and renewing power of the Holy Spirit. Unlike the Roman Catholic church, "the traditional Orthodox formula of absolution is impetrative, not declarative— 'Let God forgive thee' and not 'I forgive thee.' "[29]

The doctrine of the church. Just as the Trinity is a unity, so is the church. The Eastern Orthodox church considers itself to be the one true church of Christ in this world. It rejects the idea of one indivisible invisible church manifesting itself in numerous local churches of differing traditions. Unity is basic to the church; it has always been one and will always be one. "There can be schisms *from* the church, but no schisms *within* the church."[30]

While Orthodoxy more closely resembles Roman Catholicism in its structure than Protestantism, in that it is hierarchical, the basis of its unity is very much different. Whereas the Roman Catholic church finds its unifying principle to be an infallible pope who rules the church as Christ's direct representative on earth, the Eastern church finds its unifying principle in the Eucharist. Each local church is constituted of members together with their bishop celebrating the Eucharist. Bishops, in turn, are in collegial relation. Severance from the church occurs when one severs oneself from this collegial relationship in the church or the body of bishops.

The offices of the church are (in ascending order) deacon, presbyter, and bishop. The deacon is the entry level position among the clergy; he assists the presbyter of a parish or the bishop of a diocese. The presbyter presides over a parish under the authority of a bishop. The bishop is the diocesan head of the church. The Synod, or council of bishops, governs the church as a whole (generally presided over by an archbishop, metropolitan, or patriarch), standing under the authority of Jesus Christ who is Supreme Head of the church, which is His body. Deacons and presbyters may be married (prior to their ordination, but not following it), but the bishop is always chosen from among the unmarried clergy. The reason for episcopal celibacy is so that the bishop may devote his complete attention to the work of the church.

The emphasis on hierarchy might lead one to suspect that there is little place for the laity. Such a supposition would be misleading. In fact, with the exception of the bishop, all the church—deacons and presbyters included—are *laos*, the people of God. The bishop, as a part of the body of apostles, constitutes the laity.

Laypeople have always been heavily involved in the work of the church. They are also among the premier theologians of Eastern Orthodoxy. Photius, chief proponent of the Orthodox position in the *filioque* controversy, was a lay theologian before becoming Patriarch of Constantinople. Most bishops are advised by lay theologians, and most of the professors and students in theological seminaries are lay people.

Because the church is one, and because it is the only true church through which Christ mediates the mystery of salvation, Eastern orthodoxy holds that there is no salvation outside the church (meaning, of course, outside of the Eastern church). How, then, does Orthodoxy deal with Christians who are non-Orthodox? Are they doomed to eternal loss? Orthodox theologians fully acknowledge that "if anyone is saved, he must *in some sense* be a member of the Church; *in what sense* we cannot always say."[31]

Eschatology. The Eastern Orthodox church looks forward eagerly to the *parousia*, when Christ will come in glory for the final judgment. They refer to the Second Advent as the *apocatastasis*, or restoration, for God in Christ will transform the created order into a new heaven and a new earth.

Orthodoxy teaches the eternal bliss of the righteous and the eternal punishment of the ungodly. While some Orthodox theologians have succumbed to universalistic thinking, the overwhelming majority believe keenly in hell. Hell is a reality because human freedom of will is a reality. Human beings are free to choose or reject salvation. God has gone the second mile and further in efforts to reconcile human beings to Himself. If a person persists in rejecting God, then that individual has opted for hell, for the only alternative to God and heaven is eternal hell. Thus, for Orthodox believers, hell is not a place to which God sends the unrepentant; it is a place to which they consign themselves.

And what is the suffering of hell? It is the continuing love of God directed towards the ungodly who reside there. But what the godly experience as inexpressible joy, the unrighteous experience as inexpressible suffering. "The love of God will be an intolerable torment for those who have not acquired it within themselves."[32]

Orthodox practitioners exercise an inaugurated eschatology—an "already but not yet" concept. The coming kingdom is already impinging on this present age. In the liturgy and worship of the church, Christ is here even now.

Some Observations on Orthodox Theology

The Eastern Orthodox church preserves a very rich and ancient theological heritage extending unbroken to the apostles. Admittedly, its practice is more reminiscent of Roman Catholicism than Protestantism. Most evangelicals would feel somewhat uncomfortable in an Orthodox sanctuary with the colorful vestments, ornate icons, pungent incense, and detailed liturgy. Nonetheless, Eastern Orthodoxy is built upon the teachings of Scripture and the practices of the early church. While, for example, the Orthodox view of revelation as consisting of Sacred Tradition which includes the Bible, is not typical of evangelicals, it is built upon a convincing argument of which the Bible is the cornerstone. It is quite true that Scripture is a product of the Holy Spirit's working in and through the church, the body of Christ.

Again, while the Eastern doctrine of the Trinity has been laid aside by Protestants in favor of the Roman Catholic (*filioque*) view, it must be confessed that the former does keep the Persons of the Trinity and the work of each Member more separate and clear than the latter, which tends to blur the Father and Son. In addition, the Orthodox view promotes the biblical concept of the Father given to us by Christ (cf. John 14:26; 15:26).

As one considers the Greek doctrine of God, who could disagree with its emphasis on God the unknowable who has made Himself known to human beings through the Incarnation? Or its stress upon the unapproachable God who has approached humankind as Emmanuel, "God with us." Orthodox Christology should warm the heart of every conservative believer.

Probably the most foreign area of Greek theology for most of us would be its doctrine of salvation and the Christian life. A sacramental approach seems to rob salvation of the biblical emphasis on personal decision and action. The concept of the deification of the believer seems almost panentheistic in its scope.

Furthermore, most evangelicals would tend toward the Augustinian-Calvinistic view of original sin, believing that because of Adam's sin all humanity is born fallen and tainted with corruption; they would be somewhat suspicious of the Eastern idea that humans retain freedom of choice and (at least, some) goodness. Both views have their proof texts; it is an honest difference in interpretion. And, as noted earlier, Orthodox and evangelicals alike agree that sin has ruptured the intimacy originally existing between God and His creation.

The Orthodox insistence on being the only true church because of its history would seem to smack somewhat of the same Hebrew pride that led Paul to condemn his countrymen and insist that Abraham's children were those who imitated his faith (Rom. 9:6ff); even so, true members of the body of Christ become a part of His church by faith in Him rather than by belonging to an organization with historical roots in the first Christian century.

In defense of the Eastern Orthodox Church, it must be noted that there is, in fact, no pride or elitism in their position. Orthodox leaders pray regularly for all churches; they urge their people to practice love to all people, believers and nonbelievers alike. In spite of its adamant position, the church is extremely active in ecumenical affairs, participating in local ministerial associations, national church councils, and even in the World Council of Churches.

For Further Reading

Bogolepov, Alexander A. *Towards an American Orthodox Church.*

New York: Morehouse-Barlow, 1963.

Campbell, James M. *The Greek Fathers*. New York: Cooper Square Publishers, 1963.

Constantelos, Demetrios J. *The Greek Orthodox Church: Faith, History, and Practice*. New York: Seabury Press, 1967.

Cross, Lawrence. *Early Christianity: The Byzantine Tradition*. Sydney, Australia: E.J. Dwyer, 1988.

Florovsky, Georges. *Bible, Church, Tradition: An Eastern Orthodox View*. Belmont, Mass: Nordland Publishing, 1972.

Harakas, Stanley S. *Something Is Stirring in World Orthodoxy*. Minneapolis: Light And Life Publishing, 1978.

Lossky, Vladimir. *The Mystical Theology of the Eastern Church*. Cambridge, United Kingdom: James Clarke, 1957.

Pospielovsky, Dimitry. *The Russian Church under the Soviet Regime, 1917–1982*. 2 vols. Crestwood, N.J.: St. Vladimir's Seminary Press, 1984.

Ware, Timothy. *The Orthodox Church*. Middlesex, United Kingdom: Penguin Books, 1963.

Eight. The Charismatic Movement

The charismatic movement, also known as "the second wave of the Spirit,"[1] may be regarded as a spin-off from classical Pentecostalism among the mainline denominations. It became popular in the 1960s and has had a profound effect on both Protestant and Roman Catholic Christianity. Today it comprises some 29,000,000 mainline denominational members throughout the world.[2] In North America it represents about 18 percent of Roman Catholics, 18 percent of Methodists, about 20 percent of Baptists and Lutherans, and sizable portions of other denominations.[3]

The Origin of the Charismatic Movement

The charismatic movement has its roots in the days of World War II and some momentous happenings in traditional Pentecostalism which led to the latter's growing acceptance as a part of the mainstream of evangelical Christianity.

In 1943 the National Association of Evangelicals invited several American Pentecostal groups to join its ranks. For the first time in the history of the church a Pentecostal/charismatic movement was accepted as a part of Christian orthodoxy.[4]

Following the war, Pentecostals participated in the general economic prosperity which overtook the United States. These new financial resources were evidenced in large modern church facilities. At the same time, Pentecostals were being increasingly seen in leadership positions in industry, finance, commerce, education, and medicine. It was obvious that this charismatic brand of Christianity was no longer limited to the lower classes and the "have nots."[5]

About this same time there was a heightened interest across North America in divine healing. A number of Pentecostal evangelists—including Oral Roberts, William Branham, Jack Coe, and T.L. Osborne—held healing/evangelistic crusades which extended their ministry far beyond normal Pentecostal boundaries, attracting large numbers of mainline Christians. By the mid-1950s, Roberts was pioneering his crusades on television, and within a few years, millions of Americans were exposed to his ministry via this medium:

> Suddenly, the bishops of the Roman Catholic church became concerned by the widespread appeal of Roberts to Catholics across America. Leaders of the other mainline denominations also became aware of the large sums of money that flowed to the ministry of the Pentecostal evangelist. By 1967, computer studies showed that Roberts' largest source of financial support no longer was the Pentecostals, but his followers in the Methodist churches.[6]

The Full Gospel Business Men's Fellowship International (FGBMFI). The first organized outreach among non-Pentecostals came in 1951 with the organization of the FGBMI in southern California by layman Demos Shakarian, a wealthy Armenian Pentecostal dairyman. In 1951, after helping Oral Roberts with his Los Angeles crusade, he told Roberts that God was directing him (Shakarian) to set up a group for sharing the Gospel with businessmen. Roberts was the inaugural speaker and foretold that more than a thousand chapters would spring up and become potent vehicles for the proclamation of the Gospel. Roberts' vision was fulfilled. The FGBMFI numbered over 100,000 members in some 300 chapters by the mid-1960s and, toward the close of the 1980s, there were over 3,000 chapters in almost 90 nations.

The impetus to the charismatic movement provided by the FGBMFI has been considerable. Its thesis is that "the person who is filled with the Holy Spirit will prove more successful in business, make better tractors and automobiles than his competitors, live in a finer house . . . than the person who is . . . not baptized with the Spirit."[7] Speakers are generally laypeople who testify to the power of the Holy Spirit in their lives, either in salvation or in the miraculous. Anointing and prayer for healing are a regular part of the meeting as is the invitation to people to receive the baptism in the Holy Spirit. A large segment of those attending have not been from the traditional Pentecostal groups and have enthusiastically taken its message back to their own denominations.

David du Plessis. "The one person, above all the others, who served as a catalyst and spokesman for the new Pentecostals was David J. du Plessis, a South African. . . ."[8] Du Plessis credited his mission to non-Pentecostals to a 1936 prophecy given him by evangelist Smith Wigglesworth, that he was to leave home and take the Pentecostal message to the far corners of the earth, for God was going to perform a work which would dwarf the Pentecostal movement.

Following World War II that prophecy was fulfilled. Du Plessis became a leader in world Pentecostal circles, and in 1949 he served a brief stint as general secretary of the Pentecostal World Conference, that position being terminated because of his ecumenical activities.

During the 1950s he became Pentecostalism's "unofficial ambassador" to mainline Christianity, sharing his testimony with non-Pentecostal clergy and laity alike, many of whom were leaders in the burgeoning ecumenical movement. His loving and non-combative demeanor did much to elevate the Pentecostal image in the minds of world Protestant leaders. "By the 1950s, some mainline church leaders had even come to regard Pentecostalism as a 'Third Force' in world Christianity," thanks to du Plessis' efforts.[9]

Harold Bredesen. A young Lutheran pastor, Harold Bredesen received Spirit baptism at a Pentecostal summer camp in 1946. He volunteered to resign, but his Lutheran superiors rejected his offer. Bredesen interpreted their action as a sign that he was not to break with his denomination. He left the pastorate for other denominational endeavors and maintained a constant testimony to the power of the Holy Spirit in human life. During these years he was supported by the well-known South African Pentecostal, David du Plessis, and then by the Full Gospel Business Men's Fellowship. In 1957, Bredesen accepted the pastorate of the Mount Vernon Dutch Reformed Church, where he began a charismatic prayer meeting.

Three years later, he became chairman of the board of the newly formed Blessed Trinity Society, and was theme speaker for many of their "Christian advances." In 1963 he used the term "charismatic" as an alternative to "neo-Pentecostal," which was being employed by some media sources. In 1971, Bredesen moved to Victoria, British Columbia, where he pastored the Trinity Christian Center until 1980, when he retired to Escondido, California.

Bredesen was instrumental in the early development of the Roman Catholic charismatic movement in Latin America. He has also been cited by some noteworthy figures (such as Pat Boone, John Sherrill, and Pat Robertson) as being instrumental in their reception of the baptism of the Holy Spirit.

Agnes Sanford. The child of Presbyterian missionaries to China and the wife of an Episcopal priest, Agnes Sanford became interested in the ministry of healing after being healed of depression. This ministry was popularized in 1947 by the publication of her book, *The Healing Light*. Some seven years later, she experienced a filling of the Holy Spirit and the gift of tongues.

In 1955, she and her husband established the School of Pastoral Care, which provided seminars and conferences for clergy and medical personnel and their spouses on the ministry of healing. She continued to direct the school following her husband's death in 1960. Through this organization, Sanford actively promoted charismatic renewal in the traditional denominations. Many of her books, such as *The Healing Gifts of the Spirit* (1966) and *The Healing Power of the Bible* (1969) were well received by non-Pentecostals.

Dennis Bennett. The charismatic movement is frequently dated from November of 1959, when Dennis Bennett, rector of Saint Mark's Episcopal Church in Van Nuys, California, received the baptism in the Holy Spirit accompanied by the gift of tongues. Two members of another Episcopal church, John and Joan Baker, had received the baptism in the Holy Spirit and were quietly but steadily converting fellow church members. Their pastor, Frank Maguire, turned to Bennett for advice on how to handle the situation. Bennett met with the Bakers and, before long, experienced the Pentecostal blessing himself, followed a few days later by Maguire. During the next few months, eight clergymen and almost one hundred laity in the diocese received Spirit baptism. As of the beginning of April in 1960, about seventy members of Bennett's congregation had received the blessing.

On Passion Sunday 1960, Bennett publicly addressed Saint Mark's congregation on the events which were taking place. When challenged by an antagonistic segment of his congregation, he voluntarily resigned. Shortly thereafter, the bishop of the Episcopal Diocese of Los Angeles forbade any speaking in tongues in church-related meetings. The news of all the controversy appeared in both *Newsweek* and *Time*.[10]

Later that same year the bishop of Olympia, Washington, invited Bennett to become rector of Saint Luke's Episcopal Church in Seattle, a tiny and struggling mission work. Within a year most of Saint Luke's leadership had experienced the baptism in the Holy Spirit and, under Bennett's leadership, the church grew rapidly into one of its denomination's strongest churches and a major focus for the promotion of the charismatic renewal among mainline groups.

In 1968, Bennett and his second wife, Rita, founded the Christian Renewal Association to promote evangelism, healing, and renewal in all denominations throughout the world. In 1981 they left Saint Luke's to devote their time to writing, speaking, and conducting seminars and conferences. As the result of Bennett's testimony and especially through the written account of his experience, *Nine O'Clock in the Morning* (1970), thousands of people entered into the charismatic experience.

The Van Nuys connection. Bennett's departure from California and the interdiction on tongues effected by the bishop failed to halt the advance of the charismatic movement in southern California. Among the recipients of the Pentecostal experience at Saint Mark's Episcopal Church was Jean Stone. She organized the first charismatic renewal fellowship in Van Nuys, known as the Blessed Trinity Society (1961-66). One of the initial directors of the society was David du Plessis. It not only offered fellowship opportunities for charismatics, but it also produced a magazine, *Trinity*, to introduce the charismatic renewal to non-Pentecostals in the mainline denominations. It also marketed, beginning in 1962, charismatic teaching seminars. These activities attracted all sorts of people from all over the continent.[11]

Larry Christenson. One of the pioneer names in charismatic renewal is Larry Christenson, a Lutheran pastor from California. He had been active in the Order of Saint Luke, an interdenominational healing ministry, but in 1961 he experienced the baptism in the Spirit and accompanying glossolalia at a Foursquare Gospel Church.

Christenson attempted to relate the baptism of the Holy Spirit to the Lutheran context in which he ministered. A pamphlet he wrote, "Speaking in Tongues: A Gift for the Body of Christ," has had a strong influence on Lutherans and was even translated into German.

His denomination, the American Lutheran Church, appointed a Committee on Spiritual Gifts in 1962. Its report spurred an official statement in 1964 that tongues were to be restricted to private devotional prayer.

Into all the world. North America was the staging area for the spread of neo-Pentecostalism to Europe and the rest of the world. Much of the spadework had been done by David du Plessis in his visits the previous decade.

In Great Britain, the second wave of the Holy Spirit began about 1962, largely in the Church of England. Through the initial influence of *Trinity* magazine, a number of persons experienced Spirit baptism. About that same time, the editor of the (evangelical Anglican) *Churchman*, a highly-respected paper, visited Jean Stone in California and wrote a favorable editorial on the movement.

The following May, Frank Maguire visited England. He spoke to several Anglican groups, and a few of the people in attendance were baptized in the Spirit. "But altogether, Maguire's visit represented a mere beginning for the movement in Great Britain."[12]

More favorable growth occurred in the summer of 1963 as a result of a visit from Larry Christenson. One person he influenced who received the baptism, was Michael Harper, an Anglican curate, who in 1964 founded the Fountain Trust. This was to Britain what the Blessed Trinity Society was to the United States. It sponsored renewal conferences and seminars, published a magazine, *Renewal*, and books which promoted the charismatic movement.

Two major events in 1965 led to a dramatic increase in the numbers of neo-Pentecostals in the United Kingdom. In November, Dennis Bennett spoke at several theological colleges and churches. He was extremely well-received and substantially advanced the charismatic cause in the United Kingdom. In November, hundreds of "Full Gospel" businessmen arrived in London for a convention and stayed on to do evangelism throughout the country. By the end of that year neo-Pentecostalism was firmly ensconced throughout the British Isles.

In the British dominions of New Zealand, Australia, and South Africa, visits by Dennis Bennett, Michael Harper, and David du Plessis aided the spread of the charismatic movement in the late 1960s. The movement was solidly established in Germany, Italy, and Scandinavia by the early 1970s.

The Catholic Charismatic Renewal

The beginning of the charismatic renewal among Roman Catholics is generally taken as the formation of a student prayer group at Pittsburgh's Duquesne University in February of 1967. It was led by two lay instructors in theology, Ralph Keifer and Patrick Bourgeois, whose interest in the Holy Spirit had been piqued by reading David Wilkerson's *The Cross and the Switchblade* (1963) and John Sherrill's *They Speak with Other Tongues* (1964). Hearing that a charismatic prayer meeting was being held at the home of a Presbyterian woman, they attended and, their second time there, asked for prayer to receive the Pentecostal experience, which they did, complete with tongues.

Subsequently, they shared this experience with their friends and prayed with them for the baptism. In February of 1967 they and a group of their students agreed to spend a weekend in prayer, meditating on the Book of Acts, as they pleaded with God to reveal His will for their lives. The result was a repetition of the Azusa Street experience.

From Duquesne University the movement spread to other American centers. A participant from the Duquesne group visited Notre Dame University in early March; two students from Michigan State heard about the Duquesne experience, visited the prayer group at that university, received the baptism, and began a group at their own school.

In early April of 1967, about 100 students and faculty from Notre Dame, Michigan State, and Duquesne got together on the Notre Dame campus for prayer and a mutual debriefing on the significance of their Pentecostal experience. The story of the conference was carried in major Catholic papers and aroused national interest. Successive annual conferences at South Bend, Indiana, attracted increasing numbers. In 1973, some 20,000 persons attended; the sermon at the concluding Mass was preached by a Belgian cardinal, Leon-Joseph Suenens. Because of the huge attendances, the national conference was split into several regional meetings.

From the United States the movement spread north into Canada, first to the English-speaking provinces and, in 1969, into Quebec. It was also carried by Catholic missionaries to Latin America. In 1973, delegates from eight Latin countries met together to establish a Latin American Charismatic Catholic Center to coordinate the renewal effort.

As the renewal movement spread throughout the Roman Catholics of the world, Pope Paul VI appointed Cardinal Suenens to oversee it. Each year a conference of leaders from world Catholicism is held in Rome under the auspices of the International Catholic Charismatic Renewal Office. Though growth has leveled off, the Catholic renewal movement is solidly rooted in the church's experience and will continue to be so in the foreseeable future.

Theological characteristics of charismatic Catholicism. Because of the influence of charismatic Protestantism (and so Pentecostalism) on the Catholic charismatic renewal movement, the latter has much in common with the former. Both acknowledge that Spirit baptism is a crisis experience which must be sought through sincere prayer and which may be facilitated by others who have already had the experience. Like Protestant charismatics, Catholics expect the baptism of the Holy Spirit to be demonstrated by an accompanying gift, although (unlike Pentecostals) it may not be glossolalia. This is not to say that tongues are unimportant, for they play a vital role, especially as a devotional language. It is not unusual in charismatic prayer groups for the participants both to pray and to sing together in glossolalia. Gifts pf prophecy and healing are also held in high esteem.

One must not, however, make the mistake of thinking that Catholic charismatics are identical with Protestant charismatics in all ways. On the contrary, there are characteristics which markedly differentiate the Catholic charismatic renewal movement. Many of these differences grow out of the existing differences between Catholic and Protestant theologies.

One important area is that of revelation. Because Catholics revere not only the Bible but also certain church teachings and traditions as inspired, their experience of Pentecost is filtered through and explained in light of both Scripture and tradition.

Roman Catholic tradition teaches that the Holy Spirit is imparted to the faithful through the sacraments. Thus, to speak of the "baptism in the Spirit" apart from the sacraments would be somewhat of an anomaly. But Thomas Aquinas taught that there is the possibility of a fresh affusion of the Holy Spirit in one's life to effect a new work of grace in the performance of miracles or healing, and Catholics use this teaching as the rationale for their charismatic experience.

Catholics are also effusive in their veneration of the Virgin Mary, seeing her as an effective intercessor on their behalf before Christ. Catholic charismatics find that their renewal experience deepens their devotion to Mary. The same is true of their appreciation for the Mass.

In relation to their church, Catholic charismatics are like other Catholics. They recognize the church's authority, mediated by the clergy. Charismatic prayer and renewal groups—at individual, community, regional and national levels alike—all exist with the church's sanction and under her oversight.

The Movement Consolidates

By 1970 there were ample numbers of charismatics in all of the mainline churches. Their spiritual roots—at least as far as their new experience was concerned—were in classical Pentecostalism. But the bulk of Pentecostal leadership wanted nothing to do with these newcomers who did not, for the most part, live the separated life the former demanded. Rejected by traditional Pentecostals, neo-Pentecostal scholars began to search for an accommodation within their own denominations along with fellowship opportunities with one another.

Denominational assessments. About this same time, because of the mushrooming numbers of charismatics in their midst, many of the mainline churches felt constrained to investigate the legitimacy of this phenomenon. In 1970, the United Presbyterian Church appointed a subcommittee of behaviorists and theologians for a study. They reported back that "the practice of glossalalia should neither be despised nor forbidden; on the other hand, it should not be emphasized nor made normative for the Christian experience."[13] Studies by the

Episcopal Church (1971), the American Lutheran Church (1973), and the Lutheran Church in America (1974) were much like the Presbyterian study. The consensus was that charismatics should be permitted to remain as members in good standing in their churches.

In 1976 the United Methodist Church made its first assessment of neo-Pentecostalism. It noted that, despite the roots of Pentecostalism being deep in Wesleyan Methodism, it "has little to do with Wesley's theology." At the same time, no effort was made either to oust or bar charismatics from United Methodist churches. On the contrary, the Graduate School of Theology of Oral Roberts University, headed by Methodist theologian James Buskirk, was approved in 1982 as a seminary for the training of United Methodist clergy.[14]

The Holiness and conservative evangelical churches were not as kind in their reactions. The Christian and Missionary Alliance had already in 1963 reconfirmed A.B. Simpson's 1907 evaluation of the Pentecostal revival, "seek not, forbid not." Southern Baptists and Nazarenes rejected the movement out of hand. The Lutheran Church Missouri Synod in 1972 attacked neo-Pentecostalism as incompatible with their faith and practice.[15]

In spite of numerous promptings by David du Plessis, the World Council of Churches did not bring forth a report on the charismatic movement until 1980. It built largely on the work done by its mainline denominational components. It was a positive report, for the most part, especially in regard to the spiritual and community-building aspects of the movement.[16]

The Kansas City conference of 1977. In 1976 a group of charismatic and Pentecostal leaders called for a general conference to gather in Kansas City, Missouri the following year. This conference would include all sectors of the renewal movement. Its purpose was to demonstrate the movement's unity and to witness to the world at large of its theme, "Jesus is Lord."

The planning committee was headed by Kevin Ranaghan of the Catholic Charismatic Renewal and included members of almost every major denomination. "For the first (and only) time, all the important groups in the entire tradition met together at the same time and at the same place."[17]

The Kansas City Conference was undoubtedly "a cresting of the movement in America."[18] While various denominations continued to hold their own annual conferences, nothing on this scale has been tried since.

Basic Elements in the Charismatic Movement

Charismatics come from a multitude of different denominations worldwide. It's not surprising, therefore, that their practices differ according to the denomination in which they find themselves. Charismatic Anglicans still use the Book of Common Prayer; charismatic Presbyterians are still Calvinistic; and charismatic Methodists are still Arminian. At the same time, there are certain common views and practices that link them all.

The centrality of Christ. A strong emphasis on the lordship of Christ seems to pervade the movement. Those who have experienced the baptism in the Spirit generally speak in terms of a surrender to Christ as Lord of their life. They freely acknowledge that He is the One who immerses them in the Spirit, and their experience makes them very sensitive to His presence with them. "Jesus is Lord," the motto of believers in the early church, is equally the motto of charismatic believers.

Spiritual authority. Evangelicals and fundamentalists accept the Bible as the ultimate authority in all matters of faith and practice. Most of them would make some form of inerrancy (usually "absolute" or "full" inerrancy) a test of faith and fellowship. Thus, these groups have generally had little to do with Roman Catholics, modernists, and others who do not hold to the same standard.

Charismatic Christians find that their experience has given them a deeper love and reverence for the Bible as God's Word. Those who come from denominations which traditionally use higher critical methodology in biblical studies usually become more conservative in their interpretation of the Bible. "Liberals are not usually known for their desire to retain the miraculous.... Since ... charismatics believe in these things, a more literalistic view of Scripture usually accompanies the Pentecostal experience."[19] Charismatics have a high regard for biblical authority.

While more conservative Christians do not countenance Christian unity apart from the propositional authority of the Bible, charismatics are more likely to feel that the written source of authority, the Bible, must be subservient to the living source of authority, the Holy Spirit, who is the source of Christian unity. They note that the Book of Acts shows the Holy Spirit uniting people prior to their being united in truth. This view of unity predominates neo-Pentecostalism and is the basis for fellowship among evangelicals, modernists, and Roman Catholics.[20]

Another aspect of the subordination of the Bible to the experiential authority of the Holy Spirit is extra-biblical revelation. Many charismatics believe that God speaks just as authoritatively through prophecy in the modern day church as through Scripture. Catherine Marshall, the late inspirational writer, says, "Jesus' promise of 'further truth' gives us clear reason to believe that not all the truth and instruction Christ has to give us is contained in the canon of the Old and New Testaments."[21] Rarely, however, do these extra-biblical revelations comment on doctrinal matters; they generally relate to worship or counseling matters.

Praise. Praise is a major aspect of worship among charismatics, both in tongues and in rational speech. It is not unusual for a charismatic worship service to include an hour or more of praise choruses, testimonies, and psalms (sometimes even to the exclusion of a sermon!). Praise is often expressed not only vocally, but physically as well. Self-prostration, clapping, the raising of hands, and dancing "in the Spirit" are frequent modes of praise expression.

Direct divine communication. All charismatics are convinced that God communicates with His people in just the same fashion as in the time of the New Testament church. Those who have received Spirit baptism "experience a directness of communication and guidance from the Lord in a way that shocks or puzzles, attracts, or repels other Christians."[22] God may communicate with them through a word of wisdom, a prophecy, glossalalia (interpreted), or through the counsel of the church or its elders. Or it may be through an inner, subjective direct communication (e.g., intuition, dreams, visions).

Spiritual gifts. With the Pentecostal experience comes an openness to, and reception of, the spiritual "sign" gifts, as well as the more commonly accepted ones (that is, by non-charismatics). Tongues, interpretation of tongues, prophecy, words of wisdom and knowledge, healings, and so forth are regarded as normative gifts to be received and practiced by believers. Indeed, all the spiritual gifts of 1 Corinthians 12:8-10 are seen as basic to God's equipping of the local church for service.

Spiritual power. The baptism in the Holy Spirit is as basic to charismatic theology as it is to traditional Pentecostal theology. It is always a baptism of power for praise and service. As in the Pentecostal tradition, neo-Pentecostals see Spirit baptism as a crisis experience which comes after one's conversion. Unlike the older tradition, charismatics believe that Spirit baptism is "generally but not always identified with speaking in tongues."[23] As someone has said, "Tongues is usually a part of the package, but not always." Some other gift may be given instead which will enable the person baptized to serve the Lord ably in fulfilling the Great Commission (see Acts 1:8). As Howard Ervin writes, "Jesus' commission is still in effect and, by parity of reason, so is the charismatic enduement with power given to realize this purpose."[24] It enables the believer to glorify God as he ought and to use the spiritual gifts with which he has been endowed to their maximum potential.

Spiritual warfare. In addition to a deeper awareness of the Lord, the baptism in the Spirit also brings a deeper sensitivity to the reality of Satan and evil. Charismatics become much aware of demonic malevolence towards humanity in general and believers in particular. "Believers who have not been baptized in the Spirit are not likely to be aware enough of all the activities of Satan to be concerned about discerning of spirits, although of course, there are exceptions."[25] Charismatics realize that believers are engaged in a spiritual battle with the powers of evil. As a result, many charismatics are involved in ministries of spiritual healing, exorcism, and deliverance.

An Evaluation of the Charismatic Movement

What one thinks of the contemporary charismatic movement will depend on one's view of the more sensational—or sign—gifts and whether they are operative today. Those who believe that the sign gifts ceased with the apostles view charismatics as misled and do not see the movement as beneficial.[26]

By and large, however, most Christians see the charismatic movement as having had a positive effect on contemporary Christianity. Because it occurred within the mainline denominations, it has brought to them a renewed emphasis on the Person and work of the Holy Spirit along with a higher regard for supernatural activity at work in the everyday world. It has restored a measure of life in many denominations which had become virtually dead.

There has been a spill-over effect even in those conservative denominations which reject the relevance of the sign gifts for today. They have been forced to reconsider the Third Person of the Trinity, and He has acquired a new and greater place in their (practical) theology. New hymns and choruses in praise of the Spirit have been introduced into their worship services. New emphases on spiritual giftedness have occurred.

There are many lessons to learn from charismatics. One is that of *total worship*. The charismatic renewal aims at a total involvement of every worshiper and an openness to God at the deepest level of one's being. More time is given over to worship (as opposed to learning). Intimately tied in here is a protest against dead orthodoxy. Charismatics have done much to promote spiritual warmth and genuine fellowship.

Another lesson to be learned is that of *total ministry*. It was the Apostle Paul who first declared that every believer has a gift or gifts to be used in God's service for the upbuilding of the church. The charismatics stress (and practice, too!) that every believer must be harnessed for service. They are often innovative and daring in their worship and ministry styles, something which more mainline churches need to be.

A third lesson to be learned is that of *full community*. The concept of having Christ in common and sharing what one has from him is a quality of Christian relationship which charismatics tend to maximize. They share well, giving recklessly to help others. Their practical desire to love puts most Christians to shame!

A great spirit of openness has marked the charismatic renewal movement. These people are noted for their love, their emotion, and their enthusiastic involvement. They remind those who are more reserved that the church was not intended to be a mental mausoleum, but a hospital for sick souls and a "boot camp" for training committed disciples of Christ.

The charismatic movement, despite some flaws and in spite of some friction that it has led to, has been a great blessing to the cause of Jesus Christ in our world.

For Further Study

Basham, Don. *True and False Prophets*. Greensburg, Pa.: Manna Books, 1973.

Bennett, Dennis and Rita Bennett. *The Holy Spirit and You*. Plainfield, N.J.: Logos International, 1971.

Boone, Pat. *A New Song*. Carol Stream, Ill.: Creation House, 1970.

Burgess, Stanley M., and Gary B. McGee, eds. *Dictionary of Pentecostal and Charismatic Movements*. Grand Rapids: Regency Reference Library/Zondervan, 1988.

Christenson, Larry. *Speaking in Tongues*. Minneapolis: Bethany Fellowship, 1968.

Ervin, Howard M. *These Are Not Drunken As Ye Suppose*. Plainfield, N.J.: Logos International, 1968.

Foster, K. Neill. *The Third View of Tongues*. Beaverlodge, Alb.: Horizon House, 1982.

Hamilton, Michael P., ed. *The Charismatic Movement*. Grand Rapids: Wm. B. Eerdmans Pub. Co., 1975.

Koch, Kurt. *Charismatic Gifts*. Montreal: Association for Christian Evangelism, 1975.

MacArthur, John F. *The Charismatics: A Doctrinal Perspective*. Grand Rapids: Zondervan Publishing House, 1978.

Quebedeaux, Richard. *The New Charismatics II: How A Christian Renewal Movement Became Part of the American Religious Mainstream*. San Francisco: Harper and Row, 1983.

Synan, Vinson. *In the Latter Days: The Outpouring of the Holy Spirit in the Twentieth Century*. Ann Arbor, Mich.: Servant Books, 1984.

Vandervelde, George, ed. *The Holy Spirit: Renewing and Empowering Presence*. Winfield, B.C.: Wood Lake Books, 1989.

PART TWO

Contemporary World Trends

Nine. The Theology of Hope

The theology of hope has its origins in the existential gloom of the late 1960s, rising like a phoenix from the ashes of a quickly-discarded "God is dead" theology. At a time when ecclesiastical fortunes were at an all-time low and it seemed that much—if not most—of Christianity was headed for some form of "Christian atheism," a new school of German theologians came to the fore, propounding what has been variously termed the theology of hope or the theology of the future.[1]

The theology of hope is grounded in the eschatology of Albert Schweitzer from the early twentieth century, but with a radical redirection. It seeks to point theology toward the future, rather than toward the past or present. It places a strong emphasis on faith as it relates to history, but insists that the meaning of history can be uncovered only in its conclusion.

The theologians of hope refuse to dichotomize history into secular or sacred. For them, there is only one history and God mediates His revelation indirectly through all of it. The Christian hope is the anticipation of the historical future which will be a direct fulfillment of God's promises as given to humanity in Christ. The present is meaningful only inasmuch as it relates to future possibilities.

The theology of hope is a resurrection theology, although it sees Christ's resurrection as a "first-fruits" of the future and interprets its significance by a backward look from the future rather than vice versa. Christ's church is to be a "disturber" of society, engaged in a mission of confrontation as it awaits the eschatological fulfillment of God's kingdom.

Like Marxism, the theology of hope goes beyond traditional theological bounds, seeking to envelop the whole world, including the fields of politics, sociology, ethics, and biology. It considers itself to be a secular theology and, as such—like Marxism—has had a definite impact on Third World thinking. The pillars of this

135

school are Jürgen Moltmann (Reformed), Wolfhart Pannenberg (Lutheran), and Johannes Metz (Roman Catholic). These three will be examined as typical of the thinking of the movement.

The Theology of Jürgen Moltmann

Jürgen Moltmann (1926-), for years professor of systematic theology at Tubingen University, may be considered the father of the theology of hope. He began his fascination with the idea of human hope as a youthful prisoner of war in a camp in Britain, where hope usually made the difference between survival and death. In 1948 he began a study of theology at Tubingen where, following a short pastorate in Bremen, he earned his doctorate. Upon graduation he taught at the Church Seminary in Wuppertal and then at the University of Bonn before going to Tubingen in 1967.

The conclusion of World War II had left Europe devastated and disillusioned. The escalation of the Cold War in the 1950s and 1960s posed the threat of nuclear holocaust. Young people—especially college students—rebelled against their situation by demonstrating and protesting on campuses all over the free world. In Germany, these scenes were accompanied by debates between the proponents of communism and those of capitalism, between Marxists and Christians.

Moltmann was strongly influenced by a Marxist colleague, philosopher Ernst Bloch and by the powerful Marxist-Christian dialogue taking place on the Tubingen campus. The result was a theological trilogy: *Theology of Hope* (1965), *The Crucified God* (1974), and *The Church in the Power of the Holy Spirit* (1977).

In *Theology of Hope*, Moltmann dwelt heavily upon the Bible to formulate his concepts of eschatological hope. As Luther had with justification, Moltmann found the Bible brim full of the idea of future hope.[2] He noted that the God of the Bible has "future as his essential nature" and therefore is One who is "always only before us, who encounters us in his promises for the future."[3] This futurist theology is divided into two aspects, hope and promise.

Hope. Moltmann's whole premise was that, "from first to last, and not merely in the epilogue, Christianity is eschatology, is hope, forward looking and forward moving, and therefore also revolutionizing and transforming the present."[4] Moltmann attached a different meaning to the concept of eschatology from the traditional. As a rule, people regard eschatology as "the doctrine of last things." But he found such an interpretation inadequate.[5] Eschatology was, in fact, the two-fold doctrine of Christian hope, "the object hoped for, and also the hope inspired by it."[6] Christian hope does not speak of the mere future. It begins in a locatable reality in history and discusses the future of that reality, of its "future possibilities and its powers over the future. Christian eschatology speaks of Jesus Christ and HIS future."[7]

Hope apart from an object is a hollow utopia which is unfulfilling. Just as unfulfilling, however, is an object which cannot be believed. Moltmann emphasized the difference between hope and believing hope. In this regard he followed Calvin: "Hope is nothing else than the expectation of those things which faith has believed to have been truly promised by God. Thus, faith believes God to be true, hope awaits the time when this truth shall be manifested."[8]

If faith is based on hope, then it is reasonable to assume that "the sin of unbelief is manifestly grounded in hopelessness."[9] The sin of hopelessness is displayed in one of two ways: presumption or despair. If one is tempted to anticipate prematurely what is hoped for from God without God's promise, he or she is toying with presumption. Again, the person who anticipates the non-fulfillment of what has been promised, is toying with despair. Both sins are rooted in hopelessness.[10]

Promise. The other side of the eschatological coin is promise. "A promise is a declaration which announces the coming of a reality that does not yet exist. If it is the case of a divine promise, then that indicates that the expected future does not have to develop within the framework of the possibilities inherent in the present, but arises from that which is possible to the God of the promise. . . ."[11] It is promise which links human beings to the future and provides for them a sense of history.

Between the issuing of the promise and its fulfillment, noted Moltmann, occurs an interval of time. This interval permits persons the freedom to obey or disobey, to be hopeful or despair.[12]

Moltmann correctly observed that the above concept of promise is seen in the God of the Old Testament. While the present did not vitiate the essence of God's promises, the future clearly demonstrated that He was steadfast in keeping them.[13] These promises served to link Israel to the future more so than to the present.

The same thing is to be found in the New Testament. "Again, God is not the Absolute, but the God who demonstrates His faithfulness by bringing His promises into the future. The present is the way station on the path to the future.[14]

The focus of eschatology. Moltmann stressed that the significance of eschatology is the crucifixion and resurrection of Christ. But the true significance of these events is not to be found in the past or present so much as in the future. "All predicates of Christ . . . point believers in him towards the hope of his still outstanding future. . . . In the promises, the hidden future already announces itself and exerts its influence on the present through the hope it awakens."[15]

In true Marxist fashion, Moltmann saw the main events of Christianity as a dialectical contradiction: "For Moltmann, the cross and the resurrection of Jesus represent total opposites: death and life, the absence of God and the nearness of God, Godforsakenness and the glory of God. Jesus abandoned by his Father to death and Jesus raised by his Father to eschatological life represent an absolute contradiction. . . ."[16] The synthesis of this contradiction is the promise of the transformation of the world by God in the future. The promise of this new age has yet to be fulfilled, for Christ alone has been raised, but He is the guarantee of the promise. "Without the *future* of the risen Christ, which is the eschatological future of all reality under his lordship, his resurrection *in the past* has no meaning."[17]

The key event of the future for Moltmann is the parousia, also described as the revelation, of Jesus Christ. This revelation is more than just the unveiling of what is already reality. It is the unveiling of something which has not yet occurred, " . . . the fulfillment of the promised righteousness of God in all things, the fulfillment of the resurrection of the dead that is promised in his resurrection, the fulfillment of the lordship of the crucified one over all things that is promised in his exaltation."[18]

The place of the church. What is the role of the church in Moltmann's scheme of things? "The church participates in Christ's messianic mission and in the creative mission of the Holy Spirit."[19] While it is involved in proclamation and in the dispensing of the sacraments, its work extends far beyond these to being a vehicle for liberation and reconciliation: "The church participates in the uniting of men with one another, in the uniting of society with nature, and in the uniting of creation with God."[20] One may sum up the church's role by saying that it is "participation in the history of God's dealings with the world."[21]

Wolfhart Pannenberg

Wolfhart Pannenberg (1928-), a German Lutheran, studied philosophy and theology at Gottingen, Basel, and Heidelberg. Among his teachers were Karl Barth, Gunther Bornkamm, and Gerhard von Rad. He has taught systematic theology at Wuppertal, Mainz, and Munich, and has lectured widely throughout the world.

With the publication of *Jesus—God and Man* in English (1968), followed by *Theology and the Kingdom of God* (1969), and the more popular two-volume *Basic Questions to Theology* (1970-71), Pannenberg became a well-known name in the English-speaking theological world.

Approaching a theology. During his studies, Pannenberg had delved into philosophy and theology. A study of theology gave him a deeper acquaintance with patristics and a new appreciation for the place of history:

> The subject matter that fascinated me was the reality of God and the consequences to be derived from the affirmation of that reality in philosophy and in dogmatics. But now historical experience, tradition and critical exegesis, together with philosophical and theological reflection on their content and implications, became the privileged medium to discuss the reality of God. That meant that . . . God's presence is hidden in the particulars of history. . . . We finally arrived at the conclusion that even God's revelation takes place in history and that precisely all the biblical writings suggest this solution of the key problem of fundamental theology.[22]

Such an approach called for a new method of relating the Person and history of Jesus to the Old Testament's theology of history. It was discovered in apocalyptic thought. ". . . [I]n the end it became discernible that it is in history itself that divine revelation takes place, and not in some strange Word arriving from some alien place and cutting across the fabric of history."[23]

The kingdom as starting point. Like Moltmann, Pannenberg sees the Christian faith in an eschatological, futurist light. His starting point is the kingdom of God "understood as the eschatological future brought about by God himself."[24] God's being and His kingdom go together. It is impossible to conceive of one apart from the other. God's very "godhood" is in His rule.

While the idea of the kingdom of God was a familiar theme among the Jewish people of biblical times, Jesus' understanding that God's claim on the world should be seen completely and only in terms of His coming reign was unique.[25] In such a context, a problem arises: God's being is so interconnected with the imminence of His kingdom that He has no validity for modern man and his concept of reality. One may go so far as to say, in a qualified but very important sense, that God does not as yet exist. "Since his rule and his being are inseparable, God's being is still in the process of coming to be. Considering this, God should not be mistaken for an objectified being presently existing in its fullness."[26] The concept of His existence proves true only in the future of His kingdom.

The thought of the futurity of God's kingdom, Pannenberg cautions, should not be taken to suppose that God is only in the future, but was neither in the past nor is in the present. "Quite to the contrary, as the power of the future he dominates the remotest past."[27]

Nor does this futuristic concept exclude eternity, although it is in absolute opposition to the Greek idea of eternity as everlasting present. God's very essence suggests time: "Only in the future of his Kingdom come will the statement 'God exists' prove to be definitely true. But then it will be clear that the statement was always true. In this impending power the coming God was already the future of the remotest past. He was the future also of that 'nothing' which preceded Creation."[28]

Pannenberg lauds Whitehead and Hartshorne for their relating of time to God in process theology, but he disagrees with their idea that the futurity of His kingdom implies a development in God. While, in our finiteness, it seems that the future is undecided, "what turns out to be true in the future will then be evident as having been true all along. This applies to God as well as to every finite reality. He was in the past the same one whom he will manifest himself to be in the future."[29]

History and revelation. It is in the events of history that God discloses Himself to humanity. Nor is this revelation limited to a "sacred" history (*Heilsgeschichte*); it includes all of history, the totality of all events. In this manner God becomes known not just as "the God of Israel," but as the God of all humankind.

In Pannenberg's thought, Jesus Christ is God's ultimate revelation, but only because "in the fate of Jesus the end is not only seen ahead of time, but is experienced by means of a foretaste."[30] Pannenberg is not interested in questions of Jesus' eternal past, for it is the future which matters. It is in the eschatological significance of the Christ-event that the deity of Christ is established. The Christian should not look upon Jesus' resurrection as a past event to be experienced in the present, other than sacramentally in baptism and the Lord's Supper. "The experience of the glory of the resurrected Christ is not something that occurs in the present . . . but constitutes the future hope of Christians."[31]

The church and the world. The church, Pannenberg maintains, can be understood only in relationship to the world. But too often Christians have built up the former to the detriment of the latter. Nonetheless, "the relationship of the church to secular society is basic to a proper understanding of the church."[32]

The focal point of the church must be God's kingdom, which — as we have already seen — has to do with the world's future. It is important to remember that the church is an eschatological community:

> The Church was regarded as an anticipation of the new mankind . . . under the rule of God and his Spirit. This renewing Spirit . . . was expected to be poured out in the last days upon everyone, but it was also believed that the Spirit was now present in the Church. Therefore, in both anticipa-

tory and present senses, the Church thought of itself as the new people of God and the new Israel. Only if [we] take these eschatological titles seriously can we understand the nature and vocation of the Church in relation to the Kingdom of God, which is the future of the entire world.[33]

If the church is not to become obsolete, there must be a new stress on it as an eschatological community which pioneers the future of all humanity.[34]

The Theology of Johannes Baptist Metz

The theology of hope is not restricted to Protestant thinkers. A number of Roman Catholics have become involved in its formulation, chief among whom is a professor of theology at the University of Munster, Johannes Baptist Metz (1928-). His fundamental theological views are detailed in his *Theology of the Word* and *Faith in History and Society*.

Although he is within the broad range of the theology of hope, Metz might more particularly be viewed as a theologian of politics. He defines theology as "a defense of hope ... in the God of the living and the dead, who calls all men to be his subjects."[35] This hope is bound up in an apologetic praxis, the ultimate result of which will be the Christian's justification before the judgment seat of Christ. In the meantime, however, that praxis will demonstrate itself in Christianity's confrontation of the political and economic systems of contemporary society.

Christian faith. In light of his political theology, Metz suggests the following concept of faith:

> The faith of Christians is a praxis in history and society that is to be understood as hope in solidarity in the God of Jesus as a God of the living and the dead who calls all men to be subjects of his presence. Christians justify themselves in this essentially apocalyptical praxis (of imitation) in their historical struggle for their fellow men. They stand up for all men in their attempt to become subjects in solidarity with each other.[36]

Metz sees Christian faith as a "subversive memory" of the

incarnate Christ who established the kingdom of God among human beings by His confession of Himself as One who stood for the
outcasts of society and by His preaching of the coming kingdom of
God as "the liberating power of unconditional love."[37]

The task of the church. The church is the conservator and proclaim-
er of this memory, reminding us of God's eschatological history of
freedom purchased by Christ's death and resurrection. It is "an
emancipative memory, liberating us from all attempts to idolize
cosmic and political powers and make them absolute."[38] Without
this eschatological memory, the church will compromise its position, accepting a worldly substitute for its whole history of freedom, and moving towards the totalitarian domination of human
beings by human beings.

Metz' great hope is that the church will ultimately become one
with the world, a church which "is present for
everyone ... because all men have become subjects in it."[39] Its
identity will have evolved from the religious experiences of its
members. Its task will be to identify and combat the social
sufferings which deny identity to entire peoples and nations. This
world-church will have ceased to be an institution (a word which,
for Metz, is virtually synonymous with evil) and instead will have
become one with the world in the revolution to transform the
political, social, and economic institutions of society.

The Second Coming. Metz feels that the church has exchanged the
Christian apocalyptic symbol of time coming to an abrupt end for
"the crypto-religious symbol of evolution."[40] Thus, for much of the
church, the Second Coming has degenerated into a completely
private concern which occurs with an individual's death. Certainly,
the urgency imposed by both time and action has been suppressed
in favor of "a more stable alternative: timeless, purely individual,
timeless hopes."[41]

Metz calls for a protest against this lack of expectation in our
ecclesiastical and religious life. Only on the basis of imminent
anticipation does one truly follow Christ (especially vis-a-vis the
last judgment discourse of Matt. 25):

To live Christian hope on the basis of imminent expectation

of the second coming does not mean sacrificing its social and political responsibility but the reverse: injecting the urgency imposed by time and the need to act into a responsibility that has been robbed of its tension by extending the expectation of the second coming to infinity—one that has been diluted and deferred.[42]

Hope has its roots in Christ. It demands of contemporary Christians the expectation of the Second Coming.

An Evaluation of the Theology of Hope

When the theology (perhaps it might be more accurate to say "theologies") of hope began to emerge in the late 1960s, evangelical media tended to be quite supportive of the movement because of its opposition to Bultmann's radical existentialism, its refutation of "God is dead theology," and its strong emphases on eschatology. But as more information became available, as more articles and books appeared in English, it became apparent that theologians of hope were not the staunch defenders of orthodoxy as they had been touted. There were several vital areas in which they were perceived to be radically different from those of the orthodox faith.

Revelation. One area of concern which orthodox Christians would do well to examine is that of the doctrine of revelation (God's self-disclosure to humanity) held by theologians of hope. They oppose radical liberalism by insisting that God does indeed reveal Himself in history, a positive emphasis. But their concept of revelation in history is very much different from that of orthodoxy.

The God of Moltmann's theology, for example, is never a God who reveals Himself in the past and present, but One who reveals Himself only in the future. In fact, one may say that He is not a present Reality, but only a future possibility (or, probability?). He will not really be God until He fulfills His promises in the eschaton.[43]

While Pannenberg speaks of history as the medium of revelation, he sees all of its revelatory events as of equal value. In other words, he denies special revelation.[44] If one cannot see this revelation, it is his own fault and not that of history. As a result, the Christ-event is not God's ultimate historical self-disclosure to humankind. At best, Jesus is an anticipation of future revelation. Besides, God cannot truly be known through historical events, although His establishment of Israel and His sending of Christ demonstrate His participation in history; it is only in the completion of history that the real Person and nature of God will be apprehended.

Metz is a little more concrete in his view of revelation. He sees the Christ-event as an objective historical fact, but he does not consider it to be different in quality from any other historical occurrence.[45] There is no special revelation for him either, unless one sees all the events of history in such a light.

Christology. The Christian faith is only as good as its Christology is sound. How does the theology of hope measure up in this area?

Traditional Christianity stipulates that the Second Person of the Trinity is eternal; Christ always has been, is, and always shall be God. Moltmann's position is somewhat different; Jesus is God because He is the Bearer of the future; but when God's promises have been fulfilled, this function (that is, His deity) will be at an end.[46]

Wolfhart Pannenberg rightly confesses that the statement of Acts 4:12 (that there is no name other than that of Jesus whereby we must be saved) is the raison d'etre of the church.[47] But he questions whether Jesus claimed to be the Messiah during His earthly ministry. He attributes such claims to the early Christian community. In fact, Jesus' claim of sonship was an attitude towards God, an attitude He demanded of others: "Thus, the divine sonship was not owned exclusively by Jesus. Others before and after Jesus could and can participate in that form of relating to God as Father. But in the case of Jesus the eternal sonship became incarnate in his person."[48] Pannenberg is not really concerned with Jesus' preexistent past, but with His future. Jesus stepped out of the future back into the present and past, and thereby He has reconciled all of history in Himself.[49]

Metz' Christology is more traditional. For him, the Incarnation is an objective historical act through which God becomes the principle of history. In regard to the work of Christ, Moltmann declares that "Christology stands or falls with the raising of Jesus from the dead by God."[50] We (and all Christians) can readily affirm such a statement. But while Christians place great stress on the historicity of Jesus' resurrection as the validating factor of the faith, Moltmann considers such a matter irrelevant. He does not look from the cross to the end of history, as do most Christians, but rather from the final resurrection of the dead at the end of time back to Jesus' resurrection. The future is the validation of the past and not vice versa.[51]

For Pannenberg, the resurrection of Christ is the key to understanding history. Unlike Moltmann, he is quite prepared to call it an historical event. The survival of the community of Christian faith is evidence of Jesus' having appeared to His followers. At the same time, Pannenberg does not find the resurrection narratives entirely reliable, and he presumes (like Albert Schweitzer) that Jesus was expecting not His own individual resurrection, but "the imminent universal resurrection from the dead."[52]

Man and salvation. Orthodox Christianity holds that man fell from grace when Adam and Eve disobeyed God in the Garden of Eden. Since that time, sin has had a universal effect, disrupting communication between God and man, and leading humans to declare their independence of God. Because of the blighting of their minds and spirits by sin, they are helpless to change. Nothing short of a unilateral action by God Himself can save humanity. And God has condescended to do just that in and through Jesus Christ. As people put their trust in Christ, accepting His atonement, they are justified.

Theologians of hope tend to adopt a view of sin more in line with existentialism than with traditional Christianity, and they hold a view of salvation more akin to liberation theology. (It should come, therefore, as no surprise that most proponents of the theology of hope are also proponents of liberation theology.)

For Moltmann, hopelessness is the essential foundation of sin, either as *praesumptio* (the attempt to force the future promises without waiting for God to act) or *desperatio* (the premature expectation that God will not act in the future).[53] Hopelessness must be overcome so that humankind may achieve the *imago Dei*.

Moltmann calls for Christians to identify with the outcasts of society to help usher in the eschaton. But is not such a call *praesumptio* in and of itself, an attempt to force God's hand?

For Metz, salvation is already present as a part of the historical process. The church is to be an agent of transformation in the world: "The faith of Christians is a praxis in history and society that is to be understood as hope in the solidarity in the God of Jesus as a God of the living and the dead who calls all men to be subjects in his presence. Christians justify themselves in this essentially apocalyptic praxis (of imitation) in their historical struggle for their fellow men."[54] Salvation, then, in Metz' system is more a matter of attempting to do the things that Jesus did, rather than of faith in who He is.

Conclusions

Because of its origin as an aggressive response to those theologians of the 1960s who wished to dispense altogether with God, the theologians of hope had a ready-made audience in the people of the time who were fearful and despairing of God's future (and so, presumably, of their own!). The assurance with which these scholars proclaimed Christ's resurrection as the "firstfruits" of God's promises for the future were a breath of fresh air in the fetid context of theological despair.

Evangelicals particularly welcomed the theologians of hope, for not only did they attack the God-is-dead movement, but also neo-orthodoxy and neo-liberalism. Both Moltmann and Pannenberg, for example, decried Barth's and Bultmann's views of faith and history, demanding a more objective role for history in God's revelation. Conservatives were especially appreciative of the futurists' emphasis on Christ's resurrection as the focal point of eschatology. Many conservatives, early in the movement's life, saw the theologians of hope as fellow travelers.

Unfortunately, and contrary to popular evangelical thought, the movement provides little more hope for God's existence than does the death of God movement. While it does not declare God dead, neither does it affirm His life. It adopts a wait-and-see attitude. The future will prove or disprove God's existence.

Nor should evangelicals find much to hope for here for, in spite of a strong emphasis on eschatology, there is little more than the biblical terms that they can identify with; certainly, they would not find the content of futurist eschatology very comforting. Neither Moltmann nor Pannenberg, for example, see Jesus' relationship to eschatology in the same light as the Bible. Both assume the Bible to be in error as to its record of Jesus' resurrection and its significance for future events.

Nor can evangelicals affirm the view of revelation held by the theologians of hope. The refusal of the latter to acknowledge the existence of special revelation is a throwback to natural theology and a surrender to the more unhappy aspects of historical criticism.

In many respects, the theology of hope—at least initially—seems to be all things to all people. Because it is a futuristic theology, it can stipulate almost anything theologically, for only the never-arriving future can prove or disprove it. David Scaer has appropriately labeled it "a perpetually over-the-next-hill theology."[55]

The theology of hope is really a misnomer for this movement, for its system generates no hope at all (at least, not in the biblical sense of hope as confident assurance). At best it can be called wishful thinking for, while the orthodox Christian faith is built on the historical certainty of the life, death, and resurrection of Jesus Christ, the theology of hope has nothing sure or solid on which to build. It is to be commended for its perception of the vital importance of the future. But that future must be constructed on the solid historical facts of the past, not some wish for what may be.

For Further Reading

Alves, Rubem A. *A Theology of Human Hope*. Washington: Corpus, 1969.

Braaten, Carl E. and Robert W. Jensen. *The Futurist Option*. New York: Newman Press, 1970.

Metz, Johannes B. *Faith in History and Society*. Trans. by David Smith. New York: Seabury Press, 1980.

_____. *Followers of Christ: Perspectives on the Religious Life*. Trans. by Thomas Linton. New York: Paulist Press, 1978.

_____. *Theology of the World*. Trans. by William Glen-Doeppel. New York: Herder and Herder, 1969.

Moltmann, Jürgen. *The Trinity and the Kingdom*. Trans. by Margaret Kohl. San Francisco: Harper and Row, 1981.

_____. *Hope and Planning*. Trans. by Margaret Clarkson. New York: Harper and Row, 1971.

_____. *Religion, Revolution, and the Future* Trans. by Douglas Meeks. New York: Charles Scribner's Sons, 1969.

_____. *The Theology of Hope*. Trans. by James W. Leitsch. New York: Harper and Row, 1967.

Pannenberg, Wolfhart. *An Introduction to Systematic Theology*. Grand Rapids: Wm. B. Eerdmans Pub. Co., 1991.

_____. *Theology and the Kingdom of God*. Trans. by Richard J. Neuhaus. Philadelphia: Westminster Press, 1969.

_____. *Jesus—God and Man*. Trans. by Lewis L. Wilkins and Duane A. Priebe. Philadelphia: Westminster Press, 1968.

Ten. Process Theology

O ne of the major and most complex contemporary theological movements is known as process theology. A "theology of becoming," the process movement became particularly prominent in the late 1960s and early 1970s.

Some have claimed that process thinking extends back as far as the Greek philosopher, Heraclitus, in 500 B.C.[1] Undoubtedly, there are strands of philosophical thought from many ages which have some affinity for various segments of process thought. Those involved in the movement trace its direct origins to late nineteenth-century and early twentieth-century forces; these were the impact of two world wars and the revolution in the scientific world view on liberal theology in particular and on the contemporary culture in general.[2] World war led theological liberals to realize how dark and tragic is the human situation and how inadequate their theology; from the quagmire of hopelessness arose the neo-orthodox movement with its existentialist emphasis. The advent of Darwinian evolution followed by Einstein's theory of relativity led to the belief (in biology, physics, chemistry, psychology, and the social sciences) that all of creation is in a state of dynamic flux, each part in relation to the others.

Almost coincidentally to these events, philosophers were recasting these scientific theses into a metaphysical mold. Herbert Spencer (1820–1903) remade Darwinian evolution into a philosophy of cosmic evolution. His work, in turn, influenced Henri Bergson who in 1907 wrote *Creative Evolution*, which insisted that the evolutionary process is caused by a life force (God).

Two scientists—one turned philosopher and the other theologian—made monumental contributions to the development of process thought. Alfred North Whitehead, a mathematician and scientist, determined that "reality is not static and substantial but dynamic and in process. The real, including God, is not composed of unchanging essences but of changing activities."[3] Pierre Teilhard de Chardin, a Jesuit paleontologist (see chapter 5), formulated a radically temporalistic outlook in which evolution was no longer a theory but an added dimension of knowledge. "We live 'in a world that is *being born* instead of a world that *is*.' "[4]

The 1960s saw a special emphasis on the doctrine of God. Analytical philosophy questioned the validity of "God language." Secular theology insisted that God be presented to contemporary society in terms it could find meaningful—secular language devoid of religiosity. John A.T. Robinson, the popularizer of Paul Tillich's theology, scorned ideas of God's being "up there" as old-fashioned, and recast Him as the "Ground of our being." Thomas J.J. Altizer formulated his "God is dead" theology, proposing that God had gradually but decisively annihilated Himself, shedding His transcendence in the Incarnation.

It was in such a theological ferment that a group of theologians connected with the University of Chicago built further upon the thinking of Whitehead and Teilhard to bring process theology to full flower. The initial mover in this endeavor was Charles Hartshorne who, although never a student of Whitehead's, served as his assistant. Another leading member of the Chicago group was Bernard Meland. Other major process theologians (many of them Chicago alumni) included Schubert M. Ogden, John B. Cobb, Jr., W. Norman Pittenger, and Daniel Day Williams.

Alfred North Whitehead: Process Philosophy

Process theology is founded principally upon the philosophical system developed by Alfred North Whitehead (1861–1947). The son of an Anglican vicar, he trained in science and mathematics (although he possessed a lifelong interest in religion), and taught at the Universities of Cambridge and London. In the course of his career he investigated how mathematics is related to the real world, and from this research developed a philosophy of nature.[5]

In 1924 Whitehead accepted an invitation from Harvard University to teach philosophy. It was here and in the years following that he produced his system of process metaphysics. In 1929 he wrote his crowning achievement, the result of research for the Gifford Lectures he had given in 1927-28. *Process and Reality* "expresses his mathematical and scientific interests combined with religious, aesthetic, and metaphysical ones in a unified cosmology."[6] Other writings included *The Function of Reason* (1929), *Adventures of Ideas* (1933), and *Modes of Thought* (1938).

An overview of Whitehead's philosophy. Whitehead's system arose out of his conviction that Newtonian concepts of matter, space, and time were in error; reality is not static, but fluid. The universe is in a constant state of change. Indeed, things are in such a state of flux that nothing is ever the same twice in succession: "... the flux of things is one ultimate generalization around which we must weave our philosophical system."[7] Even God is subject to these conditions, in the process of becoming.

While Whitehead stressed flux, or process, he did not do so at the complete expense of permanence. This permanence can be found in a two-fold fashion; first, in the temporal realm and, secondly, in the eternal realm. At the temporal level, permanence is had in what Whitehead termed "eternal objects"; in the eternal arena, permanence is located in the primordial nature of God.[8]

Whitehead believed that matter is eternal. God did not create the universe *ex nihilo*. It is a continuing system. But God does have a four-fold role in it:

> (1) as source of the "eternal objects," the possible intelligible forms ... which He holds eternally in His mind and presents at the appropriate time for integration by the momentary "actual occasions" or events ..., which alone are real outside God Himself; (2) as providing the initial "subjective aim" or ideal goal of each newly arising actual occasion; (3) as providentially guiding the universe toward the greatest possible realizable value, ... by "luring" them with the persuasive power of the good; (4) as eternally preserving in His memory the objectified values achieved by the successively perishing actual entities.[9]

The dipolar nature of God. In orthodox Christianity, God is conceived as "monopolar." This means that He is unqualifiedly perfect in every respect. Whitehead rejected this traditional concept in favor of a "dipolar" God who comprises two contrasting poles, one *actual* and the other *potential*. The former is known as God's *consequent* nature; the latter, as God's *primordial* nature.

God's primordial nature may be seen as His eternal nature. It involves the abstract attributes of God, such as transcendence, absoluteness, immutability, infiniteness, and so forth. "... [B]y means of this primordial actuality, there is an order in the relevance of eternal objects to the process of creation."[10] Norman Geisler says that "God in His primordial nature is like a backstage director who organizes and lines up the actors, making them 'relevant' for their moment of 'ingression' on the stage of the temporal world,"[11] preventing chaos among those backstage.

God's consequent nature may be seen as His temporal nature. It involves the concrete attributes of God which are immanence, contingency, finiteness, changeability, and so on. "... [B]y reason of the relativity of all things, there is a reaction of the world on God. ... [God's] derivative nature is consequent upon the creative advance of the world."[12]

For Whitehead, the world was the actual pole, or consequent nature, of God. Without the potential, primordial pole which extends beyond the world, we would have pantheism. Whitehead writes concerning this aspect of God:

> It is as true to say that God is permanent and the World fluent, as that the World is permanent and God is fluent.
>
> It is as true to say that God is one and the World many, as that the World is one and God many.
>
> It is as true to say that, in comparison with the World, God is actual eminently, as that, in comparison with God, the World is actual eminently.
>
> It is as true to say that the World is immanent in God, as that God is immanent in the World.
>
> It is as true to say that God transcends the World, as that the World transcends God.
>
> It is as true to say that God creates the World, as that the World creates God.[13]

God and the world exist in a sort of "give-and-take" relationship. The temporal character of the world contributes flux to God, while God contributes durability and permanence to the world in turn. The result of the give-and-take is termed "creativity."[14] The process from God's side is referred to as His "superjective" nature.

The Process Theology of Charles Hartshorne

As we have already noted, Charles Hartshorne took Whitehead's philosophy and expanded upon it, becoming the chief articulator of process theology. An examination of his thought will plainly show Whitehead's influence. At the same time, it goes far beyond, and is uniquely his own.

Like Whitehead, Hartshorne rejected the classical theistic view propounded by Anselm, Augustine, and Aquinas of God as impassive substance. Instead, both of them held to panentheism. While classical theism emphasizes the "Otherness" of God—that is, the separateness of God from His creation—panentheism posits an interdependence between God and the universe. Process theologians relate God to the world much as the mind is related to the body.

Because of this interdependence one cannot properly speak of God's creating the world. Hartshorne suggested that "creativity, if real at all, must be universal, not limited to God alone...."[15] He cited with approval the creation hymns composed by the ancient Egyptian pharaoh, Ikhnaton. "The suggestion almost throughout is of free creatures responding to divine freedom, influencing God to delight in the spectacle they afford Him, while they delight in His benificent influence upon them."[16] For God, the world is a metaphysical necessity; without it He would be an empty abstraction.[17]

Hartshorne departed substantially from Whitehead's metaphysical concept of God. A major difference between the two is that, while the latter envisioned God as a single actual entity, the former sees God as a series of actual entities. In espousing his view, Whitehead was able to claim a relationship between God as primary actual entity and other actual entities, becoming their chief exemplification. Hartshorne, for his part, insisted that God is modally different from the world.[18]

Hartshorne differed from Whitehead, as well, on how God grounds the world. Whitehead saw God as the ground for this world, whereas Hartshorne considered Him to be the ground for all worlds. For the former, God was a universal subject; for the latter, a universal object. Furthermore, "Whitehead's God is only concretely necessary to explain this particular world, whereas Hartshorne's God is universally and logically necessary to explain this and all possible worlds."[19]

A Doctrinal Overview of Process Theology

Process theology is one of the most powerful theological movements of the latter twentieth century. It has drawn to its ranks theologians from the major Christian denominations. In looking at the essential beliefs of the movement, we shall draw on its major articulators—John Cobb, Schubert Ogden, Bernard Meland, Norman Pittenger, and Henry Wieman.

Authority. Process theology rejects the traditional Christian conviction that divine revelation is authoritatively revealed to us in and through the Bible. John Cobb suggests, "When one no longer finds it possible to accept religious doctrines that claim to be universal truths simply because some supposedly authoritative person, book, or institution proclaims them, one is inclined to ask for proof."[20] He sees that proof grounded first and foremost in universally experienced prereflective elements, and quotes Whitehead to the effect that, "Mothers can ponder many things in their hearts which their lips cannot express. These many things, which are thus known, constitute the ultimate religious evidence, beyond which there is no appeal."[21] Once these prereflective elements have been recognized and vocalized, others will recognize the truth of what is being expressed. "The verbal expression of a universally experienced fact elicits a believing response in us because we had already apprehended the fact."[22]

It is not uncommon for process theologians to refer to Scripture, for it provides provocative lures to lead us into what the future has for us. At the same time, the Bible is reliable only where and in as much as it recapitulates one's self-evident preconceptual experience. It is not always accurate and, on occasion, it must be corrected by scientific and philosophical insights.[23]

Because the real authority is not the Bible but the universally prereflective elements recognized and set forth in the Bible, then it stands to reason that other religious traditions may possess writings which do the same, and are therefore equally valid. Cobb recommends that the Christian faith of the future should incorporate into its belief system these other consciously apprehended truths. "We believe that it is possible for faith to broaden and enrich itself in this way without losing its Christian character, and that this is desirable."[24]

The doctrine of God. A substantial portion of process thinking about God has already been examined in our consideration of Whitehead's philosophy and Hartshorne's theology. The dipolar nature of God (previously considered) is basic to all process thinking, for it demonstrates the relationship of God to the created order.

Schubert Ogden, a disciple of Charles Hartshorne, has gone more deeply into the reality and nature of God. In a revolution against classical metaphysics, he has taken as a paradigm of reality the self in relationship.

To exist as a self is always to be related to one's own body. What one thinks and feels has a direct effect on one's brain and nervous system, and so on the rest of that organism which constitutes oneself. Through one's body one both affects and is affected by those things which exist beyond oneself. Temporality is basic to selfhood. Self-knowledge comes "most immediately only as an ever-changing sequence of occasions of experience, each of which is the present integration of remembered past and anticipated future into a new whole of significance."[25] As one chooses both from the heritage of past actualities and from the wealth of future possibilities, one becomes freely involved in a creative relationship with a world of other selves.

Ogden, using this "analogy of being," notes that "God, too, must be conceived as a genuinely temporal and social reality, and therefore as radically different from the wholly timeless and unrelated Absolute of traditional theism."[26] By this he does not mean that God is only one more "becoming" creature among many others. By definition God must be a unique Reality supreme to, and qualitatively different from, all others. But a valid analogy demands that the eminence attributed to God must "follow from, rather than contradict, the positive meaning of our fundamental concepts as given them by experience."[27]

Herein, according to Ogden, lies the mortal flaw in classical theism; it rests on the premise that God is neither relative nor temporal and so cannot say that He either "knows" or "loves" except by using these words in a manner unlike our use of them. In process theology, however, there is no such problem. God is seen as the perfect example of becoming, the one eminently social and temporal Reality.

Ogden continues to extend his analogy of being by pointing out that, just as the human brain is incarnated in a human body, God as the eminent Self is incarnated in the world. "God's sphere of interaction or body is the whole universe of nondivine beings, with each one of which his relation is unsurpassably immediate and direct."[28]

The process conception of God's reality, argues Ogden, incorporates all of the metaphysical attributes advanced by classical theism. It too insists that God is the Absolute. The radical difference between the two, however, is that with process theology "the traditional attributes of God are all reconceived on the analogical basis provided by our own existence as selves."[29]

Process Christology. Emil Brunner has truly declared that "the center and the foundation of the whole Christian faith is 'Christology,' that is, faith in Jesus Christ."[30] Thus, what process theology believes about the Person and work of Jesus Christ is of paramount importance.

As we consider process theology, it is well to remember the assumption it brings to the Christological task. First, it assumes a panentheistic view of God and the world. Secondly, it rules out any miraculous intrusions into the natural order of things. Norman Pittenger writes that "the notion of natural and supernatural, . . . the methods by which God was supposed to work in his world, etc., are not and cannot be ours."[31] Thirdly, process theology does not accept the Bible as uniquely authoritative, and holds that it is subject to correction by reason and science. Many process theologians belong to that school which believes that what the Bible records as the words of Jesus were actually not His, but were put in His mouth by the early Christian community.

Consistent with their rejection of the miraculous, process thinkers repudiate as "incredible and impossible the Greek idea of a god who comes down to earth and walks about as a human being."[32] To speak about Jesus as though He were an intruder from some other (even spiritual) realm would render Him supremely meaningless. Any relevant contemporary Christology must view Jesus "as a genuine man (a genuine Jew of the first century of our era), genuinely thinking the thoughts of that period in which he lived, . . . sharing fully and completely in the human experience."[33]

Pittenger also eschews the ancient confessions about the natures of Christ as being no longer meaningful. Words like *hyposta-sis, ousia*, and so forth are old-fashioned. None of the foregoing is to say that these Christological statements are unimportant. On the contrary, they preserved the Patristic view of Jesus as both the demonstration of the character and purpose of God and the supreme manifestation of human potential.

Pittenger maintains that, in attempting to reformulate the early confessions to relate them to today, we must be loyal to the *intentions* of the original authors rather than to their *words*:

> To be loyal to the intentions of our fathers in the faith may mean that we must depart from the concepts they employed and the statements they made. And if some complain that this will lead to failure in "orthodoxy," the response must be made that while it may involve departure from verbal orthodoxy it is in fact the only procedure which can retain vital orthodoxy.[34]

In attempting to relate the nature of Jesus to modernity, Pittenger stresses His humanity. He was the "authentic" man who sacrificed Himself for His fellow human beings and for God. It was in this Man that the early believers saw God at work. "Jesus is the coincidence of God's action . . . and man's responsive action . . . , not in spite of but under the very conditions of genuinely human life . . . in a degree not elsewhere known in human experience."[35]

The doctrine of salvation. Process theologians place a much heavier emphasis on the power of Jesus' life than on that of His death. They also have a radically different understanding of what salvation means. Rather than recreation of the individual from a life of corruption to a life of righteousness, process salvation is a matter of harmonizing one's life in time of health and wholeness, and of exchanging a life of self-centeredness for a concern for one's fellows. Pittenger defines it as "a unity of life, on the way to full integration, where men and women are so related to . . . the cosmic thrust of life."[36]

Henry Wieman insists that the importance of Jesus' life was not what He brought to His followers in the way of teaching, but rather what He caused to happen between them in the sense of interpersonal dynamics:

It was not something Jesus did. It was something that happened when he was present like a catalytic agent. . . . Something about this man Jesus broke the atomic exclusiveness of those individuals so that they were deeply and freely receptive and responsive to the other. . . . [Consequently] there arose in this group of disciples a miraculous mutual awareness and responsiveness toward the needs and interests of one another.[37]

Wieman is emphatic that this transforming power lay not so much in Jesus Himself as in the interaction between them. "It transformed their minds, their personalities, their appreciable world, and their community with one another and with all men."[38] Jesus was necessary to this process, but so were the disciples and the Hebrew context in which they all found themselves.

Wieman suggests that such a "creative event" as happened with Jesus' disciples is waiting for all human beings but it is usually ignored. Only when it is made the dominant factor in human life may salvation be achieved. Making it the dominant factor is by itself, however, insufficient. Without perpetuation throughout history it could not be extended universally. Such perpetuation occurs through the Bible, myth, and ritual (which accordingly become "means of grace").[39]

The Crucifixion and Resurrection were important to the universal extension of salvation. As long as Jesus was alive this creative salvation was confined to the context of Hebrew culture and religious tradition. The Resurrection shattered these restrictive barriers.

When process theologians speak of the resurrection, one must not think that they mean the literal physical resurrection of Jesus. Not at all. Wieman suggests that, with the death of Christ, hope for the future died. But about the third day after His death, that creative power came to life once more in the disciples' band. Because of its past association with Jesus, some of His followers thought that they saw Him. "But what rose from the dead was not the man Jesus; it was creative power."[40]

If Jesus was not physically raised, did anything of sigificance happen to Him following His death? Some process thinkers believe that God took Jesus' concrete experiences into Himself "to be recreated continually and afresh in God's living memory." Others simply see the resurrection in terms of the formation of the church.[41]

Process anthropology. Traditional Christianity, both Protestant and Roman Catholic, understands humankind in the light of the image of God in which they have been created. Modern theology has interpreted the significance of image in the sense of relationship. "The image of God is reflected in every aspect of man's being, not as a special entity but as the meaning of the life of man in its essential integrity."[42]

Daniel Day Williams interprets the meaning of the *imago Dei* as love. Wrapped up in this attribute we find all the nobler human aspects such as reason, moral judgment, religious awareness, and creativity. All find their purpose in life intended for community with others.[43]

In such a context the definition of sin is the failure to achieve a life of love. "It is disorder in the roots of his being. It is the disaster resulting from twisted, impotent, or perverted love."[44] In spite of this abnormal quality of love, humans are not left without reason, conscience, or God-consciousness. Within each individual is something which directs him or her toward the love of God, something which reflects his origin in God.

The love of God is the power of creation and re-creation. It brings worlds into being, sustains them, and renews them. The *imago Dei* in humanity is its call to participation in creativity. "To love is to become responsible for doing what needs to be done to make the world a more tolerable place which reflects more fully the glory of its origin."[45]

Human creativity, then, is implicitly affirmed in the *imago Dei*. Humans have the capability to rebuild their world, remold their lives, and fashion new values. We have seen much creative advances in medicine, technology, economics, and many other areas in the twentieth century.

Williams warns that these creative powers can be demonic as well as positive. "Man can end his existence on this planet. He can dehumanize as well as create."[46] Which direction we go is up to us.

An Analysis of Process Theology

As we reflect on what we have learned about process theology, we may observe a number of positive and negative points. We shall examine, first, those helpful contributions of process thought and, secondly, those which are harmful.

Positive aspects. Process theology was formulated, in part, as a protest against some severe deficiencies in classical theism. (It should
be noted here that classical theism must not be confused with biblical
theism; the former is based as much on Greek pagan philosophy as
on Scripture.) The (classical) theology of Thomas Aquinas insisted
that God is immutable and impassive; that means that He does not
change nor can He be acted upon. But the Bible speaks of God
"repenting" and being acted upon by the prayers of His people.
Classical theology presents a picture of a God who cannot get
involved in the concerns, joys, and sufferings of His children. Process
theology confronts the shortcomings of this system and demands
changes. Whether or not process thinkers have offered an adequate
alternative system, the challenge they have presented should act as a
stimulus to evangelical theologians to reconsider their doctrine of
God, and to ensure that that doctrine fully conforms to biblical
teaching.

Another positive contribution of process theology is its emphasis
on human participation in creation. Much conservative theology so
strongly emphasizes the sovereignty of God that one is led to believe
that humankind has no role to play at all in this matter. Such a view
is contrary to the biblical teaching of the *imago Dei*, an integral part
of which suggests that humans are God's stewards and representatives. Process theology reminds us that God invites us to be His
fellow laborers in the transformation of both humankind and the
world in which we live.

A third contribution is the process emphasis on natural revelation.
Some conservative theologians tend to be quite Barthian in their
theology of revelation, restricting God's self-disclosure to special revelation. Process theology brings to our attention how loudly and how
clearly creation speaks of God, His glory, and His power.

A fourth helpful aspect centers on the Incarnation. Process
thought—regardless of how helpful one considers its answers—
poses some important questions about the Person of Christ regarding
the sinlessness of Jesus in relation to humanity. We are challenged
once more to find satisfying biblical answers to the divinity of Jesus
and exactly what it meant to His humanity.

Besides doctrinal issues (which may be seen as primary concerns),
there are a number of helpful secondary contributions which may be
cited. One of these is the paramount need for pictures and analogies

in referring to God. Univocal language about God is inadequate. Process theologians soon saw that and, starting with Charles Hartshorne, willingly used analogical language to add meaning to their descriptions of God.

There are many other contributions which could be mentioned, but are precluded by space considerations. Let us take all of them to heart in formulating our theology.

Negative aspects. The numerous positive aspects of process theology are, unfortunately, far outweighed by detrimental considerations. We do well to be *aware* of them, and to *beware* of them.

The major difficulties with process theology are the assumptions with which it begins, especially its rejection of the activity of the supernatural in the created order. In this regard process theology is a child of Enlightenment liberalism.

Out of this rejection flows its low view of the Bible. Scripture becomes just one of many religious collections of myths and traditions. It has insights which are valuable to the practitioners of Judeo-Christianity, but other peoples have their own sacred writings which are equally valuable to them in their particular context. All of these writings are subject to the correction of reason. Thus, there is no divine authority; everything is subject to human determination.

From this same rejection of the activity of the supernatural comes a low view of the Person of Jesus Christ. Process theologians refuse to accept the divinity of Christ, preferring to say that God was in Christ as He is in every human being, although Jesus was more "God-conscious" than others. But the Bible proclaims that Christ is God (see John 1:1; Col. 2:9; Heb. 1:8).

Again, the panentheistic God of process is not the God of the Bible. The God of the Bible is eternal; the process God is temporal. The God of the Bible created the universe from nothing; the God of process merely cooperates with an already existent creation.

Finally, salvation in process theology is a sorry affair compared to what the Bible promises. At best, the former is the achievement of self-fulfillment or self-integration. And it all ends with death. All that is saved is the memory of the departed, a memory integrated into a host of others. How shoddy when compared to the never-ending life of bliss with God and His redeemed, as set forth in Scripture!

Conclusions. Process theology performs some valuable functions. One may appreciate its desire to repudiate "God is dead" theology and the subsequent focus on developing a contemporary and relevant doctrine of God. It does us a service, moreover, by reminding us that we have a God who is dynamically involved in creation, who loves humanity to the point of sharing in the human tragedy. It is unfortunate indeed that, as a system, process theology falls so far short. There is no reason, however, why we should not adopt its aims and develop our own theological system guided by, and built upon, God's fully-authoritative Word, the Bible.

For Further Reading

Cousins, Ewert H., ed. *Process Theology*. New York: Newman, 1971.

Cobb, John B., Jr. *God and the World*. Philadelphia: Westminster Press, 1969.

_____. *The Structure of Christian Existence*. Philadelphia: Westminster Press, 1967.

_____. *A Christian Natural Theology*. Philadelphia: Westminster Press, 1965.

Hartshorne, Charles. *A Natural Theology for Our Time*. LaSalle, Ill.: Open Court, 1967.

_____. *Reality as a Social Process*. Boston: Beacon Press, 1953.

_____. *Beyond Humanism*. Chicago: Willett and Clark, 1937.

Meland, Bernard E. *The Secularization of Modern Cultures*. New York: Oxford University Press, 1966.

_____. *Faith and Culture*. New York: Oxford University Press, 1953.

_____. *The Reawakening of Christian Faith*. New York: Macmillan, 1949.

Ogden, Schubert M. *The Reality of God and Other Essays*. New York: Harper and Row, 1966.

Pittenger, Norman W. *The "Last Things"in a Process Perspective*. London: Epworth Press, 1970.

_____. *Alfred North Whitehead*. Richmond, Va.: John Knox Press, 1969.

_____. *Process-Thought and Christian Faith*. New York: Macmillan, 1968.

_____. *God in Process*. London: SCM Press, 1967.

Schlipp, Paul A., ed. *The Philosophy of Alfred North Whitehead*. Chicago: Northwestern University Press, 1941.

Sherburne, Donald W. *A Key to Whitehead's Process and Reality*. New York: Macmillan, 1966.

Teilhard, Pierre (de Chardin). *How I Believe*. New York: Harper and Row, 1969.

_____. *The Phenomenon of Man*, rev. ed. New York: Harper and Row, 1965.

_____. *The Future of Man*. New York: Harper and Row, 1964.

Whitehead, Alfred North. *Religion in the Making*. New York: Macmillan, 1966.

_____. *Process and Reality: An Essay in Cosmology*. New York: Macmillan, 1929.

Williams, Daniel Day. *The Spirit and Forms of Love*. New York: Harper and Row, 1968.

_____. *What Present-Day Theologians Are Thinking*, 3rd ed. rev. New York: Harper and Row, 1967.

_____. *God's Grace and Man's Hope*. New York: Harper, 1949.

Eleven. Secular Theology

The 1960s occupy a memorable place in contemporary Western history. The peace marches, Black power demonstrations, "flower power," and so forth, were all symptomatic of a deepening disease—meaninglessness or despair. The people of this era were searching for a cause, for meaning.

In the period following World War II, people faced unique issues and dilemmas. It was a time of rapid advances in technology and science, of a redoubling of knowledge every decade, of a shift from agrarian to industrial society, and of movement country to city.

It was also a time of shifting religious and moral mores. Traditional beliefs and practices were under attack. Orthodox Christian teaching was being questioned by many and even abandoned by some. Young theologians were searching for a new approach to God which would be more relevant to an increasingly secular generation. The crucial issue for them was "to present Christianity intelligibly to the modern mind in order to overcome the 'God problem' in society. The alien cultural setting of the . . . twentieth century . . . [demanded] a 'contemporary understanding' of the Gospel because of the special stance of the 'godless' man of [the] times."[1] They believed that the solution to their problem would be found in the development of a secular theology.

Harvey Cox tells us that the two main marks of this new age were "the rise of urban civilization and the collapse of traditional religion."[2] Urbanization is a symbol of human maturity, of a human "coming of age," when society comes to depend on itself rather than on ancient myths and gods. It came to fruition "only with the scientific and technological advances which sprang from the wreckage of religious worldviews."[3]

The Historical Roots of Secular Theology
Even though secular theology is a child of the 1960s, its roots extend back to the Enlightenment, when a large segment of Chris-

165

tian thinkers began to question Christian doctrinal teachings. Rene Descartes in his *Critique of Pure Reason* (1781) urged that everything should be doubted which cannot be proved by reason. Friedrich Schleiermacher (1768–1834) proclaimed that true religion was not a matter of doctrines, but of man's "feeling of absolute dependence" upon God. Ludwig Feuerbach (1804–72) declared that "the secret of theology is nothing less than anthropology."[4] God is nothing more than a reflection of man's own highest characteristics.

One of the most profound minds of twentieth-century philosophy was Ernst Bloch. A professor in the United States and Germany, he had a deep appreciation for Marxism during the first part of his career, only to reject it in the latter part. Bloch's magnum opus, written in Cambridge, Massachusetts, during the 1940s, was *Das Prinzio Hoffnung (The Principle of Hope)*. It was a secular eschatology which rejected "belief in God as the most real or most perfect being, the fixed, enthroned absolute who requires and guarantees the fulfillment of his arbitrary will . . ."[5] in favor of the development and realization of human potentiality. A self-confessed atheist who credited to the world process many of the attributes of the Christian God,[6] Bloch was a forerunner of "God is dead" theology.

Secular theology owes debts, as well, to the thinking of many of the radical liberals of the second third of the century. Paul Tillich's "Ground of Being," Dietrich Bonhoeffer's "worldly Christianity," and Rudolf Bultmann's demythologization of Scripture, for example, contributed substantially to this movement. Friedrich Gogarten is also a theological ancestor of this movement, linking secular theology into the Protestant Reformation itself. Having been justified by grace alone through faith, the Christian has restored to him the stewardship of the earth and is called upon to rule it wisely. The technological advancement of contemporary times is not prohibited by God; rather, He calls the modern world to seek for completeness under His blessing. While it is threatened with His judgment should it raise its own credo or tenets, its secularity is nonetheless validated. Historian A.T. Van Leeuwen, in his *Christianity in World History* (1964), has agreed with Gogarten, declaring that secularization, confronted and animated by the Christian Gospel, is the wave of tomorrow.[7]

Secularization or Secularism?

Some definitions of the terms used by secular theologians may be of help in better understanding this movement and all that it involves. The word secular refers to a "relating to the worldly or temporal," and "not overtly or specifically religious."[8] In a more focused sense, it refers to an ungodly person; such a one is not necessarily an atheist, but nonetheless lives as though God were of no importance. The roots of this word have to do with monastic vows; the secular clergy had refrained from joining a specific order and submitting to its rules of living.

Secularism refers to a "rejection or expulsion of religion and religious considerations."[9] It is a style of thought and action which centers completely on this world. It is usually closely associated with humanistic philosophies as alternatives to religious thought forms.

The word *secularize* means "to make secular" or "to transfer from ecclesiastical to civil or lay use."[10] The latter definition may be seen in the action of the English Parliament in closing over 500 monasteries between 1536 and 1539, and turning this property over to the Crown. This was a forced secularization of church properties. In its broadest sense, the word "indicates a process by which things, persons, or institutions are separated from religious use or religious influence."[11]

In discussing secular theology, we are considering a theology of *secularization* rather than *secularism*. Secular theologians are attempting to convert ecclesiastically connected theology into "this-worldly" theology. Harold Kuhn tells us that theological secularization involves two steps: "First, there is a structured divesting of historic Christian supernaturalism of its essential qualities; and second, there is the erection of a pattern of theological premises based exclusively upon this-worldly concerns and considerations."[12] Essentially, secularization entails a repudiation of virtually all supernatural elements in Christian theology. As Dutch theologian C.A. van Peursen says, it is the attempt to deliver human beings "first from religious and then from metaphysical control over [their] reason and [their] language."[13]

Biblical Contributions to Theological Secularization

Secular theologians insist that the secularization of theology is a natural consequence of the development of biblical faith. Indeed, "the rise of natural science, of democratic institutions, and of cultural pluralism . . . can scarcely be understood without the original impetus of the Bible."[14]

Harvey Cox sees three biblical elements which fostered the secularization of theology. The first is "the disenchantment of nature."[15] The worldviews of primitive civilizations saw deity and humanity alike as integral parts of nature. The creation account of Genesis makes a radical division between the Creator God and His creation. "The Genesis account of creation is really a form of 'atheistic propaganda' "[16] intended to teach the Hebrews that nature is not a divine force. This radical separation freed science to begin its journey of successive accomplishments.

A second element which aided in the progress of secular society was the "desacralization of politics."[17] In pre-secular society the political power structure was seen as a divine appointment. The ruler was legitimated by the national or tribal religious authority and was often given divine or semi-divine status. In some of these systems, such as the Roman Empire, the ruler (emperor) was the *pontigex maximus*, high priest or direct representative of the gods.

Cox sees the Hebrew Exodus as the pivotal event in desacralizing politics. Under the direction of Yahweh, the Hebrews participated in "an act of insurrection against a duly constituted monarch, a pharaoh whose relationship to the sun god Ra constituted his claim to political sovereignty."[18] This event symbolized human deliverance from a sacral-political order where sovereignty was founded upon religion into a world where political power would be based on the ability to achieve definite social goals. Since the time of the Exodus, God's people have always moved to challenge the sacral-religious authority of those in power.

The third biblical element which aided the rise of the secular was what Cox terms the "deconsecration of values."[19] The present age is noted for the disappearance of moral constants. Truth has become increasingly subjective; human beings have lost any concrete ground on which to base their moral and spiritual decisions.

The relativization of values was initiated, Cox tells us, from the opposition of Scripture to idolatry. The prohibition against "graven images" in the Sinai Covenant forbade the making of any divine likeness. "Since, for the ancients, gods and value systems were the same thing, this interdiction against idols has real import for the question at hand."[20] The effect of this prohibition was to start the destruction of many of the religious symbols of that day; the breaking of moral and religious symbols has continued to the present.

The "Death of God"

One strand of secular theology was the "God is dead" movement of the mid-1960s. In spite of its anthropomorphic and radically immanentalist foci, the chief proponents of this movement insisted that it was a Christian theology.

Although its most ardent formulators were Americans, God is dead theology had its roots in the European humanism and skepticism of the last century. George W.F. Hegel (1770–1831) lamented that modern religion is founded on "the feeling that God himself is dead."[21] Friedrich Nietzsche (1844–1900), in his *The Gay Science*, tells of a madman who ran about the marketplace with a lantern seeking God, but who declared to bystanders: "Whither is God? . . . I shall tell you. *We have killed him* — you and I. . . . God is dead. . . . And we have killed him."[22]

The major advocates of God is dead theology included Thomas J.J. Altizer, William Hamilton, Gabriel Vahanian, and Richard Rubenstein.

Altizer's theology. The most complete and systematic exposition of God is dead theology was set forth by Thomas Altizer. He was an enthusiastic resurrector of Nietzsche's thinking, especially that of Eternal Recurrence, which holds that all of reality experiences continuous destruction and re-creation via a progressive and irresistible dialectic. "Thus, they deny all forms of traditional ontology and allow for no sovereign and unconditioned Being but only a 'God' who at some time in the dialectic wills His own self-annihilation."[23]

Altizer applied this dialectic to the doctrine of the Incarnation, dwelling on the Pauline idea of *kenosis* in Philippians 2:7-8. The transcendent Ground of all being emptied Himself of His divine attributes and became a man in the Person of Jesus Christ, in order to reconcile the world to Himself. Thus, in the Incarnation, God annihilated Himself in Christ, steadily receding into "a lifeless nothingness."[24]

In this world without God, insisted Altizer, we must do away with our traditional Western concepts and terms about God. He suggested that this could best be done by accepting Buddhist, Hindu, Taoist, and other Oriental thought forms. Uses of ideas such as *nirvana* would help contemporary North Americans better to understand the universally conceptualized All. Indeed, Altizer saw Buddha as a "primordial Christ," acceptance of whom would liberate Westerners from the fraudulent claims of the historic Christ.[25]

Hamilton's theology. William Hamilton was less systematic in his promotion of God is dead theology. But he published a number of theological books and articles and, in 1966, his theologizing was prominently featured in *Playboy* magazine.

For Hamilton, God died gradually over the last 200 years of Western history. "There was once a God to whom adoration, praise, and trust were appropriate, possible, and even necessary, but . . . there is now no such God."[26] Moreover, He died for all time and will not return.

Hamilton saw God's death as having occurred in three stages. It occurred at Calvary in the death of the Incarnate God; secondly, in the nineteenth-century collapse of faith; and, thirdly, in modern humanity's loss of the sense of God's reality.[27]

In actual fact, Hamilton had exchanged the divine transcendent God for a human, immanent Jesus. The New Testament provides information about Jesus to make Him a paradigm for truly human living in our age: "Jesus is the one to whom I repair, the one before whom I stand, the one whose way with others is also to be my way because there is something there, in his words, his life, his way with others, his death, that I do not find elsewhere. I am drawn, and I have given my allegiance."[28] Thus, the committed Christian will seek to emulate Jesus in every aspect of relating to his neighbors in every area of life.

Gabriel Vahanian's views. Gabriel Vahanian, a French-born Armenian, trained in theology at the Sorbonne and Princeton, is a solid disciple of Nietzsche, insisting that "God had to die in order that man might be what he is to become, in order that man may become the unlimited creator of culture. . . . Man cannot be while God lives."[29]

Like Gogarten, Vahanian lays the blame for the death of God at the door of the Christian faith, particularly that of the Reformation. Protestantism understood Christian faith to be a radically individual matter and thus did away with the community bond fostered by Roman Catholicism, leading to a steady erosion of faith and its replacement by religiosity. To be sure, there have been upsurges of faith (revivals) from age to age, but each one has been less intense and broad than the previous ones.

Out of the Protestant milieu, says Vahanian, has come the elimination of transcendentalism, the view that God is wholly Other. This view has been ousted in favor of immanentalism and, in effect, God has been eliminated with it. In this "leveling down" process, as he calls it, Vahanian sees three features from American Protestantism.

The first is the translation "of the Christian concept of the new man into the secular concept of the New Adam and, subsequently, into that of the Christ-figure."[30] Thus, humankind has usurped the role of Christ by arrogating to itself Christ's essential traits.[31]

The second feature is the interpretation of the kingdom of God into utopian millenarianism and the American Dream. "Millenarianism thus institutionalized God's sovereignty. As such, it was an element of petrification,"[32] devitalizing Christianity and dulling the keenness of God's sovereign presence. "Translated into purely secular terms, it led to the hope that better societies will be born when better cars are built and more gadgets (material and spiritual alike) inundate our lives."[33] Thus, God's sovereignty has been greatly trivialized.

The third feature (one attributable to Christianity as a whole and not just to American Protestantism) in the progress of secularization is the advent of the Social Gospel movement of the nineteenth century. "In a way, it became the counterpart of the earlier and more rigid Millenarianism. Whereas the latter had relied on the propositional truths of orthodoxy, the Social Gospel depended on the liberal postulate according to which, ultimately, religion and culture are identical realities."[34]

Vahanian sees this movement as a transitional one for Christianity into secularization, for it placed great confidence in science, made culture and religion synonymous, and redirected Christianity away from faith in a multitude of other, idealistic, directions.[35]

In the light of the evidence cited above, Vahanian believes that we have moved into a post-Christian era in which Christianity has become religiosity. This religiosity is apostasy from Christianity; "And it is not Christian, for we 'worship under the name of God . . . a twaddler.' This being so, 'Christianity . . . does not exist,' and God is dead—for nothing."[36]

As a result of having committed deicide, man is more alienated from himself than ever. And there is no resolution to the problem because, having disposed of that which was Other, he no longer can define or relate himself to others except as a god or as an "avenging wolf" to his fellows.

Rubenstein's theology. The death of God theology was not limited solely to Christians. American Jewish rabbi and theologian Richard L. Rubenstein claimed to hold similar views to those of Altizer and Hamilton. While he did not like the terminology "death of God" because of its Christian connections, he confessed that "I have, almost against my will, come to the conclusion that the terminology is unavoidable. . . . Death of God theology is no fad."[37]

Rubenstein attributed the death of God to the Nazis' extermination of the Jews of Europe in the Holocaust of World War II. "After Auschwitz many Jews did not need Nietzsche to tell them that the old God of Jewish patriarchal monotheism was dead beyond all hope of resurrection."[38] Rubenstein buried the historical notion of God while maintaining the psychological idea as pertinent to modern humanity. The idea of God was still needed, although in a somewhat different form. In place of the "Father-God" (now defunct) he posited a Tillichian "source and ground of being," the focus of ultimate concern. If God was indeed dead, what place did religion then have? According to Rubenstein, "It is the way in which we share and celebrate, both consciously and unconsciously, through the inherited myths, rituals, and traditions of our communities, the dilemmas and the crises of life and death, good and evil. Religion is the way in which we overcome our condition."[39]

Just as the Christian God is dead theologians replaced God with a very human Jesus, so this contemporary Jewish theologian found an alternative for God—in this case, the Torah. "I believe that in a world devoid of God we need Torah, tradition, and the religious community far more than in a world where God's presence was meaningfully experienced."[40] As a result, the synagogue, traditional guardian of the Torah and the Jewish way of life, became the vital institution of Judaism.

Rubenstein, unlike the Christian death of God theologians, did not rejoice in God's demise. On the contrary, he found it frightening and tragic, for "it heightens our sad knowledge that no power, human or divine, can ultimately withstand the dissolving onslaughts of omnipotent Nothingness, the true Lord of all creation."[41] While Altizer and Hamilton saw God's death as a sign of eschatological hope, Rubenstein saw the future without hope, only despair. According to him, there is nothing to do, however, but to accept the inevitable.

John Robinson's "Honest-to-God" Theology

John A.T. Robinson, late Anglican Bishop of Woolwich and professor of theology at Cambridge University, attempted to communicate theological values to the "man in the street" in his book, *Honest to God* (1963). His work drew for its inspiration upon the theologizing of Bultmann, Bonhoeffer, and Tillich.

Like the God is dead theologians, Robinson wanted to do away with the traditional categories of God and religion. "For I am convinced that there is a growing gulf between the traditional orthodox supernaturalism in which our Faith has been framed and the categories which the 'lay' world . . . finds meaningful today."[42] In so believing, he did not refer only to unbelievers; even Christians, he felt, have "been put off by a particular way of thinking about the world which quite legitimately they find incredible."[43] In fact, people were so put off that it would be advisable to suspend all "God-talk" for several years.

Robinson began his challenge to traditional Christian theology with the doctrine of God. Too many people think in terms of "supernaturalism," positing God as "the highest Being," existing along with and over against His creation. He is pictured as a Being who exists separately from other beings. Such views are interwoven into the very fabric of the Christian faith.

While he admitted that there was nothing intrinsically wrong with speaking of God in such a way, "I am firmly convinced that this whole way of thinking can be the greatest obstacle to an intelligent faith— . . . except [to] the 'religious' few."[44] He proposed, instead, Tillich's concept of God as pure Love, "the ground of our being, to which ultimately we 'come home.' "[45] His view here was closely akin to panentheism, the belief that the Being of God includes and penetrates all of creation.

Again, like the God is dead theologians, Robinson advocated the demythologization of the Incarnation. He accused traditional orthodoxy of Docetism, teaching that Christ only looked like a human being; in reality He was fully God. "But in practice popular preaching and teaching presents a supernaturalistic view of Christ which cannot be substantiated from the New Testament."[46]

Robinson made his case by radically reinterpreting John 1:1. The Greek words, *kai theos en ho logos*, were translated by the Authorized Version as, "And the Word was God." Not so, declared Robinson. The New English Bible better rendered it, "And what God was, the Word was." What John really meant was that, when one looked at Jesus, one saw God. "In this man, in his life, death and resurrection they had experienced God at work. . . ."[47]

He further reinterpreted the kenotic passage of Philippians 2:5-11. Christ did not strip Himself of the transcendent attributes of God. Rather, He emptied Himself not of godhood but of self. As a result, He "lays bare the Ground of man's being as love."[48]

Robinson issued a call to Christians to open themselves to the holy through worship. One worships, not to escape from this world into the "other" world, "but to open oneself to the meeting of the Christ in the common, to that which has the power to penetrate its superficiality and redeem it from its alienation."[49] It helps one to become more loving and, through Christ, to become a reconciling community. The test of worship, according to Robinson, was whether it makes one more sensitive to " 'the beyond in our midst,' to the Christ in the hungry, the naked, the homeless, and the prisoner."[50]

As one ponders Robinson's attempts to make Christianity relevant to contemporary humanity, one is reminded of Karl Barth's assessment (considering Robinson's three sources of inspiration) that he "took three German beers and got a lot of froth!"

Secular Theology

The high priest of the secular theology movement is without doubt Harvey Cox, professor of divinity at Harvard University. His little

paperback, *The Secular City,* published in 1965, became an overnight best-seller. It was easy to understand and dealt with popular
subject matter—the rise of technology and urbanization as symbols of the developing age in which we live.

Mention has already been made earlier of Cox's thesis that
Judeo-Christian tradition served as an agent of the secularization
process. It was his hope that in this way there might come about a
"constructive relativism" which "allows secular man to note the
transience and relativity of all cultural creations and of every value
system without sinking into the abyss of nihilism."[51] From these
beginnings arose the "technopolis."

The result has been the urban-secular man, who concerns himself with practical and material matters and who has little interest
in religious or metaphysical considerations. He is a pragmatic man
who sees life in terms of problems to solve and not as unfathom-
able mystery. "He does not ask religious questions because he
fully believes he can handle this world without them."[52]

Does the urban-secular man, therefore, not need the Bible? Is it
no longer relevant? Cox notes with approval Van Peursen's view
that pragmatic or functional views of truth cohere with the Bible
much more so than the ontological or mythical views they dis-
place. In the Old Testament, "God is spoken of as true because He
does what He says He will do."[53] He finds no contradiction between the biblical view of truth and emerging contemporary views.

Where does God fit into this picture, especially since Cox has
asserted that the word "God" has no relevance for secular humanity? Not to worry—God has hidden Himself for a time. But He will
reveal Himself when He is ready. It may be under a new name.
"This may mean that we shall have to stop talking about 'God' for
a while, take a moratorium on speech until the new name
emerges."[54] Perhaps society will have to do for a time without any
name for God. Ultimately, however, the name of God will be
known by the events of the future. In a later reflection on his
Secular City work, Cox reiterates this position, saying "we should
learn something from the ancient Jewish tradition of not pronounc-
ing the name of the holy One, live through a period of reverent
reticence in religious language, and wait for the Spirit to make
known a new vocabulary that is not so tarnished by trivialization
and misuse."[55]

Cox calls for a revival of the biblical doctrine of God which discerns His presence not only in a rural, agrarian setting, but also in the teeming metropolises of our world. "The Bible portrays a God who is present in the jagged reality of conflict and dislocation, calling the faithful into the crowded ways, not away from them."[56] He pleads, along with Bonhoeffer, that we as believers should "share the suffering of God in the world."

How does Cox handle the Person of Jesus Christ? Jesus so identified Himself with the kingdom of God that it may be said that its significance is embodied in His Person. Thus, "the elements of divine initiative and human response in the coming of the Kingdom are totally inseparable."[57] The question arises as to whether Jesus is God or man. Does His life represent God's activity on man's behalf or man's total response to God? The Council of Chalcedon held Him to be both.

Cox obviously is unwilling to allow that Jesus is fully God in the sense of the Definition of Chalcedon. He held that the deity of Jesus was "His readiness to accept and execute God's purposes for Him."[58] The present-day secular city may be involved in a like pursuit. Because truth is functional, rather than ontological, the kingdom may be realized in our world, as humans respond to the needs placed on them. Cox, however, has nothing to say about repentance from sin, faith in Christ as Savior and Lord, or eternal life.

An Evaluation

Secular theologians have come to the conclusion that the traditional orthodox way of interpreting the Bible is no longer helpful. Their concern may be valid; they want to present the Gospel in such a way that it is relevant to secular humanity. Unfortunately, they have sought to reshape the Gospel to fit the sinner, rather than to change the sinner.

Of course, secular theologians would not find the above statement theologically appropriate. It is no longer necessary to speak of people as sinners. Sin has no place in the "technopolis"—nor, for that matter, do most other religious or metaphysical terms. The secular city really has no place for religion.

The major problem of secularized theology is its defective view of God. It has sought to do away with the sovereignty of God. We see this desire especially in the movement's rejection of God's transcendence. The Bible contains many references to the divine transcendence (e.g., Ps. 113:5-6; 123:1; Isa. 6:1-5; 55:8-9; John 8:23). Secularists seek to yank God off of His throne with a number of New Age and panentheist ideas. God is not *the* Creator of all that exists; He is a "co-creator" along with humankind. He is not a Person, but a Feuerbachian projection from human experience.

Erickson notes that one of the implications of transcendence is that it elevates something beyond humanity. "Good, truth, and value are not determined by the shifting flux of this world and human opinion."[59] But secular theology maintains that there are no absolutes; value systems come and go, and what seems to meet the needs of a society at a given time is fitting and proper for that context.

Secular theology's view of Christ is equally flawed. Robinson, for example, declared that "Jesus never claims to be God personally."[60] But there are numerous references in Scripture which affirm His deity (as, for instance, Mark 2:8-10; John 1:1ff; Phil. 2:5-11; Heb. 1:1-10). One important aspect, or sign, of the deity of Christ is His virginal conception. Secular theology rejects this as myth. Indeed, it seeks to empty Christ of every supernatural attribute, to reduce Him to being a mere human reflection of the goodness and grace of God (albeit perhaps more fully than most other humans). Much of the supernatural work of God recorded by Scripture is seen as mythological. His transcendence, salvation, heaven, and hell are all considered in a Bultmannian light—language relevant to Bible times, but which needs reinterpretation to make it relevant to the secular scene. Any biblical terminology employed by them is a shell, not the essence, of the movement.

Although the doctrinal aspects of secular theology are fatally flawed, the desire of the movement to render the Gospel understandable to secularized humanity is laudable. Evangelicals would do well to note (and also to act upon) the jibes of secular theologians at their lack of clarity and precision in articulating the message of God's love and desire for reconciliation.

The effects of modern society on theology are widespread. One does not have to go far to notice how prevalent secular thinking is in our world. As science and technology continue to develop, it is likely that humanity will be increasingly elevated and God will be diminished in human estimation.

In the reflection on his work some twenty-five years after the fact, Cox reaffirms a statement from the book to the effect that secularization "is not the Messiah. But neither is it the anti-Christ. It is rather a dangerous liberation."[61] A better evaluation would seem to be that it is just "dangerous."[62]

For Further Reading

Callahan, Daniel, ed. *The Secular City Debate*. New York: Macmillan, 1966.

Cox, Harvey. *Religion in the Secular City: Towards a Post-Modern Theology*. New York: Simon and Schuster, 1984.

_____. *The Secular City*. New York: Macmillan, 1965.

Hadden, Jeffrey and Anson Shupe, eds. *Secularization and Fundamentalism Reconsidered*. Ann Arbor: New Era Books, 1989.

Jenkins, David. *Beyond Religion*. Philadelphia: Westminster Press, 1962.

Mehta, Ved. *The New Theologian*. New York: Harper and Row, 1965.

Newbigin, Leslie. *Honest Religion for Secular Man*. London: SCM Press, 1966.

Robinson, John A.T. *Honest to God*. Philadelphia: Westminster Press, 1963.

Smith, R.G. *Secular Christianity*. London: Collins, 1966.

Van Buren, Paul. *The Secular Meaning of the Gospel*. New York: Macmillan, 1963.

Vahanian, Gabriel. *The Death of God: The Culture of Our Post-Christian Era*. New York: George Braziller, 1961.

Williams, Colin. *Faith in a Secular Age*. New York: Collins, 1966.

Twelve. Theologies of Success

N
o other theological attitude fits in as well to the materialistic, achievement-oriented climate of the North America
of the last two decades as does what one might label the
"theologies of success." And the leaders of the success movements aptly model for their followers what they preach. They live
in opulent settings, drive top-of-the-line automobiles, and wear the
latest and most expensive designer clothing. And they teach all
who will listen that all these blessings may be theirs, as well.
Consequently:

> Many of the faithful from time to time climb into their Winne-
> bagos for cross country pilgrimages to faith conferences,
> seminars, or "world explosions" to hear "evangelists" such
> as John Osteen, Narvelle Hayes, or Kenneth Hagin. They
> send "love gifts" for booklets and tape series with titles such
> as *Living in Divine Prosperity, God's Laws of Success, Have
> Faith in Your Faith,* or *Self-Esteem, The New Reformation.*[1]

Two success theologies—both home-grown in the United
States—especially stand out. They are the theology of self-esteem
(*aka* possibility thinking) and prosperity theology (*aka* the faith
movement). Each will be examined and analyzed in turn.

The Theology of Self-Esteem
The theology of self-esteem is a unique North American "pop" theology, born in the late 1960s in California's show business milieu, and
spread largely through the medium of televangelism. It is essentially
a reaction against the "worm theology" view of humanity emphasized by late Reformation Protestantism. It seeks to affirm the personal worth of the individual and to nurture the self-esteem.

The founder of self-esteem theology. The founder and chief proponent of this school of theology is Robert Schuller, pastor (and

founder) of the Crystal Cathedral in Garden Grove, California, a "megachurch" of the Reformed Church in America. He is also the host of "The Hour of Power," the most widely watched religious television program in North America.

Schuller was born in 1926 and received his college education at Hope College, Michigan. From there he went on to train for the ministry at Western Theological Seminary. As a child, he was greatly influenced by the optimism of his father through the course of adverse circumstances. Although he did not experience grinding poverty during the Great Depression, Schuller perceived himself as living with its stigma.[2]

In 1950 Schuller was ordained by the Reformed Church and pastored his first church at Ivanhoe, a suburb of Chicago. It was there that he first began to feel God answering the prayer that he had been praying since studying at Western Seminary: "Give me a chance . . . to build a church from the bottom up. I covet no other man's job. I ask for an opportunity to create a great job for myself and leave behind something wonderful to bless generations yet unborn."[3]

In 1955 Schuller left Ivanhoe and headed West, dreaming of reaching the unchurched in southern California. He had been commissioned by the Reformed Church to begin a church in the Garden Grove vicinity. There, he found only a handful of Reformed Church people. It "was clear that he would have to appeal to the unchurched. He would have to win over people who had never before showed interest in organized religion."[4]

Schuller's first church service was held at a drive-in theater. He had advertised it, "Come as you are in the family car." A few months later, the guest speaker for a Sunday service, Norman Vincent Peale, drew over 1,700 cars and 6,000 people.[5]

Officially organized in 1958, Schuller's congregation grew by leaps and bounds. Its first building, constructed in 1961, was of a walk-in, drive-in design. Again, Peale preached the first sermon in the new facility. In 1965, the Tower of Hope was added to house staff, a counseling clinic, a telephone counseling center, and a chapel.

This facility was soon made obsolescent by numbers attending and, in 1980, was replaced by the Crystal Cathedral, which was deemed to be the ultimate in worship centers. One reporter terms it "a twenty-two-acre shopping center for Jesus Christ."[6]

Schuller soon embarked on a television ministry which grew to national prominence. His personal success became the prototype of "possibility thinking." Even today, he generates a considerable influence on North American society.

Background to self-esteem. One of the strongest influences on Robert Schuller's thought and practice of ministry has been Norman Vincent Peale. Born in Ohio in 1898, Peale became a Methodist minister in 1922, and ten years later accepted a Reformed Church pastorate in New York City.

He pioneered the combining of psychology and religion, founding a "religio-psychiatric clinic" in his church where he worked in conjunction with a psychiatrist in counseling church members. He was convinced that, "once the psychiatrist points out the basic cause, then we ministers can begin to apply the great remedies of religion: prayer, faith, and love."[7]

Peale's book, *The Power of Positive Thinking*, grew out of the idea that, "in physics, the basic factor is force; in psychology, the basic factor is a realized wish."[8] He formulated his philosophy of positive thinking with a view to fulfilling that wish.

One of his fundamental concepts was that one can achieve anything that one sets out to do. In the forward to *You Can If You Think You Can*, he gives as his purpose in writing, "to persuade you the reader, that you can if you think you can . . . by realizing the amazing possibilities inherent in the mind."[9]

Schuller began (and has continued) his work in California with his own specially-distilled flavor of Peale's positive thinking which he dubbed "possibility thinking," and which he popularized in numerous books, such as *Move Ahead with Possibility Thinking* (1967), *Peace of Mind through Possibility Thinking* (1977), and *The Be (Happy) Attitudes* (1982).

An offspring of positive and possibility thinking, Schuller's theology of self-esteem was first formulated as "self-love" in his 1969 book, *Self-Love, The Dynamic Face of Success*, but it did not really draw widespread public reaction. In 1982, he issued *Self-Esteem, The New Reformation*, which was distributed free of charge to hundreds of theological students and teachers in North America, and aroused considerable controversy.

Needed: A New Reformation?

Robert Schuller's theology cannot be separated from his life experience. Upon reading his books, one soon recognizes that Schuller himself is the most prominent example of possibility thinking,[10] which he defines as "that mental attitude which assumes that any objective that is noble, admirable, or beautiful can be realized even if it appears to be impossible."[11]

The goal of possibility thinking is the development of a positive or healthy self-esteem. Schuller defines self-esteem as "the divine dignity that God intended to be our emotional birthright as children created in his image."[12]

Schuller's theology of self-esteem grew out of his desire to reach out to the unchurched. He claims that present-day theology simply does not reach them. Our theology is the product of an age when Christianity was the major force in the world and a majority of Westerners subscribed to its creeds. As a result, it worried little about meeting the needs of the unchurched (for, officially, they were virtually nonexistent!). Its basic message was theocentric and its chief concern was theological truth—a "thus-saith-the-Lord" approach.

Today, things have changed. Christianity is in a minority position. The church has declined in numbers and in authority. Surrounded by millions of pagans, declares Schuller, it must stop "playing church" and become a missionary religion. Its focus must be anthropocentric and its chief concern must become humanity's deepest-felt needs. Religious institutions which redirect their ministries to respond to these needs will prosper. Others will continue to decline into oblivion.

It is evident, Schuller insists, that a new reformation is needed. Without it the church as the body of Christ may die. Robert Schuller sees himself as the new reformer in the tradition of Martin Luther and John Calvin, called by God to reform the present-day church.

What is wrong with the church, Schuller feels, is not so much its doctrine as its methodology. It has failed to produce emotionally healthy, vibrant Christians who are self-confident and wholly integrated individuals. Its failure is because throughout its history the church has assaulted God's foremost creation—mankind—labeling the human ego "as the ultimate sin, when, in fact, it is the mark of the image of God in people."[13] It has supposed that the deepest need of individuals was "salvation from sin," and has offered "hope for forgiveness" as the appropriate response.

Schuller will affirm such a supposition as long as it builds — rather than tears down — one's self-esteem. He maintains that all of the church's problems would be solved if it would focus all of its attention on meeting this human need which is "the uncompromising quality of humanity."[14] Just as the Protestant Reformation steered the church's focus back to the Scriptures, so this new reformation "will return our focus to the sacred right of every person to self-esteem."[15]

Schuller's Theology Described

Robert Schuller claims to be a conservative believer standing in the Reformed tradition of John Calvin and holding to the Bible as the only inerrant guide in matters of faith and practice. He also affirms the Apostles' Creed, the Nicene Creed, and the Lausanne Covenant.[16] From time to time, however, what a theologian purports to believe and what he preaches fail to be completely congruent. A brief examination of the main tenets of Schuller's theology of self-esteem will determine whether it fully measures up to the standard of conservative evangelical orthodoxy he claims. Because he is not a systematician, but a practical theologian, one must consider his work other than according to the traditional order and categories.

God the Father. Schuller's starting point claims to be the doctrine of God as Father. It is only through the recovery of the Father-child relationship that individuals may achieve a healthy and fulfilling self-image: "A high sense of self-worth based on the Fatherhood of God gives us the deep foundation for a faith and a philosophy that can build hope for human dignity."[17] Schuller's reasoning is that when a person becomes a member of God's family and realizes that he is indeed God's child, and that God is his Father, then his destructive egoism is replaced by a godly humility and feelings of inferiority are replaced by a positive self-assurance from identification with God.

Sin. The villain behind humanity's problems, Schuller declares, is sin. Traditional theology has described sin as "rebellion against

God." Because of Adam's sin, every human being is conceived in such a rebellious state (a condition known as "original sin"). Schuller rejects this idea of original sin as far too shallow. He decries traditional preaching on sin and judgment as "a destructive influence in the human personality and human life."[18] He believes that any view of sin should be rejected "that would cause me to 'feel bad about myself.' "[19] No love-needing person would naturally resist the wonderful love offered by God. Schuller defines original sin as lack of trust; because of Adam's sin, all of his descendants are born without "a trusting relationship with the heavenly Father. . . . alienated, out-of-touch."[20] He equates lack of trust with a negative self-image and emphatically decries the idea "that the central core of the human soul is wickedness. . . . positive Christianity does not hold to human depravity, but to human inability"[21] to value oneself properly.

Sin per se (as opposed to original sin) by Schuller's definition is "any act or thought that robs myself or another human being of his or her self-esteem."[22] The most serious sin, he declares, is the one which causes a child of God to say that he or she is unworthy. Sin, therefore, seems to be, at least primarily, an act against oneself or one's fellows, and only secondarily an infraction of God's standards.

Salvation. Because Schuller's definition of sin is not the classical one, neither is his concept of salvation: "To be born again means that we must be changed from a negative to a positive self-image—from inferiority to self-esteem, from fear to love, from doubt to trust."[23] Christ's death on Calvary demonstrates the value God places on a human being. As people make a faith commitment to Christ, they will realize their infinite worth and acquire self-esteem. The result is that they will feel positive about themselves. Christ's death saves one from hell which, for Schuller, is the experience of life without self-esteem.

In the resurrection Christ has commissioned humanity to continue His ministry of sharing the love which generates self-esteem with their fellow human beings. And what greater affirmation of one's self-esteem can there be? Through the leading and control of the Holy Spirit, believers join in community to infect positively the secular society about them.

The Christian life. Schuller's theology of the cross is not typical either. He agrees that God's call always includes the call to self-denial and the bearing of the cross (Matt. 16:24), but he strongly rejects the "poisonous mortification mood and message that still thrives in certain Christian literature,"[24] which fosters self-debasement and self-flagellation. God does not call the believer to attempt to think poorly of himself and to denigrate himself because he succeeds after much effort and self-sacrifice.

What, then, does Schuller see as the divine call to self-denial? It is the intentionality to become concerned with the spiritual and social solutions in society.[25] Self-esteem is a sure pathway to self-denial. Because God is our Father, we dare to dedicate ourselves, all that we have and are, to serving Him.

Bearing the cross is similar. It is not fulfilled by a "crusader complex" which aggressively accosts people in an inflammatory manner. For Schuller, the cross is offered "as an inspiring idea that would incarnate itself in a form of ministry that helps self-esteem-impoverished persons to discover their self-worth through salvation and subsequent social service in our Savior's name."[26] When one succeeds in carrying out one's mission, "much fruit" is borne and God is glorified.

The work of the church. Schuller defines the church as "a group of joyful Christians, happily sharing their glorious faith with the despairing souls of their fellow men who have never known the joy of Christ."[27] The purpose of the church is spiritual procreation. Church growth is not just one of many purposes, but the central focus of the church.

Closely connected here is Schuller's vision of the task of evangelism. The unconverted must be seen, not as evil, but as non-trusting persons who are infinitely valuable to God. They resist God's grace in Christ because of a lack of self-esteem which compels them to try to merit love and forgiveness through their actions. These people must receive substantial affirmation before they can comprehend the truth of the Gospel. Christ never called people sinners, nor should His people. The Gospel must be preached and taught as salvation from shame to glory, from self-doubt and self-vilification to self-assurance and self-avowal.[28]

Such a theology of self-esteem, Schuller maintains, leads to a revolutionary ethic which values peoples' self-worth far above all else:

> Any social act which insults another person, demeans another human being, oppresses another person's possibilities, lowers to any degree the collective level of social self-esteem, or retards the collective level of community pride is a violation of the theology of social ethics that the Kingdom of God demands from a true disciple.[29]

Racism, sexism, oppression of the poor—all must go by the board. The church will undergo a transformation from reactionary to missionary when it engages in such a thrust; it will flourish as never before.

Schuller's Theology Evaluated

Schuller's theology—like any other device or system of human construction—is neither completely edifying nor completely detrimental. It has both its positive and negative points, and these will be examined in turn.

Positive points. Much of what Robert Schuller advocates is accurate and practical. His passion to evangelize the unchurched is highly commendable. It is the driving force behind all that he has done.

Evangelicals have much to learn from his vision for the church he planted at Garden Grove. He knew whom he wanted to reach and discerned the best ways of reaching them. "Schuller has demonstrated the importance of strategy and planning to achieve the mission of the church."[30]

He has also demonstrated the importance of reaching people with a message they can understand. He communicates clearly and effectively. His message is often filled with catchy phrases and rhymes which readily imprint themselves on the listener's mind. His insistence that the sacred needs to become more secular is (in this regard) no doubt so.

Nor should we applaud only the structures for his theology. Much of the doctrine Schuller promotes is worthy of praise, as well. In his doctrine of God, his emphasis on the Father-child relationship is laudable. It is indeed vital to human spiritual and emotional well-being. Who one's Father is plays an important role in how one sees oneself, and the realization of the fatherhood of God should give a tremendous boost to one's self-esteem. The creation of humankind in and of itself shows that God values persons. But the Atonement demonstrates more highly than all else the supreme worth of humanity in God's sight.

Again, Schuller's doctrine of sin has valuable lessons to teach us. Sin surely is the basis of the human predicament. It does result in an alienation between man and God which is symbolized by a lack of trust on the part of the former.

Schuller is also correct in his perception that secular humans do not accept the Scriptures as binding, nor do they see sin from a secular perspective. Beating them over the head with the Bible, berating them for their sinfulness, will do little good. A stress on the love of God and His offer of purpose and worth for one's life should work much more effectively. And Schuller has substantiated his viewpoint very effectively, for he has evangelized more secular North Americans than anyone else.

Negative aspects. Schuller's theology begins wrongly; this wrong starting point has misdirected the whole system. Making humankind and psychology focal in his teaching is to start off on the wrong foot.[31] A correct doctrinal system begins with theology proper (God), not with anthropology (man). Until one has a right view of God, one can never see humanity in its proper perspective.

Nor is Schuller's view of sin adequate. For example, while lack of trust is a component of original sin, it is not at its core. Rebellion (contra Schuller) is that core. Human beings have chosen to go their own way rather than God's. Behind this rebellion lies inordinate pride. Of course secular man does not trust God, and has lost his self-esteem, for he has nothing in which to ground it. Nor is sin an offense primarily against oneself or one's fellows; the Bible views sin as offending God (Gen. 39:9; Ps. 51:4; Rom. 3:23).

This concept of sin as against humans results in an infraction against the biblical picture of the Atonement.[32] Instead of Christ dying on man's behalf to take away the penalty for man's rebellion against God, He evidently died to help him to become a "possibility thinker," or to improve himself.

While Schuller is correct in stating that salvation can transform one from self-loathing to self-worth, he falls short of its fullness. Christ saves us from all of the spiritual consequences of sin. In the same way, Schuller's idea of self-denial and bearing the cross is somewhat simplistic. It is far more than attempting to carry out what one considers to be a noble, divinely-inspired vision. God may call one to suffering and doing without. And while bearing the cross is not a call to indulgence in a persecution complex, it may well be a call to endure persecution.

To Summarize

Robert Schuller's theology of self-esteem is right enough as far as it goes, but it does not go far enough. His work is excellent *pre-evangelism*, helping to prepare people for the Gospel. But it fails to present Christ in His fullness, and so it fails to engage people in a full-orbed life of discipleship.

One of the chief reasons for Schuller's failure at completeness has been his formulation of theology from a human starting point. He has admitted to extensive use of polls, questionnaires, and anecdotal material to formulate his theories. He should rather have begun with a divine starting point. The theology of self-esteem is frankly and unapologetically anthropocentric. Any doctrinal approach, however, which seeks the answers to life from a human vantage point rather than from a theocentric one will tend to remake God in the image of humanity.

Another reason for Schuller's lack of completeness in his theology, as was suggested at the outset, is simply because he is not a theologian per se but a preacher-evangelist. He needs to engage someone to play Melancthon to his Luther, that is, someone to take his ideas, systematize them, and more fully develop them. Few will question this man's zeal for Christ and sincere desire to see people brought to Him. His theology, however, needs extending and maturing.

Prosperity Theology

The great "American dream" of health, wealth, and power arose as a religious philosophy concomitant to the charismatic renewal of the 1960s. Known variously as "prosperity theology," "name it and claim it," and more formally as "the faith movement," this system entails the idea that a Christian can and should live in perpetual health and material abundance and that the avenue to these blessings is the simple exercise of one's faith.[33]

Historical Roots

Although prosperity theology was made popular by American charismatic televangelists like Kenneth Hagin and Kenneth Copeland, its roots go back at least to the nineteenth-century Holiness emphasis on faith healing. Evangelist Charles Finney was a staunch proponent of the concept. He argued that, if a Christian prays in faith for something specific, expecting to obtain the blessing requested, then "faith always obtains the object."[34]

Nor were Holiness preachers the only ones emphasizing healing through faith and prayer. Episcopalians Charles Cullis and Carrie Judd Montgomery, Presbyterian-turned-Baptist A.B. Simpson, and Baptist Adoniram Judson Gordon all preached that God had given believers a means of healing through the Atonement of Christ.[35]

In addition to these Holiness and mainstream proponents of faith healing, a number of itinerants enjoyed considerable success in that area. One of these was Australian faith healer John Dowie, who had no use either for doctors or medicine, and who emphasized that authentic healings are always immediate.[36]

Pentecostal healing. While all of these advocates of faith healing exerted some influence on the early Pentecostals, Dowie's "uncompromising denunciation of the sin of 'worldliness' placed him well within Pentecostals' understanding of inspired preaching" and "they adopted a message of radical faith in God to heal their diseases without benefit of doctors or medicines."[37]

Such an emphasis was not surprising, for Pentecostals had from the earliest believed in the miraculous. The patriarch of Pentecostalism, Charles Parham, had been a faith healer with ideas much like Dowie's. Other Pentecostals, while not going to such extremes, taught healing through prayer and the laying on of hands. As believers in the reception of the gifts of the Spirit, they also held that some individuals had received the gift of healing which would allow them to command illness to leave an afflicted individual, subject to the latter's faith.

Second generation Pentecostals conducted popular healing and evangelism revivals. They included such well-known figures as

Oral Roberts, William Branham, and T.L. Osborne. All claimed to have received the gift of healing.

The "true" father of prosperity. While it has been generally accepted in the past that the faith movement began with charismatics in the late 1960s, recent research plausibly demonstrates that it actually began with a non-Pentecostal revivalist, E.W. Kenyon (d. 1948), in the second decade of the twentieth century.[38] While he believed that he was teaching "a new type of Christianity," Kenyon's long-time friend, John Kennington, declares, ". . . I have come to realize that E.W. Kenyon has simply 'baptized' many concepts from Christian Science. In so doing, he became a source for a form of 'Pentecostal Christian Science,' even though Kenyon himself was not a Pentecostal."[39]

Kenyon's writings reflected his desire to redirect Christianity which, as far as he was concerned, had taken a wrong path: *The Two Kinds of Life, The Two Kinds of Righteousness, The Two Kinds of Knowledge, The Two Kinds of Faith*, and so on:

> Living at a time when the metaphysical cults were growing rapidly, this was Kenyon's "Christian" response—a "Christianized" metaphysical cult. The mainline churches were failing because they produced no signs and wonders and Kenyon was keen to redress an anti-supernaturalistic tendency which was driving bored Christians into joining such people as Mrs. Baker Eddy. He sought to establish a teaching for Christians with all the benefits of the metaphysical cults, while remaining within the Christian fold. The result was prosperity theology, which is, with a very few embellishments, the theology of the present-day faith movement.[40]

Although much opposed to Pentecostalism in his early ministry, he seemed to come to terms with it in his latter days, and often attended the healing revivals of F.F. Bosworth and Aimee Semple McPherson. He was also widely-read by the second-generation healing revivalists.

Kenneth Hagin: Prophet of Prosperity

While E.W. Kenyon has recently been enthroned as the rightful founder of the modern faith movement, the pretender to his throne—and the man popularly recognized as the father of the movement—is Kenneth Hagin. "All of the major ministries of the Faith Movement readily admit Hagin's tutelage. He is universally recognized in the movement as both a teacher and a prophet."[41]

Born in Texas in 1917, Kenneth Erwon Hagin suffered from a congenital heart defect and so was weak and sickly throughout childhood. His emotional stability was dealt a sharp blow at the age of six when his father abandoned the family. His mother suffered a nervous breakdown as a result and was years recovering from its effects.

At age sixteen, Hagin's heart condition caused him to become bedridden and suffer bouts of delirium. During this period, two things happened to change his life greatly. The first was an out-of-body experience in which he visited hell on three occasions. He describes the experience as follows:

> ... far down below me I could see lights flickering on the walls of the caverns of the damned. They were caused by the fires of hell. The giant, white-crested orb of flame pulled me, drawing me as a magnet draws metal to itself. *I did not want to go!* I did not walk, but just as metal jumps to the magnet, my spirit was drawn to that place.... The heat beat me in the face. Many years have gone by, yet I can see it as clearly as I saw it then....[42]

Following this dreadful experience, Hagin turned his life over to Jesus Christ so that he would be able to die in peace.

The second experience of Hagin's invalid period was a revelation of the Bible passage which would become the theme of his ministry: "I tell you the truth, if anyone says to this mountain, 'Go throw yourself into the sea,' and does not doubt in his heart but believes that what he says will happen, it will be done for him. Therefore I tell you, whatever you ask for in prayer, believe that you will receive it, and it will be yours" (Mark 11:23-24). Though he received this principle of faith on January 1, 1934, he had to confess his healing from heart disease daily until a fresh and added revelation of the same passage came to him in August of that same year: "The *having* comes after the *believing*. I had been reversing it. I was trying to *have* first and then *believe*."[43] He realized that he had to believe that he was well even when lying there ill. The

Holy Spirit urged him, if he truly believed that he was well, to get out of bed. He obeyed and ultimately was healed.[44]

Ministry out of God's will. Although he grew up Baptist, Hagin's initial ministry (which began in 1934 after graduation from high school) was more Pentacostalist in tone. Because Baptists did not stress healing, he associated increasingly with Pentecostals and, in 1937, was licensed in Texas as a pastor with the Assemblies of God. In the course of this ministry, healings, "dancing in the Spirit," and even resuscitations occurred.

Even though his early ministry experience was accompanied by such miraculous spiritual phenomena, Hagin looked back on it in later years as a failure. He cited the reason that he had spent his time as a pastor without ever having been called or anointed to such a task.[45]

The prophetic teaching ministry. In obedience to a vision in which he was taken to heaven to converse with Jesus (one of many such experiences), Hagin left the pastoral ministry in 1949 to work the healing revival circuit. Sensibly, he did not attempt to compete as a healer with established revivalists like Branham and Roberts. Claiming an anointing by the Holy Spirit as a teacher and (a few years later) prophet, he stressed these aspects of ministry.

The first decade of Hagin's "anointed" ministry was less than spectacular in every way. Few people attended his services; even fewer were healed. "I preached faith and prosperity boldly with the bills stacked up all around me."[46] Another interview with Jesus led him to the realization that he had been doing ministry in his own strength and purpose, not the Lord's.

As a result of this vision (and others), Hagin redirected his ministry. In 1962 he founded his own evangelistic association, and in 1966 located his headquarters in Tulsa, Oklahoma (the site of many other similar ministries). Here he began a fifteen-minute radio program, "Faith Seminar of the Air" (now on scores of stations continent-wide) and in 1974, the Rhema Bible Training Center which would train students to propagate Hagin's word of faith theology.

During the late 1960s and 1970s, Hagin's ministry mushroomed, especially among disciples of the relatively young charismatic renewal movement. McConnell attributes the growth to disillusionment with the rather rigid Shepherding-Discipleship movement among them:

> As late as 1973, while the Shepherding-Discipleship teaching was still in vogue, his association employed only nineteen full-time workers. By the time the Shepherding-Discipleship controversy was over, Hagin's staff had tripled to close to sixty. Like some sort of overnight adolescent craze, suddenly authority and discipleship were "out" in the charismatic movement and faith and prosperity were "in." . . . it would be difficult to name a circuit ministry that grew faster in the late 1970s than that of Kenneth Hagin.[47]

The Contemporary Faith Movement

In 1979, Hagin's son-in-law, Doyle Harrison, brought together a large number of churches, pastors, and revivalists who followed Hagin's teachings to found the International Convention of Faith Churches and Ministers (ICFCM) in Tulsa. Some of those participating were Kenneth Hagin, Sr.; Kenneth Hagin, Jr.; Kenneth Copeland; John Osteen; Narvelle Hayes; and Jerry Savelle.

While the ICFCM denies being a denomination and claims to be only a point of coordination for churches and activities in the faith movement, its membership requirements suggest otherwise. To be accepted into its ranks, a church must be sponsored by a member church. Ministers must have been trained at the Rhema Bible Training Center; all of them must agree to submit to the constitution, ethics, and doctrine of the Rhema Ministerial Association International, which was founded by Hagin in 1985.[48] The ICFMC is set up to provide: "(1) a central, rational organization responsible for communication and coordination; (2) regional and national conventions; (3) a continuing education system for its ministers; (4) a missionary training board; and (5) an organizational apparatus for placing chaplains in the military."[49] As well, it has a number of affiliated primary, secondary, and post-secondary schools, a publishing concern, and numerous associated evangelistic organizations.

During the last decade considerable controversy has surrounded the faith movement, especially from fellow charismatics. In 1978

Charles Farah, a professor at Oral Roberts University, published a book which implied that the faith movement had led many to lose their faith and worse.[50] While some objected to the book, others joined the attack, including evangelist Jimmy Swaggart and authors Dave Hunt and T.A. McMahon. In spite of controversy and attacks, however, the faith movement remains a major force within North American charismatic Christianity.

Major Emphases: An Evaluation
The faith movement grounds its thematic concepts in a very literal interpretation of certain Bible verses (in the King James Version), often completely divorced from their contexts. These include:

> Beloved, I wish above all things that thou mayest prosper and be in health, even as thy soul prospereth (3 John 2).

> I am the Lord thy God which teacheth thee to profit (Isa. 48:17).

> For verily I say unto you, that whosoever shall say unto this mountain, be thou removed and be thou cast into the sea, and shall not doubt in his heart, but shall believe that those things which he saith shall come to pass; he shall have whatsoever he saith. Therefore I say unto you, what things soever ye desire when ye pray, believe that ye receive them and ye shall have them (Mark 11:23-24).

> Ye have not, because ye ask not (James 4:2).

> I am come that they might have life, and that they might have it more abundantly (John 10:10).

Three essentials. There are three essential elements to the prosperity gospel. First, there must be an awareness of the promise before it can be claimed. "If a person doesn't know that it is God's will for him to prosper, it is highly improbable that he will prosper."[51]

The second key to prosperity is obedience. Faith movement practitioners cite Job 36:11, "If they obey and serve Him, they shall spend their days in prosperity and their years in pleasures" (KJV). If one is willing to obey God's commands in every area of

life, one will prosper; otherwise, one won't.[52]
The third aspect is faith. Faith amounts to claiming authority over resources that have already been guaranteed by God. "... [Y]ou must put off all of your negative faith and believe firmly that God, who sent Jesus to be crucified for you, is good. As it is written, 'He that spared not His own Son, but delivered Him up for us all, how shall He not with Him also freely give us all things?' " (Rom. 8:32, KJV)[53]

What sets the movement apart. According to Bruce Barron, there are three basic themes emphasized by the faith movement which differentiate it from orthodox Christian understandings of the faith. They are: healing, prosperity, and positive confession.[54] These are also the areas which have engendered the greatest controversy.

Healing. That God can heal—even that God can heal miraculously—is hardly a novel idea among Christians. It is about as old as the church itself. What distinguishes the faith movement from traditional Christianity is the former's insistence that God does not intend for anyone to be sick; healing is available if one has the faith to claim it.[55] Kenneth Hagin went so far as to declare that, "when the Bible talks about suffering, that doesn't mean 'sickness.' We have no business suffering sickness and disease, because Jesus redeemed us from that."[56]

Many faith movement leaders teach that those who faithfully pray for healing will receive it because Jesus never refused (in His earthly ministry) to heal anyone who asked Him. Since He is the same yesterday, today, and forever, it stands to reason that He will heal all who come to Him in faith.[57]

Others recall that Jesus sent out His followers to preach the Gospel and endowed them with healing power: "In My name ... they will place their hands on sick people, and they will get well" (Mark 16:17-18). We see a practical fulfillment of this commissioning in the healing of the lame man at the Gate Beautiful by Peter and John (Acts 3:1-8). That commission is still given to Jesus' followers today.

Probably the major reason given for healing is that it is an integral part of the Atonement. As Kenneth Copeland puts it:

"... healing is just as much a part of the plan of redemption as salvation. ...."[58] That healing is guaranteed by the cross is clearly set forth in Isaiah 53:4-5: "Surely He took up our infirmities and carried our sorrows, yet we considered Him stricken by God, smitten by Him, and afflicted. But He was pierced for our transgressions, He was crushed for our iniquities; the punishment that brought us peace was upon Him, and by His wounds we are healed."

Because healing is effected through the shed blood of Christ on the cross, it can be activated only by faith. While healing revivalists do use the laying on of hands in their services, they note that such a practice is only ritual and has no healing efficacy. It serves simply to motivate the sick person to release his faith to allow healing to occur.[59]

Jerry Savelle has set out the movement's position on healing quite succinctly:

Not only is it God's will to heal, it is God's will to heal all! Satan is the author of sickness and disease.

By the authority of His word, God has made provision for our healing. It is not the will of God that anyone be sick with any sickness or disease or pain whatsoever—from hangnails to tuberculosis![60]

The problem. That Jesus cured all with whom He came in contact seems, at first, like a very potent argument—until one realizes that it is not completely true. The miracle at the pool of Bethesda is a case in point; there were many ill people at the pool, but Jesus passed them by to heal only one individual. Again, while the apostles healed some people, these were few and far between. There were many—including some of the apostolic band (see 2 Tim. 4:20)—who were not healed. It seems that the further away the church moved (in time) from Christ's earthly ministry, the less healings took place. To base a theology of healing, furthermore, on Mark 16:16-18 is unwise, for that text is generally rejected as a part of the original (inspired) Gospel written by Mark.

When discussing the efficacy of the Atonement, one must keep in mind that the effects of the kingdom of God will not be felt in their completeness until Jesus comes again. Salvation, in the New

Testament Greek, is synonymous with healing. Spiritual healing is available at once in the form of the forgiveness of sins, but healing both physical and emotional may not happen until the fullness of the kingdom of God is realized.[61]

Prosperity. The faith movement believes that the kingdom of God already exists on earth and that it is our responsibility as Christians to take back from Satan the good things of life (mostly material) and to live a prosperous life. According to Charles Capps, "You can have the kingdom, and the benefits right here on earth."[62] Jerry Savelle writes, "There is no reason for you to wait until you get to heaven to receive the blessing of God. . . . the time for prosperity is now."[63]

Although prosperity has to do with being successful in all areas of life, most of those who are bound up in the movement see financial prosperity as the sure and certain sign of God's blessing and approval of those with the requisite portion of faith. The movement bases its views upon Old Testament covenantal theology. Material wealth was an integral part of the covenant God made with Abraham (Gen. 24:35). Since Abraham is the father of the faithful and a prototype of the child of God who lives by faith, it makes sense to suppose that, as God blessed Abraham, so He will bless all whose lives are modeled after his. "If Abraham prospered by paying his tithes," writes Paul Cho, "modern believers should also receive the same blessings."[64]

Another crucial passage for prosperity teachers is Malachi 3:10, " 'Bring the whole tithe into the storehouse, that there may be food in My house. Test Me in this,' says the Lord Almighty, 'and see if I will not open the floodgates of heaven and pour out so much blessing that you will not have room enough for it.' " This has been made an axiom of success: tithe and God will reward you abundantly. Another axiom of success is Mark 10:29-30, which promises a hundred-fold return to those who have sacrificed for Christ's sake. Gloria Copeland comments on this passage: "Give one house and receive one hundred houses or one house worth one hundred times as much. Give one airplane and receive one hundred times the value of the airplane. Give one car and the return would furnish you a lifetime of cars. In short, Mark 10:30 is a very good deal."[65]

The problem. Even a casual examination of the biblical facts will lead one to conclude that such promises or "axioms" cannot be taken literally. None of the disciples who were fishermen received hundreds of boats in return for leaving all to follow Christ. Zaccheus actually lost money for turning to Him. And the Apostle James was executed for his faith!

When one looks at the Two-Thirds World, the majority of Christians are impoverished. Does that mean that they are lacking in faith? Of course not!

In all fairness to many of the movement's teachers, it must be admitted that they teach that there is a purpose for prosperity. Kenneth Copeland observes that "true prosperity is the ability to use God's power to meet the needs of mankind in any realm of life."[66] And Kenneth Hagin, Jr., in addressing students at the Rhema Bible Training Center, told them that if they had come to learn in order "to help you get more faith so that you can have Cadillacs,"[67] they should resign and leave at once.

In recent years some have mellowed even more. Since 1985, for instance, Kenneth Copeland has admitted that prosperity may come in forms other than financial. It may take the form of a bountiful harvest or a plentiful rainfall.[68]

Positive confession. Prosperity theology teaches that health and wealth come as the result of what is called "positive confession." The idea is based on two New Testament passages. Romans 10:10 tells us that "it is with your mouth that you confess and are saved." Other confessions will provide other blessings. Mark 11:23-24 (cited earlier in this chapter) is fundamental, to the effect that whatever you say without doubting will come to pass and whatever you pray for, believing, you will have it. It is from this passage that the cliche, "name it and claim it," is derived. The Christian finds an appropriate "success" passage in the Bible and claims it as his own. Then he or she acts as if God has already granted it.

The line between positive confession and a manipulation of God is very thin. The positive confession is another "axiom" and must be followed, even by God. Robert Tilton says it well: "Success is here and readily available . . . it is up to us to come and get it. If you are not a success, it is your fault, not God's. You determine your level of success. You make the choice. . . . He has placed the ball in your court . . . it's your move."[69]

If positive confession brings success, failure is induced by negative confession. Great harm may be done by a critical tongue, a bitter heart, or a negative attitude. Faith movement teachers are adamant that the Christian's destiny is in one's own hands: "God is not going to override your authority. . . . He has given you authority in the earth. . . . He will let you die sick if you choose to do so . . . you have the authority to go ahead and die. God will not stop you."[70]

The problem. This prosperity doctrine detracts from the sovereignty of God. It deifies humanity in God's stead. Even though some of the teachers would limit what one can demand of God, there is really nothing in their interpretation of the positive confession texts which would put a cap on human expectations. Kenneth Hagin gives four steps to receiving God's bounty — "say it, do it, receive it, and tell it."[71] Such teaching clearly appeals to the lowest level of human greed and lust. James Goff aptly notes that positive confession has reduced God "to a kind of 'cosmic bellhop,' attending to the needs and desires of His creation."[72]

Conclusions

In the areas of healing, prosperity, and positive confession, the faith movement's teaching is radically different from that of Christian orthodoxy. The former places all the onus for success on humankind. Other than having set forth certain spiritual laws to govern human actions, God has little to do with man's situation; he is captain of his own destiny.

Quite evident behind these teachings is a system based on dualistic thought, somewhat reminiscent of first-century Gnosticism. "This involves a belief in two mutually exclusive realms — the spiritual and the material. The former . . . is under the governance of God, and is the proper domain for people. The latter is ruled over by its own god and is in eternal conflict with the former."[73] As with Gnosticism, all humans begin in the lower, or material, realm with the hope of moving upward to the spiritual plane. Such upward mobility can be achieved only through the acquisition of special knowledge from an external agency (in this case, the above "axioms," given by God to believers).

Prosperity theologians follow the Gnostics in their teaching that the "true" human being is a "spirit man" trapped in a physical body. Kenneth Hagin writes, "The real man is the spirit. The spirit operates through the soul. . . . And the soul operates through the body. The real you (your spirit) and your soul live in a physical body."[74]

The faith movement's concept of healing (namely, that you claim health and act as though you are not ill) may be traced back to E.W. Kenyon's flirtation with Christian Science. That cult claims that healing is just the triumph of "mind over matter." Sickness is a condition of the mind, not of the body. Ern Baxter notes that one day he found Kenyon reading from Mary Baker Eddy's *Key to the Scriptures*, "Then I made a comment and *he responded very positively that there was a lot of good that could be gotten from Mary Baker Eddy*. That alerted me . . . to the fact that he probably wasn't formulating his faith positions from *sola Scriptura* and that he was influenced by the metaphysicians."[75]

McConnell has said, with considerable accuracy, that the faith movement is cultic; not a cult, but cultic; "it has certain doctrines and practices that are cultic in thought and historical origin."[76] Because so many who are involved in, or who flirt with, this movement are active evangelical Christians, it is all the more vital to expose such a fact. It is well for us to be encouraged that God loves us, wants us to be healthy and wants us to prosper (in a qualified—certainly spiritual—manner). But these things can be affirmed without turning to heresies like Christian Science and Gnosticism.

Success Theologies: A Summary

Both the theology of self-esteem and prosperity theology were hatched in the incubator of the "American dream." Without the visions of success which came to the United States via the concept of manifest destiny, the writings of Horatio Alger, and the Hollywood promotions of a variety of media, it is doubtful that these two theologies would ever have attained any sort of prominence.

Both of them suffer from severe deficiencies in their ideas of how God and humanity relate to one another. Both operate on the assumption that humans are entitled to well-being and happiness. But the Bible teaches that, because of sin, they are "entitled" to nothing except God's wrath. Anything good they receive is not the result of entitlement, but of God's free and unmerited grace. Schuller's idea that God sent Christ to the cross in order to cause humans to become better "possibility-thinkers" belittles the enormity of Jesus' sacrifice. Prosperity theology deifies humanity at God's expense. God becomes a supernatural slot machine; all one has to do to win a jackpot of health or wealth is to lever in the right sequence of steps. Both of these theologies fall dismally short of New Testament church thinking and practice.

Undoubtedly, both the theology of self-esteem and prosperity theology will survive, in spite of criticism. As long as there are materialistic and carnal Christians who have never accepted that being saved involves—as Dietrich Bonhoeffer puts it—"costly grace" both on God's part and on ours, theologies of success will flourish. The idea of "health, wealth, and happiness" in this world without awaiting the next is simply too alluring for too many.

For Further Reading
The Theology of Self-Esteem

Peale, Norman Vincent. *The Positive Power of Jesus Christ,* Carmel, N.Y.: Guideposts, 1980.

_____. *You Can If You Think You Can.* Old Tappan, N.J.: Fleming H. Revell, 1967.

_____. *The Power of Positive Thinking.* Westwood, N.J.: Fleming H. Revell, 1956.

Schuller, Robert H. *Self-Esteem, The New Reformation.* Waco, Tex.: Word Inc., 1982.

_____. *The Peak to Peek Principle.* Garden City, N.Y.: Doubleday Co., 1980.

_____. *Self-Love, The Dynamic Force of Success.* New York: Hawthorne Books, 1969.

_____. *Move Ahead with Possibility Thinking.* Old Tappan, N.J.: Fleming H. Revell, 1967.

Voskuil, Dennis. *Mountains into Gold Mines: Robert Schuller and the Gospel of Success*. Grand Rapids: Wm. B. Eerdmans Pub. Co., 1983.

Prosperity Theology
Barron, Bruce. *The Health and Wealth Gospel*. Downers Grove, Ill.: InterVarsity Press, 1987.

Copeland, Gloria. *God's Will Is Prosperity*. Fort Worth, Tex.: KC Publications, 1978.

Copeland, Kenneth. *You Are Healed*. Fort Worth, Tex.: KC Publications, 1979.

Farah, Charles. *From the Pinnacle of the Temple*. Plainfield, N.J.: Logos International, 1978.

Hagin, Kenneth E. *Understanding the Anointing*. Tulsa, Okla.: Faith Library, 1985.

_____. *Godliness Is Profitable*. Tulsa, Okla.: Faith Library, 1982.

_____. *I Believe in Visions*. Old Tappan, N.J.: Fleming H. Revell, 1972.

McConnell, D.R. *A Different Gospel: A Historical and Biblical Analysis of the Modern Faith Movement*. Peabody, Mass.: Hendrickson Publishers, 1988.

Savelle, Jerry. *Godly Wisdom for Prosperity*. Tulsa, Okla.: Harrison House, 1986.

Tilton, Robert. *God's Laws of Success*. Dallas: Word of Faith Publications, 1983.

Thirteen. Liberation Theology

Over the last two decades liberation theology has captured considerable attention. Much of it has come from technical theological journals for, while it is popular in the Two-Thirds World, it is less well-known in North America, except to the theologically informed.

Fundamental characteristics. Liberation theology is not a monolithic movement. It would probably be more accurate to speak of liberation "theologies." In spite of a diversity of approaches, there are common aspects which allow all to be labeled "liberation."

The movement rejects a developmental approach to global problems. This view suggests that all peoples could and should attain to the high living standard of the most advanced nations of the world; it is simply a matter of aiding the less fortunate in their development. Liberationism, however, is adamant that only divine instruction in human affairs can effect real and enduring change in this world.[1]

Liberation theology strongly emphasizes the unity of history. It rejects the traditional separation of history into sacred and secular. God is active in *all* of history; He has not devised a separate strand of history in which to achieve His salvific will.[2]

The movement is eschatological in nature. Closely allied to the theology of hope, it is futuristic in its orientation. "What God will do helps explain the partial fulfillment of His will in the present."[3] God's liberating power coupled with His promise furnish the basis for hope and understanding.

Liberation theology maintains a consummate concern in the political implications of the human relationship to God. It grounds itself in the Old Testament prophetic notions of injustice, oppression, and alienation. It acknowledges that God is able to confront the sordidness of societies, but it proclaims that human beings act as mediators of divine aid. The Christian has an obligation to work out the lordship of Christ in the political arena.[4]

Salvation is linked to the political and social venues of life. Liberationism teaches that salvation is to be had, not by trusting in Christ, but by denouncing the world and living for others.[5]

Fundamental methodology. Just as important as theological content is the theological methodology of the liberation movement. Its theologians declare that the proper starting point must be with "the view from below," that is, "where the pain is";[6] that means, in the context of the pain of the downtrodden and outcast. We are called to see the world from their viewpoint.

While traditional theology relies on philosophy for its structure, liberation theology goes toward the social sciences. "Through them theology gains a concrete understanding of the world in which faith is lived, and, therefore, of the questions which it must respond to in order to enable Christians to test and strengthen the *efficacy* of their obedience."[7]

In this new context, liberationism stresses as its methodology critical reflection on praxis:

> Meaning something quite different from the familiar "practice," praxis describes the circular traffic that is always going on between action and reflection. . . . It is the never ending dialectical process . . . in which action forces me to reflection and reflection forces me to action again. . . . Through praxis, people seek not merely to understand the world but to change it.[8]

Theology follows praxis. In the latter, one commits oneself to the tranformation of society on behalf of and along with the oppressed. Then, in the former, one reflects on what has happened and works to bring it into a right relationship with the revelation of God in Christ Jesus.[9]

A definition of liberation theology. We see, then, that liberation theology by definition consists of both content and methodology. It originates from many contexts but carries the common aspect of God's liberating power. "Liberation theology may be defined as that theological endeavor which sees God's continuing work in the world from the viewpoint of the oppressed and understands that work to involve the reconstruction of persons and societies according to the mold of the Master."[10]

A Historical Overview of Liberation Theology

Liberation theology had its inception in the oppression and colonialism of Latin America. Christianity was brought to Latin America by the Spanish whose purpose was to conquer the world for God and Spain. From the native inhabitants, "obedience to the great king of Spain and submission to the King of Heaven was demanded as one single act."[11]

For some four centuries the Roman Catholic church had a dominant role in Latin American history. Society was divided into various classes. At the top were the leaders of both church and state (these were usually appointed from Spain); their offspring frequently filled the second level of governmental positions. The third stratum was filled from the Spanish masses (soldiers, merchants, farmers); then came the Amerindians, and at the very bottom, mestizos and blacks.[12]

There were a few missionaries of note who promoted the cause of the Amerindians. A priest, Bartolome de Las Casas, freed his African slaves and sought peacefully to evangelize the Indians. He went to Spain to plead before the king for them, arguing that they were free human beings and conquest was not a rightful means of conversion. To many—especially the poor—Bartolome de Las Casas is the "Moses" of Latin America.[13]

With the decline of imperial Spanish power from the seventeenth century on, there was a similar decline in colonial control. But the power of the Roman Catholic church increased, and it amassed substantial wealth. As the Spanish colonies gained their independence during the nineteenth century, they sought to attain control over the church, a situation which strained relations between these governments and the Vatican for decades.[14]

British economic power quickly filled the vacuum left by the retreating Spanish, to be succeeded by the United States in the twentieth century. While Latin American nations gained political independence, they remained in economic bondage.

The full impact of Latin America's poverty and suffering was realized in the 1950s with the United Nations' proclamation of the "decade of development." In 1961, John F. Kennedy launched the

Alliance for Progress, but Latin Americans recognized its failure from the outset for, "... the expected minimum measure of growth was never reached. ... The terms of trade continue[d] to be unfavorable. ... Production [was] unable to cope with the increase of population."[15]

The rise of populist governments during the 1950s and 1960s—Peron in Argentina, Vargas in Brazil, and Cardenas in Mexico—raised nationalistic pride and increased industrial development. While this benefited the middle classes and some of the urban workers, it sank huge sectors of the peasantry into bare subsistence living in rural hovels or makeshift urban shanties. In sharp contrast, the social revolution of Fidel Castro in Cuba stood out as an alternative. In many countries armed rebellions occurred, directed towards the overthrow of rulers and a redistribution of wealth.[16]

By the mid-1960s a number of Latin American theologians had become disillusioned with the failure of the West to relieve the poverty and oppression of the people. They decided that new, more radical directions must be followed. One of them, Gustavo Gutierrez, writes, "When I discovered that poverty was something to be fought against, that poverty was structural, that poor people were a class, it became crystal clear that in order to serve the poor, one had to move into political action...."[17] Gutierrez believed that Marxism provided the means for responding to the class struggle he perceived as necessary to throw off the capitalist oppression and liberate the masses. At that time, Cuba and China seemed powerful examples of the social gains possible under Marxism, and Brazil was a sterling example of the failure of the capitalist development plan.[18]

That these theologies used Marxism as a tool of social analysis should not be taken to mean that they assumed it as a philosophy or plan of political action. Economically, they believe that "the notion of communism is in the New Testament, right down to the letter. ... In fact, the definition Marx borrowed from Louis Blanc, 'From each according to his needs,' is inspired by, if not directly copied from, Luke's formulation eighteen centuries earlier."[19]

Latin American Liberationism

As we have noted, Latin America was the cradle of liberation theology. Latin Americans were the first to formulate a system on behalf of the downtrodden. Roman Catholicism was the nurturing context.

Two key events in Roman Catholicism were elemental in the formulation of Latin American liberation theology: Vatican II and Medellin.

Vatican II. The second Vatican Council represented Catholicism's response to the challenges of the modern world. (For a more detailed consideration of its actions, see chapter 6.) The documents issued by Vatican II emphasized the responsibility of Christians toward "those who are poor or in any way afflicted."[20] One document, *Gaudium et Spes* (1965), underscored the universal mandate "to count social necessities among the primary duties of modern man."[21] Pope Paul VI built upon these ideas in his 1967 encyclical, *Populorum Progressio*, on the oppression of Latin America: "There are certainly situations where injustice cries to heaven. When whole populations destitute of necessities live in a state of dependence barring them from all initiative and responsibility and all opportunity to advance culturally and share in social and political life, recourse to violence, as a means to right these wrongs to human dignity, is a grave temptation."[22]

The freedom and creativity engendered by the Second Vatican Council spurred several Latin American theologians to begin thinking about pastoral problems involving their countries. The ecumenical atmosphere encouraged frequent meetings between Catholic thinkers (such as Gustavo Gutierrez, Juan Luis Segundo, and Lucio Gera) and Protestant thinkers (such as Emilio Castro, Ruben Alves, and Jose Miguez-Bonino), who deliberated together on the relationship between faith and poverty and the Gospel and social justice.

Medellin. In 1968 the Second General Conference of Latin American Bishops was held in Medellin, Colombia. The conference placed the Roman church squarely on the side of the outcasts. Its duty was "to defend the rights of the poor and oppressed according to the Gospel commandment, urging our governments and upper classes to eliminate anything which might destroy social peace. . . ."[23]

In a document, "Poverty of the Church," the bishops isolated three meanings of poverty: "... real poverty as an evil—that is, something that God does not want; spiritual poverty, in the sense of readiness to do God's will; and solidarity with the poor, along with protest against the conditions under which they suffer."[24]

The conference concluded that "Latin American underdevelopment, with its own characteristics in the different countries, is an unjust situation which promotes tensions that conspire against peace,"[25] and that the continent would, in due course, undertake its own liberation no matter what the cost.

Ecclesial communities. While the documents of Vatican II and Medellin acted as spurs to the liberation movement, they did not produce it. The movement itself was birthed from the lives of the downtrodden themselves in the context of the *comminidados ecclesiales de base* ("basic ecclesial communities"), Christian communes of the outcast who were attempting to relate their faith in a practical manner. Alvaro Barreiro describes the work of these communities of the "poor in action": "When the oppressed poor accept the Gospel as good news of liberation, and actually strive to become liberated from the oppression that is being suffered, they are, ipso facto, battling against the sin of the oppressor, inviting the latter to conversion."[26]

Major Proponents and Their Theology
A brief look at the major proponents of Latin liberation theology and their doctrinal thrusts should serve to give us a clearer picture of the movement and what it stands for.

Gustavo Gutierrez. The preeminent Latin American theologian is Gustavo Gutierrez. His book, *A Theology of Liberation*, is considered by many to be the classic text for liberation studies.

Born in 1928 in Lima, Peru, Gutierrez experienced racial discrimination early in life because of his mestizo blood. As a student at San Marcos University in Lima he was involved in several Christian groups protesting oppression and inequities in certain segments of Peruvian society. In his undergraduate years he combined the study of medicine with courses in the thought of Karl Marx before turning to theology, graduating in 1959 with a doctorate from the University of Lyons in France.

Returning home in the early 1960s, Gutierrez became priest of a parish in Lima and an instructor of theology at the Catholic University. He found his European theology inadequate to deal with the impoverishment of his parishioners and, during the latter 1960s, he began to formulate his liberation principles.

During the 1970s and 1980s Gutierrez became very popular as a lecturer and visiting professor in the United States and Europe. He also began to run afoul of the magisterium in matters of doctrine. He was forbidden to attend the 1979 conference of Latin American bishops in Mexico. In 1983 the Vatican investigated his theology, but he was never officially censured.

Gutierrez evidently affirms Karl Rahner's view of the "anonymous Christian," for he says very simply that "persons are saved if they open themselves to God and to others, even if they are not clearly aware that they are doing so."[27] He defines saving faith in a very practical manner as "an act of trust, a going out of one's self, a commitment to God and neighbor, a relationship with others."[28]

Sin, for Gutierrez, is the negation of one's fellow human being as a brother. "Sin is regarded as a social, historical fact, the absence of fellowship and love in relationship among persons, the breach of friendship with God and with other persons, and therefore, an interior, personal fracture."[29] Sin is fundamental alienation, the root of instances of injustice and oppression. "Sin demands a radical liberation, which in turn necessarily implies a political liberation."[30]

Eschatologically, through political, economic, and cultural revolution, humans forge the kingdom of God. "The humiliation of misery and exploitation is a sign of the coming of the Kingdom."[31]

Jose Miguez-Bonino. The leading Protestant liberation theologian is Argentinian Methodist, Jose Miguez-Bonino. Born in 1924, the child of a shipyard foreman, he was well-acquainted with the poverty of dock workers' and also went to school with children from a nearby barrio. The Methodist church his family attended was very active in social outreach; thus, the need to help the poor was impressed upon him early in life.

Miguez-Bonino began his university studies in medicine, but he was strongly influenced by socialist professors and committed himself to social action. He became interested in theology and, in

1948, graduated from the Evangelical Faculty of Theology and was ordained to the Methodist ministry.

After serving parishes in Bolivia and Argentina, he returned for further studies, securing a doctorate in 1960 from Union Theological Seminary in New York. His area of specialization was in Roman Catholic thought. He has been deeply involved in ecumenical affairs and has served as President of the World Council of Churches. From 1970–85 he was professor of theology and ethics at the Protestant Institute for Higher Theological Education in Buenos Aires, and he has been visiting professor at schools in Europe and North America. His book, *Doing Theology in a Revolutionary Situation* (1975), is seen as a superb overview of the development of liberation theology.

In his paper, "Violence: A Theological Reflection," Miguez-Bonino sets forth his view of revelation to the effect that "Scripture almost always takes the form of a call to create a new situation, to transform and correct present conditions—a summons to conversion and justice."[32]

His foundational theme is love. He does not see love as an abstract emotion; it is "inextricably interwoven with hope and justice. . . . It is not content to express and demonstrate, it intends to accomplish."[33] Any confrontation of oppression, he insists, is an act of love. "*Orthopraxis*, rather than orthodoxy, becomes the criterion for theology."[34]

Leonardo Boff. The leading expert in Christology in liberationism is Leonardo Boff. His *Jesus Christ Liberator* (1972) was the first work on that topic by a liberation theologian. Upon publication it aroused immediate controversy and was hotly attacked by Brazil's Vincente Cardinal Scherer because of its humanistic view of Christ to the detriment of His transcendence.

Born in 1938 in Brazil, Leonardo Boff studied systematic theology in Europe as a student of Jürgen Moltmann. He joined the Franciscan order and after graduation served as professor of theology at Petropolis in his native land.

Boff tells us that liberation theology occurred when faith confronted the oppression of the poor. The poor he describes as "all this mass of the socially and historically oppressed."[35] Through the eyes of faith believers can see in these folk the face of the Suffering Servant, Jesus Christ. In serving the oppressed, in struggling on their behalf, we are in fact performing an act of love for God in Christ.[36]

Boff takes the Exodus of Israel from bondage in Egypt as a paradigm for doing liberation theology. "The living God sides with the oppressed against the pharaohs of this world."[37] He hears the cries of the downtrodden in their suffering and resolves to liberate them (Ex. 3:7-8). God will not passively stand by; He will act. "The biblical authors often present God as *Go'el*, which means: he who does justice to the weak, father of orphans, and comforter of widows...."[38]

Jesus came to earth to inaugurate the kingdom of God which is not only future but is even now in our midst (Luke 17:21). This announcement of the kingdom calls for a revolution not only in thought and attitude, but also against all those forces that oppress and depress humanity. "The kingdom or reign of God means the full and total liberation of all creation, in the end, purified of all that oppresses it, transfigured by the full presence of God."[39]

(American) Black Theology

Liberation theology among American blacks developed almost simultaneously to the Latin American liberation movement in the 1960s. It emerged from the civil rights movement founded by Martin Luther King, Jr. Although King was a strong advocate of nonviolence, his marches—especially the one on Washington in 1963—stirred many black Americans to confrontation with the authorities.

The emergence of black theology. From this troubled time came the term "black theology." It was used in 1966 by the Committee on Theological Perspectives of the National Conference of Black Churchmen in the United States: "Black theology is a theology of black liberation. It seeks to plumb the black condition in the light of God's salvation in Jesus Christ, so that the black community can see that the Gospel is commensurate with the achievement of black humanity.... It is the affirmation of black humanity that emancipates black people from white racism...."[40]

J. Deotis Roberts described black theology in Tillichian terms: "The black Christian is concerned about the relation between faith and life. His 'ultimate concern' has to do with life-and-death decisions. His 'situation' is the racism that affects his total life and the experiences of his loved ones."[41]

Black power. To describe this new self-awareness of black humanity, Stokely Carmichael, in the spring of 1966 coined what was to become a popular term, "black power." The phrase was not clearly defined. But it was a sign that blacks were beginning to take ownership of their lives and destiny.

Black theologians reacted to the idea of black power in different ways. Martin Luther King, diagnosing it as an advocacy of violent revolution, opposed it. Albert B. Cleage, Jr., pastor of the Shrine of the Black Madonna in Detroit and one of the fathers of black theology, enthusiastically endorsed it; in 1968, he published a volume of sermons entitled *The Black Messiah* in which he claimed that Jesus was really a black Jewish revolutionary, a member of the fanatic anti-Roman Zealots.[42] James Cone, another black theology pioneer, embraced the black power concept in his first book, *Black Theology and Black Power* (1968). He saw it as an opportunity to call blacks in America to do whatever might be required to stop the white intrusion on black dignity. Cone wrote, "For me, it was a choice between satisfying the theological values of white people's racism and saying a word of encouragement for the black freedom struggle."[43] Deotis Roberts, on the other hand, seemed to feel that involvement with black power would draw a theologian away from his true task of interpreting the Gospel. Black power might be religiously motivated, but it was not therefore Christian. "A theologian," he wrote, "is not an interpreter of the religion of Black Power. He, as a black theologian, may be the interpreter of Afro-American Christianity. . . . But he is attempting to understand the Christian faith in the light of his people's experience."[44] He recognized that steering such a course might well run the risk of misunderstanding "by black militants and moderates as well as by white radicals and liberals,"[45] but it was part of one's Christian commitment.

Other black theologians reacted against black power by seeking to relate black theology to reconciliation, approaching a kind of political pietism. Others moved toward a consideration of sociopolitical action, attempting to relieve the socio-economic exploitation of blacks and other minorities.

The role of Marxism. Unlike Latin American liberationists, Afro-American theologians underplayed Marxism. It was not really foundational to their system. But the goals of the two theologies differed markedly. Latin American liberation theology was seeking relief from economic oppression; black theology, from social oppression. Consequently, Marxism has spoken more clearly to the former than to the latter.

Major Emphases of Black Theology

It would be inappropriate to suggest that the major black theologians have a uniform approach to doctrinal matters. They do not. Much of their differences are concerned with the "blackness" of God. Some, like James Cone, insist that "there is no place in Black Theology for a colorless God in a society where people suffer precisely because of their color."[46] Others, like Roberts, while directing their theology primarily toward the black situation, nonetheless recognize that right theology "leaves the way open for reconciliation between men of goodwill, whether black or white."[47] With the exclusion of black nationalism/racism from the theological mix, there is a remarkable commonality to their thought.

The doctrine of God. The Christian God is One who discloses Himself, His will, and His purpose to human beings. He reveals Himself in an existential "I-thou" encounter with human beings through the agency of the Holy Spirit. What God has to say to humans will depend on the context in which He finds them. What He says to the suburban dweller will be vastly different from the message for a slum inhabitant. "We are making the point that when the human condition and the self-awareness that makes the difference known to the one who experiences it changes, then what God is revealing to man is understood in a different light."[48]

God speaks to the black man in his "blackness," letting him know that he is "somebody." In the society where people are oppressed because of their color, God takes on the color of the victim, proclaiming that "black is beautiful."[49]

The outstanding attribute of God for black theologians is His sovereignty or power, not surprising since blacks are overwhelmingly conscious as a group of their powerlessness. Another important and accompanying attribute is God's goodness. Roberts asserts, "I submit that a God who is absolute in both power and goodness makes sense to black men. Absolute goodness is important as well as absolute power. Absolute power ensures the ultimate triumph of the good; but absolute goodness assures us that absolute power will not be abused."[50]

Just as God reached out to rescue Israel in the Exodus, so He is reaching out to His people today, the American blacks. This knowledge that the God of the Exodus is also their God serves as a great reassurance for black people.

The Person and work of Christ. God has supremely revealed Himself to humankind through the Messiah, Jesus Christ. Blacks see Jesus as one with them, for the New Testament depicts Him as the oppressed One. He associated with the downtrodden, beggars, and the homeless. He had little use for the upper classes who robbed the poor of their dignity.[51]

Black theologians are unanimous in their view of Jesus as black. Most would not choose Cleage's idea of Jesus as literally and historically black (part of a black faction of the Hebrew people). Roberts is typical when he writes that "Christ conceived in a black image is one of us and in a real sense he becomes our Lord and our God."[52] As they shoulder the cross existentially, the black people know that the Crucified One understands their pain and burden. They look forward to their own existential resurrection, their triumph over the evil that currently besets them.

As Messiah, Christ is King. This kingship is not just future; it is present. Blacks place great hope in 1 Corinthians 15:25, "For He must reign until He has put all His enemies under His feet." Cone remarks, "Jesus' work is essentially one of liberation. Becoming a slave himself, he opens realities of human existence formerly closed to man."[53] The teaching of Christ as Liberator is a major theme of black theology.

Eschatology. Black theology is a theology of hope. It places stress on realized eschatology (present) as opposed to unrealized (future). The promise of future reward (such as heaven) or punishments (hell) make little impact on one who is hungry, ragged, and destitute. Roberts comments that "hell-future makes little impression on blacks living in a hell-present...."[54] Cone agrees: "The idea of heaven is irrelevant for Black Theology. The Christian cannot waste time contemplating the next world (if there is a next)."[55] The true Christian will not squander his time thinking of heaven and hell, but will invest it in the struggle for human rights and freedoms. That is the better way of life—helping to usher the kingdom into reality in the present time.

African Liberation Theology

Christianity has been in Africa since the first century. Until the fifteenth century, however, it was largely limited to Africa north of the Sahara. At that time, Portuguese Roman Catholics brought their faith to the main body of Africa along with exploration and commerce. Beginning in the nineteenth century, Protestants evangelized central, western, and southern Africa.

Throughout its history the growth of the African church has been dependent upon its European progenitors. Only in the last quarter-century or so have attempts been made to redirect the church towards indigenization. The formulation of an African liberation theology may be seen as a part of this Africanization process.

African theology and black theology. Some may assume that black theology (as formulated in the United States) would be an appropriate doctrinal vehicle for black Africans. Others may even suppose that black theology and African theology must be one and the same (especially since some African theologians are wont to use the term "black theology" of their own context). While there are similarities, the two are not the same. Desmond Tutu explains:

> Both African and Black Theology have been firm repudiations of the tacit claim that white is right, white is best. In their own ways these theologies are giving the black man a proper pride in things black and African. . . . [But] there must be differences because the two theologies arise in a sense from different contexts. African theology on the whole can probably afford to be a little more leisurely. . . . There is not the same kind of oppression which is the result of white racism except in South Africa. . . . Black theology arises in a context of black suffering at the hands of rampant white racism.[56]

Liberation theology is popular throughout all of Christianized

Africa, but it is most newsworthy in South Africa because of the apartheid problem in that nation. White Reformed Christians created Afrikaaner nationalism and equated it with the kingdom of God. In the experience of millions of blacks the Afrikaaners are responsible for untold misery, degradation, and exploitation; in short, an utter disregard for human dignity.[57]

African theology seeks to liberate African Christians from the oppression of white (Western) Christianity. It "is concerned to interpret essential Christian faith in authentic African language in the flux and turmoil of our time, so that there may be genuine dialogue between the Christian faith and African culture."[58]

In South Africa the question of violence has been raised. Some of those who are affiliated with the African National Congree—like Allan Boesak—have not totally rejected violence, even though they do not affirm it either. Others, like Archbishop Desmond Tutu, openly eschew it.

Doctrinal Aspects of African Theology

The themes and theological emphases of the African liberation movement are little different from those of Latin American and black liberation theology.

The African concept of God. Until very recently European theological views of God prevailed to such a degree that He was seen almost universally as "white." Only in the last few decades have black theologians dared to think of God as black, or artists depict Him in that color. In South Africa the "whiteness" of Christianity has been heavily underscored. Things black have been associated with evil; it has been easy to project this view onto people. As a result, a new concept of God is needed which is distinct from existing views. Sabelo Ntwase and Basil Moore suggest a new, relational, image of God as freedom. "God is the freedom fleetingly and incompletely known in our own experience. But God is also the freedom beyond anything we have yet known, the freedom that calls us out of our chains of oppression into a wholeness of life."[59]

Jesus Christ Liberator. A main preoccupation of Africans is the threat to them of evil forces. Deliverance is a common theme among believers and unbelievers alike. Thus, it should come as no surprise to discover that Jesus is seen as Savior, Redeemer, and Power.

Closely tied in is the concept of Christ as Liberator. "Liberation must be understood in its totality, as removal of all that which keeps the African in bondage, all that makes him less than God intended him to be."[60] The idea is that Jesus has the power to liberate from fear, illness, and evil, as well as from oppression, racism, and exploitation. That Jesus identified in His own earthly life with the poor, needy, and defenseless endears Him all the more to black Africans.

The African view of salvation. The traditional African worldview is a wholistic one. Life is a whole which includes both the sacred and the secular. Not even death can rend its fabric. African theologian Manas Buthelezi, accordingly, describes the character of life as "sacramental."[61]

Man's relationship with God is something which is given along with his life; "to live means to receive life from outside himself."[62] To be made in God's image is one means to expressing that relationship. God created man as a whole being; part of being God's image is having dominion over one's creaturely self. But there are many factors in life which can take a person's selfhood prisoner. Black Africans in particular are subject to conditions which render their selfhood less than ideal.

Salvation is a sacrament whereby man accepts and acknowledges the good and perfect gifts of God even if he has not received them in totality. He realizes that God sends good things, although they may end up at times with someone else. This believing is one aspect of faith.

Another aspect of faith is the acceptance of others as people whom God has accepted. "To be sure, some of these may be the ones who have displaced him from 'his place'; that is, they may be his exploiters."[63] Thus, a crucial part of faith involves being reconciled with one's exploiters.

The church and society. The role of the church in the liberation of humanity is most important. It must realize that human development—both spiritual and personal—cannot be isolated from society and the economy. Julius Nyerere suggests that the church must accept that human development involves rebellion:

> At a given and decisive point in history men decide to act against those conditions which restrict their freedom as men. . . . Unless we participate actively in the rebellion against those social structures and economic organizations which condemn men to poverty, humiliation and degradation, then the Church will become irrelevant to man and the Christian religion will degenerate into a set of superstitions accepted only by the fearful.[64]

The world is divided between the haves and have-nots, the rich and the poor, the advantaged and the disadvantaged. There are those with power and without. The former are a small minority, most of whom are set apart by their color and race. The church must not allow such a state of affairs to continue. It must push for the world to become one and for social justice to prevail.[65]

Liberation Asian-Style: Korean Minjung Theology

One of the more recent types of liberation theology to have appeared on the scene is Korean. Minjung theology is a movement focused on human rights; it originated in the 1970s.

Historical roots. The term "minjung" comes from two Chinese characters, *min*, meaning "the people," and *jung*, "the mass." It refers simply to "the mass of people." It was first used during the Korean Yi dynasty (1392–1960) when the ruling class (*yangban*) oppressed the common people. Any person who was not of the elite *yangban* was a *minjung*. In contemporary usage the term denotes all those who are excluded from the select dictatorship group.[66]

As a movement, minjung theology made its appearance about 1975. The movement may be defined as "an accumulation and articulation of theological reflections on the political experience of Christian students, laborers, the press, professors, farmers, writers, and intellectuals as well as theologians in Korea in the 1970s. It is a theology of the oppressed in the political situation, a theocentric response to the oppressors, and it is the response of the oppressed to the Korean church and its mission."[67]

The history of Korea is a long tale of oppression. For more than four millenia the people of Korea were subjugated by the greater powers which surrounded them. After suffering terrible agonies during World War II, the country was liberated only to be divided into two sectors and overcome by Communism. Freed by Allied troops in 1952, South Koreans were quickly enslaved by a series of dictatorships. Though the country prospered economically, there was a massive group who remained at a subsistence level or worse, bereft of a voice or recognition socially.

The birth of an awareness. The beginnings of the minjung movement as a theology may be traced to the activities of the Urban Industrial Mission in the early 1960s. A core of dedicated Christians volunteered under this mission to serve a minimum of six months as worker-evangelists in the urban industrial complex. This was initially intended to be a foray into conventional personal evangelism, but the conditions they found as common laborers forced them to reevaluate both their theology and methodology.[68] They recognized the need for including a struggle against injustice and exploitation in the workplace. In the early 1970s additional Urban Industrial Mission groups were established to help found labor unions and further workers' rights. Simultaneously, other Christian groups—the Christian Ecumenical Youth Council, Church Women United, and the Catholic Young Workers Organization—cooperated in the struggle for greater rights.[69]

Reaction to these efforts was swift on the part of the government administration. Those who were in positions of leadership were removed from their seminary, college, or church positions by the regime of the current dictator, Park Chung-Kee; numbers were tortured or imprisoned.[70] But such treatment served only to further identify them with the minjung in their suffering and so provided impetus for the movement's progress.

Theological Formation of Minjung

Minjung theology may be seen as the child of several modern theological systems. The development of liberation theologies in the Two-Thirds World focused attention on the plight of the underdog. Because of Korean government restrictions and censorship of literature and other media, only a few Korean theologians came to a limited knowledge of liberation theology and so developed their own indigenous form.

Coupled with liberation theology was the introduction of revolutionary ideas into Catholicism by Vatican II. Karl Rahner's "anonymous Christianity" declared that even those who were not yet aware of Christ might be a part of the community of the redeemed and demonstrated how Christian minjung might relate to those in the non-Christian political minjung movement. Hans Kung taught them an openness to universalism and ecumenical cooperation with the practitioners of Korean folk religions.[71]

From process theology came an emphasis on humanity as the foundation of the doctrinal process, along with the blessing of cooperation with other movements on points of common outlook.[72] From Japanese theology, minjung learned to stress socio-political conflict between the ruled and their rulers.[73]

The "mainline" Christian leadership of Korean Christianity were mostly conservative in their theological orientation. They were slow to respond socially and politically to the violation of human rights. Thus, there was a gap, which was filled by more radical groups like the minjung. "Considering the influence of modern theological thought, it can be said that minjung theology is an alien, mosaic product of theology."[74]

Minjung methodology. Like other liberation theologies, minjung theology is contextual, with an emphasis on a reflection on the praxis of its struggle for freedom. Of central importance is socio-political hermeneutics.

Socio-political hermeneutics centers on the relation between the development of Hebrew society and its religious development, focusing on the social position of the underdogs. The revolt of the Hebrew slaves against the bondage of the pharaohs serves as a paradigm. Koreans see a repetition of this event in the Donghak rebellion against Japanese oppression, which is seen as an act of God in liberating the minjung.

The act of liberation itself is the starting point of minjung theology, for the movement uses an inductive methodology rather than the typical deductive method of Western theology. The act of liberation reveals God's nature and character.[75]

Minjung theology arising from this inductive method is formulated in stories. The Gospels are essentially narratives about how God revealed Himself in and through Jesus. Thus, our theological contemplation is based on stories about Jesus told by ordinary people.

Minjung theology comes in two types of narrative, the *silwha*, or "real story," and *mindam*, or folk tale. It is not easy to distinguish between the two. Both are effective instruments to communicate intimacy, profanity, and oppression in a realistic fashion. "If traditional theology is transcendental and deductive, storytelling theology is immanent and inductive. The former is the theology of rulers, while the latter is the theology of the minjung."[76]

Minjung Themes and Emphases

As mentioned above, minjung theology owes much to the liberation movement, although it has gone in its own particular direction. As we examine minjung emphases, therefore, we shall find evidences of strong similarities to liberation thinking, but with some quite unique twists.

The Trinity. Minjung theology looks at God from a socio-political standpoint. It considers traditional theology as dogmatism and rejects it. Its major concern is not really God at all, but oppressed humanity. Its God is revealed not in the Bible so much as in the oppressive situation in the suffering person. Minjung practitioners tend towards pantheism. "God is the immanent historical force of the process of humanization."[77]

The Jesus-event is the principle foundation of minjung theological reflection (not the *kerygma* or proclamation of the Atonement as is central in traditional theology, but the event itself). This is the event of the suffering, death, and resurrection of Jesus. It was this event that freed the oppressed of His day. The Jesus-event has become the liberating event. The presence of a liberating event signifies the presence of the living Christ.

All minjung struggles for liberation in past history are viewed as manifestations of the Jesus-event, from the peasant rebellion in A.D. 1176 to the present. The Jesus-event is seen as the archetype of these and all liberation events. These occurrences are animated by the movement of the Holy Spirit.[78]

Because God works as the Holy Spirit, His work is not confined by time or space. Consequently, He is present in all of history, and so whatever has happened in time past—whether Christ was physically present or not—may be seen as the Spirit at work. Undergirding this view is the influence of Shamanism which holds that the spiritual presence is everywhere and is the cause back of all events. This "pneumaticalogical" or "spiritual" approach gives minjung theology a broad inclusivity.[79]

Salvation: han and dan. Minjung people experience a distinctive form of suffering which they refer to as *han*. Like *minjung* itself, the term is hard to define. Moon Hee-suk Cyris, a minjung theologian, has defined it as "the anger and resentment of the minjung which has been turned inward and intensified as they become the objects of injustice upon injustice."[80]

Han is the psychical accumulation of innocent suffering. The oppression and exploitation of those who are blameless causes *han* in their fellows. Christ came to save Koreans by liberating them from the power of *han*.

The method of redeeming people—of cutting off the vicious *han* cycle—is called *dan*. *Dan* is the restoration of justice (rather than the mediation of forgiveness and love, as in orthodox theology). "Justice alone heals the wound of *han* and restores the minjung to their rightful place."[81]

There are two means of resolving *han*, one at the personal level, and the other at the social level. The former is accomplished by self-denial or self-sacrifice, the latter—a collective affair—can lift the entire community or society to a better existence. It is accomplished through four stages (borrowed from *Chondokyo*, the Heavenly Way): (1) to realize God in our heart, (2) to allow the divine consciousness to root within us, (3) to practice our faith in God, and (4) to overcome injustice by transforming the world.[82] These four stages are the process of salvation in the minjung movement.

Liberation Theology: An Evaluation
Liberation theology is a serious attempt to deal with some real and long-neglected needs in the world. Sincere efforts, however, are not sufficient unless they measure up to biblical standards. We shall try to discover to what degree liberation theology meets the requirements of biblical Christianity.

Positive aspects. There is much of value that liberation theology has to teach the church (evangelicals included). There are those aspects of the movement which can lead us to renew, refine, and rededicate our commitment to the Lord Jesus and His cause in this world.

One positive aspect of liberation theology—regardless of its content—is its universal appeal. There is no area of the Christian world which does not have some form of liberationism. Our Westernized evangelical theology appeals almost entirely to middle and upper class people of European stock.

What is it in liberation theology that can help us to give our own theology universal appeal? The secret ingredient is a concern for the condition of the poor, suffering, and outcast. Leonardo Boff says, "Underlying liberation theology is a prophetic and comradely commitment to the life, cause, and struggle of these . . . debased and marginalized human beings, a commitment to ending this historical-social iniquity."[83] When evangelical theology shares a similar commitment, it too will be embraced all over the world by a variety of classes and societies.

A second lesson that we might learn from liberation theology is the need for theological contextualization. Theology cannot be effective unless and until it is formulated to function in a concrete or specific situation. Karl Barth once said that the best theology is created with the Bible in one hand and the newspaper in the other! Exegesis must be related to the contemporary scene. Liberation theology does this well.

Probably the most important contribution we can glean from the liberation movement is its model of theology as praxis. What is in mind here is not so much "reflection on praxis but . . . reflective commitment in praxis."[84] Too often theology has lost this praxeological aspect. We have allowed it to become an abstract discipline rather than a practical instrument to prick our consciences and direct our lives.

Detrimental aspects. Many of the doctrinal teachings of liberationism must raise questions in our minds. They fall short of what the Bible sets forth.

The movement exists first and foremost to combat injustice. Their cure appears to focus on a more zealous and effective humanism. Just as humans created the injustice, so they can rectify it. There is a strong emphasis on love; love is demonstrated in one person reaching out to help another.

While it is fitting and proper for each of us to help our fellows, liberation theology seems to have forgotten the need for divine aid. Injustice and oppression have been with us since shortly after the Fall, and do not seem to be lessening. Utopia has long been sought but never attained. Without intervention on the part of an omnipotent, sovereign God to transform and redeem, it is impossible that society should be bettered.

Liberationists generally base their argument for human liberation of human beings on a panentheistic concept of God. Because God is in every person, human efforts at ending injustice should be successful.

Again, liberation theologians have a view of sin which falls short of the biblical definition. The Bible teaches that sin is an offense against the holiness of God; it is disobedience to His law and a rebellion against His will. To the liberationist, sin is to be wealthy in the face of someone else's poverty; it is not so much a personal failure as a societal situation. Liberation theologians frequently speak of the "sinful structures of society" much more than individual moral shortcomings.[85]

In regard to salvation, liberation theology has been tainted by the pronouncements of Vatican II and subsequent Catholic directions towards universalism. People may be saved if they open themselves to God, whether they know they are doing so or not. The view is common, furthermore, that this life is a test— one will be judged according to one's treatment of one's fellow human beings.

The Bible, of course, teaches that the shed blood of Christ is the basis for human salvation. Salvation is always by faith, and never by meritorious actions (Eph. 2:8-9).

Where does Jesus Christ fit in here? The Christian holds Him to be God come in the flesh to die for the sins of humanity. He is even now preparing a place in heaven for those who trust Him in faith. Liberationism holds Christ to be the "Liberator" from the oppressive, sinful structures of society. In some theologies, this occurs sacramentally. In others, He is the archetype, or model, for liberation.

Conclusions

Liberation theology has some excellent ideas and stimulating themes. The coupling of commitment and community in the struggles to throw off oppression is a particularly attractive one, as is its ability to relate biblical interpretation to contemporary events. When all is said and done, however, it falls short of the mark because it depends on human beings in space and time to achieve its redemptive goals. One wonders how and why God is at all necessary to the achievement of liberation goals. To this movement Jesus Christ is a political liberator, but more in a community or societal sense than in an individual connotation. It seems to overlook the need for individuals to be transformed before the society can be changed. Jesus Christ is not an archetype of political liberation, as they would make Him out to be, but the sovereign, personal Redeemer. Liberation theology neglects almost completely the eternal and transcendental dimension.

We would, nonetheless, conclude with Gutierrez's own conclusion in his *A Theology of Liberation:*

> To paraphrase a well-known text of Pascal, we can say that all the political theologies, the theologies of hope, of revolution, and of liberation, are not worth one act of genuine solidarity with exploited social classes. They are not worth one act of faith, love, and hope, committed in one way or another—in active partcipation to liberate humankind from everything that dehumanizes it and prevents it from living according to the will of the Father.[86]

God commands the Christian to help those who are in need and to fight injustice and oppression wherever he finds it. All believers should be moved by the plight of the weak and the poor to help to alleviate their distress. At the same time ultimate liberation will occur only when Jesus comes again to establish the kingdom of God in its fullness.

For Further Reading

Boesak, Allan. *Farewell to Innocence: A Socio-Ethical Study on Black Theology and Power.* Maryknoll, N.Y.: Orbis Books, 1976.

Boff, Leonardo and Clodovis Boff. *Introducing Liberation Theology.* Maryknoll, N.Y.: Orbis Books, 1987.

Brown, Robert McAfee. *Theology in a New Key: Responding to Liberation Themes.* Philadelphia: Westminster Press, 1978.

Cone, James H. *Black Theology and Black Power.* New York: Seabury Press, 1969.

Ferm, Deane W. *Third World Liberation Theologies: An Introductory Survey.* Maryknoll, N.Y.: Orbis Books, 1986.

_____, ed. *Third World Liberation Theologies—A Reader.* Maryknoll, N.Y.: Orbis Books, 1986.

Gutierrez, Gustavo. *A Theology of Liberation,* rev. ed. Maryknoll, N.Y.: Orbis Books, 1988.

_____. *The Power of the Poor in History.* Maryknoll, N.Y.: Orbis Books, 1983.

Lee, Jung Young, ed. *An Emerging Theology in World Perspective.* Mystic, Conn.: Twenty-Third Publications, 1988.

Miguez-Bonino, Jose. *Doing Theology in a Revolutionary Situation.* Philadelphia: Fortress Press, 1975.

Moore, Basil, ed. *The Challenge of Black Theology in South Africa.* Atlanta: John Knox Press, 1974.

Parrott, John, ed. *A Reader in African Christian Theology.* London: SPCK, 1987.

Roberts, J. Deotis, Sr. *A Black Political Theology.* Philadelphia: Westminster Press, 1974.

_____. *Liberation and Reconciliation: A Black Theology.* Philadelphia: Westminster Press, 1971.

Fourteen. Third Wave Theology: The Vineyard Movement

O ne of the latest and fastest-growing theological developments of the last decade is that phenomenon known as
the "Signs and Wonders" or "Third Wave" movement.
The Pentecostal revival of 1906 and the charismatic renewal of the
1960s were the first and second waves respectively. This new
movement is composed largely of Reformed and Dispensationalist
evangelicals who preferred not to identify with the Pentecostals or
charismatics but who are very much interested in the work of the
Holy Spirit, holding that the miraculous (or "sign") gifts of the
New Testament have continued into the present.[1]

The Origins of the Third Wave Movement
The Third Wave movement came about as the result of the inter-
secting ministries of C. Peter Wagner, professor of missions at
Fuller Theological Seminary in Pasadena, California, and John
Wimber, pastor of the Vineyard Christian Fellowship in Anaheim,
California.

Peter Wagner. As a missionary for some sixteen years in Latin
America, Wagner—who had been awakened to the importance of
church growth as a student of Donald McGavran—noticed that the
fastest-growing churches in his mission area were Pentecostal.
Upon his return to the United States, he became involved with
Pentecostals and, "in some Church of God meetings I was ministered to more than ministering."[2] His Pentecostal associations
combined with his ongoing research in church growth (in 1971 he
had been appointed professor of church growth at Fuller) caused
him to give increasing consideration to the New Testament teaching on spiritual gifts and the possibilities of the miraculous.

John Wimber. John Wimber was a fourth-generation unbeliever
who was converted to the Christian faith as an adult in 1962. His

wife, Carol, was converted that same year. Both came to Christ seeking freedom from guilt and despair and the opportunity to begin life anew. As a result of the liberating power of the Gospel within their lives, both became ardent (and successful) personal evangelists.[3]

In 1970, Wimber became a staff member of the Yorba Linda (California) Friends' Church. He had a successful ministry and the church grew; nonetheless, "I was dissatisfied with my life and did not understand why."[4] Consequently, when he was invited to join Peter Wagner in church growth work with the Fuller Evangelistic Association, he seized the opportunity.

A crisis point in his personal theology occurred in 1977 when Carol Wimber one night dreamt that she was filled with the Holy Spirit and awoke speaking in tongues.[5] Wimber, a Dispensationalist, had to this point held that the "sign gifts" had ceased at the end of the first century. His wife's experiences, coupled with challenges from Wagner and the writings of Donald Gee, Morton Kelsey, and George Ladd, led him to accept the premise that all the spiritual gifts of New Testament times are valid today, and that evangelism will be most potent when the Gospel is combined with a demonstration of these gifts in what he termed "power evangelism."[6]

Feeling that he had to test his new theology in a practical manner, he resigned from the Fuller Evangelistic Association and accepted the pastoral oversight of a group of fifty people in what is now the Vineyard Christian Fellowship of Anaheim.

Signs and wonders. The experiment did not go well at first. Wimber preached regularly on healing, but the church prayed for months for healing without any results. Many people left in frustration. Finally, after ten months, a woman was healed and growth began.

In 1981 the church launched a ministry of power evangelism. The results were startling: ". . . at one point it looked like a battlefield scene, bodies everywhere, people weeping, wailing, speaking in tongues."[7] Growth skyrocketed.

During that same year, Wimber gave a lecture to Wagner's doctoral class on the relationship between church growth and signs and wonders. In 1982 he began a course at Fuller entitled, "Signs, Wonders, and Church Growth (MC510)." "It was taught on ten successive Monday nights throughout the quarter. For these hours John Wimber lectured on topics such as the relationship of program evangelism to power evangelism, the kingdom of God, biblical records of the miraculous, spiritual gifts, contemporary faith healers, and many others."[8] Throughout the classes there were healings, Spirit anointings, and the manifestation of other spiritual phenomena. ". . . [T]he course broke all enrollment records at Fuller."[9]

The course continued over four years, but was the target of increasing attacks. Many faculty members were unhappy with these charismatic displays and were successful in 1986 in having the course replaced by MC550, "The Ministry of Healing in World Evangelization."

Into all the world. By 1985, the Vineyard Christian Fellowship at Anaheim had grown to 5,000 members and another 120 congregations had been established. Wimber made his "Signs, Wonders, and Church Growth" into a seminar and conducted it in centers throughout North America, Europe, South Africa, Australia, and New Zealand. Thousands of people attended and fellowships began in many of these areas.

Wimber published a number of books, as well. Immediate successes were *Power Evangelism* in 1985 and *Power Healing* the following year. In addition, tapes, videotapes, songbooks, and other materials were marketed by his church headquarters.

Although Wimber had indicated initially that he had no desire to turn the Vineyard into a denomination, in 1986 he founded the Association of Vineyard Churches. It is informed by *The Vineyard Newsletter* and is supervised by regional pastoral coordinators. John Wimber is the governor of the church. His goal is 10,000 Vineyard Fellowships "in our generation."[10]

Emphases of the Movement

Because the movement terms itself the "Third Wave," suggesting a link to the other two "waves"–Pentecostalism and the charismatic movement–but declares itself to be non-charismatic, a certain amount of confusion is engendered. Just what does the Vineyard movement stand for? And what emphases does it provide that differ from evangelicalism? Some of these emphases are philosophical; others are theological.

Worldview perspective. John Wimber cites the Western worldview as an obstacle to our understanding of the spiritual or supernatural. Charles Kraft explains the concept of worldview as follows:

> Cultures pattern perceptions of reality into conceptualizations of what reality can or should be; what is to be regarded as actual, probable, possible, or impossible. These conceptualizations form what is termed the "worldview" of our culture. The worldview is the central systematization of conceptions of reality to which the members of this culture assent (largely unconsciously) and from which stems their value system. The worldview lies at the very heart of the culture, touching, interacting with, and strongly influencing every aspect of the culture.[11]

Wimber is in profound disagreement with what he considers to be the church's "Western worldview," which is so chained to secularism, rationalism, materialism, and mechanism that it excludes any practical concept of the supernatural's intrusion into everyday life. He builds on the work of Paul Hiebert, professor of mission anthropology at Fuller Seminary School of Missions, who teaches that a Far Eastern worldview is much more the context of the biblical writers. Both Orientals and the biblical writers, Hiebert claims, have a three-tiered view of reality. Occidentals have only a two-tiered system, one which excludes a vital "middle," which allows for supernatural forces on this earth, including spirits, ghosts, ancestors, demons, earthly gods and goddesses who inhabit trees and rivers and hills and villages; as well as supernatural forces such as mana and evil eyes and sorcery, along with angels, signs, and wonders. He cites his own problems on the mission field by way of example:

> As a Westerner, I was used to presenting Christ on the basis of rational arguments, not by evidences of his power in the lives of people who were sick, possessed and destitute. In particular, the confrontation with spirits that appeared as a natural part of Christ's ministry belonged in my mind to a separate world of the miraculous—far from ordinary everyday experience.[12]

Wimber draws on this teaching to insist that we need to recover that "excluded middle" tier lost during the Enlightenment. We need to "rediscover, develop, and practice a theology which includes ... God in human history, *now*, in the affairs of nations, or peoples and individuals; a theology of divine guidance, provisions, *Signs and Wonders*, healings, invisible powers,"[13] and so forth.

The Vineyard movement practices what Wimber preaches. It seeks to recover the worldview of the Middle Ages (and what still is the worldview of the East) by proclaiming a Gospel undergirded by dreams, visions, and miracles.

The kingdom of God. This practice of the supernatural and miraculous is inextricably linked to a particular view of the kingdom of God on earth. Wimber's theology has, by his own admission, been much influenced by the eschatological views of the late George Eldon Ladd.[14] A historical premillennialist, Ladd held that the kingdom is both a present reality and a future event. Ladd wrote:

> The Kingdom of God belongs to the Age to Come. Yet the Age to Come has overlapped with This Age. We may taste its powers and thereby be delivered from This Age and no longer live in conformity to it. ... The Kingdom of God is future, but it is not only future. ... the Kingdom of God has invaded this evil Age that man may know something of its blessings even while the Evil Age goes on.[15]

Wimber teaches that the works and words of Jesus reveal what the kingdom is and will be. The kingdom of God came in power in Jesus and it still comes in power today with those who are open to the filling of the Holy Spirit.[16] It is the manifestation of the power of God which is the sign of the presence of the kingdom of God.[17] For Wimber, that power is not the perseverance of the church in the world or the winning of persons to Jesus Christ so much as the sensational wonders: "Casting out demons, raising people from the dead, healing the sick, providing food where there is none, stilling the elements, these are the *Signs of the Kingdom*."[18]

Power evangelism. There can be no question that John Wimber has a deep concern for the unsaved and a zeal for reaching out to them with the Gospel. When he talks about evangelism, however, he does not mean traditional evangelistic ministries in which most evangelical churches are engaged. For this type of program he has little use. "By its very nature and assumptions, programmatic evangelism tends to have as its goal decisions for Christ, not disciples."[19] Programmed evangelism does not have the demonstrable power of the Holy Spirit.

Instead, Wimber espouses what he terms "power evangelism." He defines power evangelism as:

> . . . a presentation of the Gospel that is rational but which also transcends the rational. The explanation of the kingdom of God comes with a demonstration of God's power. It is a spontaneous, Spirit-inspired presentation of the Gospel. It is usually preceded and undergirded by demonstrations of God's presence and frequently results in groups of people being saved.[20]

Power evangelism, Wimber declares, is a continuation of the New Testament practice of evangelism as defined by the Apostle Paul in 1 Corinthians 2:45: "My message and my preaching were not with wise and persuasive words, but with a demonstration of the Spirit's power, so that your faith might not rest on men's wisdom, but on God's power."

People who are engaged in power evangelism, says Wimber, see themselves as soldiers in God's army, signed up to do battle against evil. They look for conflict because they know that Satan must be overcome in order to free people from his domination:[21]

> In Power Evangelism, people who are constantly in communion with the Holy Spirit receive insights, inklings, sometimes even strange thoughts about complete strangers, and act on them with startling results. Is this really that different from the way the disciples operated in the Book of Acts? I think not.[22]

Power evangelism practitioners rely on "divine appointments" with those whom they evangelize. "A divine appointment is a meeting arranged by God in which his Gospel will find favor in an individual or group through the manifest expression of spiritual gifts or other supernatural phenomena."[23]

Power healing. Wimber emphasizes the need for believers to follow James 5:13-14 in regard to those who are sick. And few evangelicals would not willingly affirm such a practice. But Wimber wants more than that; he expects the healing power of the Holy Spirit to follow the believing prayer and to restore the sick.[24] "That is why," notes Tim Stafford, "when Wimber prayed for healings over ten months and saw none, he was so devastated. The power of God was not being demonstrated."[25]

Healing is important because it is a sign of the power of the in-breaking of the kingdom of God. Do miraculous healings take place in the context of the Vineyard movement? Wimber exults, "Today we see hundreds of people healed every month in the Vineyard Christian Fellowship services. Many more are healed as we pray for them in hospitals, on the streets, and in homes. The blind see; the lame walk; the deaf hear. Cancer is disappearing."[26]

We know, however, that all who are prayed for are not healed. What of those who do not receive the healing power of God? On this aspect, Wimber seems of two minds. In his book, *Power Healing*, he cautions, "There are many reasons why people are not healed when prayed for. Most of the reasons involve some form of sin and unbelief."[27] Elsewhere, in the same volume, he declares, "I never blame the sick person for lack of faith if healing does not occur."[28]

That Wimber believes in miraculous healing does not diminish his respect for modern medicine. He freely acknowledges that it can be lifesaving. In fact, it is reported that he carries nitroglycerin for a heart problem!

Spiritual warfare. "Among the supernatural realities we encounter in the movement of the Holy Spirit that I call the Third Wave . . . is the work of demons."[29] The Bible tells us that we do not strive against flesh and blood, but "against the rulers of the darkness of this age, against spiritual hosts of wickedness in the heavenly places" (Eph. 6:12, NKJV). Those who accept the supernatural as a standard aspect of kingdom living come into conflict with the kingdom of evil on a daily basis. The conflict occurs in the hearts and minds of human beings.

Wimber states that Christians are becoming aware of territorial spirits. They are "powerful fallen angels . . . who exercise influence over cities, regions, even nations (Eph. 1:21; 6:12; Col. 2:15). They influence every aspect of a culture much as soil types determine which crops can be grown in different regions."[30] The ultimate enemy, however, is Satan. He is the "enemy general." The territorial demons may be considered his officers. Christians are mostly in conflict with the "foot soldiers" of evil—"low-level demons."[31]

The Christian's defensive weapons are described in Ephesians 6:10-18. Our offensive weapon "is the sword of the Spirit which is the Word of God" (Eph. 6:17). Another weapon is praying in the Spirit. God answers prayers for boldness in Christian action.

Wimber laments the apathy of much of the church: ". . . many Western Christians are unaware of the conflict, because in large part they have been secularized."[32] Church leaders simply are not aware of the extent to which our society has, in the last twenty-five years especially, been infiltrated by the occult, oriental mysticism, satanism, the New Age movement, and the like. An entire generation dwells in a world which is not the world of the majority of Christian leaders.[33]

An Evaluation of Vineyard Theology

While the roots of the Third Wave movement are largely Dispensational and Reformed, its affinity for the charismatic aspects of faith have caused emphases which are dissimilar to traditional evangelical practice. We shall examine these differing emphases, some of which are positive and some of which are detrimental to the Christian cause.

Positive aspects. (1) The work of the Holy Spirit. Wimber's disciples are essentially following in the footsteps of the charismatics of the 1960s and 1970s. What we could affirm about the latter we may affirm in the Vineyard movement. There is a joy and confidence in the work of the Holy Spirit which is set over against the formalism of many of our mainline and evangelical groups. Too often we give only lip service to what the Holy Spirit can do in human lives; those who follow Wimber's teachings go well beyond that. Clark Pinnock notes, "Like Saint Paul, Wimber wants to see people's faith resting not in the wisdom of words, but in the power and demonstration of the Spirit of God."[34] While we may not wish to accept everything that Wimber is teaching about the work of the Holy Spirit, we should rejoice in an emphasis which leads people to seek Spirit-filled and Spirit-led lives.

(2) The healing ministry. While the bulk of Christian people pay

lip service to healing through prayer, Wimber does more than that. As Philip Collins points out:

> ...it's a good sign when individuals are healed. We should expect and pray for healing in our churches, spiritually, relationally, redemptively, and, yes, physically. It is a proper biblical expectation, a gift from God in Christ, when by the Spirit the devil has been defeated once again.[35]

(3) Evangelism. John Wimber cares about the lost. His desire to carry out the Great Commission is commendable. Would that more Christians had a similar zeal!

Wimber notes that the most difficult person to convince of the effectiveness of spiritual gifts in evangelism are conservative evangelicals and fundamentalists. He declares that they have been taught to be leery about anything outside of their normal experience.[36] Much of the blame for this condition he lays at the door of the church leadership which expects ministry to be exercised by the professionals rather than the laity.

He also blames the failure of effective evangelism on the increasing secularization of the church. He quotes Gallup's report, "1984 Religion in America," to the effect that "Religion is growing in importance among Americans but morality is losing ground.... There is very little difference in the behavior of the churched and the unchurched on a wide range of items including lying, cheating, and pilferage."[37] It should come as no surprise, then, that churches are relying more on "program" evangelism and less on New Testament power.[38]

Once again, we stand condemned, for what Wimber says in this regard is true. We are not capable evangelists. We do not rely on the power of the Holy Spirit. We are timid and afraid. And our lives far too frequently are so worldly that we could not hear the Holy Spirit's direction even if we wanted to.

(4) The equipping ministry. Closely tied in to evangelism is Wimber's emphasis on the equipping of the laity for daily ministry in and to the world. He includes in this ministry that of evangelism, noting that "every Christian has been called to the harvest."[39] He also calls for the reeducation of lay people, to make them more effective in dealing with those who have problems, whether demonism, illness, or serious sin.

Donald Lewis of Regent College, in an evaluation of the Vineyard Fellowship, observes that Wimber not only "wants to see individuals moving out in faith and trusting God to work in new and exciting ways," but that he also "has a strong emphasis upon the organic nature of the church and urges all of its members to develop their own gifts of ministry."[40] One can only heartily agree with such an emphasis.

(5) The church as a caring community. Wimber emphasizes that one of the signs of the kingdom of God among us "is the people of the kingdom. They represent an alternate society."[41] This society is the faith community, the family of God. They exist to provide loving care for one another. They are a form of "extended family in which people are taught to be intimate, supportive, and accountable to one another."[42]

That every church should be such a kingdom community should go without saying. Only in such a context of mutual love and accountability can proper Christian discipleship and growth take place. And once again we are rightly taken to task by Wimber for our failure to be what Christ has demanded.

Detrimental emphases. While there is much in the Vineyard movement which is laudable, there are also a number of emphases which must surely and firmly be rejected, for they do not stand in the orthodox Christian tradition.

(1) Kingdom doctrine. Wimber's doctrine of the kingdom is either defective or somewhat premature in its expectations. He quotes Ladd's teaching that the kingdom is impinging on the present but is still future,[43] but he seems to expect things to happen which would be representative of the kingdom's arrival in full force. He anticipates that all believers should be mediating sensational "power" gifts which will throw Satan on his back to the canvas and will destroy the works of evil. But is such a view compatible with the biblical teaching?

Wimber's former colleague at Fuller Seminary has put the case well:

The New Testament warns us against anticipating too much worldly benefit for the present time. Jesus himself told us that the call of a disciple is to a life of the cross, of self-denial, not to a life of reliance upon miracles to free us from the ailments and agonies we are heir to on earth.[44]

Nor is it biblical to expect that every believer can and should be evincing "power" gifts of the Spirit. After Jesus' ascension, there were few miracles recorded in Scripture, and those involved a very few disciples. As far as we can tell, the overwhelming majority of believers did not receive such sensational powers. Why, then, should such things be the norm today?

(2) Eschatology. Connected to the view of the kingdom, one may say that Wimber's eschatology is somewhat defective, as well. In his review of John Wimber's *Power Evangelism*, Pinnock writes, "John Wimber has a vision for a restored church, a church in which people will again encounter a Gospel of power accompanied by signs and wonders as they did in the first century."[45] The whole thrust of Wimber's teaching is that of preparing the church for Christ's return, of making it purified and holy. Such a view of necessity rejects the idea of the imminency of the Parousia. Wimber seems to be espousing an ancient heresy, namely, that Christ will not return until the church is spotless and the apostolic ministry has been reclaimed. Restorationism was not uncommon in the nineteenth-century American frontier, and it produced a myriad of new sects convinced that they had the key to the regaining of the New Testament church.[46]

(3) Theology of suffering. This is an area of great concern to many theologians. It is obvious from his writing and teaching that John Wimber has a concern for the sick and longs to see people made well. And that is as it should be in any believer's life. Every Christian should pray for and devoutly desire that day when sickness and suffering will be no longer a part of the human condition. But for the moment, in our fallen state, they are very much a part of our existence.

Vineyard teaching regarding illness and pain has been somewhat ambivalent. "At a ministers' seminar led by one of Wimber's team, one of us asked the question 'Is it ever in the loving will of God to allow his children to suffer for a greater good?' *We received no reply.*"[47]

Wimber's own teaching on this matter is inconsistent. On the one hand he declares that perfect health cannot be achieved until "after Christ's second coming, in the fullness of the kingdom of God."[48] He also determines that the victim's faith is not necessarily the criterion for healing: "we have no right to presume that unless God heals in every instance there is something wrong with our faith or his faithfulness."[49] Having said that, however, he goes ahead to note that the failure to be healed generally is caused by one's lack of faith. "There will be more grace, more mercy, more power, and more divine healing . . . if only we persist in seeking him."[50]

He suggests, furthermore, that sickness and suffering take the toll they do because Christians are not exercising a ministry of healing. Such a ministry is the privilege of every believer.[51] His view is that Jesus never refused to heal the sick and His desire is for everyone to be well. There simply is no need for sickness and suffering to exact the price they do.

Wimber's views plainly do not square with biblical teaching. Jesus healed a great many people, but there were people with whom He had contact who were left ill.[52] Nor was His primary purpose in healing works of compassion (though that element was assuredly present!); it was a manifestation of His fulfillment of messianic prophecy. And an examination of the epistles shows that there were within Paul's immediate company (e.g., Timothy and Epaphroditus) those who were sick but were not healed.

The Vineyard movement needs to develop a more ample view of suffering, for it is evident that only a few are ever healed and many thousands are not. It is well to have a strong healing emphasis, but there must also be for those not healed an equally strong theology of the cross which stresses that God through Christ suffers along with us, that we have a God "who understands our suffering, not by observation, *but by participation.*"[53]

(4) Elitism. The disciples of John Wimber have frequently been accused of causing schism within many congregations. The attitude that "we are the ones with the keys to the kingdom" inevitably does that. When sensational signs and wonders are proclaimed as the norm for the Lord's work on this earth, then it is implicit that those who do not embrace such a theology are acting primarily in their own power in attempting to do ministry. "Thus the great lights of the church—Augustine of Hippo, Luther, Calvin, Pascal, Jonathan Edwards, John Wesley—seem pretty dim, for the

Wimber brand of unction was absent from their ministries."[54]

Conclusions

John Wimber calls us to a fresh awareness of the presence and power of the Holy Spirit. God the Spirit is actively at work in the world today, healing people both physically and spiritually. And we as Christians must remain open and available to what He wants to do in us and through us.

Wimber's desire that Christians must invite the Holy Spirit to fill and use them is refreshing. It is absolutely true that those who minister to their fellow human beings should do so as instruments of God's power rather than simply as instruments of a particular church program.

That said, however, we must recognize that the Spirit of God is not limited in the way He works. That includes being forced into the Vineyard mold. A study of the church will show that, once established, the church has moved more powerfully and successfully along the way of personal holiness and suffering servanthood (the demonstration of the fruit of the Spirit as evidenced by the New Testament church at Ephesus) than by the exercising of signs and wonders (the demonstration of sensational gifts of the Spirit as evidenced in the New Testament church at Corinth). Too often, whether with the Montanists of the early church era or the Branhamites of the mid-twentieth century, an emphasis on the sensational has brought division and strife rather than wholeness and growth. Such has been the preliminary evidence of this movement.

At the same time, one should not completely condemn the Vineyard movement, for there are many fine emphases within it that we would do well to emulate. It may well be that with time and an ongoing, developing theology—and an openness to the leading of the Holy Spirit—the elitism and excesses of Third Wave theology will moderate. Christian orthodoxy would be wise at this point in time not to make any snap decisions as to the validity and worth of this movement, but to adopt a "wait and see" attitude.

For Further Reading

Blue, Ken. *Authority to Heal.* Downers Grove, Ill.: InterVarsity Press, 1988.

Coggins, James R. and Paul G. Hiebert, eds. *Wonders and the Word*. Winnipeg: Kindred Press, 1989.

Smedes, Lewis B., ed. *Ministry and the Miraculous: A Case Study at Fuller Theological Seminary*. Waco, Tex.: Word Inc., 1987.

Wagner, Peter C. *The Third Wave of the Holy Spirit: Encountering the Power of Signs and Wonders Today*. Ann Arbor, Mich.: Servant Publications, 1988.

_____. *Signs and Wonders Today*. Altamonte Springs, Fla.: Creation House, 1987.

White, John. *When the Spirit Comes with Power: Signs and Wonders Among God's People*. Downers Grove, Ill.: InterVarsity Press, 1988.

Wimber, John and Kevin Springer. *Power Points*. San Francisco: Harper and Row, 1991.

_____. *Power Healing*. San Francisco: Harper and Row, 1987.

_____. *Power Evangelism*. San Francisco: Harper and Row, 1986.

Fifteen. Feminist Theology

L ike so many other theological movements current today, feminist theology is a product of the turbulent 1960s. Those years were characterized by a general questioning of the regulations and mores of society. Among those desiring changes in their treatment were many women who, having perceived the freedom and advantages enjoyed by men, began to agitate for those same rights for themselves. As their efforts progressed and became more formally organized, Christian scholars began to investigate the spiritual and theological aspects of their struggle. So theological feminism was born.

One may define feminism as the struggle in every area of life to obtain rights for women equal to those enjoyed by men. Theological feminism is the same effort in the context of religion, an attempt to put into practice Paul's statement in Galatians 3:26-28 that in Christ all human beings are one.

The Historical Roots of Feminism

The historical roots of women's rights extend back to the Protestant Reformation of the sixteenth century. Both Martin Luther and John Calvin (though hardly pro-feminist) on the basis of Scripture refuted the Roman Catholic position that women were unclean pawns of the devil who lured men to sins of lust. They also taught, on the same basis, that both men and women were created in the image of God and therefore stood before God as equals. These views, combined with an emphasis on the priesthood of all believers, established a religious milieu in which women could find a place. This awareness of place was demonstrated in seventeenth-century Puritan England where girls were educated along with boys, and women were theologically aware and discussed spiritual issues with men. The Methodists and the Quakers of the eighteenth century permitted women to teach and preach and hold office in their churches.

From the Enlightenment. Certain individuals and groups in the Enlightenment period reinforced the emphasis on the rightful place of women, not because of an emphasis on the rights of the individual, but on equality of place within a community. In the early nineteenth century Robert Owen had a vision of establishing a utopian community where all the inhabitants would live in peace and love, all on an equal footing. From about 1812 Owen circulated books and pamphlets promoting his views of marriage, family, and community life. Some years later he founded the New Harmony community from which all power relationships had been removed. Women were equal with men and children enjoyed equality with adults.

The Victorian era also provided advocates of women's rights. John Stuart Mill was influenced by his wife, Harriet Taylor, to issue a host of tracts and pamphlets insisting that society reconsider its treatment of women. In 1869 he published *On the Subjection of Women* which, within a year, had been translated into eight languages and distributed in twelve countries. Women all over Europe met to discuss it.

In the latter part of this period women in Canada, the United States, and Britain became involved in the temperance movement. In 1869 the Women's Christian Temperance Union was established. Its leader was Frances Willard, a fervent Christian and advocate of women's suffrage. A number of other activists in this movement—Susan B. Anthony, Elizabeth Blackwell, and the Grimkes—were also heavily involved in the suffrage movement.

The twentieth century. Efforts by those interested in women's rights continued into the early twentieth century with a good measure of success. By 1920 women in Canada, the United States, Great Britain, Germany, Holland, Austria, and the Soviet Union had gained the vote. Even Pope Benedict XV, the previous year, had supported the right of women to the franchise. By 1925 they had been admitted to most of the professions and were standing for election to government legislative positions. It appeared that women would soon come to possess true equality with men in Western (Protestant) society.

The Great Depression, unfortunately, began a slowdown in the progress of women's rights. It was felt by most employers (and by society at large) that, because of the severe economic recession, women should not be allowed to deprive men of jobs they needed to support their families (in other words, men were still considered to be the major breadwinners). World War II brought a turnaround in employment as women filled jobs in plants, stores, and offices (jobs vacated by men going off to fight). The post-war years, however, brought a reaction against working women and a renewed emphasis on the woman as homemaker, wife, and mother.

Vatican II. As they had with liberation theology, developments in the Roman Catholic church played a large part in the encouragement of feminism. With the accession of John XXIII to the throne of Peter, the Roman Catholic church was headed by a man who was sympathetic to the aspirations of women to equality. In his 1963 encyclical *Pacem in Terris*, he wrote: "Since women are becoming ever more conscious of their human dignity, they will not tolerate being treated as mere material instruments, but demand rights befitting a human person both in domestic and in public life."[1] Elsewhere in the encyclical he wrote sympathetically of equal rights for men and women and even of the right for all to follow a vocation to the priesthood.[2]

This Pope's influence was seen in the documents of Vatican II concerning men and women. *Gaudium et Spes* observes without comment that, "where they have not yet won it, women claim for themselves an equity before the law and in fact."[3] It also declared that all discrimination, including sexual, "is to be overcome and eradicated as contrary to God's intent. . . . Such is the case of a woman who is denied the right and freedom to choose a husband, to embrace a state of life, or to acquire an education or cultural benefits equal to those recognized for men."[4] *Apostolicam Actuositatem* was equally optimistic for women: "Since in our times women have an ever more active share in the whole life of society, it is very important that they participate more widely also in the various fields of the Church's apostolate."[5]

Not long after Vatican II, several major Catholic journals began to call for changes in the church's treatment of women. Serious scholarly work dealing with the problems of women appeared, exposing anti-feminist strains in the church and calling for its theological purification.[6]

Modern feminism in the 1960s. The feminism of the 1960s found its origin in two basic arenas—politics and commerce. Younger women who were involved in the civil rights and anti-war movements often found themselves regarded as inferior to the male participants. Many of them, well-educated and influenced by Marxist and socialist ideals were unwilling to tolerate what they saw as oppression and so became advocates of radical change. Business and professional women found similar attitudes on the part of their male colleagues, which often led to restrictions on their advancement and, in 1966, formed NOW, the National Organization of Women. Working class and ethnic women, though they rejected the feminist label, organized around issues such as urban renewal and became the National Congress of Neighborhood Women. In many denominations, Christian women's organizations demanded greater roles for women in church affairs. In 1972 a major magazine for women, *Ms.*, was published and it became an immediate success. It was followed by many others, and many existing women's publications adopted feminist overtones.[7]

Political Feminism as a Movement
As the fight for women's rights grew and spread in the 1960s and 1970s, important divisions emerged among the different groups. As a rule, issues pertaining to employment, education, and politics brought women together. But sexual concerns, particularly related to morality (such as abortion), tended to fracture their unity. And even those originally united over the former concerns became split over questions of tactics and style. As early as the latter 1960s there were distinct political factions among those who sought essentially the same goals.

Liberal feminism. The mother of liberal (or, moderate) feminism is Betty Friedan whose book, *The Feminine Mystique* (1963), challenged those ideas and institutions which pushed American women to become homemakers at the cost of their own self-fulfillment. In 1966 she became founding president of the National Organization of Women, which was designed to obtain equal rights and job opportunities for women.

The early liberal feminists were, for the most part, well-educated, middle-class housewives who were appealing to others in their own set. They were not anti-men and demonstrated such by including the opposite sex in NOW membership. When some women went to extremes, they were shocked. Friedan writes:

> For us, with our roots in the middle American mainstream and our fifties' families, equality and the personhood of women never meant the destruction of the family, repudiation of marriage and motherhood, or implacable sexual war against men. That "bra-burning" note shocked and outraged us, and we knew it was wrong—personally and politically—though we never said so, then, as loudly as we should have.[8]

This moderate wing of the feminist movement begins with the principle that all people are created equal and that equal opportunity should be available to all. They realize this principle has not been fully applied to women and they demand that it must be, at once.[9]

The liberal wing frequently uses the vocabulary of the movement as a whole—talking, for example, about the oppression of women—and it recognizes many of the same problems, but its analysis of the functions served by sexism is somewhat different. Sexism, as they see it, is dysfunctional for society; it deprives society of benefiting from the skills of half of its constituency. It also emphasizes that sexism harms men too. They are the fellow victims of this "half-equity," not the enemy.[10]

While liberal feminists speak of a "revolution," they do not really mean it. They desire change through a moderation of the existing system. A radical overturning of the existing order should not be necessary.

Although many liberal feminists have an increasing sympathy for the poor women of society, for the social outcasts, and for women in prison, they tend to draw back from a radical embracement of "sexual politics." Instead, "there should be a rediscovery of the values which linked people together in community. Man-hatred had no place in this program: cooperation and partnership between the sexes should be stressed."[11]

Barbara Deckard evaluates the liberal position as being extremely ineffective: ". . . when the difficulty of bringing about truly significant changes becomes apparent, moderates will settle for palliatives and tokens or get discouraged and give up the struggle completely."[12]

Marxist-socialist feminism. One strand of feminism draws its inspiration from European socialism, including that of Marx and Engels. Those feminists see the class system as the underlying cause of the oppression of women. Women, blacks, and the working class are caught up in the snare of a powerful minority who oppress and exploit them.

It was not always so. In very primitive times, Marxist feminists tell us, women were the socio-cultural leaders in a society of equals. They found and prepared the vegetable staples of people's diets. They were the developers of art, pottery, and weaving. What was it that caused their downfall? "The downfall of women coincided with the breakup of the matriarchal clan commune and its replacement by class-divided society with its institutions of the patriarchal family, private property, and state power."[13] Society, initially homogeneous, began to break up into groups which differed in the labor in which they participated. These groups ultimately became classes where some produced and others took the surplus. This surplus became the private wealth of a hierarchy of men, which in turn, necessitated the establishment of marriage and family to fix the legal ownership of this property and its inheritance. "Through monogamous marriage the wife was brought under the complete control of her husband who was thereby assured of legitimate sons to inherit his wealth."[14]

Women's inferior status, then, is because of the institution of private property and the class system. Indeed, women are doubly exploited, for they are expected, like men, to produce goods which are commodities; but further, "within the social division of labor in capitalism the task of maintaining and reproducing commodity producers is largely given to women."[15] Thus, child-bearing, marriage, and family are all primarily a part of the support of the capitalistic superstructure and only secondarily for the fulfilment of human needs for mutual companionship.

One must realize that—in spite of a frank recognition of sexist oppression—the central emphasis of Marxist-socialist rhetoric is not anti-sexist but anti-class and anti-capitalist. Society needs to be democratized both politically and economically. The means of production would be publicly owned and its output equally distributed. Race and sex would no longer determine one's status. The family's normal functions would be performed by other workers and consequently its oppressiveness would be terminated.

Radical feminism. Radical feminists are a group of women's rights activists who see all men as oppressors and wish to exclude them altogether. They came about as a result of disillusionment with the treatment of women active in the radical, left-wing, anti-war student groups of the 1960s. The male activists in these groups treated their female counterparts largely as sexual objects whose ideas were valueless. The latter reacted by moving into a radical stance in women's rights which saw men as a totally dominating group. Hostility towards men varied from excluding them from their meetings to the writing of a manifesto for an organization called SCUM—Society for Cutting Up Men.[16]

In 1971 Germaine Greer wrote a popular book, *The Female Eunuch,* which reiterated many of these anti-male attitudes. One of her chapters, entitled "Loathing and Disgust," declared that women have no idea how much men really hate them; they are valued not as persons but only as available sex objects.[17]

Radical feminist Shulamith Firestone in her book, *The Dialectic of Sex* (1970), sets out a comprehensive theory of how women's oppression originated. It came directly from a biological reality; in short, women can become pregnant. Their biology has forced on them a dependence on men for physical survival.[18]

Modern birth control methods have made it possible for women to free themselves from male enslavement and exploitation. But the supporting structures for continuing oppression are still in place. Only a feminist revolution can permanently free women from bondage to males.

Female homosexuals have also been an aggressive faction in the radical movement. Each seems tailor-made to the other. If one wishes to exclude men, how much more can one do so than through lesbianism? "To be a lesbian is thus the most personal and the most political stand a radical feminist can make. It is the final refusal."[19] Lesbianism drives home with a vengeance the point of radical feminism—"men are irrelevant."[20]

One must, of course, question the main plank of radical feminism. Casual observation demonstrates that all men are not oppressors; some are clearly among the oppressed. Similarly, all women are not the oppressed; some are clearly oppressors.

Mainstream Theological Feminism

Theological feminism is as diverse in its outlook as its political counterpart. As with the latter we may wish to isolate three general types which we may term mainstream (or, liberal), radical, and evangelical feminism. The theological paths they follow toward women's liberation turn in vastly different directions. The mainstream, liberal, feminist faction will be examined in some detail and evaluated. The other two will be considered in later sections with reference to where they deviate either from mainstream feminism or orthodox Christianity.

Feminist hermeneutics. Feminist theology is involved in a critique of what feminists consider "the androcentrism and misogyny of patriarchal theology."[21] These two flaws are considered characteristic of Christian patriarchal theology, dating back to the dictum of 1 Timothy 2:12 (considered by most women's liberationist theologians not to be genuinely Pauline in authorship): "I do not permit a woman to teach or have authority over a man; she must be silent." The flaws have continued throughout Christian history.

The Bible shares (or even exemplifies) this patriarchalism, say feminists. How strong its anti-female bias is and how it should be treated are matters on which they differ.

Some feminist theologians follow liberation theology and argue for "a 'prophetic-liberating tradition of biblical faith' present in texts ... that can then function as a norm by which other biblical texts are judged."[22] That prophetic tradition then determines which other biblical texts may be authoritative. We have here a version of the "canon within the canon" argument, but it sets out criteria to undercut the misogynist bias of other texts. Feminists insist that men and women alike must realize that the essence of the Christian faith is the prophetic call for the liberation of the downtrodden.[23]

A second feminist position attempts to regain passages overlooked or distorted by patriarchal hermeneutics. It seeks to uncover the counter-cultural aspects of the passage, focusing its attention on those texts concerning women characters and exploring their functions apart from the patriarchal presumption of their marginality.[24] One scholar who has had considerable success in this area is Phyllis Trible, whose research with Eve in Genesis 2–3 is worthy of note.[25] Since such materials are much limited and those possessing counter-cultural values even scarcer, this is known as the "remnant position."

The third position rejects the canon almost completely and instead attempts to reform biblical history, seeking to demonstrate that the actual situation of Judeo-Christianity permitted a greater latitude for women than the writings of the time (the Bible included) suggest.[26] The presupposition involved in such a view is that the Scriptures are the product of patriarchal hermeneutics and are a vessel filled with ideas of female inferiority.

Some feminists are so disillusioned by their failure to build a strong theology for their position from the Bible that they seek new directions. Rosemary Ruether is typical. She writes:

> Feminist theology, then, is not just engaged in a reformation to some original good moment in the past, some unblemished period of origins, because no such period can be discovered for women, either in the Judeo-Christian tradition or before it. Even for those who claim some continuity with the Jewish or Christian traditions, feminist theology must stand as a new midrash or a third covenant, that . . . makes a new beginning, in which the personhood of woman is no longer at the margins but at the center. . . .[27]

Feminism and God. The majority of biblical references to God are masculine. Even Jesus referred to Him as "Father," teaching us to do the same. Feminists are fond of reminding us that "the problem is that we've forgotten that the same Jesus also spoke about God as mother and female."[28]

That the Bible does not give greater place to the feminine, they tell us, is because of the cultural context of its writers: ". . . in a patriarchal culture, where men hold all the religious and political power, the way to honor anything is to make it masculine."[29] Despite that, there are many female images of God in the Bible. Such images remind us that God is not limited to one sex. They should also lead women to embark on whatever spiritual leadership roles for which they have been gifted and men to admit the so-called feminine traits within themselves.[30]

The Bible refers to God in female imagery a great many times. Isaiah 49:15 depicts Him as a woman tenderly breast-feeding her infant. Psalm 123:2 portrays God as the chief woman of a household. In Luke 15:8-10, Jesus speaks of God as a woman sweeping her floor in search of a lost coin. These are but a few of many depictions of God in a feminine aspect.

Feminists have also retranslated names and characteristics of God to identify with women. Theologian Phyllis Trible, for example, notes that the Hebrew name *El Shaddai*, "God of the mountains" (and normally rendered "God Almighty"), can be as well translated "God of the breasts." And Exodus 33:19 and 34:6, which use the Hebrew *rehem* to speak of God as "compassionate," may be rendered as "womb-love." Jack Rogers of Fuller Seminary notes that many of the terms describing the immanence of God are feminine in Hebrew grammar: *torah* (teaching), *chokmah* (wisdom), *shekinah* (God's indwelling presence), *batkol* (the voice of God), and *ruach* (spirit of God).[31]

Christ and salvation. Mainstream liberal feminists see Christ as the representative of God. Some would reject Him along with God as being too patriarchal in nature, but most adopt the view of Letty Russell that, "there has been a lot of rejection of the Bible as the basis for theology. . . . Yet those who do Christian theology cannot abandon the story of Jesus of Nazareth."[32] Consequently, He is able to liberate human beings, "exemplifying the divine acceptance of all and the inclusion of even the most oppressed in the divine kingdom."[33] Christ's salvation is one of liberation from spiritual and earthly enslavement be it political, social, or personal.

Women's liberationists acclaim Christ by two of His New Testament titles, Lord and Suffering Servant. This dialectic underscores the uniqueness of His relationship to God and humanity: "As Lord of love, who serves others, Christ shows us the basis for genuine partnership, in which we are partners with God in liberating the world, but also partners with each other, overcoming the bonds of race, sex, class."[34]

Many feminists adopt a liberation stance in regard to salvation. It is liberation from the oppression of patriarchal institutions and attitudes. Some, like Letty Russell, are universalist in their views, seeing in Christ God's acceptance of all of the oppressed.[35]

Other feminists depict Jesus as a mother who seeks to find and heal her children. Julian of Norwich, the (female) mystic of the

Middle Ages, wrote a book, *Showings*, of meditations on Christ's motherhood. She linked the crucifixion to childbearing. "The crucifixion is the moment of cosmic travail, when the creation that has been born—in love and in God—fully enters into the painful process of transformation."[36]

The historical Jesus appeals to many women because He rejected the patriarchal establishment of His day. He openly accepted the oppressed and outcasts—tax-collectors, prostitutes, Samaritans, lepers, and women:

> Though the observation is frequently made by those who oppose women in leadership roles that Jesus chose no women to be among his twelve disciples, by any reading of the Gospels Jesus' attitude toward women was revolutionary. Contrary to Jewish custom, he freely socialized with women.... In the home of Mary and Martha (Luke 10:38-42), Jesus related to Mary as a teacher to a disciple and tacitly defended her right to a role which was commonly denied to Jewish women. In talking to the Samaritan woman at the well (John 4:1-42), Jesus broke conventions again in the freedom with which he related to this woman whom he would have scorned had he followed the conventions of his day.... But it is not only his actions which were positive towards women, his teachings were also revolutionary.... By declaring that a man commits adultery in his heart when he looks at a woman for the purpose of lusting after her (Matt. 5:28), he affirmed that women have rights of their own and are not things to be used.[37]

The Holy Spirit. Many women's rights advocates find the Holy Spirit the Person of the Trinity with whom they are the most comfortable. They often speak of the Holy Spirit in feminine terms. Many are fond of associating the Spirit with the divine Wisdom principle, described by the writers of Proverbs as female.[38] The Holy Spirit is the One who guides, comforts, and nurtures, like a loving, caring mother.

Feminist anthropology. A major question among feminists is whether to think of people primarily as human beings or as male and female. Many answer the latter. "Male persons are identified as the oppressors who have consciously or more often unconsciously lived in and promoted a social and religious system in which they perceived and presented themselves as normative humanity."[39] The majority, however, see sex as but one factor among many which qualify a common humanity. They point to Galatians 3:28, that in Christ there is no male or female, but all are one.

The Bible is clear that both male and female are created in the image of God (Gen. 1:26–27). A part of that imaging is their stewardship over creation. Humankind is the link between the lower creation and its Creator. All human beings share the responsibility for the created order — both males and females. They are one in this respect. "To assert that male and female persons are radically different, as some feminists do, . . . would create divisions in the role of humanity in its cosmic responsibility."[40]

Many feminists follow liberation theology in their view of sin. Sin is that which estranges us from others, which destroys relationship with our fellows. The establishment of patriarchy, for example, created a sinful structure which alienated men from women, cutting off the normative relationship God had intended. Mainstream feminists would, for the most part, agree with Dorothee Soelle, who writes:

> According to a Christian understanding of the world, sins are not particular things we do as individuals — the infringement of sexual norms, for example. They are structures of power which rule over us, something to which we are subjected, from which we have to be liberated. It is not primarily a question of the violation of individual commandments. It is life under a different God, the God whom the New Testament calls mammon.[41]

Women and the church. For many feminists the church signifies oppression. It is the ultimate patriarchal oppressor. "After 2,000 years the Church remains an institution structured by men for men. Whilst proclaiming eternal freedom in Christ, it endorses temporal bondage for women."[42] It proclaims that in Christ there is only oneness and no male or female, but it practices subjugating women to the authority of men. Women are given the menial and tedious tasks; men make the vital decisions.

One of the major areas of controversy in the church is the ordaining of women to professional ministry. If all are one in Christ, why should there be any question of ordaining women who have felt the call of God to the pastorate?

Ordination is the affirmation of God's giftedness and call to a person. To refuse ordination to women is to waste some half of the church's resources. Molly Marshall-Green writes:

> It is the growing conviction of many that the Church cannot do without all that women have to offer through its ministries. Viewing women in ministry as a creative possibility (whose time has come) will allow unhindered reception of their varied contributions. Not only will women's gifts complement and complete the Body of Christ, but a new credibility in the eyes of an increasingly egalitarian society will be gained. Indeed, the Church should strive to be the most egalitarian expression of human relatedness because of its theological understanding of greatness as servanthood and leadership as self-emptying to others. It should not be characterized by what Letty Russell has called a "pyramid of domination," which is a hierarchical view of authority and relationships, for Christ is the authority for the Church, and his authority was as one among friends (John 15:15).[43]

To counter the anti-feminist argument that the church has not historically ordained women, feminists argue that the New Testament speaks of several women in prominent church leadership roles. Phoebe was both a deacon and administrator (Rom. 16:1-2). Junia was an apostle (Rom. 16:7). Priscilla was a prominent teacher (Acts 18:24ff). And in the early church the Montanists, a charismatic group, had prophetesses and ordained women ministers.

Radical Theological Feminists

A large portion of the women's liberation movement have come to reject the Christian faith because the church since its inception has aided and abetted the oppression of women. They advocate the substituting of new forms coming out of women's experience.

"In theology, at the root of such distortions as anti-feminism is the problem of conceptualization, images and attitudes concerning God."[44] God is interpreted as a patriarchal deity who is male. Preachers and theologians may protest that they believe God is asexual, but they nonetheless use the pronoun "He" in referring to this non-sexed Deity.

Radical feminists, consequently, reject this God, insisting that "we can no longer limit God's work in history to the deliverance of the Hebrews from bondage nor to the Incarnation in Jesus Christ. That lens is just too narrow."[45] Instead, they substitute the term Goddess to denote Ultimate Reality. Carol Christ, a radical feminist, lists three possible definitions of the Goddess:

(1) The Goddess is divine female, a personification who can be invoked in prayer and ritual;
(2) the Goddess is symbol of the life, death, and rebirth energy in nature and culture, in personal and communal life; and
(3) the Goddess is symbol of the affirmation of the legitimacy and beauty of female power.[46]

Other radical feminists have delved into witchcraft, using the symbol of the Goddess in a pantheistic fashion. Wiccan leader Starhawk rejects any parallelism to God the Father. "The Goddess does not rule the world. She *is* the world."[47] Other Wiccan feminists recognize a duality in deity—God and Goddess, of whom the earth is the physical manifestation of their deity.[48]

Evangelical Feminism

Evangelical feminists seek to emulate the English Quakers by combining women's rights and biblical Christianity. They are unwilling, as many feminists have done, to abandon the historic Christian faith. They accept the Bible as God's authoritative Word. Doctrinally, they are evangelical, following the directions of the mainstream movement in the areas permitted by Scripture, but refusing to follow it beyond Scriptural bounds. At the same time, they recognize inequities in the church's treatment of women. Letha Scanzoni and Nancy Hardesty, two evangelical feminists, write:

As Christians we can no longer dodge the "woman problem." To argue that women are equal in creation but subordinate in function is no more defensible than "separate but equal" schools for the races. The church must either be consistent with the theology it sometimes espouses and oppose all

forms of women's emancipation—including education, political participation, and vocations outside the home—or it must
face up to the concrete implications of a Gospel which liberates women as well as men.[49]

Evangelicals recognize that men and women are different. Wom-
en do not wish to become men, but they do want to be full human
beings. "We ask for the right to make our own choices, to define
our own lives, not out of selfish motivations, but because God calls
us and commands us to develop the gifts he has given us."[50]

Evangelical feminists admit that women's liberation may mean a
loss of power for men, but Scripture cautions Christians against
seeking power and privilege. God has shared His power and responsibility with us and redeemed men must learn to share the
same with women.[51] Galatians 3:28 must become a practical fact.

Conclusions

That the church has abused women in many areas of life and/or
treated them as inferior to men for many centuries is a virtual
"given." The patristic church, because of its warped views of sexuality, taught that women were in league with the devil, using
their bodies to lure hapless men into the pit. These views were
continued for centuries through the medieval church and into the
Renaissance period. As a result, women were allowed to occupy
most servile and menial positions. It was a rare woman who ever
achieved any authoritative status other than among women.

Although the Reformers made some far-reaching changes in the
theology of women, raising their status in theory, in actual practice
little was achieved. They did, however, lay the foundation for the
English and American Puritans who had a more liberated and
egalitarian practice than any who had preceded them. The Methodists and Quakers of the eighteenth century and the Baptists of the
nineteenth century all advanced the cause of equality for women,
but they were a minority in the church.

The present century has seen an escalation in the battle for
equal rights for women in politics, society, and economics, as well
as in the church. In this last area, sadly, gains have not been as

great as in other sectors. As the century draws to a close, women still fail to enjoy a position equal with men in the church.

The last three decades have spawned a variety of feminist groups. They range from mild to extreme radical. Marxist-socialist feminism appeals only to the politically and economically naive and is as bereft of value as is its political counterpart. Radical feminism, which would do away with men altogether and which tends to exalt female homosexuality, approaches the ludicrous. At the same time, along with the less extreme, more credible varieties of feminism, they serve to illustrate the seriousness with which the movement needs to be taken.

Feminist hermeneutics (excepting those of evangelical feminists, for the most part) are somewhat flawed. They evidently do not see the Bible in the light of Reformation theology, namely, as the Word of God. The movement's attacks on Scripture as patriarchal and therefore anti-female are at best attempts to deal simplistically with what the text says rather than to wrestle with its difficulties; at worst, they are a rejection of supernatural revelation.

Should one object to the emphasis given by women's rights advocates to the feminine in God? Not at all, for it is there. The Bible does indeed refer to God in female imagery on many occasions. Our insistence should be—like that of evangelical feminism—that such emphases be kept within the biblical bounds. When feminism ventures beyond the pale of Scripture to proclaim a "Goddess" as Ultimate Reality, then it has gone too far.

In the same mode of thought, we must applaud the emphasis on Jesus as the Liberator of every facet of life. Those, however, who would carry this liberation concept to the point of universalism, go beyond reason. We must keep in mind Letty Russell's caution that, "for Christians, all ideologies must be subject to constant critique in the light of the Gospel."[52]

Feminists have a case to make in their criticism of the church. If the male/female equality of pre-Fall history is restored in Christ, then why does the church seek to force women to be subordinate to men? Women's liberationists are correct in their insistence that the church must practice consistency in its theology. And the argument over Galatians 3:26-28—while we must recognize that some would interpret it differently—makes a good case. If slavery has been abandoned as antithetical to the preaching of the Gospel, if racism has been outlawed for the same reason, is it not sound to suppose that misogyny should go out the window as well?

There is no question that feminism is an issue still hotly debated among evangelicals today (and that it is still largely a closed book among fundamentalists). Both men and women of good faith and conscience interpret what the Bible has to say in diametrically opposite manners. Consequently, some of these people will grant women a say in the church—while refusing them parity with men. In that regard, women's rights advocates must continue to speak out, while maintaining an attitude of love and humility which characterized Christ Himself in His relationship to others.

For Further Reading

Christ, Carol P. *Living Deep and Surfacing: Women Writers on a Spiritual Quest*. Boston: Beacon Press, 1980.

Christ, Carol P., and Judith Plaskow, eds. *Womanspirit Rising*. New York: Harper and Row, 1979.

Daly, Mary. *Gyn/Ecology: The Metaethics of Radical Feminism*. Boston: Beacon Press, 1978.

_____. *Beyond God the Father: Toward a Philosophy of Women's Liberation*. Boston: Beacon Press, 1973.

Deckard, Barbara. *The Women's Movement*. New York: Harper and Row, 1975.

Evans, Mary J. *Woman in the Bible*. Downers Grove, Ill.: InterVarsity Press, 1983.

Friedan, Betty. *The Second Stage*. New York: Summit Books, 1981.

Greer, Germaine. *The Female Eunuch*. New York: Bantam Books, 1972.

Hayter, Mary. *The New Eve in Christ*. Grand Rapids: Wm. B. Eerdmans Pub. Co., 1987.

Loades, Ann. *Searching for Lost Coins, Explorations in Christianity and Feminism.* Allison Park, Pa.: Pickwick Publications, 1987.

Russell, Letty M. *The Future of Relationship.* Philadelphia: Westminster Press, 1979.

Russell, Letty M. *Human Liberation in a Feminine Perspective—A Theology.* Philadelphia: Westminster Press, 1974.

Scanzoni, Letha, and Nancy Hardesty. *All We're Meant to Be.* Waco, Texas: Word Inc., 1975.

Spencer, Aida Besancon. *Beyond the Curse.* Nashville: Thomas Nelson, Inc., 1985.

Starhawk (Miriam Simos). *The Spiral Dance.* New York: Harper and Row, 1979.

Trible, Phyllis. *God and the Rhetoric of Sexuality.* Philadelphia: Fortress Press, 1978.

Wilson-Kastner, Patricia. *Faith, Feminism, and the Christ.* Philadelphia: Fortress Press, 1983.

Sixteen. Reconstructionist (Dominion) Theology

O ver the last three decades or so, a movement has arisen from among evangelicals which has aroused both consternation and fear on the part of those from whom it came. Dominion theology—also called the Christian Reconstructionist movement—follows a system of thinking about God's law and how it works out in the world which is radically different from that accepted and practiced by the majority of conservative Christians. Increasing numbers, however, are entering the movement, seeing it as a means of reestablishing the greatness and former glory of the Christian faith, and even of ushering in the kingdom of God in the here and now.

Reconstruction defined. Gary DeMar, a Christian Reconstructionist theologian, characterizes the movement as follows:

> Christian Reconstructionists believe that the Word of God, that is, "*all* Scripture," should be applied to *all* areas of life. With such faithful application, Christian Reconstructionists expect that God will bless the efforts of His people in both "this age" and in the "age to come" (Mark 10:29-31). It is obvious that the "all Scripture" Paul mentions in 2 Timothy 3:16 is the *Old* Testament, since at the time of his writing, the New Testament canon had not been completely formulated. ... The Old Covenant order, with its types and shadows did not pass away. This vital distinction is often missed by today's Christians.[1]

Also known as theonomy (from *theos*, "God," and *nomos*, "law"), the movement holds that the civil laws of Old Testament Israelite society are normative in all societies for all time. Under this system, for example, crimes such as homosexuality or adultery would become capital offenses.[2]

Leaders in the Reconstructionist movement insist that establishing such a theocracy (their foremost goal in the United States) would necessitate democratic action by the populace. They are quite adamant that their views on this matter are ethical. Christian reconstruction "does not come automatically, nor is it imposed top-down by a political regime or by an army of Christians working frantically to overthrow the governments of the world."[3] But, they add, it would be expedited by a virtually universal spiritual revival with a myriad of conversions to Christ.[4]

Dominion theologians are unapologetically postmillennial. They believe that there will be a long utopian era here on earth before Jesus comes again. In the interim believers must make every attempt to reclaim the nations—starting with the United States— for Christ. Politics, therefore, is important, for it is one device for remodeling society. The followers of this movement recognize that such vast change will not take place overnight; it may take centuries to achieve.[5]

Historical Roots

According to Reconstructionist leader Gary North, "Twenty years ago, the Christian Reconstruction movement did not exist."[6] Today, the movement has grown substantially both in following and influence. Its growth may be traced, for the most part, to three individuals: R.J. Rushdoony, Greg Bahnsen, and Gary North.

R.J. Rushdoony. The father of Christian Reconstructionism, Rousas John Rushdoony, was born to Armenian immigrants in New York City in 1916. He claims to be one in an unbroken family line of pastors from the fourth Christian century.[7] His education included a Bachelor and Master of Arts degree from the University of California, religious training at the Pacific School of Religion, and the Doctor of Philosophy from Valley Christian University. Following graduation he worked as a missionary to Chinese youth in San Francisco and then with Shoshone and Paiute natives. With the conclusion of his missionary service, he pastored a succession of Presbyterian churches.

In 1959 his first book, *By What Standard?* was published, followed by some thirty others.[8] His initial books, which were not related to dominion theology, were well-received, but his 1973 work, *The Institutes of Biblical Law*, a theonomic appeal to Scripture, aroused the ire of the Reformed community.[9]

Rushdoony founded the Chalcedon Foundation in 1965 in Vallecito, California, to promote "Christian Reconstructionism." He also established a newsletter, *Chalcedon*, and a scholarly review, *Journal of Christian Reconstruction*, to disseminate the message of the foundation. *Newsweek* has referred to the Foundation as "the think tank for the religious right."[10]

Greg Bahnsen. The most brilliant of the Christian Reconstruction thinkers, Greg Bahnsen began reading Rushdoony's books as a youth. He attended Westminster Theological Seminary (M.Div. and M.Th.) and received his doctorate from the University of Southern California. Following graduation he began to teach at the Reformed Seminary in Jackson, Mississippi.

In 1977 he published *Theonomy in Christian Ethics*, whose thesis was that all of the Mosaic Law should be applied directly to American life. It caused so much uproar among evangelicals that he was dismissed from his post.[11]

Bahnsen became pastor of an Orthodox Presbyterian church in southern California. He also serves as a dean of graduate studies at a local teachers college. Even though most people outside of his movement disagree with his views, his scholarly thoroughness has won their admiration.[12]

Gary North. Gary North is Rushdoony's son-in-law. A Ph.D. in economics from the University of California, Riverside, he assisted the latter by editing the *Journal of Christian Reconstruction* from 1974 until the two had a falling out in 1981.

At that point North moved to Tyler, Texas, because he believed that the American economy would soon collapse and a rural setting would be the best place for the survival of his "remnant."[13] There, his Institute for Christian Economics was founded, followed by a sister group, Geneva Ministries, which publishes a monthly *Geneva Review*.

Gary North is a prolific writer. Among his varied publications through the years are *An Introduction to Christian Economics* (1973), *The Dominion Covenant: Genesis* (1982), and *Inherit the Earth: Biblical Principles for Economics* (1987). He is well-known for a pugnacious rhetoric in his literary style.

North was able to penetrate the charismatic movement with the message of dominion theology when Robert Tilton's wife read one of his books and persuaded her husband to invite North to address a conference of some 1,000 pastors and their wives. There, he made many converts.

Other prominent figures. One of North's associates and the dominion theologian most responsible for popularizing the movement's teaching on prophecy is David Chilton. His books, *Paradise Restored* (1985) and *Days of Vengeance* (1987), have spread the Reconstructionist view of biblical prophecy to new converts of the movement.

Gary De Mar, one of Bahnsen's students at Reformed Seminary, is director of the Institute of Christian Government in Atlanta. He leads seminars on God and Government from the theonomic perspective, and has authored several books.

Other prominent figures include theonomist Joseph Kickasola, professor of international studies and Hebrew at Regent University, and Ray Sutton, a Dallas Seminary graduate and Episcopal priest whose book, *That You May Prosper*, is considered the standard on the dominion view of biblical covenants.

The rise of dominion theology. The Reconstructionist movement began in the 1960s under the influence of the late Cornelius Van Til, Reformed philosopher at Westminster Theological Seminary. Van Til has been called the "patron philosopher" of the movement (though he vigorously denied any affiliation with it).[14]

Dominion theology proponents insist that their principles are based on logical deductions from the character of God. They have isolated three basic concepts:

1. The immutability (changelessness) of God.
2. God's character is perfectly reflected by His law.
3. As a consequence, His laws are eternal and are binding on all peoples of all times.[15]

That God's laws are changeless and eternally binding on all is reflected by Jesus in Matthew 5:17-19, which is foundational to the reconstructionist movement:

Do not think that I have come to abolish the Law or the Prophets; I have not come to abolish them but to fulfill them. I tell you the truth, until heaven and earth disappear, not the smallest letter, not the least stroke of a pen, will by any means disappear from the Law until everything is accomplished. Anyone who breaks one of the least of these commandments and teaches others to do the same will be called the least in the kingdom of heaven, but whoever practices and teaches these commandments will be called great in the kingdom of heaven.

Theonomist Greg Bahnsen declares that the best translation of the word "fulfill" in this verse is "confirm," and that Jesus is asserting that He has come to confirm and restore the Old Testament Law in its fullness.[16]

It was not until 1973 that dominion theology began to grow among intellectuals. It was then that R.J. Rushdoony wrote his *Institutes of Biblical Law,* a 900-page two-volume work which propounded the implications of Scripture for every aspect of life. Despite a low view of Calvin, he obviously patterned the title of his book on the reformer's *Institutes of the Christian Religion.*[17]

The growth of Christian Reconstructionism was aided and abetted by the deterioration of American society. The movement's conservative agenda promises a return to Christian morality, decency, and security. "Reconstructionists leave little doubt that they are consciously imitating the Puritans of the early seventeenth century in establishing 'a city on a hill' and calling on the New Testament (e.g. Matt. 5:14; 28:18) for justification."[18]

The burgeoning Reconstructionist movement aroused the ire of many church groups. In 1988 the Assemblies of God responded to the thrust of dominion theology by denouncing postmillennialism as a heresy. Dave Hunt, co-author of *The Seduction of Christianity,* suggested that Reconstructionism has New Age overtones. Mainline denominations and non-Christian religions are equally disturbed, for dominion theology threatens religious liberty as they know it. "Rushdoony, for example, sees no place in a Reconstructed society for the panoply of Jews, Buddhists, Muslims, Hindus, Baha'is, humanists, atheists, and non-reconstructionist Christians that make up American religious pluralism."[19]

Reconstructionist Emphases

The Christian Reconstruction movement rests upon three distinctive doctrinal foundations: (1) personal regeneration, (2) the application of biblical law to all areas of life (theonomy), and (3) the advance of the already-present kingdom of God in history (postmillennialism).[20] The foregoing is not to suggest that the movement ignores the other basic doctrines of the Christian faith:

> Reconstructionists do not cast aside prayer, evangelism, and worship. Instead, we emphasize long-neglected doctrines like application of biblical law in the New Covenant order and the advance of God's kingdom in the world. Reconstructionists subscribe to the basics of the Christian faith: from the inerrancy of Scripture to a literal heaven and hell and everything in between.[21]

Regeneration. Reconstructionists are quick to point out that society cannot be transformed unless and until the individuals who compose it are transformed. Thus, the starting point for the movement must be regeneration. "God's Spirit must be in us *before* we can walk in His statutes (Rom. 8:3-4, 7)."[22]

Before they are able to change, people must be given the will to change. The means of that change is evangelism, the preaching of the Gospel. R.J. Rushdoony declares that "the key to remedying the situation is not revolution. . . . The key is regeneration, propagation of the Gospel, and the conversion of men and nations to God's law-word."[23]

Regeneration, which is the main step in one's salvation, restores a person to his original purpose. That purpose, David Chilton tells us, is to have dominion over all the earth.[24] That was the significance of God's creating humankind in His own image. With the Fall that image was stripped of God's glory and tragically disfigured. The earth, which God had intended to serve as His "Garden-Temple," became a wilderness. But regeneration begins a threefold pattern in the work of God in us: ". . . we *have been* remade in God's image (Eph. 4:24), we *are being* progressively remade in His image (2 Cor. 3:18), and we look forward to the day when we *will be* perfectly remade in His image (Phil. 3:20-21)."[25] Regeneration, then, both restores human beings to their original purpose and guarantees the fulfilling of their original mandate under God to exercise dominion.

Reconstructionists point out that their opponents have misinterpreted their teaching on God's mandate to suppose that they want to establish His kingdom by force of politics or arms. Not so, they protest. The Bible is clear that the kingdom is already here, having been inaugurated by Jesus. Entry into (or participation in) the kingdom is the automatic consequence of regeneration, and cannot be achieved apart from regeneration. Jesus warned Nicodemus that one cannot even "see the kingdom" until having been "born again," or regenerated (John 3:3).[26]

Theonomy. Greg Bahnsen defines theonomy as the obligation of the Christian "to keep the whole law of God as a pattern for sanctification and that this law is to be enforced by the civil magistrate where and how the stipulations of God so designate."[27] By the whole law of God, he means the law as codified in the Old Testament. Rushdoony concurs, declaring that "apart from biblical law, there is no standard for our behavior in this world."[28]

Dominion theologians chide those who would deny that God's law is not applicable to our world, especially to civil government. They quote with disdain Norman Geisler's contention that "government is not based on special revelation, such as the Bible . . . [but] on God's general revelation to all men. . . . Thus, civil law . . . lays no specifically religious obligation on man."[29] A fallen and distorted creation, they argue, is incapable of formulating a moral code to govern the nations. The natural order, which is also fallen, cannot be depended on to give us an ethical code from observing it.[30]

The theonomic goal of Reconstructionists for the United States and all nations is the establishment of a theocracy:

> Now by *theocracy* I do not mean a government ruled by priests and pastors. . . . A theocracy is a *government ruled by God*, a government whose law code is solidly founded on the laws of the Bible. Civil rulers are required to be God's ministers, just as much as pastors are (Rom. 13:1-4). According to God's holy, infallible Word, the laws of the Bible are the *best* laws (Deut. 4:5-8). They cannot be improved upon.[31]

Consequently, they have a vision for a reconstructed America which would be ruled under Old Testament law. It would include a general decentralization of government, strong private property rights protected against state encroachment. The government would have no part in business, education, or social welfare. To aid the poor, voluntary slavery would be established along with gleaning on private farms after the harvest. Society would return to the patriarchal system.[32]

Criminal law would also follow the Old Testament. The death penalty would be applied to all those crimes listed in the Old Testament as capital offenses: adultery, homosexuality, fornication, apostasy, incorrigibility in older children, blasphemy, rape, murder, and kidnapping. For such crimes as robbery, embezzlement, and vandalism (those against property), restitution would be required and, when impossible, those guilty would be indentured into servitude.

Postmillennialism. Postmillennialism, the victorious advance of God's already present kingdom throughout history, is the third distinctive of dominion theology. Its advocates joyfully proclaim that the kingdom of God has arrived. We are presently in the Millennium. It was inaugurated when Christ entered Jerusalem on Palm Sunday (Matt. 21:5), and He was enthroned in heaven upon His ascension (Acts 2:30-36).[33] "In one sense, both Christians and non-Christians alike are now living in God's kingdom: Christians as sons and daughters of the King, non-Christians as rebels."[34] The Apostle Paul, in Ephesians 1:20-22, writes that at Christ's ascension, God "seated Him at His right hand in the heavenly realms, far above all rule and authority, power and dominion, and every title that can be given, not only in the present age but also in the one to come." Chilton asks, "Now if Christ is seated *now* above all rule and authority and power and dominion, if all things are now under His feet, *why are some Christians waiting for His kingdom to begin?*"[35]

While the kingdom has been established in Christ's earthly ministry, it has not yet attained its full growth. Like leaven in bread it will grow unobtrusively but continually until it ultimately engulfs the whole world.[36] When all the nations own the rule of God, then Christ will return. But such a state of affairs may take many centuries more. Biblical postmillennialism, declares

DeMar, is a long-term hope in which Christians may exercise the basic ingredient of genuine biblical faith: patience.[37]

Gary North describes the differences in the millennial views and why, in his perception, postmillennialism is the appropriate view:

> While neither premillennialism nor amillennialism teaches a specific timetable regarding the return of Christ to earth, their adherents generally believe that time remaining is very short. Their cultural battle cry is this: "Come quickly, Lord Jesus." The postmillennialists' cry is this: "Come quickly, but only after your Church has achieved its role in fulfilling the Great Commission." ... The first is either a call to retreat from most of the battlefields of life, or else a call to launch a kamikaze-type attack against the prevailing humanist culture. The second is a call to historical victory.[38]

Dominion Hermeneutics

Biblical hermeneutics is the science of interpreting the Bible. What the Bible says to a person will depend upon one's interpretation of the text. When one looks at the variety of interpretations on millennial events, the importance of a correct hermeneutic is obvious. What composes the hermeneutics of the Christian Reconstructionist movement? And how adequate is that method of interpretation?

Interpreting symbolic language. A major area of dispute between the Reconstructionists and their premillennialist opponents is the question of how to interpret symbolic language. While the latter stick as closely as possible to the *sensus literalis* (literal meaning), the former see symbolic terms "as a set of patterns and associations. . . . Biblical symbolism is not a code . . . [but] a way of seeing, a perspective."[39]

Chilton warns against taking an allegorical approach to Scripture and he illustrates with the example of the word, "water":

> We can suddenly decide, "Aha! Water is a special code word which means *eternal life*. That means that whenever the Bible talks about water symbolically, it is *really* talking about eternal life; whenever someone takes a drink, he is *really* becoming a Christian." It doesn't work that way (as you will see if you try to apply it to the Bible). Besides, what sense would it

make for the Bible simply to put everything in code? The Bible is not a book for spies and secret societies; it is God's *revelation* of Himself to His covenant people.[40]

Such allegorizing is, at best, "speculative; it does not pay sufficient attention to the way the Bible itself speaks."[41]

Chilton notes that Scripture is intended to be read "visually." The evangelists presented us with a series of pictures or images which seeks to evoke a response from their readers. Thus, the Bible must be read visually:

> So, when the Bible tells us a story about water, it is not "really" telling us about something else; it is telling us about *water*. But at the same time we are expected to see the water, and to think of the *biblical associations* with regard to water. The system of interpretation offered here . . . takes the "water" seriously and literally, but it also takes seriously what God's Word associates with water throughout the history of biblical revelation.[42]

When it comes to numbers, Reconstructionists tend to view them more symbolically than literally. Certain numbers, such as 40 or 1,000, are seen as ancient Near Eastern "round numbers." Consequently, the 1,000 years of the millennium are not necessarily literal, but refer to a very long time, perhaps several thousand years. It refers, essentially, "to the entire era between the ascension of the resurrected Christ to heaven and the final judgment."[43]

Dominion Theology: An Evaluation

Dominion theology has been praised as the salvation of a deteriorating degenerate society, and damned as a false system of prophecy which provides the philosophical basis for anti-semitism. The truth probably lies somewhere between these extremes.

Theological system. The overwhelming position of dominion theology appears to be orthodox. As we have already observed, Reconstructionists claim to be conservative evangelical inerrantists.

When one examines the first of their proclaimed distinctives, regeneration, nothing negative appears. The movement's declaration that society cannot be transformed apart from the transformation of those who compose it is only common sense. Who can argue with such biblically based reasoning?

The second distinctive, theonomy, is undoubtedly the most controversial of the three. At first glance, a return to biblical law might seem to be just what our obviously fallen society needs. To wipe out unemployment, most crime, much poverty, high taxation, and other evils would be to create a virtual utopia.

Further thoughts, however, raise serious concerns. The Old Testament gives us a picture of failure. Fallen humanity could not keep the law then; why should they be any more successful today? The Apostle Peter puts it well in addressing the Jerusalem Council on the very matter of the Gentiles' keeping the Old Testament Law: "Now then, why do you try to test God by putting on the necks of the disciples a yoke that neither we nor our fathers have been able to bear?" (Acts 15:10). While Reconstructionists would argue that the majority of the population would be regenerated and hence empowered by the Holy Spirit to keep the law, many people would still be unsaved and incapable of meeting its demands.

Questions have been raised, as well, about religious liberty. Theocracies have existed before. And while one would not question the rulership of Christ, one might think twice about that of His human representatives. One of the more famous (or, infamous) theocracies, John Calvin's Geneva, was responsible for a multitude of executions (one of a disobedient child, another of a man who had mocked Calvin), the most nefarious of which was the burning of Michael Servetus, a Unitarian, for heresy (his greatest sin seems to have been deriding Calvin's *Institutes!*). Such theocracies appear to work well only for those at the top.

What of those people who are not Christians? Wayne House and Thomas Ice properly ask, "Bahnsen, Rushdoony, and others typically list apostasy and idolatry as capital crimes. . . . Their definition of such acts is quite broad. Would a Buddhist be allowed to erect a public shrine? Would there be synagogues and mosques?"[44] To be sure, Christian Reconstructionists insist that totalitarianism is absolutely certain when authority is invested in an individual, powerful elite, whether it be church or state, and they hold to a substantially decentralized view of government, consisting of family, church, schools, other institutions, and civil government all holding together in a loose federation.[45] But small elite groups can be just as discriminatory and cruel as large ones. The underlying principles, to a major degree, are what will constitute their directions.

What about Christians of non-dominion persuasion? House and Ice speculate that they would surely be excommunicated and would be considered at war with law and order. They quote Rushdoony to the effect that "the rights have the rights"[46] (the reverse of which would seem to be that "those not right have no rights").

The third distinctive—postmillennialism—is part of an ongoing argument about the correct interpretation of the Book of Revelation which usually emits more heat than light. Such a position is hardly heretical. The Puritans, steadfast guardians of Christian orthodoxy in early New England, were postmillennialists. There are devout believers who are postmillennialist, amillennialist, and premillennialist, and there are cultists who hold these differing views, as well. The Millennium is one of those issues on which Christians of good faith must agree to disagree.

Hermeneutics. It would appear that the Reconstructionists apply different methodology to different parts of the Bible. While they apply their "visualization" approach to the Book of Revelation, they interpret the books of Old Testament law quite literally. One must question the rationality of such an inconsistent approach.

Equally problematic is their numerology. Either certain numbers must always be seen as "round," or else they must be taken literally. One is led to question whether the millennium is 1,000 years (quite literally) in duration as premillennialists declare, or the "long time" of dominion theology.

Conclusions

Christian Reconstructionism is a conservative, evangelical movement. It cannot properly be regarded as a cult or even as a heresy. It is part and parcel of the resurgence of evangelical involvement in society. It offers what appears to be a Christian salvation from the mess in which Western civilization finds itself. At the same time, as theologian Richard John Neuhaus points out, "To turn the Bible into a code book or a blueprint for societal reordering is to deny what the Bible itself presents itself to be, which is the story of God's salvation of a sinful world in Jesus Christ."[47]

Dominion theologians rightly point out that there is a battle going on in the world for control of our society; the most important aspect is control of thought patterns and worldview. Combatants include humanists, atheists, New Agers, and various Christian groups. The Reconstructionists criticize Christians for either turning to a "natural law ethic" or for gutting the Bible of much of its blueprint for living. They insist that they (the Reconstructionists) are striving for a "revolution from the inside out," not—as their critics suggest—the violent overthrow of government.[48]

That the United States will have such a revival establishing a theocracy does not seem likely in the near future. At the same time, with some of the amazing things that have happened in the last few years—such as the fall of Communism—one never knows. As undoubtedly the Christian Reconstructionists themselves would point out, "With God all things are possible" (Mark 10:27, NKJV).

For Further Reading

Bahnsen, Greg. *Theonomy in Christian Ethics*. Phillipsburg, N.J.: Presbyterian and Reformed Publishing, 1984.

_____. *By This Standard: The Authority of God's Law Today*. Tyler, Texas: Institute for Christian Economics, 1985.

Chilton, David. *The Days of Vengeance: An Exposition of the Book of Revelation*. Fort Worth, Texas: Dominion Press, 1987.

_____. *Productive Christians in an Age of Guilt-Manipulators: A Biblical Response to Ronald J. Sider*, 4th ed. Tyler, Texas: Institute for Christian Economics, 1986.

_____. *Paradise Restored: An Eschatology of Dominion*. Fort Worth, Texas: Reconstruction Press, 1985.

DeMar, Gary. *The Debate over Christian Reconstruction*. Fort Worth, Texas: Dominion Press, 1988.

_____. *Ruler of the Nations: Biblical Blueprints for Government*. Ft. Worth, Texas: Dominion Press, 1987.

_____. *God and Government*, 3 vols. Atlanta: American Vision Press, 1982-86.

DeMar, Gary and Peter Leithart. *The Reduction of Christianity: A Biblical Response to Dave Hunt*. Ft. Worth, Texas: Dominion Press, 1988.

Grant, George. *The Changing of the Guard: Biblical Blueprints for Political Action*. Fort Worth, Texas: Dominion Press, 1987.

House, H. Wayne and Thomas Ice. *Dominion Theology: Blessing or Curse?* Portland, Ore.: Multnomah Press, 1988.

North, Gary. *Millennialism and Social Theory*. Tyler, Texas: Institute for Christian Economics, 1990.

_____. *Unconditional Surrender: God's Program for Victory*, rev. ed. Tyler, Texas: Institute for Christian Economics, 1987.

_____. *Dominion and Common Grace: The Biblical Basis of Progress*. Tyler, Texas: Institute for Christian Economics, 1987.

_____. *Conspiracy: A Biblical View*. Fort Worth, Texas: Dominion Press, 1986.

Rushdoony, Rousas J. *Christianity and the State*. Vallecito, Calif.: Ross House, 1986.

_____. *The Institutes of Biblical Law*. Phillipsburg, N.J.: Presbyterian and Reformed Publishing, 1973.

_____. *Thy Kingdom Come: Studies in Daniel and Revelation*. Phillipsburg, N.J.: Presbyterian and Reformed Publishing, 1970.

Rushdoony, Rousas J. and Ed Powell. *Tithing and Dominion*. Vallecito, Calif.: Ross House, 1979.

Sutton, Ray. *That You May Prosper: Dominion by Covenant*. Tyler, Texas: Institute for Christian Economics, 1987.

Seventeen. The New Age Movement

N ot since Gnosticism at the dawn of the Christian era has there arisen a philosophy as pervasive and threatening to orthodox Christianity as the New Age movement. Like Gnosticism, it comes from the East and is extremely eclectic, either mixing with or assimilating other disciplines or world views. Philosophy, science, politics, music, medicine, and theology (even Christian theology) have all been infected by New Age thinking. It would be difficult to find any area of life which has not been touched or redirected to some degree by the concepts of this movement.

Defining the New Age Movement
It is no small task to adequately describe the New Age movement. It has been compared to the elephant which the three blind men of Indostan attempted to describe:[1] one felt its leg and categorized it as tree-like; another, its trunk and argued that it was really like a hose; and the third grabbed its tail and insisted that it was a rope-like creature. What is true of parts of the movement is not necessarily true of it as a whole.

The New Age movement may best be described as a *metanetwork*, or network of networks. "Networks are composed of self-reliant and autonomous participants — people and organizations who simultaneously function as independent 'wholes' and as interdependent 'parts.' "[2] Consequently, one may find a whole series of concentric or intersecting networks (in other words, a *metanetwork*). While these networks may share certain common features, each one has its own unique thrust, and some may differ sharply in emphasis from others. What the New Age movement has to say, then, on a given topic will depend on which of its constituent networks is speaking. While such a feature may make the movement appear somewhat nebulous or in a state of confusion, it also increases its ability to speak to, or connect with, a

273

much more varied spectrum of interests. Hence, its utterly persuasive ability.

The term, "New Age," suggests that modern humanity stands at the threshold of a new era in history, one as momentous as the shift from the Middle Ages to the Industrial Revolution. "All around us there are signs that we are entering a new age of peace, where death does not exist and spiritual harmony rules. And we have the potential to make it happen."[3] Nor is the movement known only as New Age; it also works under aliases such as the Age of Aquarius, the One World Order, the New Consciousness, Cosmic Consciousness, and the New Globalism, to name a few.

The amazing advance of communications technology has been a key factor in the rise of New Age thinking. Douglas Groothuis notes:

> The computer chip is hailed by many as a vital evolutionary impetus. Mass media and modern communications serve to "globalize" and unify consciousness. Technological innovation accelerates the rate of evolution and provides a needed context for the New Consciousness. . . . The "electronic envelope" that now surrounds and permeates the earth is the fulfillment of Teilhard de Chardin's prophecy of the development of the "nousphere" (the expanding layer of consciousness on earth).[4]

Electronic bulletin boards, modern transfers, conference calls, desk-top publishing, and audio and video communications are all the stuff which foment and comprise networking.

The goal of the New Age movement as a whole is to create the new world view necessary to usher in the new age. It therefore advocates different means of altering human consciousness to enable people to come to enlightenment, or union with God. In the experience of such a union, the world will become an ideal place, true paradise.

Historical antecedents. While the New Age movement has made a popular appearance in the Western world only in the last few decades, its roots extend far back into Eastern mysticism. It may be said to be an updated, westernized version of Vedanta Hinduism with bits of Taoism, Zen, and ancient Babylonian and Egyptian religions thrown in for good measure.

The basic message of Hinduism being communicated by New Age people is pantheistic: "God is all and all is God." Many Eastern religions hold this view, that God is impersonal energy; any human being who knows how may connect with that energy to his own benefit, for we are all one with the universe to begin with.

Oriental mysticism was imported into North America in 1875 under the name, Theosophy, by Helena Blavatsky. The wife of a Polish general, Madame Blavatsky (as she preferred to be known) spent some time in the Orient after his death, learning from the gurus of the ancient Eastern religions. She then settled in the United States, where she founded the Theosophical Society. She claimed to receive spiritual direction from superhuman "masters" who held the keys to the secrets of universal wisdom and power.

Theosophists stressed the universal brotherhood of humanity and used the teaching of these "masters" to uncover unexplained laws of nature and the powers latent in humankind. They defined their creed as "the body of truths which forms the basis of all religions."

When Madame Blavatsky died, she was succeeded by Mrs. Annie Besant as president of the Theosophical Society. Mrs. Besant claimed that a protege, Krishna Murti, was the reincarnation of one of the great masters, Lord Maitreya.

Another Blavatsky disciple, Mrs. Alice Bailey, wrote some twenty books which she claimed were dictated by her "spiritual guide." One of these, *The Externalization of the Hierarchy*, predicted that 1975 would mark the commencement of a fifty-year period at the end of which the masters would begin to appear. Their appearance would culminate with the coming of the Christ.

Another important figure in the popularization of Eastern mysticism (and one highly regarded by New Age practitioners) was Edgar Cayce, a soothsayer and sage of the first half of the twentieth century. He was known as "the sleeping prophet" because he would enter a trance-state to receive answers to people's illnesses and problems.

Cayce was a staunch believer in reincarnation and considered himself to be the reincarnation of an Egyptian high priest who had helped to direct the building of the Great Pyramid. He also believed that Jesus was the reincarnation of Adam (of Old Testament fame) and that He had gained salvific knowledge through the Fall in Eden.

Pierre Teilhard de Chardin,[5] though a Jesuit priest and not a New Age proponent, formed a vital link between Roman Catholic and Eastern mystical thinking. He taught that all of creation is moving toward the "Omega Point," when all of the universe will be melded into the One to form a single cosmic consciousness.

The stormy sixties produced an ideal climate for the introduction and popularization of Oriental mysticism into the West. When the Beatles went to India to sit under the Maharishi Mahesh Yogi, the news was communicated all over Europe and North America, and myriad young people (and not a few older ones) hastened to follow suit. George Harrison's "My Sweet Lord" was bought and sung by thousands, who did not realize that it was an ode to the Lord Krishna, and not to the Lord Jesus Christ. David Carradine's portrayal of the Buddhist priest in the television series, "Kung Fu," popularized the martial arts and schools for their instruction sprang up everywhere. By the late 1960s, there were groups throughout the Western world practicing Buddhism, Shinto, Zen, Taoism, Transcendental Meditation, and Yoga. Groothuis declares that "what was open and irregular in the sixties—the 'love-ins,' 'happenings,' Eastern religious disciplines, occultism—became less ostentatious and quite well-integrated into the general culture by the mid-1970s and on into the 1980s."[6]

The disillusionment of the 1960s was, in part, a disillusionment with the failure of the Christian faith to deal adequately with the problems of the time. The result was a looking for answers in other belief systems and philosophies. Pluralism became the order of the day. Many formerly fringe heresies such as Unity School of Christianity, Christian Science, and Mormonism became respectable. Esoteric Eastern movements were welcomed and investigated as possible ways of life.

In the 1970s hippies were assimilated by the culture of the day. They did not drop their Eastern thought patterns, but blended them to fit in with society. Those who were well-educated often found professional positions (such as teaching in the universities) where they could spread their beliefs without opposition.

In the mid-1970s, Jerry Rubin, a hippie agitator of the previous decade, prophesied, "Perhaps the 1980s will see the activism of the sixties combined with the awareness of the seventies. In the next flurry of activity we will come from a deeper psychological and spiritual base."[7] That deeper base is what people call the New Age movement, and it poses a greater hazard to contemporary Christianity than any other movement this century.

Contemporary components. Erwin Lutzer and John DeVries list four basic components of the New Age philosophy.[8] They are:

(1) Pantheism
(2) Reincarnationism
(3) Relativism
(4) Esotericism

(1) As mentioned earlier, pantheism teaches that all is God and God is all. Another term which could serve equally well is monism. In realistic considerations there is no difference between entities. God, a rock, a tree, and a human being are only perceived to be different; they are, however, all a part of the same reality.

Pantheism is a variation of monism. It states that the whole universe is a partaker of the divine essence (God). Here, God is not a personal Being, but a force or energy.

Similarly, if all creation shares in the essence of God, then every human being *is* God! One New Age proponent puts the case well: "In dropping God, man recovers himself. It is time that God be put in His place, that is, *in man*, and no nonsense about it."[9] And Actress Shirley MacLaine declares, "We already know everything. The knowingness of our own divinity is the highest intelligence."[10]

(2) One of humankind's greatest fears is of death. New Age thinking caters to that fear with its teaching of reincarnationism. Hinduism and Buddhism teach that all of life is reincarnated. One life form may transmigrate in a future life into a completely different form. For example, a person may return as a toad or a housefly or a pig, and vice-versa. In what form one returns to this life depends upon one's *karma*. "By the law of karma it is understood that whatever a person does — good or bad — will return to him in an exact proportion good or bad."[11] Thus, a person who has done harm to others may be downgraded in his next life to a lower form (Hindus regard those humans who are less fortunate as lower forms!) until such time as the bad karma has been paid off.

The New Age thinkers have tended to overlook these more negative aspects of reincarnation. They teach that it will give every human being the opportunity for a further, richer self-development—a natural conclusion in evolutionary thinking. The next life provides the opportunity to avoid the mistakes of the last one and to progress towards the ultimate goal of union with the One.

(3) Relativism is foundational in New Age philosophy. There are no absolutes either in truth or morality. What is true or right for one person is not necessarily so for another. Miller notes that "it is the height of presumption to think that one knows the key truth for all people. . . . it is the apex of love to 'allow' others to have their own 'truth.' "[12]

Morally, situation ethics rules New Age thinking. What is right is what is best for me. Nothing is right or wrong in and of itself. It may hurt you, but if it pleases me or feels good to me, then it is right for me.

(4) Like the Gnostics of old, New Age people believe that they have received a special knowledge or guidance which has been hidden from the ordinary person. "This philosophy, known as esotericism, lies at the heart of the New Age Movement. We are told that there is a 'transformation of consciousness' that initiates us into true spirituality."[13]

New Age philosophers downgrade theology (because the doctrinal beliefs of the major world religions are irreconcilable) in favor of religious experience. By experience they mean the feeling of being one with Ultimate Reality, with the One. Some have termed this process an "altered state of consciousness." It does not mean "turning off" reality, but rather transcending it. Through this mystical experience, it is claimed, one gains absolute certainty about procedures and processes in any area involving reasoning, be it philosophical, religious, or scientific.[14]

The last decade, as a result of New Age emphasis on esoteric experience, has witnessed many attempts to wed mystical modes of thought to various disciplines of science. Quantum physics is one such area. The University of California at Berkeley took the lead; one of its professors, Fritjof Capra, published *The Tao of Physics* which, while heavily criticized, was nonetheless well-received by his colleagues in the field.

Parapsychology is another area which has gained considerable ground in the last several years. In the mid-1970s, the University of California at Berkeley began a doctoral program in the area and, in 1979, several respected physicists published "The Icelandic Papers," which detailed reports of physical experiments with psychics.[15]

New Agers have been very keen in attempting to isolate varying sources of natural energy and harnessing it for other purposes. In this pursuit they have resorted more to ancient techniques rather than modern scientific ones. Pyramids and crystals are favorite objects of experiment. "No longer built of stone, modern-day pyramids are constructed from wire, copper tubing, wood, and cardboard. If we can believe the claims, pyramid shapes help tomatoes grow bigger, razor blades stay sharper and spiritual seekers rise higher."[16] Amazing anecdotes are set forth by New Age practitioners of relief from stress and new, higher levels of energy as a result of sitting in or beneath pyramids. When used in conjunction with crystals, the effects are greatly heightened.[17] Many New Age proponents regard crystals (quartz is the stone of choice) as the most therapeutic natural healing device available. These stones are supposed to exude or channel cosmic energy; they are used by natural healers to heal all manner of maladies; they are worn as jewelry by people to keep healthy; they are even used in farming to provide better and healthier crop yields. They are said to be especially useful when accompanied by meditation.

Nowhere has New Age influence been more evident than in the development of holistic medicine. Western physicians have traditionally seen human beings as physical machines, completely ignoring their spiritual aspect. Holistic medicine views the body in its interrelated totality and seeks to treat the whole person — spirit, mind, and body — not just one part of it.

While there is nothing wrong with a holistic approach per se to medicine (certainly, Christians should adopt such a view!), much treatment follows New Age directions, such as the use of transcendental meditation to quiet the mind and allow it to be reoriented toward the emitting of healing power, or the use of positive mental imaging (visualization) to stimulate healing through the untapped power of the mind. Psychic diagnosis and healing are also popular holistic techniques and are undoubtedly connected to New Age concepts.

Some primary proponents. Every area of life has prominent members of the New Age connection. No "who's who" listing would be lacking those who are active in promoting some aspect of the New Age cause. The list would be far too long to include here, but a partial listing of the best-known in some of the more important fields is given for information purposes.

In the spiritual realm, one may find representatives from many different religious groups. These include Peter and Eileen Caddy, founders of the Findhorn Community, a renowned New Age learning center in northern Scotland; Benjamin Creme, founder of the Tara Center and author of many New Age books; Matthew Fox, a Catholic theologian and developer of "creation spirituality";[18] and Terry Cole-Whittaker, a California televangelist turned New Age author.

Numerous show business personalities are involved in New Age practices, such as Dennis Weaver, Sharon Gless, and the late Jim Henson. The one person who has served to popularize New Age ideas more than anyone else is Shirley MacLaine, whose books on channeling, reincarnation, and other spiritual practices have been best sellers. Her book and television mini-series, *Out on a Limb*, introduced thousands of people to New Age metaphysics.

Science has its share of New Age participants, as well. One of the best-known is Dr. Elizabeth Kubler-Ross, the noted expert on death and dying. Others are former Harvard professor of psychology, Richard Alpert; Thomas Kuhn, whose work on how paradigm shifts occur in the scientific realm, *The Structure of Science*, has been well-received by New Age practitioners; and biologist Jonas Salk.

Other well-known figures who support New Age concepts include Jesuit theologian Thomas Berry, mythology researcher Joseph Campbell, retired United Nations assistant secretary Robert Muller, cultural historian Theodore Roszak, and futurist Alvin Toffler.

New Age Doctrines

Because the New Age movement is a "network of networks," its practitioners hold a variety of beliefs and many different emphases according to the particular group to which they belong. There are, however, certain theological views common to most of them, and it is these which we shall delineate.

Revelation. Because of its eclectic nature, the New Age movement rejects any single source as the only authoritative supernatural revelation. Wisdom of any kind—ancient or modern—is revered for what it can teach about the mysteries of the ages. Lola Davis, a New Age mentor, writes:

> Among these are the Dead Sea scrolls, the vast treasures of religious writings found in the Potola in Tibet; Christian writings deleted from the Bible during the fourth century; writings of Teilhard de Chardin; and previously carefully guarded knowledge of the Ancient Wisdom, including the writings of the Tibetan in the Alice Bailey books; writings of the mystics from various religions; the materials offered by the Rosicrucians; and many books on Buddhism and Hindu philosophies and practices. . . .[19]

These, of course, are all in addition to the sacred books of the major world religions (e.g., the Bible, Koran, Bhagavad Gita).

The New Age is quite permissive in regard to regulatory sources. Followers may listen to whatever voices they wish, provided they do not hold their source to be unique, the only source of authority (such as most Christians proclaim the Scriptures to be). Nor is revelation of a necessity written or historical. There are many current sources of revelation demonstrating themselves.

Probably the most popular form of superhuman revelation is channeling. New Age psychologist Jon Klimo describes channeling as "an *identity* (the source), apparently foreign to that of the channel, exercising *control* over the perceptual, motor, cognitive, or self-reflective capacities of that person once he or she has relinquished . . . control or sense of self-identity."[20] Those who believe in channeling accept it even more uncritically as "gospel" than Christians do the Bible; the former believe the spirit absolutely.

What is it that these spirits want to teach human beings in the present age? Maxine Hondema, a channeler from Grand Rapids, Michigan, and a leader of the (New Age) Spiritual Frontiers Fellowship, tells us that "they try to explain to us both what Cosmic Law is (or God's law if you prefer that term) and how if we try to understand and use that knowledge it will eliminate most of the difficulties that beset us. . . ."[21] These "spirit guides" evidently perform much the same sort of task as Christians claim for the Holy Spirit's guidance, except that they would claim a greater and more direct personal preciseness for the individual who is being guided (often in the material realm).

Many of these channelers—for example, J.Z. Knight who channels for "Ramtha," an ancient giant warrior; Jack Pursel, channel for "Lazaris," a multi-dimensional non-physical being; and Kevin Ryerson, who acts as a medium for several disembodied spirits between incarnations—advise wealthy and famous people on their future activities and make thousands of dollars per month for their spiritual direction. Some have waiting lists of two years and more.

Spirit guides are not really new to the occultic scene. Socrates, Theresa of Avila, Joan of Arc, Adolf Hitler, and Emmanuel Swedenborg were all guided by spirit voices. The difference is that present day spirit guides come through a third party, rather than directly to the individual being guided.

Another source of revelation for New Age practitioners is through the revival of the ancient practice of shamanism. In primitive times a shaman was the "medicine man," soothsayer, or seer of the tribal unit. While that role is still in vogue today, it has been expanded. ". . . [I]t means a world healer, . . . the being that's there when it's time. . . . they bring prayer to the people and teach them to sing in their own voice and use their own drum. . . ."[22] The shaman often undergoes an altered state of consciousness in which he or she comes into contact with a spirit or animal guide who reveals special knowledge for difficult situations. Modern shamans, like channelers, have a tendency to engage in very lucrative "private practice."

Astrology is another very old, but current, source of divine revelation. The most famous user of astrological revelation in recent times is undoubtedly Nancy Reagan, who is alleged to have relied on prophetess-astrologer Jeanne Dixon while her husband was governor of California. During the Reagan White-House era, it is said that she relied on a San Francisco clairvoyant named Joan Quigley for psychic direction, and that these forecasts were used on occasion to time foreign policy actions in the United States.[23]

The doctrine of God. We have already noted that New Age disciples are pantheistic in their concept of God. The late Jane Roberts of

Elmira, New York was a channel for an entity named Seth, who described God as "not one individual, but an . . . absolute, ever-expanding, instantaneous psychic gestalt, . . . so secure in its existence that it can constantly break itself down and rebuild itself."[24] In this notion, God is at best an "it," impersonal energy. George Lucas, producer of the *Star Wars* films, popularized this view of God as "the Force." The expression, "May the Force be with you," became a favorite expression of many young people in the early 1980s. The Force had a good side and an evil side, and every human being could decide which side he would seek.

Some New Age followers, disillusioned with Western Christianity, have abandoned God altogether in favor of paganism. By "pagan" is meant "the pre-Christian nature religions of the West . . . in new forms."[25]

Of these, the most adored is the cult of the *Goddess*. Espoused particularly by feminists who find Christianity too patriarchal and male-dominated, the Goddess is a reconceptualizing of the One, or the All, from a female perspective. Modern New Age feminists express their spiritual ideals in the symbols of the ancient pagan goddesses—Diana, Hecate, Isis, and so on. These ancient goddesses are symbols of their liberation from spiritual subjugation to men and a sign of their new-found power in all realms of life. Wicca (witchcraft) is one form of devotion to the Goddess; its devotees claim to be "white witches," concerned only with the betterment of creation.

Some have incorporated the Goddess into the Trinity. She displaces the Holy Spirit, giving a supernatural model for the family—Father, Mother, and Son. Benjamin Creme, a disciple of Alice Bailey, has followed ancient Gnostic teaching, positing Intelligence and Force as male and female emanations of the One, who gives birth to a child, Love. "And thus the Triune God stands forth, whom men call Father—Mother—Child."[26]

The doctrine of Christ. New Age followers claim to have a very high regard for "the Christ" (it is rare for a New Age practitioner to use the noun "Christ" without the preceding direct article). But the New Age Christ is not synonymous with the New Testament's Jesus of Nazareth. Judith Skutch, president of the Foundation for Inner Peace, describes the difference: "Jesus was an historical person, but the Christ is an eternal transpersonal condition."[27] Once again, Gnosticism is a convenient vehicle for christianizing pantheism. Like the New Age movement, Gnosticism saw the major human problem not as sin, but as ignorance. For Gnostics — and now, for New Agers — the Christ revealed wisdom which helped His followers to see that they could become one with the One just as He is: "He who will drink from my mouth will become like me. I myself shall become he. . . ."[28]

Jesus was a prime example of one human being who was able to achieve "Christ consciousness," that divine principle which lies dormant within every human being. In a book entitled *The Aquarian Gospel of Jesus Christ*, supposedly the revelations of a spirit-guide named "Levi," Ohio channeler Eva Dowling chronicles some 170 chapters of the life of Christ who, according to the spirit, traveled to India to sit at the feet of Hindu gurus and learn about reincarnation (among other things).[29] Levi states that "Edward was not always king, and Lincoln was not always president, and Jesus was not always Christ. Jesus won his Christship by a strenuous life."[30] Now, He is numbered among the spiritual Masters who operate on the timeless, higher plane. But what He has attained is open to, and possible for, every other person: "What I have done, all men can do, and what I am, all men shall be."[31]

Man, sin, and salvation. Redemption is a "given" in New Age philosophy because of its pantheistic foundation. Pantheism teaches that God is all and all is God; human beings, therefore, are God too.

Because all human beings share in the divine nature, all are in command of their own destiny. What happens to people happens because they will it. Werner Erhard, founder of *est*, writes: "You're God in your universe. You caused it. You pretended not to cause it so you could play in it."[32] Thus, human beings have it within their grasp to save themselves if they will.

New Age perceptions of sin and salvation follow Eastern mystical philosophies but, as always, with a westernizing touch to make it palatable to our society. Sin is a matter of ignorance more than of transgression and — because of karma — will bring its own punishment.

New Agers deny that humanity ever fell. What Christians call the Fall was really a separation of the unity called God into matter and mind. "Salvation means that these two aspects of God become united once more."[33] But humanity will save God (and not vice versa) by being the means of reuniting these separated aspects!

Because sin stems from a lack of knowledge and brings its own reward, it follows that God does not punish the wicked; such punishment would be redundant. Similarly, the idea of having Someone atone for another's sin is unnecessary. The crucifixion is seen by New Age people as a myth which symbolizes the arrival of the cosmic Christ on a higher spiritual plane where He can speed the evolutionary process of ultimate union with the One.[34]

Salvation is achieved through a series of physical reincarnations culminating in the experience of enlightenment. It is a very impersonal affair: a person realizes at long last his true identity or self, only to lose it by being absorbed into the One.

The person of Satan. The New Age movement has rehabilitated Satan. Instead of the Accuser of Scripture who seeks to lead people astray, he has become Lucifer, a god on a par with the Christ, who "works within each of us to bring us to wholeness as we move into the New Age."[35] Lucifer is seen as a "Christ spirit" who will initiate human beings into spiritual progress. In his book, *The Ultimate Frontier*, Eklal Kueshna declares that "Lucifer is the head of a secret Brotherhood of Spirits, the highest order to which man can elevate himself."[36]

New Age disciples believe that Lucifer acted in humanity's best interests by tempting Eve. Because of the Fall, humankind was able to begin the evolutionary path to wisdom and godhood. The present-day Church of the Process, a New Age-Satanic cult in North America and Europe, teaches that Lucifer is a convivial, peace-loving god, whereas Jehovah is a legalistic, demanding killjoy. It claims that the end of the present millennium will see a reconciliation between Jehovah and Lucifer.

The Parousia. Because sin is essentially nonexistent, and karma brings reward and punishment according to one's prior life, there is little place in New Age thinking for judgment and, consequently, really no place for a coming of Christ.

Just as the crucifixion is rejected in favor of mythological symbolism, so the Parousia is seen in symbolic terms as that event in which human beings gain access to the spiritual secrets of the universe. Emmett Fox, a liberal theologian turned New Age writer, maintains that: "In the history of all races the Cosmic Christ has incarnated in man—Buddha, Moses, Elijah. . . . However, in his New Age, the Cosmic Christ will come into millions of men and women who are ready to receive it. This will be the Second Coming of Christ for them."[37]

New Age thinkers have taken the final judgment and made it into an evaluative and reconciling process. "The Last Judgment might be called a process of right evaluation. It simply means that everyone will finally come to understand what is worthy and what is not."[38]

For most New Age practitioners the Messiah who will inaugurate the age to come is not Jesus of Nazareth, called the Christ, but the Lord Maitreya, revealed by the spirit-guide known as "the Tibetan" through Alice Bailey. He has been strongly promoted in American media by Benjamin Creme who, in 1986, divulged that for some millennia Maitreya had inhabited a small village in the Himalaya mountains; on July 8, 1977, however, he descended from the mount in a self-created body and came to live in the slums of London's east end. (Creme sees himself as playing John the Baptist to Maitreya's Christ.) When Maitreya makes known his messiahship the world will enter into a new era of economic, social, and political transformation.[39]

An Evaluation of New Age Theology

The foregoing overview of New Age theology demonstrates that none of it, other than in terminology, resembles orthodox Christian theology in any way. Most of the theology of that movement is either Eastern mysticism or ancient Gnostic heresy in Western garb.

The Person of God. The New Age God of pantheism even dressed up for Western consumption is only a pale imitation of the God and Father of our Lord Jesus Christ. The former is an impersonal energy field undifferentiated from the created order. The latter is an all-powerful, all-knowing, all-loving Person who is Creator of all, but who transcends His creation.

There is one God who manifests Himself in a three-fold fashion as Father, Son, and Holy Spirit. There are no Goddesses and there is no "Mother" in the Christian Trinity.

Revelation. We know about God and His nature and work through His Son, Jesus Christ, and through His Word, the Bible. The Bible is both the record of God's revelation in Christ and special revelation from God to us. Outside of what the Bible records, there is no special revelation of and from God in human possession. All truth must conform to the Scriptures or it is a lie. New Age claims that authoritative revelation may be gleaned from other sources— whether they be from other world religious writings, from channels of ancient spiritual "masters," or from modern visionaries— must be categorized as false.

The Person of Jesus. The New Age movement rejects Christianity's claim that Jesus Christ is the unique Son of God (the Greek *monogenes* in John 3:16 means "the only one of the same kind" as God), sacrificed by the Father to redeem humankind from sin. Nor will it accept that "there is no other name under heaven given to men by which we must be saved" (Acts 4:12). For them, there are many other names far greater than His which will serve to lead human beings to redemption.

The atonement of Christ has been reinterpreted by New Age teachers. It does not refer to God's attempt in Christ to reconcile humans to Himself, but rather to a final reconciliation of all creation in the One.

Sin and salvation. The New Age movement teaches that humankind is already divine in nature. There is no sin from willful transgression, only from a lack of knowledge. In contrast, the Bible teaches that human beings are creatures of God, mortal in their nature, and fallen by willful and disobedient choice. Sin is the result of prideful rebellion against God's will.

The New Age teaches that human transformation is a matter of knowledgeable choice. Humans have the ability to save themselves. The Bible, on the other hand, teaches that humankind can do nothing to save themselves; it is beyond their spiritual capacity.

Only God has the power to save and He has done so in Christ. Human beings may be saved only as they trust Christ as personal Savior and Lord and, in faith, follow Him.

The person of Lucifer. New Agers put Satan (Lucifer) on a par with Jesus. For many of them, he is merely another agent or avenue of "Christ consciousness." He is really a god of light and goodness who tempted Eve for her own future well-being. Orthodox Christianity, however, sees Lucifer as the original rebel who, in his pride, tried to usurp God's place (Isa. 14:12ff), and was cast out of heaven. He is now the Accuser of God's people and desires their rejection of God and destruction.

Last things. The New Age movement teaches that all human beings, after numerous physical reincarnations, will be saved by becoming one with Ultimate Reality, the One. That is the destiny of the universe. There is no other course. Any punishment for evil or reward for goodness will occur in one's subsequent reincarnation, prior to absorption into the One.

The Bible, on the other hand, teaches that — at the close of the age — Christ will return to claim His people and to punish the evil (those who have rejected Him). The righteous will enter eternal blessing with Him in heaven; the unrighteous will be cast into the eternal punishment prepared for Satan and his demons (Matt. 25:31ff).

Some Conclusions on the New Age Movement

Because New Age teachers are prone to use Christian terminology which they have loaded down with different meanings from that of Christian orthodoxy, some Christians and many who are merely "Christianized" will be led astray. New Age emphases in politics, medicine, education, ecology, and other fields offer attractive techniques for improving people's life-styles which may open the door to New Age religion. Without being aware of the dangers, Christians may find themselves drawn in.

Some researchers have suggested that some Christian churches and leaders have become a party to New Age techniques.[40] Mysticism, visualization, and positive mental imaging are common practices in some Christian groups. While the church does not need a new series of witch-hunts for those who have been tainted by New Age teachings, there is a tremendous necessity for the spiritual gift of the discernment of spirits in our churches.

The New Age stress on an experiential religion as opposed to an objective one, and to feeling over against rationality, will find a ready ear in the modern generation. Contemporary sociological studies demonstrate that the "twenty-plus" generation, as it is often called, is affective rather than cognitive in style. It responds much more deeply to emotion and feelings than to reasoned objectivity.

As with any other heresy, Christians can best counteract the philosophy of the New Age movement by knowing what the Bible teaches, what Christian orthodoxy believes, and how these differ from New Age teaching. Prayerful probing of the New Age philosophy in light of sound biblical teaching is recommended.

A New Age conspiracy? Many conservative writers have taken seriously the title of consciousness researcher Marilyn Ferguson's popular 1980 book, *The Aquarian Conspiracy*. They see in the New Age movement an organized effort to oust Christianity as the foundation of modern Western culture and replace it with the New Age philosophy.[41]

That members of the movement are heavily involved in seeking political and religious unity may help to emphasize such a notion. Mark Satin, in his book on *New Age Politics*, declares that "this unity is on the point of being politically expressed in a world government that will unite nations and regions in transactions beyond their individual capacity."[42] Walter Martin insists that "the new ideological base of the New Age political agenda is *a unity of all religions* . . . teaching the same core truth: mankind is divine."[43]

Unquestionably, the New Age movement has pervaded every area of life endeavor. Some New Age groups, such as Greenpeace and the "Green Party" (of several nations) are politically active, and there are those within most political groups quietly working to promote and achieve the movement's general aims. To what degree this movement constitutes an organized conspiracy, however, is questionable.

At the same time, that society is gradually being directed toward New Age thinking is unquestionable. There are physicians who (unknowingly) employ New Age techniques, believing that they will be of genuine help to their patients. There are school teachers who use New Age methods out of a desire to create an optimum learning climate for their classes. There are counselors who prescribe New Age visualization and meditation procedures whose goal is the well-being of their clients. All of these promote New Age ideas and advance the New Age cause without being aware of so doing.

But whether ignorantly or deliberately, the New Age cause is advanced. It now poses a major threat to the progress of the Gospel as proclaimed by orthodox Christianity. All believers would do well to be deeply informed in the methods and beliefs of this *metanetwork* and its multitude of subsystems, and the degree to which it has invaded all parts of our society.

For Further Reading

(Books marked with an asterisk * are critical of the New Age movement.)

Bailey, Alice. *The Externalization of the Hierarchy*. New York: Lucis Publishing, 1957.

_____. *The Reappearance of the Christ*. New York: Lucis Publishing, 1948.

Creme, Benjamin. *The Reappearance of the Christ and the Masters of Wisdom*. North Hollywood, Calif.: Tara Center, 1980.

Ferguson, Marilyn. *The Aquarian Conspiracy*. Los Angeles: J.P. Tarcher, 1980.

*Groothuis, Douglas R. *Unmasking the New Age*. Downers Grove, Ill.: InterVarsity Press, 1986.

*Hunt, Dave, and T.A. McMahon. *The Seduction of Christianity*. Eugene, Ore.: Harvest House, 1985.

Levi. *The Aquarian Gospel of Jesus the Christ*. Santa Monica, Calif.: De Vorss, 1907.

*Lutzer, Erwin W. and John F. DeVries. *Satan's Evangelistic Strategy for This New Age*. Wheaton, Ill.: Victor Books, 1989.

*Martin, Walter. *The New Age Cult*. Minneapolis: Bethany House, 1989.

*Miller, Elliot. *A Crash Course on the New Age*. Grand Rapids: Baker Book House, 1989.

Roberts, Jane. *The Seth Material*. Englewood Cliffs, N.J.: Prentice-Hall, 1970.

Spangler, David. *Reflections on the Christ*, 3rd ed. Moray, United Kingdom: Findhorn Publications, 1981.

*Tucker, Ruth. *Another Gospel: Alternative Religions and the New Age Movement*. Grand Rapids: Zondervan Publishing House, 1989.

Eighteen. Creation Spirituality

The latest theology to make its appearance on the North American scene is creation spirituality. An attempt to call the church back to its radical and mystical roots, it has begun to exert a strong influence on clinical pastoral education and care both in Canada and the United States.

Matthew Fox

The founder and prime proponent of creation spirituality (also known as creation-centered spirituality in its earlier days) is a Dominican priest named Matthew Fox. Fox became a Dominican in 1960 after graduating from college and was ordained in 1967. That same year, as a result of Thomas Merton's influence, he entered the doctoral program at the Institut Catholique de Paris, graduating with a degree in the history and theology of spirituality.

Fox's early goal was to make spirituality and theology palatable to the public at large. He became known through the publication of several books with somewhat quixotic titles: *On Becoming a Musical, Mystical Bear: Spirituality American Style* (1972); *Whee! We, Wee All the Way Home: A Guide to a Sensual Prophetic Spirituality* (1976); and *A Spirituality Named Compassion* (1979). Other major works included *Original Blessing: A Primer in Creation Spirituality* (1983); *The Coming of the Cosmic Christ* (1988); and *Creation Spirituality* (1991).

In 1977, Fox established the Institute of Culture and Creation Spirituality on the campus of Holy Names College in Oakland, California (*Original Blessing* sets out the principles on which the Institute's program is based). Students are mostly Roman Catholic, although many denominations are represented. He also established a bimonthly magazine, *Creation*, which represents the Institute's views.

Fox has been greatly influenced by the thought of medieval Christian mystics. Two of the most formative for him have been

Hildegard of Bingen and Meister Eckhart. (He also wrote *Break-through: Meister Eckhart's Creation Spirituality in New Translation* in 1980 and *Illumination of Hildegard of Bingen* in 1985.) It is to them and to some of the earlier, mystically inclined church fa-thers—along with a few moderns like Einstein and Teilhard de Chardin—that Fox attributes his creation spirituality theology.

The church investigates. In July of 1984 the Vatican Congregation for the Doctrine of the Faith (successor to the defunct Holy Office of the Inquisition) raised questions as to the orthodoxy of Fox's work. A commission of three theologians from the Dominican order examined his writings and the following May gave a report to Joseph Cardinal Ratzinger (head of the Congregation), declaring that "there should be no condemnation of Father Fox's work."[1]

When Fox invited Starhawk, a member of Wicca (therefore a witch) to join the Institute's faculty, concerns were raised once more. In December of 1985 Cardinal Ratzinger questioned the conclusions of the Dominican report and demanded public condem-nation of "Father Fox's seeming espousal of witchcraft and the harm which his published books and teaching activities have al-ready brought to the faithful."[2] He further accused Fox of denying the validity of infant baptism and objected to his calling God "Mother" and "child."

Despite a spirited defense of Fox by the Provincial of his order, Cardinal Ratzinger in September of 1987 notified the Dominican Master General that his own office would do an investigation and, a year later, he insisted that the Master General take steps to terminate Fox's position as director of the Institute along with his public appearances and further writings.

Fox agreed to the ban—although he and hundreds of others protested the action—and from December 15, 1988 to August 1989 he was silent, sure that "silencing me will not destroy Creation Spirituality any more than silencing Leonardo Boff destroyed Lib-eration Theology."[3] And it has not. The publicity served only to increase Fox's popularity and spread his work more widely.

Mysticism Defined

Fox sees mysticism as that type of religious procedure which centers on a personal experience of the divine. All religions possess mystical aspects; "believers retain vital belief in a transcendent reality only as long as they communicate with that reality by direct experience."[4] Since every human being has the potentiality for religious experience, every person possesses mystical possibilities.

Mysticism, Fox tells us, has two essential bases which correspond to the two English renditions of the Greek *mystikos*: to "shut one's senses" and to "enter the mysteries." These two meanings are related. One cannot enter the mysteries without closing down one's senses in order to cleanse and restore them.[5]

Fox's foci are the "primal sacraments" of the universe itself (earth, fire, wind, water). He hopes to create a sacramental liturgy which experiences both God and the primal creation at once. Hence, the term "creation spirituality."

Creation Spirituality Defined

Creation spirituality, says Fox, is both a tradition and a movement. Its context is to be found in a properly defined cosmology (indeed, Fox often seems to use creation spirituality and cosmology almost synonymously). A living cosmology is constituted by "the holy trinity of science (knowledge of creation), mysticism (experiential union with creation and its unnameable mysteries), and art (expression of our awe at creation). . . ."[6] These three would all seem to be components of creation spirituality.

The tradition. Fox claims that creation spirituality is nothing new, except for twentieth-century Westerners. It is an ancient tradition, "for it is the basic spiritual knowledge of Native Americans [and] . . . the basic spiritual heritage of native peoples everywhere."[7] All of these peoples have centered their existence on cosmology.

Creation spirituality is also, he declares, the most ancient tradition in Judaism and in Scripture. "The Yahwist (or J) source in the Hebrew Bible is the oldest tradition in the Bible, and its theology is creation-centered theology."[8] Because the Old Testament is the Scripture Jesus knew so well, the creation spirituality tradition has been carried on in the New Testament:

> . . . from the parables of Jesus so steeped in creation imagery
> and experience to the preaching of Jesus about the "king-

dom" of God—a phrase that biblical scholar Krister Stendahl says deserves to be translated as "creation"; from hymns to the Cosmic Christ... which Paul invokes in his letters, to the birth narratives in the Gospels of Matthew and Luke.[9]

The tradition is carried on by the Greek fathers, such as Basil of Caesarea and Gregory Nazianzus. But it reaches a high point with the mystic prophets, such as Hildegard of Bingen, Francis of Assisi, and Thomas Aquinas. Further masters of this spiritual movement, claims Fox, were Mechtild of Magdeburg, Meister Eckhart, Julian of Norwich, and Nicholas of Cusa. With the condemnation of Eckhart, however, in 1329, mystical spirituality came under attack and even a determined effort by the sixteenth-century reformers to revive it met with only limited success. But with the renewal of interest by science in the spiritual, our days are witnessing a revival of interest in creation spirituality which serves as a bridge between the two.[10]

The movement. Creation spirituality is not only a tradition; it is a movement as well. Fox declares that those people who discover creation spirituality "want the spirit that liberates their souls to be put to good use in liberating others."[11] Thus, they promote its concepts in the institutions, work places, and communities to which they relate:

> As a movement, creation spirituality becomes an amazing gathering place, a kind of watering hole for persons whose possession has been touched by the issues of our day—deep ecologists, ecumenists, artists, native peoples, justice activists, male liberationists, gay and lesbian peoples, animal liberationists, scientists seeking to reconnect science and wisdom, people of prophetic faith traditions—all these groups find in the creation spirituality movement a common language and a common ground on which to stand.[12]

Four Paths to Creation Spirituality

Fox has determined four paths which lead to creation spirituality. They delineate those things of ultimate importance in life. They are not ladderlike in their course, but spiral, interwoven and interconnected with each other.

The first path. Path One may be termed the *via positiva*. This is a joyous and friendly attitude toward Mother Nature. It is demonstrated in the stimulation of sensuality — eating and drinking, dancing and singing, affirming creation through the erotic and playful. "The experience of ecstasy is the experience of God."[13]

Fox cites as a commandment for the first path, "Thou shalt fall in love at least three times a day."[14] This kind of falling in love has little to do with the Western perception of seeking a mate. It may be falling in love with a star, or a flower, or a bird. "Or a homosexual if one is proud of being heterosexual. Or a black, if one is white, and vice versa."[15] This path to creation spirituality has to do with a love for creation and its components.

The second path. Path Two may be called the *via negativa*. On this path we discover the creation's mystery and darkness, in its silence and emptiness, in its pain and suffering. Fox quotes Meister Eckhart to the effect that "God is superessential darkness."[16] As we allow ourselves to sink into that darkness and silence, we shall find Him.

Fox's second command, relating to the *via negativa*, is: "Thou shalt dare the dark."[17] In so doing, one allows the darkness and nothingness to work its mystery, and learns from pain badly needed lessons.

A part of this path is what the mystics call "the dark night of the soul." It is in the pain and solitude of this darkness that our hearts are broken and so opened to become channels of compassion.

The third path. Path Three is known as the *via creativa*. In this path we come to the realization that we are cocreators with God, ". . . [W]e trust our images enough to birth them and ride them into existence."[18] Fox claims that all of creation spirituality finds its apex in this path. The first two lead into it ("for we create only what we have beheld of light and darkness"), and the fourth flows from it, "since we are putting our imaginations and creativity at the service of compassion."[19]

To walk along this third path it is necessary to develop more fully the right-brain functions, or the artistic side, of the individual. This, Father Fox tells us, is "that dimension of the child, of play, of imagination, of creativity and art that is intrinsic to the creation tradition of Scripture...."[20]

Creativity, however, is more than the development of the aesthetic (though it certainly includes it). It is exposing and naming the demons inside of us—embracing the shadow side of our natures as well as our greatest visions. Fox commands "art-as-meditation" as a foundational form of prayer in the practice of creation spirituality.[21]

The fourth path. Path Four is called the *via transformativa*. This pathway is based in a doctrine of realized eschatology which calls for the creation of a new world order in which peace and justice rule supreme. Fox challenges people following this path "to be instruments for this new age, this new creation."[22] Otherwise, "humanity will exterminate itself and put an end to twenty billion years of providential art and history."[23]

Fox has a commandment for those disciples who follow this way of transformation: "Be you compassionate as your Creator in heaven is compassionate."[24] It is his rendering of Matthew 5:48 which, he declares, summarizes Jesus' teaching in the Sermon on the Mount. He prefers replacing the KJV rendition of "perfect" with "compassionate," for the latter more clearly expresses the true sense of what Jesus was saying in Hebrew, namely, "mature" or "ripe."

To follow the *via transformativa* is to be prophetic. The prophet is one who "interferes" with injustice, suffering, and neglect:

> It is important to recall that justice is a cosmic category as well as a human one. All creation is ruled by justice or homeostasis, the quest for equilibrium that is intrinsic to all atoms, galaxies, the earth, the whole history of the universe. The human call to compassion and justice making...is a matter of the human species joining the dance of all creation in the quest for balance.[25]

Theological Emphases of Creation Spirituality

Some theologians have labeled Matthew Fox as a New Age practitioner;[26] others depict him as a dedicated Christian who is attempting to recover the long-lost tradition of radical Christian mysticism.[27] An examination of the theological emphases of his movement may indicate which is true.

Doctrine of God. Fox rejects a label of pantheism in favor of panentheism. The former claims that God is everything and everything is God; the latter, that God is in everything and everything is in God. Panentheism leaves some room for God to be greater than His creation: "The second is not only not heretical; it's constantly referred to in the Scriptures. For example, Jesus' image of the vine; God is in us and we are in God. Or Paul saying that God is the one in whom we live, move, and have our being. So panentheism is certainly scriptural."[28]

Fox posits Jesus as the supreme model of panentheism in Scripture. Matthew's stress in his Gospel on Jesus as Emmanuel (Matt. 1:22) is an accent on the immanence of deity within His person and subsequently in the created order through His presence.[29]

Fox rejects the classical Christian view which, he declares, posits a "phallic" location of a "peeping-tom" God who stands apart from and above humanity.[30] Rather, God is within us, located in the unconscious mind.

Is Matthew Fox a trinitarian? When asked if he believed in Jesus Christ as Lord and Savior, he replied, "I am a trinitarian Christian."[31] But he then qualified his statement by noting that "those who think that Christianity is exclusively about Jesus are in fact heretics. They deny the trinitarian divinity."[32]

Claiming to represent Martin Luther's trinitarian theology, Fox sees "the Creator, parent God; Jesus the Liberator; the Holy Spirit who sanctifies."[33] The Creator God illuminates the cosmos in perpetual creativity. He is divine Mind, divine Heart, and divine Artist. Because humanity is the *imago Dei*, they too are imagining, loving, suffering, and creating.

Jesus, as God in human form, has proclaimed Himself to be the Liberator of humanity (see Luke 4:18ff). In turn, He liberates us, calling us to be God's sons and daughters. The Beatitudes are given by Him to allow us to become all that we can be.

The Holy Spirit is for Fox the essentially feminine part of the Trinity: "the spirit who is 'evergreen' (Hildegard) and who is the 'transformer' (Eckhart) is essentially a feminine spirit."[34] He sees the Holy Spirit in Old Testament terms, and refers to the Spirit's description as "Mother Sophia" from Wisdom literature texts, "which come from North Africa where a Mother Goddess was worshiped before the Israelite people were formed."[35]

The Person and work of Jesus. What role does Jesus Christ play in Fox's creation spirituality? He serves as our prototype for the new creation. He is a model for how we renew the image of God which we are:

> Jesus invites people to renew a tarnished, guilt-ridden, lacking-in-confidence image of God. Namely, ourselves. All persons are "the image and glory of God" (1 Cor. 11:7-8; cf. Gen. 1:27-28), but Jesus comes to remind us of what this means, to reawaken us to our beauty (*doxa*) and our responsibility for beauty. . . . An image of God does what God does, which is to birth beauty in all its forms.[36]

Jesus is also "a way" to God, but certainly not "the only way." Fox states that:

> I believe God is not bound by any one way but that God has sent Jesus as a very special way precisely to make the way easier and more accessible for all people. I think Jesus does this first by teaching us but also by being the way. . . . And he's the way in so far as his death on the cross liberates us along with his resurrection.[37]

The Jesus of Matthew Fox is not so much a literal, historical person as He is a principle of divine potentiality which may be found in every living creature. This principle he refers to as "the Cosmic Christ." It is in this Christ, he declares, that one becomes joined to the universe in a new and meaningful way. On the cross a cosmic disruption follows the most brutal possible disturbance between humanity and divinity as the Father abandons the Son, letting Him suffer alone. But from this, the power of sin is fractured and God raises Christ from the grave; through the New Man, or Cosmic Christ, Christians are reconnected to the whole universe—not only to their fellow human beings, but to the rest of the cosmos (e.g., animals, land, and water). Fox sees this as the meaning of Colossians 1:15-17, which depicts Christ as "the first-born of all creation" in whom all things hold together.[38]

Creation spirituality and sin. Fox holds a very radical view of sin. He finds any idea of original sin quite distasteful, and prefers to concentrate on "original blessing" as the basis for his theology:

> Whatever is said of original sin, it is far less hallowed than are love and desire. . . . Our origin in the love of our parents, . . . and the celebration of creation at our birth, are far, far more primeval and original in every sense of that word than is any doctrine of "original sin."[39]

Human beings may sin, but they do not have to. They may refrain from sin and recover their original blessed state. All acts which are sensual, creative, and aesthetic are steps toward the recovery of the original blessing.

Fox does not deny the reality of sin, but he believes that it has received far too much emphasis. He blames Augustine for having seduced the church away from its real biblical heritage. Most Western Christians, he suggests, believe more in Augustine than in Christ.[40] As far as Fox is concerned, sin is not the acts of life which the church has condemned as morally evil. It is, rather, false thinking about God and His creation.[41] Evil is not to be found so much in human behavior as within those institutions, such as the church, which perpetuate wrong ideas of the ecosystem, women, and native peoples.[42]

Much of Fox's work seems to identify Western Christian tradition in its teaching of Fall/redemption theology as the basis of sin. He refers to it as "the way of idolatry."[43] Its picture of God "is necessarily a vengeful, sadistic deity — peeping and judging, denouncing and spying: a God of guilt."[44]

The doctrine of humankind. Fox calls for a Copernican revolution in religion. Human beings must be led to see themselves in a new light. They are no longer to consider themselves fallen, lost creatures. Such a view will interfere with their true mission in life, which is to be agents of transformation.

Because God is in everything and everything is in God, creation is pulsing with what Fox calls *Dabhar*, or divine energy. *Dabhar* is usually translated into English as "the word," but Fox hesitates to use that term, for he believes that the Western theology of the Word has virtually destroyed the biblical significance of the term. The Enlightenment, he charges, robbed our society of the value of the word by inundating us with the verbal; he calls for a return to the time when there was so much silence that words still had significance. *Dabhar* signifies more than mere words; it indicates deeds and actions; it connotes all that God did in Genesis 1–2. As human beings immerse themselves ecstatically in creation, they may become a "uniquely sacramental receptacle" filled with that spiritual energy and take on the Creator's characteristics.[45]

There are many ways of attaining unity with God. These include "natural ecstasies," such as listening to music, enjoying the arts, dancing, and lovemaking. There are also the "tactical ecstasies" of asceticism—fasting, Yoga, Transcendental Meditation, and the like. Fox himself commends the technique of "art-as-meditation." One develops the mystic in oneself by awakening the right-brain hemisphere through dance, clay sculpting, or painting. "People have some of the deepest conversions of their lives on the dance floor, when giving and receiving massage, in painting, in music."[46] Fox cites Jesus' statement that one must become like a child before one may receive the kingdom of God—"that means taking up crayons, working with images, playing games."[47]

Indeed, human beings may become so highly divinized that they may not only be cocreators with God, but even creators of God! ". . . God can be a baby, a child, a new creation. . . in some sense God is not born yet. . . humanity is responsible for the birthing and nurturing of God."[48]

Eschatology. Fox looks forward to the creation of a new age, the Aquarian age which, he estimates, should replace the Piscean (or Christian) era by the year 2000.[49] His agenda for the new age is overtly political, for creation spirituality demands "a new kind of society with new economic goals and political means."[50] Fox warns that the "Gods of the past" will continue to haunt and beckon his followers and they must be kept suppressed.[51] "To look back long-ingly is to commit adultery."[52]

The creation of the new age, the ushering in of the kingdom of God, is not so much God's work as humanity's. "Our era leaves us to create the first global civilization on earth. We are that genera-tion that begins the creative transformation of the whole world into a single community out of the diverse peoples of the planet."[53]

Jesus is a model for the inbreaking of the kingdom. His mystic preaching of the inbreaking kingdom was calculated to help His hearers realize what was happening around them. "Jesus' shocking parables have as their primary purpose," says Fox, "to *get people to behold*, to get people to wake up and see, to behold what is already in their midst."[54] That kingdom is a panentheistic realm. The mustard seed, the leaven in the lump, the dragnet are all panentheistic images Jesus uses to rouse all to the "kingdom/queendom" of God.[55]

Fox cites Albert Schweitzer as one of the few modern Christians to cite Jesus as a mystic, though he erred in allowing Him to be a mystical teacher only in the future Son of Man. But Jesus proclaimed the kingdom both present and future. "This is not so much eschatology as a future event as it is the future come home, the future starting here and now."[56]

A Critical Evaluation of the Movement

Matthew Fox is at the very least the proponent of a movement very heavily influenced by New Age principles. Creation spirituality is assuredly a Christian heresy which is laced through and through with Eastern mystical thought. Christian mystics are evident, but they are not alone.

While Fox claims to be a panentheist in his doctrine of God, it is hard to see how his views differ greatly from pantheism. He has removed the God of Scripture and substituted in His place a deified man and creation. He teaches that humankind is creator—even of God Himself.

But the Bible teaches that God is transcendent; He is Other. He is the Creator, and neither we nor the world in which we live are extensions of His Being. We have been created by God and He acts upon us; we do not act upon Him.

One may affirm Fox's desire to love and care for creation. One function of the *imago Dei* in humanity is to represent God in creation; we are stewards of creation. The goodness of creation, however, is not intrinsic; it is good because God has declared it so. That earth is created and not divine does not detract from its goodness.

Again, we may agree with Fox that human beings are imbued with creativity. It is a part of the human makeup. We may also agree that humans are invited by God to participate with Him in the creative endeavor. But to call humans cocreators is to go too far. Anything that we may create is never *ex nihilo*, but it is from already existing materials previously created by God.

Jesus Christ occupies too small a place in Matthew Fox's system. One wonders whether He is necessary at all. If faith in Christ is not the only way to God—and Fox allows for many ways—then He could be dropped without being missed. Fox claims that the crucifixion of Christ is of major importance. But we find that His death has only symbolic value to the degree that it serves as a model for others in their effort to transform humanity. As an objective victory over sin and death it has no value. In all of this, creation spirituality goes against the teaching of Scripture which posits Jesus as the only way to God (John 14:6) and His death as the means of reconciling humans to God (Rom. 5:10).

Nor is Fox's understanding of the Holy Spirit an orthodox one. His linking of the Third Person of the Trinity with the Goddess of pagandom in an effort to include a feminine person in the Godhead is pagan, not Christian. Nor does the Holy Spirit indwell all human beings, as Fox claims.[57] The Bible notes that the Spirit indwells those who are in Christ Jesus (Acts 2:38).

When it comes to sin, the movement is topsy-turvy, calling good bad and bad good. Fox suggests that those things condemned by the Bible as evil—such as homosexuality, drug-use, astrology, and witchcraft—are really potentially helpful spiritual aids. And he condemns the church as the bastion of evil.

Not all may agree with Augustine, but the Bible—not he—is responsible for noting the Fall and depravity of humanity. And while we should be sympathetic to Fox's desire to give the environment, women, and native peoples their rightful and respected place in the world, infractions against these groups— admittedly evils—are not the only evils in the world. Human behavior which falls short of God's standards is also sin (see Gal. 5:19ff).

Nor is humanity capable of transforming itself. Meditation—of whatever kind—is not the key to union with God or to a changed life. Only Jesus Christ can effect either. Wayne Boulton criticizes Fox as "simplistic," somewhat "like a Robert Schuller of the left."[58]

When the new age, or kingdom, is ushered in, it will be on God's timetable and not as the result of human initiative. No amount of human effort will bring about a universal transformation of this world. Fox's theology is works-oriented, falsely trusting in humanity to pull itself up by its bootstraps to save itself.

Boulton notes that "Fox's most damaging flaw is that in Christian terms he is not mystical enough."[59] When it comes to some of the most important areas of the New Testament teaching—heaven, an afterlife, and the judging of this world—"Fox is silent about these things; his creation-centered spirituality excludes them."[60]

Conclusions

Matthew Fox's theology is indeed radical. But it is not, as he would have us believe, radical in the spirit of the early Christian tradition, for he does not subscribe to the idea of Jesus Christ as the only way to God, a notion on behalf of which thousands of early believers joyfully went to their deaths. Rather, it is radical in the spirit of heretical Gnosticism which sought to dethrone the God of heaven in favor of an esoteric, topsy-turvy scheme based on meditative techniques and human efforts.

Some have suggested that the real value of creation spirituality lies not in theology but in pastoral care.[61] Indeed, the movement's teaching has become very much a fad among many associations of pastoral education and pastoral care practitioners. Fox's rejection of "worm theology" is lauded, as is his desire to assist human beings in recovering the "original blessing." Certainly, any discipline which seeks to alleviate human misery, elevate the downtrodden, and emphasize compassion would enjoy a high place in the esteem of the average person.

Fox may have contributed to the affirmation of self-esteem and the value of personhood. At the same time, one must wonder how any spiritual endeavor which is built on a rotten foundation can ultimately be of any worth. It has been demonstrated how faulty are Fox's panentheistic doctrine of God and his upside-down doctrine of sin. How can any theology be helpful if its direction is totally wrong from the start?

For Further Reading

Fox, Matthew. *Creation Spirituality*. San Francisco: Harper and Row, 1991.

_____. *The Coming of the Cosmic Christ*. San Francisco: Harper and Row, 1988.

_____. *Original Blessing: A Primer in Creation Spirituality*. Santa Fe, N.M.: Bear Publishing, 1983.

_____. *Whee! We, Wee All the Way Home*. Santa Fe, N.M.: Bear Publishing, 1981.

_____. *On Becoming a Musical, Mystical Bear*. New York: Paulist Press, 1972.

Appendix. Some Third-World Theological Directions

The "Two-Thirds World," as it is increasingly called, is a fertile field for innovative theologians. Many interesting and esoteric directions have been taken by church leaders from this region. From their evangelization dependent upon European theology, the developing regions have attempted to replace this "colonial theology" with theologies which square more completely with their own cultural and historical viewpoints.

Asian Directions

It is primarily in the last three decades or so that Asian theology has begun to come into its own. The initial attempts at the task utilized indigenization. When the Gospel is moved from one culture to another it must be "demythologized" and then reencapsulated to relate to its new context. The danger with such an approach is in becoming so enculturated that it cannot be applied in any other environment.

In reaction to this difficulty, younger theologians have shifted their emphasis from indigenization to contextualization:

> Contextualization has to do with how we assess the peculiarity of Third World contexts. Indigenization tends to be used in the sense of responding to the Gospel in terms of a traditional culture. Contextualization, while not ignoring this, takes into account the process of secularity, technology, and the struggle for human justice, which characterize the historical moment of nations in the Third World.[1]

A major danger in contextualizing theology is syncretism. Those attempting contextualization may become too accepting of the culture. Accepting elements of a culture which are false or sinful are a syncretistic accommodation.[2] A second danger is that major paradigm shifts in the culture may leave a contextualized Christianity, which has failed to keep up somewhere on the fringes of society, as nothing more than an irrelevant anachronism.[3]

The primary goal of Asian theologians has been to create an Asian expression of Christianity. ". . . [T]heology's responsibility is not so much to restate Asian traditions in terms of Christian faith as to restate the Christian faith in terms of Asian traditions."[4]

Waterbuffalo theology. One attempt to translate the Christian faith into Asian tradition is Japanese theologian Kosuko Koyama's "waterbuffalo theology" in Thailand. His concept is based on 1 Corinthians 9:22: "To the weak I became weak, to win the weak. I have become all things to all men so that by all possible means I might save some." In order to reach people, the Gospel must be shared with them on their own level of thinking.

Koyama's target group are Thai farmers who spend their days in the rice fields. They would not comprehend the Gospel if it were presented to them in our common theological terms. Koyama, therefore, has related theology to them in their own language.

One example of such theologizing has to do with nature. Nature is cyclically oriented. One season is succeeded by the next. The monsoon season begins in May and continues until October in Thailand. Thai peasants believe that hope and salvation come with the monsoon rain. "*Every year* at about the same time the faithful monsoon arrives, impressing the people that mother nature does not forget them and that she is, in all that she does, dependable and benevolent."[5] The Thai view of nature spills over into their view of God and salvation. They believe that "there are always second, third, fourth, fifth . . . chances for man and nature to accomplish what they intend to do."[6]

Koyama helps to incorporate Christianity into the Thai way of thinking by pointing out that the God of the Bible is in an anti-monsoon orientation. He is not cyclical, but linear. He is not many times, but once for all. The Thai farmers must realize that God has created this regularity in nature; Mother Nature is not God. "The monsoon orientation (cyclical movement) is placed within the purpose of God (linear movement)."[7]

Since most Asians are Buddhists, Koyama has incorporated Buddhism into his theology. Seasoning Christianity with Buddhism will help Asians, he claims, to understand the Christian faith more completely. Accordingly, instead of using Christian terms such as "salvation through the blood of Jesus," Koyama substitutes "salvation through the dharma."[8]

In his call to self-denial based on Jesus' words in Matthew 16:24 — "If anyone would come after Me, he must deny himself and take up his cross and follow Me" — Koyama borrows much from Buddhism. In his book, *No Handle on the Cross*, he notes that "a Buddhist monk who lives as a sign of self-denial is highly praised."[9] Since Asians have been taught to revere such a state of life, they can understand the Christian position more easily.

Koyama believes in "the slow God." The traditional method of slow approach has been disturbed by the impact of technology. While there are certain values in modernity, "I find that God goes 'slowly' in his educational process of man. 'Forty years in the wilderness' points to his basic educational philosophy."[10]

God's love is shown in Jesus Christ's coming to a full stop. "He was nailed down! He is not even at three miles an hour as we walk. He is not moving."[11] It is at this point of "full stop" that God's love for humankind is fully revealed.

Water buffalo theology is not systematic and so is sometimes hard to grasp. Koyama's desire to reach Asians in general and Thais in particular is commendable. Because he is Asian he can think as they think; he knows their culture and worldview. Through stories and analogies, theology is made simple.

Koyama's incursions into Asian religions and his attempt to meld them into Christianity are less commendable. It is indicative of a tendency towards syncretism — and even universalism — for he feels that one cannot define where the adherents of those religions stand in relation to Jesus Christ. He suggests that "we cannot compare religions because they are like different cuisines, no better or worse, just different."[12] Such reasoning flies in the biblical and historical exclusivity of Christianity.

Yin-yang theology. Yin-yang theology is the brainchild of an American-educated theologian from North Korea. Jung Young Lee, a graduate in systematic theology from Boston University and professor of religious studies and humanities at Drew University, first applied this yin-yang principle to Christian anthropology in 1971 in his book *The I: A Christian Concept of Man*, and in 1979 to the doctrine of God in his work, *The Theology of Change: A Christian*

Concept of God in an Eastern Perspective.

Lee sees the major problem of Western theology as being not one of faith but of thinking in absolutist terms of "either-or." Such thinking came from Greek Aristotelianism, the foundation of Western thought patterns. Easterners quickly see some obvious examples: "What is not good must be evil, and what is not evil must be good; and what is not wrong must be right, and what is not right must be wrong. But it is possible that what is not wrong may be neither right nor wrong, and what is not right may be both right and wrong at the same time."[13] Such Aristotelian thinking, however, excludes the latter, middle possibilities as invalid.

Lee argues that this either-or type of thinking has shaped the absolute dogma of God and forced Him to become less than the God of the Christian faith. He has been made into an ideal of intellectual display.[14]

Again, the either-or kind of theological thought, declares Lee, has prevented Christianity from a coexistence with other major world religions. Its isolation from these religions is caused by the absolute claims of human doctrines which exclude any possibility of harmony and compromise with other faiths.[15]

Either-or thinking has also destroyed Western mysticism. Consequently, Christianity—especially Protestant Christianity—has failed to meet the needs of the whole person, for these needs include the arcane.[16]

This absolutist form of thinking contributes towards environmental pollution. "Man must *either* conquer nature *or* nature will conquer him. . . . Man gradually overcomes nature . . . but he never conquers it completely. Ultimately neither of them survives."[17]

Lee sees his theological task as two-fold: to confine the role of either-or theological thinking, and to seek the most comprehensive category of thinking to round it out. Its function must be limited because unequivocal thinking "is no longer compatible with the contemporary understanding of the world."[18] Einsteinian physics, which sees everything—time and space included—as relative has done away with the Newtonian worldview of absolute categories of time and space.

We must therefore find an inclusive category of thinking. Since a relativistic worldview has been part of the fabric of Eastern society for centuries, Lee suggests that one should seek there for a symbol of relativistic thinking. He commends to us the idea of yin-yang as set forth in the ancient *Book of Change* or *I-Ching*, whose cosmological view is normative for the Chinese people.[19]

The yin and the yang principles go back into history too far to trace. "The concept of yin originally came from the imagery of shadow, while that of yang came from brightness. Yin then came to signify female, receptive, passive, cold, etc., and yang male, creative, active, warm, etc."[20] This symbol's characteristic nature is the complementarity of opposites. Each requires the other. Thus, the symbol is a method of both-and which allows as well for either-or thought.

The yin-yang category of thinking brings fresh insights to theology, argues Lee. For example, Western thinking—with its either-or emphasis—has problems expressing the divine immanence and transcendence. But it is no difficulty for yin-yang thinking. In this category, "the God of transcendence is also the God of immanence."[21]

In the same way, when one asks whether God is personal or impersonal, the response is "yes" under the yin-yang view. A God who is only personal would be a limited One. He is God both of personal and impersonal entities.[22]

Nor can Jesus Christ be seen in either-or terms as both God and man. How can a man be God? But in yin-yang terms, in Christ God and man are not separated. "They are in complementary relationship. He is God because of man; he is man because of God."[23]

Lee concludes that the yin-yang category deals with ultimate matters to which either-or cannot apply. The latter has to do with penultimate affairs. Both viewpoints are necessary to accomplishing successfully the theological task.[24]

To the degree that Lee has developed this system, it seems to make considerable sense. And is it any less legitimate to use categories from Chinese religious culture than from pagan Platonic and Aristotelian categories? Certainly, the idea of both/and in and of itself is not unreasonable as a viable category. There are, however, places in Scripture which limit us to either-or categories (such as salvation being in Christ alone); where that occurs, yin-yang must stand rejected. Christianity is indeed exclusive, and that is indubitably an either-or category.

Conclusions. Asian theologians must be lauded for attempting to do everything in their power to make the Gospel relevant to the various Asian cultures. That there are dangers inherent in the method used—contextualization—have already been demonstrated, the major threat being syncretism. The two theologies surveyed reveal the danger of trying to restate Christianity in terms of another tradition.

Waterbuffalo theology attempts to relate the Gospel to Thai farmers. Koyama's analogy of "the slow God," for example, is very apt. He has done well here in his efforts to effectively contextualize. Unfortunately, he seems to have gone an unnecessary "second mile" in formulating Christian doctrine in Buddhist terms and concepts. He appears, like so many others, to have forgotten that the early church proclaimed the Christian faith in absolute opposition to the cultures into which it sought to make inroads.

Jung Young Lee's yin-yang theology is perhaps easier for us to relate to than the former, for Lee is a product of the American university system. He seeks to decontextualize the Christian faith from its Greek traditions and recontextualize it in Chinese concepts. He also endeavors to combine the two traditions for Westerners the better to express Christian truth. Once again, however, he goes too far in attempting to make salvation a "both-and" category.

The major failure of these two theologies is their developers' excesses when it comes to the doctrine of salvation. Historically and biblically, Jesus Christ is the sole way of salvation. To attempt to posit an additional way is to wander from the narrow way.

None of the above should be taken as a negation of contextualization. It is a necessary exercise if the peoples of other cultures are to understand the Gospel and be saved. But those who perform this exercise must take care to remain within the boundaries established by the Bible. To go beyond those limits, as have Koyama and Lee, is to harm rather than help needy cultures, for it deceives them into thinking that there are means other than Christ whereby they may be saved. To recontextualize the Bible within the biblical borders, is to perform an inestimable service. And we salute those who seek to do so.

African Theological Directions
African theology has come to the fore only in the last three decades or so. Prior to that time it was believed that there was but a

single form of Christian theology which permeated all aspects of society. This theology was of European construction. Attempts up to that time—such as that of Mojola Agbebi of Nigeria—to integrate Christianity with African culture were largely disregarded.[25]

The 1950s and 1960s brought independence to most African nations. With the departure of the colonial powers, Africa was left alone to deal with the question of her identity. The church in Africa also began to question its identity. The main task of African theology was seen as the discovery of a genuine African character.[26]

Many Africans regarded Christianity as a form of European imperialism. The missionary establishment on that continent was regarded as a form of spiritual oppression in much the same fashion as political oppression had been imposed from the exterior. The early years of independence were a time of distrust for things Western. As a result, African theologian Mercy Oduyoye wrote not of a theology of liberation, but of the liberation of theology, hailing the freeing of the church in Africa from Western thought forms and irrelevant "predigested theologies."[27] Similarly, the early works of African theologians like Mbiti, Mulago, and Tshibangu were "theologies of antithesis: African theology is what European theology is not."[28]

African theologies, then, tend to be reactionary in nature. Sempore aptly observes that "the tendency to reflect by reaction against or opposition to the white world is still strong in many African theologians; similarly the tendency still to study the problems of the fifties."[29] Their theologies may generally be categorized either as cultural or political. The former attempt to relate Christianity to African culture; the latter are "decolonization" theologies rooted in liberation thought.

John S. Mbiti. One of the most important African theologians is John S. Mbiti. Born in Kenya in 1931, he was educated at Makerere University College in Uganda and completed studies for a doctor of theology degree at Cambridge University. He served as a clergyman in England and then as a teacher at the Universities of Birmingham and Hamburg respectively, before returning to Africa as a professor of religious studies at Makerere University College and then as a pastor in the Reformed Church of Switzerland.

In 1969 Mbiti wrote *African Religions and Philosophy*, which sought to encourage Christians to appreciate traditional African religions and culture more deeply. As stated earlier, he works in a context of reaction against differing experiences of European colonialization:

> Africans . . . were overcome by Europeans who slaughtered them like beasts, who burned down their villages, . . . who forced them to quit their lands and become laborers on European farms or "house boys" for European masters and mistresses. The new change started and continued in blood and tears, . . . through honest and dishonest means, . . . by choice and by subjection. . . . So the revolution came by both peace and force, and Africa could not remain the same way any more.[30]

The results of European imperialism were detribalization for the African natives—removal from the land, urbanization, and the destruction of tribal and clan structures.

Mbiti attempts to approach these troubles from a Christian perspective. He holds that authentic human identity may be found in unity with Christ. As a result of this Christocentric identity, one is liberated to be seen as an African or whatever else one may wish to become. "That is the height to which Christianity in Africa must soar."[31]

This commitment to uncovering authenticity in Christ, however, does not mean a radical disconnection from one's African past, religious or cultural. Mbiti considers other religious systems "to be preparatory and even essential ground in the [African] search for the Ultimate."[32] He calls upon Christians to be more open to the traditional religions and philosophy of Africa and to incorporate into Christian practice rites that are familiar to Africans, such as dreams and visions, exorcisms, healings, traditional modes of dance and song, and even esteem for ancestors. "Mbiti, of course, realizes that openness to modes of traditional African religiosity is also openness to anciently traditional Christian religiosity."[33]

One must not think that Mbiti is totally one-sided. He freely acknowledges that what he terms "mission Christianity" (as opposed to indigenous independent African churches) has made an exceptional effort to ameliorate poor conditions in Africa. He does feel, however, that the independent churches come closer to traditional African religious practices than does the former.

Mbiti is one of the more moderate theologians who are attempting to inculturate Christianity into African tribal practices. For the most part, one cannot fault his motives. The familiar is easier to accept than the unfamiliar. To the degree that African practices such as dreams, visions, healings, and the like do not venture beyond the bounds of Scripture, they should be encouraged. But all practices must come under the authority of Scripture and not vice versa.

E. Bolaji Idowu. Another outstanding African theologian who has combined both political and cultural aspects is E. Bolaji Idowu, professor of religious studies at Nigeria's University of Ibadan. A graduate of Cambridge University and an ordained Methodist clergyman, Idowu majored in the concept of God among the Yoruba people, and in 1962 published *Olodumare: God in Yoruba Belief.*

As a practicing theologian, Idowu's chief efforts have been in attempting to reconcile the Christian faith and traditional African religions. His major work, *African Traditional Religion* (1973), argues for "theology which bears the stamp of original thinking and meditation of Africans."[34]

For some years Idowu has promoted the idea that Christianity must be clothed in, or complemented by, traditional tribal beliefs if it is to make any meaningful impact on native Africans. He writes of the church: "It is time for her to realize that in order to be effective in her life and mission in Nigeria, she must respect, preserve and dedicate to the glory of God anything that is of value in the culture and institutions of the country."[35]

He has become increasingly syncretistic and supports in Ibadan's Department of Religion a journal entitled *Orita.* The word means in the Yoruba language "where the ways meet," and presupposes that Christian, Muslims, and African traditionalists all worship the same God. "The impression one gains is that they have received the same revelation, and are bound for the same destiny. . . . This being the case, they should live at peace with all men of all religions."[36]

Idowu declares that the sovereign God is in control of all of the earth. He speaks to all peoples, each in their own context. He writes that, although there are differences between religions, the

Christian should recognize that his doctrinal system is but "one *homo religiosus* as meeting another *homo religiosus*."[37]

Idowu draws upon Tillich and Baillie to insist that God's revelation to humankind occurs in an "I-thou" encounter between Himself and humanity.[38] ". . . [R]evelation cannot be limited in scope . . . it is meant for all mankind, all rational beings, irrespective of race or color."[39] Revelation implies response, maintains Idowu, and he borrows this time from Otto and Eliade to posit this response as "a creaturely feeling, a sense of the fact that there is in the universe a 'Wholly Other' than the creature and the world of ordinariness,"[40] or what Otto refers to as the "numinous."[41]

While all people experience this noumenal Reality, how they express it differs according to their cultural context. African people express the experience in their tribal rites. It may be that the picture the tribes have of God is flawed somewhat, but that does not make it less valid than the Christian experience. The tribal African awareness of the sovereign God is as genuine as that of the Western believer.

The chief factor of African religion is the doctrine of God. "We find that in Africa, the real cohesive factor of religion is the living God and that without this one factor, all things would fall to pieces."[42] When someone objects that Africans are polytheists and believe in many gods, Idowu protests that these gods are not "gods" at all, but divinities whom God has ordained as ministers. In answer to suggestions that African tribalists are, in fact, idolaters, he argues that:

> the material has no meaning apart from the spiritual; it is the spiritual that informs the material and gives it whatever quality and meaning it has. The material therefore can only be, at best, technically, a symbol. It is the divine entity that is represented by the material object to whom worship is rendered. The material symbol can rot away, become destroyed, be carried away, and be replaced, but not so the divine being. Symbols may change. Deity or his ministers remain.[43]

Idowu has come a long way from his evangelical Methodist beginnings. He has evidently turned away from orthodox Christianity to embrace a universalist syncretism. The concern for an indigenous Nigerian church free of European colonialist control is laudable; the intense African nationalism which has attempted to exalt traditional African religion by rationalizing it into a form of "implicit monotheism" which is acceptable to God is much less so.

When it comes to revelation, that the animists of Africa have an awareness of God is unquestionable. But their knowledge is not the legitimate type which comes about as the result of God's revelation in Christ Jesus. One is reminded of Paul's statement in Romans 1:21 that such people know who God is but do not give Him the glory which is His due. "The awareness of God is there. But Idowu does not need to baptize depravity into dignity. That the natural man is aware of God is one thing but that he worships God through images is entirely another."[44]

It seems clear that Jesus has no significant place in Idowu's philosophy. If Christianity, Islam, and African traditional religions are all acceptable ways to God, then Jesus is not "*the* way, and *the* truth, and *the* life" (John 14:6, emphasis mine), but only *a* way to God.

Although Idowu seeks to emancipate African theology from European dependence, his new directions lean heavily on liberal European theologians from Schleiermacher to Tillich. Such dependence will serve only to lead his people away from Christ to a deep and sorry servitude to ungodly spiritual forces.

Conclusions. There are many African theologies which have sought to be different from traditional European systems by seeking indigenization or inculturation. E.W. Fashole-Luke insists that "conversion to Christianity must be coupled with cultural continuity." Kofi Appiah-Kubi declares that the mission church has brought healing without consideration for traditional African worldviews and so has failed to heal many elements of the whole human being. He advises serious study of traditional African beliefs and practices, and the attainment of their holistic approach. Burgess Carr holds that Africans must liberate Christianity from its Western trappings so that it may become universal in its scope. Christian Mwolaka is committed to Tanzanian *Ujamaa,* or East African style of political and economic socialism, as a practical way of imitating the work of the Trinity.[45]

The seeming assumption of those who place great value on African culture is that biblical religions and African ones are similar. Tienou observes, "Sadly, the work of some Christian theologies has actually strengthened traditional religions by stressing continuity rather than diversity with the Gospel."[46] As noted above, where contextualization can be made within the biblical boundaries, well and good; but to stretch and rationalize those boundaries illegitimately—as some of these theologians have—is an engagement in heresy and can do no good to the Christian cause or to those who are the objects of conversion attempts.

For Further Reading

Anderson, Gerald H., ed. *African Voices in Christian Theology.* Maryknoll, N.Y.: Orbis Books, 1976.

Dickson, Kwesi A. *Theology in Africa.* Maryknoll, N.Y.: Orbis Books, 1984.

Elwood, Douglas J., ed. *Asian Christian Theology: Emerging Themes.* Philadelphia: Westminster Press, 1980.

Imasogie, Osadolar. *Guidelines for a Christian Theology in Africa.* Achimota, Ghana: African Christian Press, 1983.

Kato, Byang H. *Theological Pitfalls in Africa.* Nairobi, Kenya: Evangel Publishing, 1987.

Koyama, Kosuke. *Waterbuffalo Theology.* London: SCM Press, 1974.

Moore, Basil, ed. *The Challenge of Black Theology in South Africa.* Atlanta: John Knox Press, 1973.

Oduyoye, Mercy Amba. *Hearing and Knowing: Theological Reflections on Christianity in Africa.* Maryknoll, N.Y.: Orbis Books, 1986.

Ro, Bong Rin, and Ruth Eshenreer, eds. *The Bible and Theology in Asian Contexts.* Taichung, Taiwan: Asian Theological Association, 1984.

Song, C.S. *Theology from the Womb of Asia.* Maryknoll, N.Y.: Orbis Books, 1986.

Notes

Chapter 1: Fundamentalism

1. Sydney E. Ahlstrom, *A Religious History of the American People* (New Haven, Conn.: Yale University Press, 1972), 815.

2. Bill J. Leonard, "The Origin and Character of Fundamentalism," *Review and Expositor* 79 (Winter 1982): 12. Cf. Walter B. Shurden, *Not a Silent People: Controversies That Have Shaped Southern Baptists* (Nashville: Broadman Press, 1972), 93.

3. Stewart G. Cole, *The History of Fundamentalism* (1931; repr., Hamden, Conn.: Archon Books, 1963), 283.

4. *Southern Baptist Convention Annual, 1926,* 18 as quoted by Shurden, *Not a Silent People,* 99.

5. From this point on, "fundamentalist" or "fundamentalism"—unless specified to the contrary—will be used as equivalent to "neo-fundamentalism."

6. George W. Dollar, *A History of Fundamentalism in America* (Greenville, S.C.: Bob Jones University Press, 1973), 221.

7. L. Russ Bush and Tom. J. Nettles, *Baptists and the Bible* (Chicago: Moody Press, 1980), 379-80.

8. It should be noted here that Landmarkism is still practiced by some Southern Baptist churches, whose views would be essentially the same as the American Baptist Association, while still retaining the Southern Baptist Connection.

9. Earl E. Cairns, *Christianity through the Centuries,* rev. ed. (Grand Rapids: Zondervan Publishing House, 1981), 465.

10. Carl McIntire, *The Modern Tower of Babel* (Collingswood, N.J.: Christian Beacon, 1949), 196.

11. There is some question among fundamentalist writers on the legitimacy of including the Conservative Baptists under the heading of fundamentalist. While Jerry Falwell, ed., *The Fundamentalist Phenomenon* (Garden City, N.Y.: Doubleday-Galilee, 1981), 124-25 sees them as fundamentalists, Dollar, *Fundamentalism in America*, 283 accuses them of "complete capitulation to new-evangelical attitudes and methods."

12. Falwell, *Fundamentalist Phenomenon*, 126.

13. *Baptist Bible Tribune*, 23 June 1950, as quoted by Falwell, *Fundamentalist Phenomenon*, 127.

14. See Jerry Falwell and Elmer Towns, *Church Aflame* (Nashville: Impact Books, 1971), 74-75.

15. One interesting media example of such a battle is John R. Rice's book, *Bobbed Hair, Bossy Wives, and Women Preachers*.

16. Falwell, *Fundamentalist Phenomenon*, 156.

17. Martin E. Marty, "Fundamentalism as a Social Phenomenon," *Review and Expositor* 79 (Winter 1982): 19.

18. Ibid.

19. The rationale for, and manifesto of, the Moral Majority may be found in Jerry Falwell, *Listen, America!* (New York: Doubleday, 1980).

20. See Falwell, *Fundamentalist Phenomenon*, 7; Cole, *History of Fundamentalism*, 67; and many others.

21. Morris Ashcraft, "The Theology of Fundamentalism," *Review and Expositor* 79 (Winter 1982): 39.

22. See Charles Hodge, *Systematic Theology* (1872; repr., Grand Rapids: Wm. B. Eerdmans Pub. Co., 1960), 1.152ff.

23. Many scholars would claim that Warfield was the first to posit inerrancy in the *autographa*, but it may be argued that he was simply voicing what others had already held, perhaps from the time of the Lutheran scholastics.

24. James Barr, *Fundamentalism* (Philadelphia: Westminster Press, 1977), 52.

25. Greg L. Bahnsen, "The Inerrancy of the Autographs," in *Inerrancy*, ed. Norman L. Geisler (Grand Rapids: Zondervan Publishing House, 1979), 154.

26. Falwell, *Fundamentalist Phenomenon*, 8.

27. James Orr, "The Virgin Birth of Christ," in *The Fundamentals*, ed., R.A. Torrey et al. (1917; repr. Grand Rapids: Baker Book House, 1970), 2.259.

28. Ashcraft, "Theology of Fundamentalism," 41.

29. Ibid., 42.

30. There are notable exceptions. The late John R. Rice, for example, while not hesitating to condemn tongues as unbiblical, willingly cooperated with Pentecostals and charismatics in evangelistic ventures as fellow Christians.

Chapter 2: Neo-orthodoxy
1. Delving back into historical theology, one may readily see the thought of Soren Kierkegaard as a strong influence on both Barth and neo-orthodox theology.

2. Karl Barth, "On Systematic Theology," *Scottish Journal of Theology* 14 (September 1961): 225.

3. Karl Barth, *Church Dogmatics: A Selection,* trans. and ed. G.W. Bromiley (New York: Harper and Row, 1961), 50.

4. Ibid., 53.

5. Ibid., 94.

6. Karl Barth, *Church Dogmatics,* trans. G.W. Bromiley et al. (Edinburgh: T. and T. Clark, 1957), 2/2.3.

7. Karl Barth, *The Faith of the Church,* trans. Gabriel Vahanian (London: Fontana Books, 1960), 40.

8. Barth, *Church Dogmatics,* 4/1.618.

9. Ibid., 70.

10. Barth, *Church Dogmatics,* 1/2.507.

11. Ibid., 529.

12. Bernard L. Ramm, *The Evangelical Heritage* (Waco, Tex.: Word Inc., 1973), 109-10.

13. Colin Brown, *Karl Barth and the Christian Message* (Downers Grove, Ill.: InterVarsity Press, 1967), 132.

14. Emil Brunner, *The Christian Doctrine of God, Dogmatics,* trans. Olive Wyon (Philadelphia: Westminster Press, 1950), 1.19.

15. Ibid., 23.

16. Ibid., 110.

17. For this concept, Brunner was indebted to the ideas of Jewish theologian, Martin Buber.

18. Brunner, *Christian Doctrine,* 168.

19. Barth responded to Brunner with a stinging reply in *Nein! Antwort an Emil Brunner* (No! Answer to Emil Brunner).

20. Emil Brunner, *The Christian Doctrine of Creation and Redemption, Dogmatics,* trans. Olive Wyon (Philadelphia: Westminster Press, 1952), 2.104.

21. Ibid., 354-55.

22. Ibid., 360.

23. Reinhold Niebuhr, *The Nature and Destiny of Man* (New York: Scribners, 1964), 1.13.

24. Ibid., 17.

25. Ibid., 188.

26. Ibid., 142.

27. Ibid., 148.

28. Dietrich Bonhoeffer, *The Cost of Discipleship*, 2nd ed., trans. R.H. Fuller (New York: Macmillan, 1959), 54.

29. Ibid., 273.

30. Edwin H. Robertson, "Bonhoeffer's Christology," in Dietrich Bonhoeffer, *Christology*, trans. John Bowden (London: Collins, 1966), 9-26 charges that any concept of Bonhoeffer as a "theologian who would have done away with all the religious elements of the church and perhaps even with the church itself" (9) is the result of quoting his *Letters and Papers from Prison* out of context.

31. For a fuller treatment of this concept, see Paul Schrotenboer, "Emil Brunner," in *Creative Minds of Contemporary Theology*, ed. Philip E. Hughes (Grand Rapids: William B. Eerdmans Pub. Co., 1966), 104-07.

32. Karl Barth, *Church Dogmatics* 1/1.188 as cited by Charles C. Ryrie, *Neo-Orthodoxy* (Chicago: Moody Press, 1956), 36.

Chapter 3: Pentecostalism
1. See Steve Durasoff, *Bright Wind of the Spirit: Pentecostalism Today* (Englewood Cliffs, N.J.: Prentice-Hall, 1972).

2. Much as some Baptists hold to "the trail of blood."

3. Sarah E. Parham, *The Life of Charles F. Parham* (Joplin, Mo.: Tri-State Printing, 1930), 52-53.

4. John Thomas Nichol, *The Pentecostals* (Plainfield, N.J.: Logos International, 1966), 28. It is as a result of this event that Pentecostalism cherishes its belief that the initial evidence of Spirit baptism is the reception of glossolalia.

5. Klaude Kendrick, *The Promise Fulfilled: A History of the Modern Pentecostal Movement* (Springfield, Mo.: Gospel Publishing, 1961), 59.

6. Nichol, *The Pentecostals*, 31.

7. Ibid., 33.

8. Frank Bartleman, *How "Pentecost" Came to Los Angeles* (Los Angeles: n.p. 1925), 64 as quoted by Vinson Synan, *In the Latter Days* (Ann Arbor, Mich.: Servant Books, 1984), 49.

9. William M. Menzies, "The Movers and Shakers," in *Pentecostals from the Inside Out*, ed. Harold B. Smith (Wheaton, Ill.: Victor Books, 1990), 31-32.

10. Nichol, *The Pentecostals,* 112.

11. Douglas J. Wilson, *The Church Grows in Canada* (Toronto: Canadian Council of Churches, 1966), 185.

12. Nils Bloch-Hoell, *The Pentecostal Movement* (Oslo, Norway: Universitets-forlaget, 1964), 75.

13. Synan, *Latter Days,* 60-61.

14. David J. duPlessis, "Pentecost in South Africa," *Pentecostal Evangel* 26 (1938): 2-4, as cited by Nichol, *The Pentecostals,* 50-51.

15. L. Grant McClung, Jr., "New Culture, New Challenges, New Church?" *Pentecostals from the Inside Out,* ed. Harold B. Smith

(Wheaton, Ill.: Victor Books, 1990), 108-9.

16. Ibid., 68.

17. Block-Hoell, *The Pentecostal Movement,* 52.

18. Ibid., 161.

19. Alvyn J. Austin, *Saving China: Canadian Missionaries in the Middle Kingdom, 1888-1959* (Toronto: University of Toronto Press, 1986), 125-26.

20. Nichol, *The Pentecostals,* 50.

21. Now officially the Pentecostal World Conference.

22. David J. du Plessis, "Golden Jubilees of Twentieth Century Pentecostal Movements," in *Azusa Street and Beyond,* ed. L. Grant McClung, Jr. (South Plainfield, N.J.: Bridge Publishing, 1986), 42-43.

23. Bloch-Hoell, *The Pentecostal Movement,* 97.

24. Gordon F. Atter, *The Third Force* (Peterborough, On.: College Press, 1962), 132.

25. Lewi Petrus, *Hur jag fick Andens dop,* 2.14 as quoted by Bloch-Hoell, *The Pentecostal Movement,* 103.

26. Thomas Barrett, *When the Fire Fell,* 114 quoted by Bloch-Hoell, *The Pentecostal Movement,* 105-6.

27. Ibid., 118.

28. Atter, *The Third Force,* 294.

29. Gloria G. Kuhlbeck, *What God Hath Wrought* (Toronto: Pentecostal Assemblies of Canada, 1958), 355.

30. They will, however, acknowledge that a believer may be op-

pressed by a demon, especially if he has dabbled in the occult.

31. Durasoff, *Bright Wind,* 244.

32. Gordon L. Anderson, "Pentecostals Believe in More Than Tongues," in *Pentecostals from the Inside Out,* Smith, 62.

Chapter 4: Evangelicalism

1. Harold J. Ockenga, "The New Evangelicalism," *The Park Street Spire,* February 1958, 7.

2. Bruce Shelley, *Evangelicalism in America* (Grand Rapids: Wm. B. Eerdmans Pub. Co., 1967), 70.

3. Joel A. Carpenter, "From Fundamentalism to the New Evangelical Coalition," in *Evangelicalism and Modern America,* ed., George Marsden (Grand Rapids: William B. Eerdmans Publishing Co., 1984), 12.

4. Shelley, *Evangelicalism in America,* 82.

5. Harold J. Ockenga, "From Fundamentalism, through New Evangelicalism, to Evangelicalism," in *Evangelical Roots,* ed. Kenneth S. Kantzer (Nashville: Thomas Nelson Publishers, 1978), 42.

6. Gordon Clark in the preface to Carl F.H. Henry, *Remaking the Modern Mind* (Grand Rapids: Wm. B. Eerdmans Pub. Co., 1946), 13.

7. Carl F.H. Henry, *The Uneasy Conscience of Modern Fundamentalism* (Grand Rapids: Zondervan Publishing House, 1947), preface.

8. Ockenga, "New Evangelicalism," *The Spire,* 5-6.

9. Edward J. Carnell, *The Case for Orthodox Theology* (Philadelphia: Westminster Press, 1959), 113ff. For the fundamentalist reaction, see Robert Lightner, *Neo-Evangelicalism* (Findlay, Ohio: Durham, n.d.).

10. Carpenter, "From Fundamentalism," 15.

11. Donald G. Bloesch, *The Evangelical Renaissance* (Grand Rapids: Wm. B. Eerdmans Pub. Co., 1973), 30ff.

12. Ibid., 30.

13. Richard Quebedeaux, *The Young Evangelicals* (New York: Harper and Row, 1974), 37-39.

14. Bloesch, *Evangelical Renaissance, 36.*

15. Ibid.

16. See Dietrich Bonhoeffer, *The Cost of Discipleship,* rev. ed. (New York: Macmillan, 1962).

17. Richard Quebedeaux, "The Evangelicals: New Trends and New Tensions," *Christianity and Crisis,* 20 September 1976, in Deane William Ferm, ed., *Contemporary American Theologies II, A Book of Readings* (New York: Seabury Press, 1982), 282.

18. Ibid.

19. Quebedeaux, *Young Evangelicals,* 150.

20. I have deliberately used the term "authority" here rather than "inerrancy" because the latter has become so hackneyed—it can mean whatever anyone wishes it to mean. I also recognize that many evangelicals (especially in Europe) do not like "inerrancy" and refuse to use it. I agree wholeheartedly with the statement of Kenneth S. Kantzer, "Evangelicals and the Inerrancy Question," in *Evangelical Roots,* ed. Kenneth S. Kantzer (Nashville: Thomas Nelson Publishers, 1978), 95-96: "Evangelicals today assert the truthfulness and divine authority of the Scripture—all of it.... "

21. For a helpful overview of qualified inerrancy terms, see Millard J. Erickson, *Christian Theology* (Grand Rapids: Baker Book House, 1983-85), 222-24.

22. James Davison Hunter, *Evangelicalism, The Coming Generation* (Chicago: Univ. of Chicago Press, 1987), 25.

23. Donald G. Bloesch, *The Future of Evangelical Christianity: A Call for Unity Amid Diversity* (Garden City, N.Y.: Doubleday Co., 1983), 118.

24. Clark H. Pinnock, "Three Views of the Bible in Contemporary Theology," in *Biblical Authority,* ed. Jack Rogers (Waco, Tex.: Word Inc., 1977), 65-68. Cf. Pinnock, *The Scripture Principle* (San Francisco: Harper and Row, 1984), 70-79.

25. Millard J. Erickson, *The New Evangelical Theology* (Westwood, N.J.: Fleming H. Revell, 1968), 82.

26. Robert P. Lightner, *Evangelical Theology, A Survey and Review* (Grand Rapids: Baker Book House, 1986), 47.

27. Erickson, *New Evangelical Theology,* 91.

28. A variation of this view sees the days of Genesis 1–2 as a literary device demonstrating only that Creation was effected in six stages.

29. Bernard Ramm, *The Christian View of Science and Scripture* (Grand Rapids: Wm. B. Eerdmans Pub. Co., 1955), 113.

30. Ibid., 116.

31. Ibid.

32. Carnell, *Orthodox Theology,* 92.

33. Ibid., 95.

34. For a more recent treatment of the same kind, see Robert Brow, "The Late-Date Genesis Man," *Christianity Today,* 15 September 1972, 128-29.

35. See Henry Morris, *The Beginning of the World* (Denver: Ac-

cent Books, 1977). Cf. Morris, *Scientific Creationism* (San Diego: Creation-Life Publishers, 1974).

36. Morris, *The Beginning,* 8.

37. Davis A. Young, "Scripture in the Hands of Geologists," as quoted by Clark H. Pinnock, "Climbing Out of a Swamp," *Interpretation,* 42 (April 1989): 146. Cf. Howard J. Van Till, Davis A. Young, and Clarence Menninga, *Science Held Hostage: What's Wrong with Creation Science and Evolution* (Downers Grove, Ill.: InterVarsity Press, 1988).

38. Pinnock, "Climbing Out," 150.

39. Lightner, *Evangelical Theology,* 181.

40. Hunter, *Evangelicalism,* 105.

41. Robert G. Clouse, ed., *The Meaning of the Millennium* (Downers Grove, Ill.: InterVarsity Press, 1977).

42. See David L. Edwards and John R.W. Stott, *Essentials: A Liberal-Evangelical Dialogue* (London: Hodder and Stoughton, 1988), 312-29. Cf. Edward Fudge, *The Fire That Consumes* (Houston: Providential Press, 1982) for a more detailed exegetical-theological examination of annihilation.

43. See Neal Punt, "All Are Saved Except," *Christianity Today,* 20 March 1987, 43ff.

44. For an up-to-date evaluation of this whole controversy, see Larry Dixon, *The Other Side of the Good News* (Wheaton, Ill.: BridgePoint/Victor Books, 1992).

45. Carnell, *Orthodox Theology,* 121.

46. Lightner, *Evangelical Theology,* 126.

Chapter 5: Neo-liberalism
1. William E. Hordern, *A Layman's Guide to Protestant Theology,*

rev. ed. (New York: Macmillan, 1968), 95.

2. Harry Emerson Fosdick, *Dear Mr. Brown: Letters to a Person Perplexed about Religion* (New York: Harper and Row, 1961).

3. Ibid., 43.

4. Ibid., 44.

5. Ibid., 55.

6. Ibid., 62-63.

7. Ibid., 60.

8. Ibid., 88.

9. Ibid., 89.

10. Henry P. Van Dusen, *The Vindication of Liberal Theology: A Tract for the Times* (New York: Charles Scribner's Sons, 1963).

11. Ibid., 17.

12. Ibid., 151.

13. Ibid.

14. D.M. Baillie, *God Was in Christ* (New York: Charles Scribner's Sons, 1943), 82 as quoted by Van Dusen, *Liberation Theology*, 129.

15. Van Dusen, *The Vindication of Liberal Theology*, 130.

16. Ibid., 133.

17. Ibid., 135.

18. Ibid., 137.

19. Ibid., 139.

20. Ibid., 143.

21. Ibid., 146.

22. Rudolf Bultmann, *New Testament Mythology and Other Basic Writings,* trans. and ed. Schubert M. Ogden (Philadelphia: Fortress Press, 1984), 1.

23. Ibid., 2.

24. Ibid., 7.

25. Ibid., 21.

26. Ibid., 147.

27. Vernon C. Grounds, "Pacesetters for the Sixties and Seventies," in *Tensions in Contemporary Theology,* 2nd ed., ed. Stanley N. Gundry and Alan F. Johnson (Grand Rapids: Baker Book House, 1976), 56.

28. Paul Tillich, *Systematic Theology* (Chicago: University of Chicago Press, 1967), 1:21.

29. Ibid., 211.

30. Paul Tillich, as cited by John Hick, *Philosophy of Religion* (Englewood Cliffs, N.J.: Prentice-Hall, 1963), 67.

31. Ibid., 205.

32. Ibid., 109.

33. Ibid., 112-13.

34. Ibid., Part 2, 44.

35. Ibid., 45.

36. Ibid., 61.

37. Ibid.

38. Ibid., Part 1, 49.

39. Ibid., Part 2, 148.

40. Ibid.

41. Ibid., 159.

42. Ibid., 177.

43. Ibid., 178.

44. Ibid., 179-80.

45. Pierre Teilhard de Chardin, *The Phenomenon of Man,* trans. Bernard Wall (New York: Harper, 1959), 35.

46. Ibid., 71.

47. Ibid., 257-60.

48. Ibid., 293.

49. Ibid., 294.

50. Ibid.

51. Teilhard, as quoted by Ian G. Barbour, "Teilhard's Process Metaphysics," in *Process Theology,* ed. Ewert H. Cousins (New York: Newman Press, 1971), 344.

52. It should come as no surprise that Teilhard is revered by New Age practioners as one of their "saints." E.g., Lola Davis, *Toward*

a World Religion for a New Age (Farmingdale, N.Y.: Coleman Publishing, 1983), 25, places his works on a par with the great religious writings of the ages, including the Bible.

53. George Marsden, "The Plight of Liberal Protestantism," *Fides et Historia,* 20 (1988): 49.

54. Clark H. Pinnock, "Where Is North American Theology Going?" *TSF Research* (1979): 2.

55. Schubert M. Ogden, *Christ without Myth* (New York: Harper and Row, 1961), 127.

56. Langdon Gilkey, *Reaping the Whirlwind* (New York: Seabury Press, 1976), 247.

57. Langdon Gilkey, *Message and Existence* (New York: Seabury Press, 1979), 41.

58. David Tracey, *Blessed Rage for Order: The New Pluralism in Theology* (New York: Seabury Press, 1975).

59. Ibid., 8.

60. Ibid., 44.

61. Ibid., 32.

Chapter 6: Post-Vatican II Catholicism
1. See Bruce Demarest, *General Revelation* (Grand Rapids: Zondervan Publishing House, 1982), 183-84.

2. For the full text, see Walter M. Abbott, ed. and Joseph Gallagher, trans., *Documents of Vatican II* (Piscataway, N.J.: New Century Publishers, 1966), 14-101.

3. Ibid., 49.

4. Ibid., 57. For a fuller picture of Conciliar thinking on the laity,

see *Apostolicam Actuositatum,* "Decree on the Apostolate of the Laity," in same document, 489-521.

5. Ibid., 60.

6. Ibid., 114-15.

7. Ibid., 661.

8. Ibid., 115.

9. Frederick C. Grant, "A Response," ibid., 129.

10. For the full text, ibid., 341-66.

11. For the full text, ibid., 373-86.

12. For the full text, ibid., 584-632.

13. For the full text, ibid., 660-68.

14. For the full text, ibid., 675-96.

15. Ibid., 346.

16. Ibid.

17. Ibid., 661-62.

18. Ibid., 662.

19. Ibid., 35.

20. Ibid.

21. Ibid., 665.

22. Ibid., 598.

23. Karl Rahner, *Foundations of Christian Faith* (New York: Seabury Press, 1978), 17.

24. Ibid., 18.

25. George Vandervelde, "The Grammar of Grace: Karl Rahner as a Watershed in Contemporary Theology," *Theological Studies* 49 (1988): 446.

26. Ibid.

27. David H. Johnson, "The Theological Method of Karl Rahner," (Class paper, Trinity Evangelical Divinity School, 1989), 10.

28. Karl Rahner, "Philosophy and Theology," in *A Rahner Reader,* ed. Gerald A. McCool (New York: Seabury Press, 1975), 78.

29. Rahner, *Foundations*, 34.

30. Ibid., 176.

31. Ibid., 39.

32. Ibid., 201-2.

33. Ibid., 318.

34. Rahner, "Christianity and the Non-Christian Religions," *A Rahner Reader*, 219.

35. For a documented account of Kung's conflict with Rome, see Leonard Swidler, ed. and trans., *Kung in Conflict* (Garden City, N.Y.: Image Books, 1981).

36. Hans Kung, *On Being a Christian* (Garden City, N.Y.: Doubleday Co., 1976), 83-84.

37. Ibid., 84.

38. Ibid., 91.

39. Ibid., 92.

40. Ibid., 98.

41. Ibid.

42. Ibid., 66.

43. Ibid., 85.

44. Ibid., 76.

45. Ibid., 123.

46. Ibid., 126.

47. Ibid., 602.

48. Edward Schillebeeckx, *The Church and Mankind, Concilium Theology in an Age of Renewal* (Glen Rocks, N.J.: Paulist Press, 1965), 1:72.

49. Ibid., 73.

50. Ibid.

51. Ibid., 74.

52. Ibid., 75.

53. Ibid., 81.

54. Ibid., 88.

55. Ibid., 100.

56. Excerpts from Gregory Baum, *Man Becoming God in Secular*

Experience (New York: Seabury Press, 1970) in *Contemporary American Theologies II—A Book of Readings,* ed. Deane William Ferm (New York: Seabury Press, 1982), 316.

57. Ibid., 317.

58. Ibid.

59. Ibid., 325.

60. Ibid., 326.

61. Ibid., 327.

62. Excerpts from Raimundo Pannikar, *The Intra-Religious Dialogue* (New York: Paulist Press, 1978) in Ferm, *Contemporary American Theologies,* 356.

63. Ibid., 357.

64. Ibid., 360.

65. Ibid., 362.

66. Ibid., 364.

Chapter 7: Eastern Orthodox Theology
1. Demetrios J. Constantelos, *The Greek Orthodox Church: Faith, History, and Practice* (New York: Seabury Press, 1967), 34.

2. Lawrence Cross, *Early Christianity: The Byzantine Tradition* (Sydney, Australia: E.J. Dwyer, 1988), 9.

3. Constantelos, *The Greek Orthodox Church,* 46.

4. Timothy Ware, *The Orthodox Church* (Middlesex, United Kingdom: Penguin Books, 1963), 98.

5. Ibid.

6. Earle E. Cairns, *Christianity through the Centuries,* rev. ed. (Grand Rapids: Zondervan Publishing House, 1981), 268.

7. Ibid., 385.

8. Ibid.

9. Frank S. Mead and Samuel S. Hill, *Handbook of Denominations in the United States,* 8th ed. (Nashville: Abingdon Press, 1985), 186.

10. Alexander A. Bogolepov, *Towards an American Orthodox Church* (New York: Morehouse-Barlow, 1963), 80.

11. Ibid., 87.

12. Joseph Meyendorff, "Orthodox Unity in America: New Beginnings?" *St. Vladimir's Theological Quarterly,* 35 (1991): 6.

13. Ibid., 7.

14. Ibid., 12-13.

15. Ware, *Orthodox Church,* 204.

16. Ibid., 206.

17. Constantelos, *The Greek Orthodox Church,* 97.

18. As quoted by Cross, *Early Christianity,* 47.

19. See Cross, *Early Christianity,* 48 and Ware, *Orthodox Church,* 205.

20. Ware, *Orthodox Church,* 219.

21. Ibid., 221.

22. Cross, *Early Christianity,* 29.

23. Ibid., 30.

24. Joseph M. Roya, *The Face of God* (Denville, N.J.: Dimension Books, 1976), 22.

25. As quoted by Ware, *Orthodox Church,* 233.

26. P.D. Steeves, "The Orthodox Tradition," in *Evangelical Dictionary of Theology,* ed. Walter A. Elwell (Grand Rapids: Baker Book House, 1984), 807.

27. *Orthodox Spirituality,* 2nd ed. (Crestwood, N.Y.: St. Vladimir's Seminary Press, 1978), 30.

28. Like Baptists, the Eastern church baptizes by immersion, but generally practices infant baptism.

29. Ibid., 46.

30. Ware, *Orthodox Church,* 249.

31. Ibid., 252.

32. Vladimir Lossky, *The Mystical Theology of the Eastern Church* (Cambridge, United Kingdom: Clarke, 1968), 234.

Chapter 8: The Charismatic Movement

1. The "first wave" being the Pentecostal movement.

2. See David B. Barrett, "A Survey of the Twentieth Century Pentecostal/Charismatic Renewal in the Holy Spirit, with Its Goal of World Evangelization," in *Dictionary of Pentecostal and Charismatic Movements,* ed. Stanley M. Burgess and Gary B. McGee (Grand Rapids: Zondervan Publishing House, 1988), 812-13.

3. See Burgess and McGee, *Dictionary of Pentecostal and Charismatic Movements,* 49, and Kenneth S. Kantzer, "The Charismatics Among Us," *Christianity Today,* 22 February 1980, 25.

4. Vinson Synan, *In the Latter Days: The Outpouring of the Holy Spirit in the Twentieth Century* (Ann Arbor, Mich.: Servant Books, 1984), 83.

5. Ibid., 84.

6. Ibid., 85.

7. Walter Holenweger, *The Pentecostals: The Charismatic Movement in the Churches* (Minneapolis: Augsburg Publishing House, 1972), 6-7.

8. Synan, *In the Latter Days,* 86.

9. Richard Quebedeaux, *The New Charismatics II: How a Christian Renewal Movement Became Part of the American Religious Mainstream* (San Francisco: Harper and Row, 1983), 60.

10. See "Rector and a Rumpus," *Newsweek,* 4 July 1960, 77 and "Speaking in Tongues," *Time,* 15 August 1960, 53-55.

11. Quebedeaux, *New Charismatics,* 65.

12. Ibid., 68.

13. Synan, *In the Latter Days,* 123.

14. Ibid., 124.

15. Ibid., 125.

16. Ibid., 125-26.

17. Ibid., 127.

18. Ibid., 130.

19. Grant L. Anderson, "Pentecostals Believe in More than Tongues," in *Pentecostals from the Inside Out,* ed. Harold B. Smith (Wheaton, Ill.: Victor Books, 1990), 57.

20. Quebedeaux, *New Charismatics,* 132.

21. Catherine Marshall, *Something More* (New York: McGraw-Hill, 1974), 270.

22. P.D. Hocken, "Charismatic Movement," in *Dictionary of Pentecostal and Charismatic Movements,* ed. Stanley M. Burgess and Gary B. McGee (Grand Rapids: Zondervan Publishing House, 1988), 156.

23. Walter Hollenweger, "Charismatic and Pentecostal Movements: A Challenge to the Churches," in *The Holy Spirit,* ed. Dow Kirkpatrick (Nashville: Tidings Press, 1974), 225 as quoted by Quebedeaux, *New Charismatics,* 155.

24. Howard M. Ervin, *These Are Not Drunken as Ye Suppose* (Plainfield, N.J.: Logos International, 1968), 51.

25. Dennis and Rita Bennett, *The Holy Spirit and You: A Guide to the Spirit-Filled Life* (Plainfield, N.J.: Logos International, 1971), 143.

26. See John F. MacArthur, *The Charismatics: A Doctrinal Perspective* (Grand Rapids: Zondervan Publishing House, 1978).

Chapter 9: The Theology of Hope
1. Some theologians wish to dichotomize these terms into two separate schools of theological thought, but they have enough similarities to retain them as a single entity.

2. David Scaer, "Jürgen Moltmann and His Theology of Hope," *Journal of the Evangelical Theological Society,* 13 (Spring 1970): 71.

3. Jürgen Moltmann, *Theology of Hope,* trans. James W. Leitch (London: SCM Press, 1965), 16.

4. Ibid.

5. Ibid., 15.

6. Ibid., 16.

7. Ibid., 17.

8. John Calvin, *Institutio*, III.2.42 as quoted by Moltmann, *Theology of Hope*, 20.

9. Moltmann, *Theology of Hope*, 20.

10. Ibid., 23.

11. Ibid., 103.

12. Ibid.

13. Ibid., 216-17.

14. David P. Scaer, "Theology of Hope," in *Tensions on Contemporary Theology*, 2nd ed., ed. Stanley N. Gundry and Alan F. Johnson (Grand Rapids: Baker Book House, 1976), 211.

15. Ibid., 19-20.

16. Richard Bauckham, "Moltmann's *Theology of Hope* Revisited," *Scottish Journal of Theology*, 42 (1989): 202-3.

17. Ibid., 203.

18. Moltmann, *Theology of Hope*, 229.

19. Jürgen Moltmann, *The Church in the Power of the Spirit* (London: SCM Press, 1977), 65.

20. Ibid.

21. Ibid.

22. Wolfhart Pannenberg, "God's Presence in History," in *Theologians in Transition*, ed. James M. Wall (New York: The Crossroad Publishing Co., 1981), 95.

23. Ibid., 96.

24. Wolfhart Pannenberg, *Theology and the Kingdom of God,* ed. Richard J. Neuhaus (Philadelphia: Westminster Press, 1969), 53.

25. Ibid., 56.

26. Ibid.

27. Ibid., 62.

28. Ibid.

29. Ibid, 63.

30. Wolfhart Pannenberg, *Revelation as History,* trans. David Granskou (New York: The Macmillan Co., 1968), 131.

31. Wolfhart Pannenberg, *Jesus — God and Man,* trans. Lewis L. Wilkins and Duane A. Priebe (Philadelphia: Westminster Press, 1968), 114.

32. Pannenberg, *Theology,* 72-73.

33. Ibid., 74.

34. Ibid., 75.

35. Johannes B. Metz, *Faith in History and Society,* trans. David Smith (New York: Seabury Press, 1980), 3.

36. Ibid., 73.

37. Ibid., 90.

38. Ibid., 91.

39. Ibid., 151.

40. Johannes Baptist Metz, *Followers of Christ* (New York: Paulist Press, 1978), 76.

41. Ibid., 78.

42. Ibid., 79.

43. Jürgen Moltmann, *Religion, Revolution, and the Future*, trans. M. Douglas Meeks (New York: Scribner, 1969), 209.

44. Wolfhart Pannenberg, *Basic Questions in Theology*, trans. George H. Kehm (Philadelphia: Fortress Press, 1970), 22ff.

45. Metz, *Faith in History*, 75.

46. Moltmann, *Religion, Revolution*, 213.

47. Wolfhart Pannenberg, *An Introduction to Systematic Theology* (Grand Rapids: Wm. B. Eerdmans Pub. Co., 1991), 53ff.

48. Ibid., 60.

49. Wolfhart Pannenberg, "The Revelation of God in Jesus," in *New Frontiers in Theology*, vol. 3 of *Theology as History*, eds. James M. Robinson and John B. Cobb, Jr. (New York: Harper and Row, 1967), 130.

50. Moltmann, *Theology of Hope*, 165.

51. Moltmann, *Religion, Revolution*, 52.

52. Pannenberg, *Jesus — God and Man*, 66.

53. Moltmann, *Theology of Hope*, 22ff.

54. Metz, *Faith in History*, 73.

55. David P. Scaer, "Theology of Hope," in *Tensions in Contemporary Theology*, 230.

Chapter 10: Process Theology

1. See Norman L. Geisler, "Process Theology," in *Tensions in Contemporary Theology*, 2nd ed., ed. Stanley N. Gundry and Alan Johnson (Grand Rapids: Baker Book House, 1976), 238.

2. See Ewart H. Cousins, "Process Models in Culture, Philosophy, and Theology," in *Process Theology*, ed. Ewart H. Cousins, (New York: Newman Press, 1971), 4.

3. Geisler, "Process Theology," 239.

4. Ian G. Barbour, "Teilhard's Process Metaphysics," in Cousins, *Process Theology*, 325.

5. Set out in *An Enquiry Concerning the Principles of Natural Knowledge* (Cambridge: University Press, 1919) and *The Concept of Nature* (Cambridge: University Press, 1920).

6. John B. Cobb, Jr. and David Roy Griffin, *Process Theology, An Introductory Exposition* (Philadelphia: Westminster Press, 1976), 163.

7. Alfred N. Whitehead, *Process and Reality* (New York: Macmillan, 1929), 317.

8. Ibid., 70-73.

9. W. Norris Clarke, "Christians Theism and Whiteheadian Process Philosophy," in *Process Theology*, ed. Ronald H. Nash (Grand Rapids: Baker Book House, 1987), 220.

10. Alfred N. Whitehead, "God and the World," in Cousins, *Process Theology*, 88.

11. Geisler, "Process Theology," 246.

12. Whitehead, "God and the World," 89.

13. Ibid., 93.

14. Ronald H. Nash, "Process Theology and Classical Theism," in Nash, *Process Theology*, 20.

15. Charles Hartshorne, "The Development of Process Philosophy," in Cousins, *Process Theology*, 53-54.

16. Ibid., 54.

17. Donald Bloesch, "Process Theology and Reformed Theology," in Nash, *Process Theology*, 42.

18. Geisler, "Process Theology," 255.

19. Ibid., 255-56.

20. Cobb and Griffin, *Process Theology*, 36.

21. Whitehead, *Religion in the Making* (New York: Macmillan, 1926), 65 as quoted by Cobb and Griffin, *Process Theology*, 36.

22. Ibid.

23. Bloesch, "Process Theology," 39.

24. Cobb and Griffin, *Process Theology*, 37.

25. Schubert M. Ogden, "The Reality of God," in Cousins, *Process Theology*, 121.

26. Ibid., 122.

27. Ibid.

28. Ibid., 124.

29. Ibid., 125.

30. Emil Brunner, *The Mediator* (Philadelphia: Westminster Press, 1948), 242.

31. Norman Pittenger, *Christology Reconsidered* (London: SCM Press, 1970), 15.

32. Norman Pittenger, *The Lure of Divine Love* (New York: Pilgrim Press, 1979), 11.

33. Norman Pittenger, "Bernard E. Meland, Process Theology, and the Significance of Christ," in Cousins, *Process Theology*, 210.

34. Ibid., 209-10.

35. Ibid., 211.

36. W. Norman Pittenger, *Unbounded Love: God and Man in Process* (New York: Seabury Press, 1976), 54.

37. Henry N. Wieman, "The Human Predicament," in Cousins, *Process Theology*, 220.

38. Ibid., 221.

39. Ibid., 221-22.

40. Ibid., 223.

41. Bruce Demarest, "The Process Reduction of Jesus and the Trinity," in Nash, *Process Theology*, 75.

42. Daniel Day Williams, "God and Man," in Cousins, *Process Theology*, 178.

43. Ibid.

44. Ibid., 179.

45. Ibid., 184.

46. Ibid., 186.

Chapter 11: Secular Theology

1. Editorial, "Modern Theology at the End of Its Tether," *Christianity Today*, 16 July 1965, 20.

2. Harvey Cox, *The Secular City* (New York: Macmillan, 1966), 1.

3. Ibid.

4. Ludwig Feuerbach, *The Essence of Christianity* (London: John Chapman, 1854), 206.

5. S. Paul Schilling, *God in an Age of Atheism* (Nashville: Abingdon Press, 1969), 63.

6. Ibid., 64.

7. Charles C. West, "Secularization," in *Dictionary of the Ecumenical Movement,* ed. Nicholas Lossky, Jose Miguez Bonino, John Pobee, et al. (Grand Rapids: Wm. B. Eerdmans, Pub. Co., 1991), 917.

8. *Webster's New Collegiate Dictionary* (Springfield, Mass.: Merriam-Webster Inc., 1981), 1037.

9. Ibid.

10. Ibid.

11. Harold B. Kuhn, "Secular Theology," in *Tensions in Contemporary Theology*, 2nd ed., ed. Stanley N. Gundry and Alan F. Johnson (Grand Rapids: Baker Book House, 1976), 160.

12. Ibid.

13. As quoted by Cox, *Secular City*, 2.

14. Ibid., 17. For a contrary view, see Bernard Murchland, "How Do We Speak of God without Religion?" in *The Secular City Debate*, ed. Daniel Callahan (New York: Macmillan, 1967), 17-22.

15. Ibid., 21-24.

16. Ibid., 22-23.

17. Ibid., 25-30.

18. Ibid., 25-26.

19. Ibid., 30-36.

20. Ibid., 32.

21. G.W.F. Hegel, *Erste Druckschriften, Samthiche werke,* ed. Georg Laaon, (Leipzig: Felix Meiner, 1928), 1.344 as cited by Schilling, *Atheism,* 101.

22. Walter Kaufmann, ed. *The Portable Nietzsche* (New York: Viking Press, 1965), 95-96, cited by Schilling, *Atheism,* 135-36.

23. Kuhn, "Secular Theology," 162.

24. Schilling, *Atheism,* 107.

25. Thomas J.J. Altizer, *The Descent into Hell* (Philadelphia: J.B. Lippincott, Co., 1980), 202.

26. William Hamilton, "The Death of God," *Playboy,* August 1966, 84.

27. Ibid., 137.

28. William Hamilton, "The Shape of a Radical Theology," *Christian Century* 82 (1965): 1221.

29. Gabriel Vahanian, *The Death of God* (New York: George Braziller, 1961), xvi-xvii.

30. Ibid., 15.

31. Ibid., 20.

32. Ibid., 23.

33. Ibid.

34. Ibid., 29.

35. Ibid., 32-33.

36. Ibid., 230.

37. Richard L. Rubenstein, *After Auschwitz: Radical Theology and Contemporary Judaism* (Indianapolis: Bobbs-Merrill, 1966), 151-52.

38. Ibid., 227.

39. Ibid., 263.

40. Ibid., 153.

41. Ibid., 257.

42. John A.T. Robinson, *Honest to God* (London: SCM Press, 1963), 8.

43. Ibid.

44. Ibid., 43.

45. Ibid., 49.

46. Ibid., 70.

47. Ibid., 71.

48. Ibid., 75.

49. Ibid., 87.

50. Ibid., 90.

51. Cox, *Secular City*, 33.

52. Ibid., 63.

53. Ibid., 65.

54. Ibid., 266.

55. Harvey Cox, *"The Secular City* 25 Years Later," *The Christian Century* 107 November (1990): 1026.

56. Ibid., 1028.

57. Cox, *Secular City,* 111.

58. Ibid., 112.

59. Millard J. Erickson, *Christian Theology* (Grand Rapids: Baker Book House, 1985), 317.

60. Robinson, *Honest to God,* 73.

61. Rhoda Dueck, "Secular Theology" (Paper prepared for Contemporary Theological Trends, Winnipeg Bible College, February 1991), 12.

62. Cox, "25 Years Later," 1029.

Chapter 12: Theologies of Success
1. Mark Hellstern, "The 'Me Gospel': An Examination of the Historical Roots of the Prosperity Emphasis within Current Charismatic Theology," *Fides et Historia,* 21 (October 1989): 78.

2. Dennis Voskuil, *Mountains into Gold Mines: Robert Schuller and the Gospel of Success* (Grand Rapids: Wm. B. Eerdmans Pub. Co., 1983), 9.

3. Ibid., 11.

4. Ibid., 15.

5. Ibid., 18-19.

6. David Singer, "The Crystal Cathedral: Reflections of Robert Schuller's Theology," *Christianity Today*, 8 August 1980, 28.

7. Arthur Gordon, *Norman Vincent Peale Ministers to Millions* (Englewood Cliffs, N.J.: Prentice-Hall, 1958), 178.

8. Ibid., 228.

9. Norman Vincent Peale, *You Can If You Think You Can* (Old Tappan, N.J.: Fleming H. Revell, 1974), 10.

10. Glen W. Siemens, "A Study and Overview of the Theology of Self-Esteem" (Paper prepared for Contemporary Theological Trends, Winnipeg Bible College, March 1991), 7.

11. Voskuil, *Mountains into Gold Mines*, 5.

12. Kenneth S. Kantzer, "Hard Questions for Robert Schuller About Sin and Self-Esteem," *Christianity Today*, 10 August 1984, 20.

13. Robert Schuller, *Self-Esteem, The New Reformation* (Waco, Texas: Word Inc., 1982), 31.

14. Ibid., 15.

15. Ibid., 35.

16. Kantzer, "Hard Questions," 16-17.

17. Schuller, *Self-Esteem*, 57.

18. Richard N. Ostling, "Power, Glory—and Politics," *Time*, 17 February 1986, 68.

19. Jeffrey Gibbs, "The Grace of God as the Foundation for Ethics," *Concordia Theological Quarterly* (April–July 1984): 189.

20. Schuller, *Self-Esteem*, 65.

21. Ibid., 67.

22. Ibid., 14.

23. Ibid., 68.

24. Ibid., 163.

25. Ibid., 116.

26. Ibid., 118.

27. Voskuil, *Mountains into Gold Mines,* 39.

28. Schuller, *Self-Esteem,* 161.

29. Ibid., 161-62.

30. Siemens, "The Theology of Self-Esteem," 13.

31. Voskuil, *Mountains into Gold Mines,* 25.

32. Robert L. Reymond, "A Reply in the Form of an Open Form Letter to Dr. Robert B. Schuller," *Covenant Seminary Review* 10 (1984): 121.

33. Hellstern, "The 'Me Gospel,' " 78.

34. James R. Goff, Jr., "The Faith That Claims," *Christianity Today,* 19 February 1990, 19.

35. Ibid.

36. Ibid.

37. Ibid.

38. See D.R. McConnell, *A Different Gospel: A Historical and Biblical Analysis of the Modern Faith Movement* (Peabody, Mass.: Hendrickson Publishers, 1988), 3ff.

39. Quoted by McConnell, *A Different Gospel,* 15.

40. Robert Jackson, "Prosperity Theology and the Faith Movement," *Themelios* 15 (October 1989): 16.

41. Ibid., 57.

42. Kenneth E. Hagin, *I Believe in Visions* (Old Tappan, N.J.: Fleming H. Revell, 1972), 13.

43. Ibid., 27.

44. Ibid., 28-30.

45. Kenneth Hagin, *Understanding the Anointing* (Tulsa, Okla.: Faith Library, 1985), 58-59.

46. Kenneth Hagin, *Godliness is Profitable* (Tulsa, Okla.: Faith Library, 1982), 16.

47. McConnell, *A Different Gospel,* 78.

48. Jackson, "Prosperity Theology," 21.

49. McConnell, *A Different Gospel,* 86.

50. See Charles Farah, *From the Pinnacle of the Temple* (Plainfield, N.J.: Logos International, 1978).

51. Jerry Savelle, "True Prosperity, What Is It?" *Christian Life,* July 1983, 47.

52. Ken L. Sarles, "A Theological Evaluation of the Prosperity Gospel," *Bibliotheca Sacra* 143 (July 1986): 335.

53. Paul Y. Cho, *Salvation, Health, and Prosperity* (Altamonte Springs, Fla.: Creation House, 1987), 15.

54. Bruce Barron, *The Health and Wealth Gospel* (Downers Grove, Ill.: InterVarsity Press, 1987), 9.

55. Dennis Hollinger, "Enjoying God Forever: An Historical/ Sociological Profile of the Health and Wealth Gospel," *Trinity Journal* 9 (1988): 133.

56. Kenneth E. Hagin, *Must Christians Suffer?* (Tulsa, Okla.: Rhema Bible Church, 1983), 2.

57. Jackson, "Prosperity Theology," 19.

58. Kenneth Copeland, *You Are Healed* (Fort Worth, Texas: KC Publications, 1979), 2.

59. Hollinger, "Enjoying God Forever," 133.

60. Jerry Savelle, *God's Provision for Healing* (Tulsa, Okla.: Harrison House, 1981), 8 as quoted by Hollinger, "Enjoying God Forever," 134.

61. Hollinger, "Enjoying God Forever," 20.

62. Charles Capps, *The Tongue: A Creative Force* (Tulsa, Okla.: Harrison House, 1976), 109.

63. Jerry Savelle, *Godly Wisdom for Prosperity* (Tulsa, Okla.: Harrison House, 1980), 18.

64. Cho, *Salvation, Health, and Prosperity*, 77.

65. Gloria Copeland, *God's Will to Prosperity* (Fort Worth, Texas: KC Publications, 1978), 54.

66. Kenneth Copeland, *The Laws of Prosperity* (Fort Worth, Texas: KC Publications, 1974), 26.

67. Hollinger, "Enjoying God Forever," 135.

68. Ibid.

69. Robert Tilton, *God's Laws of Success* (Dallas: Word of Faith Publications, 1983), 28, 60.

70. Gloria Copeland, *God's Will to Prosperity*, 72.

71. Hollinger, "Enjoying God Forever," 136.

72. Goff, "Faith that Claims," 21.

73. Jackson, "Prosperity Theology," 20.

74. Kenneth E. Hagin, *Redeemed from Poverty, Sickness, and Death* (Tulsa, Okla.: Kenneth Hagin Ministries, 1983), 25.

75. A taped conversation with Ern Baxter, cited by McConnell, *A Different Gospel*, 26.

76. McConnell, *A Different Gospel*, 19.

77. See Dietrich Bonhoeffer, *The Cost of Discipleship*, rev. ed. (New York: Macmillan, 1959).

Chapter 13: Liberation Theology

1. Steven Phillips, "Liberation Theology: Hope or Hoax?" *Search* 12 (Winter 1982): 17.

2. Wolfhart Pannenberg, "Redemptive Event and History," in *Basic Questions in Theology: Collected Essays*, trans. George H. Kahm (Philadelphia: Fortress Press, 1970), 1.78.

3. Phillips, "Liberation Theology," 17.

4. Ibid.

5. Gustavo Gutierrez, *The Power of the Poor in History* (Maryknoll, N.Y.: Orbis Books, 1983), 49.

6. Frederick Herzog, *Liberation Theology* (New York: Seabury Press, 1972), 258.

7. Orlando Costas, "Liberation Theology: A Solution?" *The Mennonite*, 11 July 1978, 434.

8. Harvie M. Conn, "Theologies of Liberation: Towards a Common View," in *Tensions in Contemporary Theology*, 2nd ed., ed. Stanley N. Gundry and Alan F. Johnson (Grand Rapids: Baker Book House, 1976), 400.

9. Ibid.

10. Phillips, "Liberation Theology," 19.

11. Rebecca S. Chopp, *The Praxis of Suffering* (Maryknoll, N.Y.: Orbis Books, 1986), 7.

12. Deane William Ferm, *Third World Liberation Theologies: An Introductory Survey* (Maryknoll, N.Y.: Orbis Books, 1986), 1.

13. Cindy Giesbrecht, "Liberation Theology in Latin America," (Paper prepared for Contemporary Theological Trends, Winnipeg Bible College, March 1991), 3.

14. Ferm, *Introductory Survey*, 5.

15. Robert McAfee Brown, *Theology in a New Key: Responding to Liberation Themes* (Philadelphia: Westminster Press, 1978), 72.

16. Leonardo Boff and Clodovis Boff, *Introducing Liberation Theology* (Maryknoll, N.Y.: Orbis Books, 1987), 67.

17. Quoted by J. Deotis Roberts, Sr., *A Black Political Theology* (Philadelphia: Westminster Press, 1974), 9.

18. Conn, "Theologies of Liberation," 334.

19. Jose Miranda, "Christianity is Communism," in *Third World Liberation Theologies—A Reader*, ed. Deane William Ferm (Maryknoll, N.Y.: Orbis Books, 1986), 160-61.

20. Ferm, *Introductory Survey*, 7.

21. Ibid.

22. Quoted by Ferm, *Introductory Survey,* 8.

23. Latin American Episcopal Council (CELAM), "Medellin Document on Peace," in Ferm, *A Reader,* 3.

24. Gustavo Gutierrez, *A Theology of Liberation,* rev. ed. (Maryknoll, N.Y.: Orbis Books, 1988), xxv.

25. "Medellin Document on Peace," 3.

26. Alvaro Barreiro, *Basic Ecclesial Communities: Evangelization of the Poor* (Maryknoll, N.Y.: Orbis Books, 1982), 67.

27. Gutierrez, *A Theology of Liberation,* 84.

28. Ibid., 6.

29. Ibid., 103.

30. Ibid.

31. Ibid., 97.

32. Jose Miguez-Bonino, "Violence: A Theological Reflection," in *Mission Trends No. 3: Third World Theologies,* eds. Gerald H. Anderson and Thomas F. Stransky (Grand Rapids: Wm. B. Eerdmans Pub. Co., 1976), 111.

33. Jose Miguez-Bonino, *Doing Theology in a Revolutionary Situation* (Philadelphia: Fortress Press, 1975), 114.

34. Ibid., 81.

35. Boff and Boff, *Introducing Liberation Theology,* 4.

36. Ibid.

37. Ibid., 50.

38. Ibid., 51.

39. Ibid., 52.

40. Brown, *Liberation Themes*, 110.

41. J. Deotis Roberts, Jr., *Liberation and Reconciliation: A Black Theology* (Philadelphia: Westminster Press, 1971), 16.

42. See Albert B. Cleage, *The Black Messiah* (New York: Sheed and Ward, 1968).

43. James H. Cone, "The Gospel and the Liberation of the Poor," in *Theologians in Transition*, ed. James M. Wall (New York: Crossroad Publishing, 1981), 189.

44. Roberts, *Liberation and Reconciliation*, 21.

45. Ibid.

46. James H. Cone, *A Black Theology of Liberation* (Philadelphia: J.B. Lippincott Co., 1970), 120.

47. Roberts, *Liberation and Reconciliation*, 193.

48. Ibid., 79.

49. James H. Cone, "Black Theology and Black Liberation," in *The Challenge of Black Theology in South Africa*, ed. Basil Moore (Atlanta: John Knox Press, 1974), 55.

50. Roberts, *Liberation and Reconciliation*, 88.

51. Cone, "Black Theology and Black Liberation," 54.

52. Roberts, *Liberation and Reconciliation*, 137.

53. James Cone, *Black Theology and Black Power* (New York: Seabury Press, 1969), 35.

54. Roberts, *Liberation and Reconciliation*, 157.

55. Cone, *Black Theology and Black Power*, 39.

56. Desmond M. Tutu, "Black Theology and African Theology: Soulmates or Antagonists?" in *A Reader in African Christian Theology*, ed. John Parrott (London: SPCK, 1987), 53.

57. Allan Boesak, "Black and Reformed: Contradiction or Challenge?" in Ferm, *A Reader*, 274.

58. John Pobee, "The Sources of African Theology," in Parrott, *African Christian Theology*, 34.

59. Sabelo Ntwase and Basil Moore, "The Concept of God in Black Theology," in Moore, *Black Theology in South Africa*, 27.

60. Kofi Appiah Kobi, "Christology," in Parrott, *African Christian Theology*, 96.

61. Mana Buthelezi, "Salvation as Wholeness," in Parrott, *African Christian Theology*, 96.

62. Ibid.

63. Ibid., 100-1.

64. Julius Nyerere, "The Church's Role in Society," in Parrott, *African Christian Theology*, 119.

65. Ibid., 120-21.

66. Jung Young Lee, "Minjung Theology: A Critical Introduction," in *An Emerging Theology in World Perspective*, ed. Jung Young Lee (Mystic, Conn.: Twenty-Third Publications, 1988), 4.

67. Yong Wha Na, "A Theological Assessment of Korean Minjung Theology," *Concordia Journal* 14 (April 1988): 138.

68. For a detailed account of this mission endeavor, see George

Ogle, "A Missionary's Reflection on Minjung Theology," in Lee, *An Emerging Theology*, 59-72.

69. Lee, *An Emerging Theology*, 7.

70. Ibid.

71. Yong Wha Na, "A Theological Assessment," 140.

72. John Cobb, Jr., "Minjung Theology and Process Theology," in Lee, *An Emerging Theology*, 56.

73. Yong Wha Na, "A Theological Assessment," 140.

74. Ibid., 141.

75. Lee, *An Emerging Theology*, 86.

76. Ibid., 18.

77. Yong Wha Na, "A Theological Assessment," 144.

78. Lee, *An Emerging Theology*, 12.

79. Ibid.

80. Ibid., 8.

81. Ibid., 10.

82. Ibid.

83. Boff and Boff, *Introducing Liberation Theology*, 3.

84. Harvie M. Conn, "Theologies of Liberation: Towards a Common View," in Gundry and Johnson, *Contemporary Theology*, 424.

85. Dave Breese, "Will We Succumb to 'Liberation Theology'?" *Confident Living*, May 1982, 2.

86. Gutierrez, *A Theology of Liberation*, 174.

Chapter 14: Third Wave Theology: The Vineyard Movement

1. Ken Sarles, "An Appraisal of the Signs and Wonders Movement," *Bibliotheca Sacra* 145 (Jan.–Mar. 1988): 57-58.

2. C. Peter Wagner, *The Third Wave of the Holy Spirit* (Ann Arbor, Mich.: Servant Publications, 1988), 23.

3. John Wimber and Kevin Springer, *Power Evangelism* (San Francisco: Harper and Row, 1986), xv-xvi.

4. John Wimber and Kevin Springer, *Power Healing* (San Francisco: Harper and Row, 1987), 23.

5. Ibid., 31.

6. Wimber, *Power Evangelism*, xxix-xxx.

7. John Wimber, "A Hunger for God: A Reflective Look at the Vineyard's Beginnings," *The Vineyard Newsletter* 2 (Fall 1987): 7.

8. Wagner, *Third Wave*, 27.

9. David A. Hubbard, foreword to *Ministry and the Miraculous,* ed. Lewis B. Smedes (Pasadena, Calif.: Fuller Theological Seminary, 1987), 15.

10. *The Vineyard Manual (1986),* quoted by James R. Coggins and Paul G. Hiebert, "The Man, the Message, and the Movement," in *Wonders and the Word,* ed. James R. Coggins and Paul G. Hiebert (Winnipeg: Kindred Press, 1989), 22.

11. Charles Kraft, *Christianity and Culture* (Maryknoll, N.Y.: Orbis Books, 1979), 53.

12. Paul G. Hiebert, "The Flaw of the Excluded Middle," *Missiology* 10 (January 1982): 35.

13. John Wimber, *Signs and Wonders, and Church Growth,* rev. ed. (Placentia, Calif.: Vineyard Ministries International, 1985), 3.7.

14. See George E. Ladd, *The Gospel of the Kingdom* (Grand Rapids: Wm. B. Eerdmans Pub. Co., 1959) and *A Theology of the New Testament* (Grand Rapids: Wm. B. Eerdmans Pub. Co., 1974).

15. Ladd, *Gospel of the Kingdom*, 42.

16. Wimber, *Signs and Wonders*, 2.7.

17. Ibid., 2.12.

18. Ibid., 2.16.

19. Wimber, *Power Evangelism*, 56.

20. John Wimber and Kevin Springer, *Power Points* (San Francisco: Harper and Row, 1991), 172-73.

21. Wimber, *Signs and Wonders*, 1.7.

22. Ibid., 1.9-10.

23. Ibid., 1.11.

24. Ibid., 2.15.

25. Tim Stafford, "Testing the Wine from John Wimber's Vineyard," *Christianity Today*, 8 August 1986, 20.

26. Wimber, *Power Evangelism*, 44.

27. Wimber, *Power Healing*, 164.

28. Ibid., 186.

29. Wagner, *The Third Wave*, 57.

30. Wimber and Springer, *Power Points*, 182.

31. Ibid.

32. Wimber, *Power Evangelism,* 73.

33. Philip Collins, "Tasting the Vineyard's New Wine" (Paper presented at the Baptist Union of Western Canada, Carey Hall Baptist College, Vancouver, 1986), 10.

34. Clark H. Pinnock, "A Revolutionary Promise," *Christianity Today,* 8 August 1986, 19.

35. Collins, "Tasting the Vineyard's New Wine," 9.

36. Ibid., 11.

37. Wimber, *Power Evangelism,* 36-37.

38. Ibid., 37-39.

39. Ibid., 32ff.

40. Donald Lewis, "John Wimber: Signs and Wonders," *Channels* (Fall 1986): 8ff, as quoted by Collins, "Tasting the Vineyard's New Wine," 8.

41. Wimber, *Signs and Wonders,* 2.14.

42. Ibid.

43. Wimber, *Power Evangelism,* 5-6.

44. Smedes, *Ministry and the Miraculous,* 26.

45. Pinnock, "A Revoluntary Promise," 19.

46. Donald Lewis, "Signs and Wonders (Assessing the Vineyard Movement)," *Mennonite Brethren Herald,* 19 September 1986, 4.

47. Wallace Benn and Mark Burkhill, "A Theological and Pastoral Critique of the Teachings of John Wimber," *Churchman* 101 (1987): 103.

48. Wimber, *Power Healing,* 157.

49. Ibid.

50. Ibid., 159.

51. Wimber, *Signs and Wonders,* 5.11.

52. John 5:2ff notes that when Jesus visited the pool of Bethesda, there were many sick, but He approached only one individual.

53. Collins, "Tasting the Vineyard's New Wine," 14.

54. Ben Patterson, "Cause for Concern," *Christianity Today,* 8 August 1986, 20.

Chapter 15: Feminist Theology
1. Pope John XXIII, *Pacem in Terris,* Encyclical of 11 April 1963, no. 41 quoted by Mary Daly, *The Church and the Second Sex* (New York: Harper and Row, 1975), 118.

2. Ibid.

3. "Pastoral Constitution on the Church in the Modern World," in *The Documents on Vatican II,* ed. Walter M. Abbott (Piscataway, N.J.: New Century Publishers, 1966), 207.

4. Ibid., 228.

5. "Decree on the Apostolate of the Laity," *The Documents of Vatican II,* 500.

6. Daly, *The Second Sex,* 126.

7. *The Encyclopedia Americana,* 1985, s.v. "Women's Rights Movement."

8. Betty Friedan, *The Second Stage* (New York: Summit Books, 1981), 47.

9. Barbara Deckard, *The Women's Movement* (New York: Harper and Row, 1975), 426.

10. Ibid., 428.

11. Elaine Storkey, *What's Right with Feminism?* (Grand Rapids: Wm. B. Eerdmans Pub. Co., 1985), 69.

12. Deckard, *The Women's Movement*, 429.

13. Ibid., 415.

14. Ibid.

15. Sheila Rowbotham, *Women's Consciousness in Man's World* (Penguin, 1974), 59 as quoted by Storkey, *What's Right*, 79.

16. Storkey, *What's Right*, 93.

17. Germaine Greer, *The Female Eunuch* (New York: Bantam Books, 1972), 249-51.

18. Deckard, *The Women's Movement*, 420.

19. Storkey, *What's Right*, 107.

20. Ibid.

21. Rosemary Ruether, "Feminist Theology in the Academy," *Christianity and Crisis*, 4 March 1985, 58.

22. Mary Ann Tolbert, "Defining the Problem: The Bible and Feminist Hermeneutics," *The Bible and Hermeneutics, Semeia 28*, ed. Mary Ann Tolbert (Chico, Calif.: Scholars Press, 1983), 122.

23. Ibid.

24. Ibid.

25. See Phyllis Trible, *God and the Rhetoric of Sexuality* (Philadelphia: Fortress Press, 1978), 72-143.

26. Tolbert, *Semeia 28,* 123.

27. Ruether, "Feminist Theology," 61.

28. Virginia Ramey Mollenkott, "Unlimiting God," *The Other Side,* November 1983, 11.

29. Ibid., 12.

30. Ibid.

31. Ibid., 13.

32. Letty M. Russell, "Human Liberation in a Feminist Perspective—A Theology," in *Contemporary American Theologies II, A Book of Readings,* ed. Dean William Ferm (New York: Seabury Press, 1982), 185.

33. Patricia Wilson-Kastner, *Faith, Feminism, and the Christ* (Philadelphia: Fortress Press, 1983), 31.

34. Ibid., 32.

35. Letty M. Russell, *The Future of Partnership* (Philadelphia: Westminster Press, 1979), 61.

36. Wilson-Kastner, *Feminism and the Christ,* 102.

37. Roger L. Omanson, "The Role of Women in the New Testament Church," *Review and Expositor* 83 (Winter 1986): 15-16.

38. Ann Loades, *Searching for the Lost Coin: Explorations in Christianity and Feminism* (Allison Park, Pa.: Pickwick Publications, 1987), 91.

39. Wilson-Kastner, *Feminism and the Christ,* 55-56.

40. Ibid., 60.

41. Dorothee Soelle, *Choosing Life* (London: SCM Press, 1981), 39-40.

42. Storkey, *What's Right*, 47.

43. Molly Marshall-Green, " 'When Keeping Silent No Longer Will Do': A Theological Agenda for the Contemporary Church," *Review and Expositor* 83 (Winter 1986): 30.

44. Daly, *The Second Sex*, 180.

45. Sheila Collins, "A Different Heaven and Earth," in Ferm, *Contemporary American Theologies II*, 197.

46. Carol P. Christ, "Why Women Need a Goddess," in *Womanspirit Rising*, ed. Carol Christ and Judith Plaskow (New York: Harper and Row, 1979), 278.

47. Starhawk (Miriam Simos), *The Spiral Dance* (New York: Harper and Row, 1979), 9.

48. Christy Revere, "The Gentle Craft of Wicca," *The New Age Connection* 4 (Spring 1991): 1.

49. Letha Scanzoni and Nancy Hardesty, *All We're Meant to Be* (Waco, Texas: Word, Inc., 1975), 205.

50. Ibid.

51. Ibid., 207.

52. Russell, "Human Liberation," 187.

Chapter 16: Reconstructionist (Dominion) Theology
1. Gary DeMar, *The Debate over Christian Reconstruction* (Fort Worth, Texas: Dominion Press, 1988), 59.

2. Randy Frame, "The Theonomic Urge," *Christianity Today* 21 April 1989, 38.

3. Gary DeMar and Peter Leithard, *The Reduction of Christianity: A Biblical Response to Dave Hunt* (Ft. Worth, Texas: Dominion Press, 1988), 24.

4. Ibid.

5. Anson Shupe, "The Reconstructionist Movement on the New Christian Right," *Christian Century* 106, (1989): 880.

6. Gary North, "Cutting Edge or Lunatic Fringe," *Christian Reconstruction,* 11 (January-February 1987): 1 quoted by Thomas D. Ice, "An Evaluation of Theonomic Postmillennialism," *Bibliotheca Sacra* 145 (July-September 1988): 282.

7. Ibid.

8. Hal Lindsay, *The Road to Holocaust* (New York: Bantam Books, 1989), 32.

9. Ice, "Theonomic Postmillenialism," 283.

10. "The Right: A House Divided?" *Newsweek,* 2 February 1981, 60 as cited by Ice, "Theonomic Postmillenialism," 283.

11. Lindsay, *Holocaust,* 33.

12. Ibid.

13. Ice, "Theonomic Postmillenialism," 283.

14. Shupe, "The Reconstructionist Movement," 881.

15. H. Wayne House and Thomas Ice, *Dominion Theology: Blessing or Curse?* (Portland, Ore.: Multnomah Press, 1988), 32-33.

16. Ibid., 33.

17. Ibid.

18. Ibid.

19. Ibid.

20. DeMar, *The Debate,* 62.

21. Ibid., 63.

22. Ibid.

23. Rousas J. Rushdoony, *The Institutes of Biblical Law* (Phillipsburg, N.J.: Presbyterian and Reformed Publishing, 1973), 113.

24. David Chilton, *Paradise Restored, A Biblical Theology of Dominion* (Fort Worth, Texas: Dominion Press, 1985), 23.

25. Ibid., 24-25.

26. DeMar, *The Debate,* 65.

27. Greg L. Bahnsen, *Theonomy as Christian Ethics* (Nutley, N.J.: Craig Press, 1979), 34.

28. As quoted by John Frame, *"The Institutes of Biblical Law:* A Review," *Westminster Theological Journal,* 30 (Winter 1976): 201.

29. See DeMar, *The Debate,* 65.

30. Ibid., 66.

31. Chilton, *Paradise Restored,* 219.

32. Shupe, "The Reconstructionist Movement," 881.

33. Chilton, *Paradise Restored,* 70-76.

34. DeMar and Leithard, *The Reduction of Christianity,* 192-93.

35. Ibid., 71.

36. Ibid., 74.

37. DeMar and Leithart, *The Reduction of Christianity*, 205.

38. Gary North, *Millennialism and Social Theory* (Tyler, Texas: Institute for Christian Economics, 1990), 24.

39. Chilton, *Paradise Restored*, 18.

40. Ibid.

41. Ibid.

42. Ibid.

43. North, *Social Theory*, 21.

44. House and Ice, *Blessing or Curse?*, 78.

45. DeMar and Leithart, *The Reduction of Christianity*, 323.

46. House and Ice, *Blessing or Curse?*, 79.

47. As quoted by Frame, "The Theonomic Urge," 40.

48. DeMar and Leithart, *The Reduction of Christianity*, 333.

Chapter 17: The New Age Movement

1. See Elliot Miller, *A Crash Course on the New Age Movement* (Grand Rapids: Baker Book House, 1989), 13.

2. Jessica Lipnack and Jeffrey Stamps, *Networking* (Garden City, N.Y.: Doubleday Co., 1982), 7 as cited by Miller, *A Crash Course*, 14.

3. Erwin W. Lutzer and John F. DeVries, *Satan's Evangelistic Strategy for This New Age* (Wheaton, Ill.: Victor Books, 1989), 15.

4. Douglas R. Groothuis, *Understanding the New Age* (Downers Grove, Ill.: InterVarsity Press, 1986), 32.

5. For a more extensive consideration, see chapter 5.

6. Groothuis, *Understanding the New Age,* 40.

7. Jerry Rubin, *Growing (Up) at Thirty-Seven* (New York: M. Evans & Co., Inc. 1976), 199.

8. Lutzer and DeVries, *Satan's Evangelistic Strategy,* 9.

9. Lancelot L. Whyte, *The Universe of Experience* (New York: Harper and Row, 1974), 6.

10. As quoted by Lutzer and DeVries, *Satan's Evangelistic Strategy,* 17.

11. Miller, *A Crash Course,* 17.

12. Ibid., 207.

13. Lutzer and DeVries, *Satan's Evangelistic Strategy,* 20.

14. See physicist Fritjof Capra, *The Turning Point* (Toronto: Bantam Books, 1982), 78.

15. Miller, *A Crash Course,* 50.

16. Anna Olsen, "Pyramids through the Ages," *The New Age Connection* 2 (Spring 1989): 1.

17. Ibid.

18. For a detailed examination of Fox, see chapter 18.

19. Lola Davis, *Towards a World Religion for the New Age* (Farmingdale, N.Y.: Coleman Publishing Inc., 1983), 25.

20. Jon Klimo, *Channeling* (Los Angeles: Jeremy P. Tarcher, 1987), 185.

21. As quoted by Ruth A. Tucker, *Another Gospel: Alternative Religions and the New Age Movement* (Grand Rapids: Zondervan Publishing House, 1989), 328.

22. Patricia Armstrong, "The Making of a Shaman," *The New Age Connection* 4 (Winter 1990/91): 6.

23. Ruth Tucker, *Another Gospel,* 343-44.

24. Jane Roberts, *The Seth Material* (Englewood Cliffs, N.J.: Prentice-Hall, 1970), 237-38.

25. Margot Adler, *Drawing Down the Moon: Witches, Druids, Goddess Worshippers, and Other Pagans in America Today* (Boston: Beacon Press, 1979), v.

26. Benjamin Creme, *The Reappearance of the Christ and the Masters of Wisdom* (London: Tara Press, 1980), 10.

27. John White, "A Course in Miracles: Spiritual Wisdom for the New Age," *Science of Mind,* March 1986, 80.

28. James M. Robinson, ed., "The Gospel of Thomas (II, 2)," *The Nag Hammadi Library* (San Francisco: Harper and Row, 1981), 129.

29. See Levi, *The Aquarian Gospel of Jesus the Christ* (Santa Monica, Calif.: DeVorss, 1907).

30. Ibid., 14.

31. Ibid., 265.

32. As quoted by Lutzer and DeVries, *Satan's Evangelistic Strategy,* 93.

33. Ibid., 62.

34. David Spangler, *Reflections on the Christ* (Moray, United Kingdom: Findhorn, 1981), 7.

35. Ibid., 44.

36. As quoted by Tucker, *Another Gospel*, 342.

37. Emmett Fox, *Diagrams for Living: The Bible Unveiled* (New York: Harper and Row, 1968), 158-59.

38. Helen Shucman, *A Course in Miracles* (New York: Foundation for Inner Peace, 1975), 30.

39. Tucker, *Another Gospel*, 336-37.

40. See Dave Hunt and T.A. McMahon, *The Seduction of Christianity* (Eugene, Ore.: Harvest House, 1985). Cf. Walter Martin, *The New Age Cult* (Minneapolis: Bethany House, 1989), 74-79 and Miller, *A Crash Course*, 187-89.

41. See Constance Cumbey, *The Hidden Dangers of the Rainbow* (Shreveport, La.: Huntington House, 1983) and Texe Marrs, *Dark Secrets of the New Age* (Westchester, Ill.: Crossway Books, 1987).

42. Mark Satin, *New Age Politics* (New York: Dell, 1979), 142.

43. Martin, *The New Age Cult*, 70.

Chapter 18: Creation Spirituality
1. As quoted by Ted Peters, "Matthew Fox and the Vatican Wolves," *Dialog* 28 (Spring 1989): 139.

2. Ibid.

3. Ibid., 140.

4. Wayne G. Boulton, "The Thoroughly Modern Mysticism of Matthew Fox," *The Christian Century* 107 (1990): 428.

5. Ibid.

6. Matthew Fox, *The Coming of the Cosmic Christ* (San Francisco: Harper and Row, 1988), 78.

7. Matthew Fox, *Creation Spirituality* (San Francisco: Harper and Row, 1991), 14.

8. Ibid.

9. Ibid., 14-15.

10. Ibid., 15.

11. Ibid., 16.

12. Ibid., 16-17.

13. Matthew Fox, *Whee! We, Wee All the Way Home* (Santa Fe, N.M.: Bear Publications, 1981), 76.

14. Fox, *Creation Spirituality*, 19.

15. Ibid.

16. Ibid.

17. Ibid.

18. Ibid., 18.

19. Ibid.

20. Philip Harden, "Matthew Fox, Playful Prophet of Creation Spirituality" (an interview), *The Other Side*, May 1987, 14.

21. Fox *Creation Spirituality*, 21.

22. Matthew Fox, *Original Blessing: A Primer in Creation Spirituality* (Santa Fe, N.M.: Bear Publications, 1983), 251.

23. Ibid.

24. Fox, *Creation Spirituality,* 22.

25. Ibid., 23.

26. See Robert Brown, "The Taming of a New Age Prophet," *Christianity Today,* 16 June 1989, 28; Elliot Miller, *A Crash Course in the New Age Movement* (Grand Rapids: Baker Book House, 1989), 188.

27. See Harden, "Matthew Fox, Playful Prophet," 16.

28. Ibid., 17.

29. Matthew Fox, *The Coming of the Cosmic Christ* (New York: Harper and Row, 1988), 69.

30. Fox, *Whee! We, Wee,* 89-90.

31. Fox, *Creation Spirituality,* 55.

32. Ibid.

33. Ibid.

34. Ibid, 62.

35. Ibid., 107.

36. Fox, *Original Blessing,* 242.

37. Harden, "Matthew Fox, Playful Prophet," 15.

38. Boulton, "The Thoroughly Modern Mysticism," 429.

39. Fox, *Original Blessing,* 50.

40. Harnden, "Matthew Fox, Playful Prophet," 13.

41. Fox, *Whee!, We, Wee,* 37.

42. Matthew Fox, *On Becoming a Musical, Mystical Bear* (New York: Paulist Press, 1972), 136-37.

43. Fox *Whee! We, Wee,* 107.

44. Ibid., 90.

45. Fox, *Original Blessing,* 40.

46. Harden, "Matthew Fox, Playful Prophet," 15.

47. Ibid.

48. Fox, *Original Blessing,* 225-26.

49. Fox, *Whee! We, Wee,* 31.

50. Ibid., 229.

51. Ibid., 240.

52. Ibid.

53. Matthew Fox, *Manifesto for a Global Civilization* (Santa Fe, N.M.: Bear Publishing, n.d.), 45 as quoted by Texe Marrs, *Dark Secrets of the New Age* (Westchester, Ill.: Crossway Books, 1987), 42.

54. Fox, *The Cosmic Christ,* 70.

55. Ibid., 71.

56. Ibid., 72-73.

57. Fox, *Creation Spirituality,* 105.

58. Boulton, "The Thoroughly Modern Mysticism," 432.

59. Ibid., 431.

60. Ibid.

61. See Peters, "Matthew Fox," 141.

Appendix: Some Third-World Theological Directions
1. Theological Education Fund (TEF), *Ministry in Context: The Third Mandate Programme of the TEF, 1970-77* (London: TEF, 1972), 19 as quoted by Douglas J. Elwood, "Asian Christian Theology in the Making: An Introduction," in *Asian Christian Theology: Emerging Themes* (Philadelphia: Westminster Press, 1980), 26.

2. John H. Connor, "When Culture Leaves Contextualized Christianity Behind," *Missiology: An International Review* 19 (January 1991): 21.

3. Ibid., 23.

4. Ibid., 27.

5. Kosuke Koyama, *Waterbuffalo Theology* (London: SCM Press, 1974), 30.

6. Ibid.

7. Ibid., 41.

8. Ibid., 82.

9. Kosuke Koyama, *No Handle on the Cross: An Asian Meditation on the Crucified Mind* (Maryknoll, N.Y.: Orbis Books, 1977), 100.

10. Kosuke Koyama, "Three Mile an Hour God," in Elwood, *Asian Christian Theology,* 126.

11. Ibid.

12. Koyama, *No Handle on the Cross,* 100.

13. Jung Young Lee, "The Yin-Yang Way of Thinking," in Elwood, *Asian Christian Theology*, 52.

14. Ibid.

15. Ibid.

16. Ibid., 82-83.

17. Ibid., 83.

18. Ibid.

19. Ibid., 85.

20. Ibid.

21. Ibid., 87.

22. Ibid.

23. Ibid.

24. Ibid., 88.

25. Tite Tienou, "Indigenous African Christian Theologies: The Uphill Road," *International Bulletin of Missionary Research* 14 (April 1990): 74.

26. Bonita Friesen, "Third World Theology—Africa" (Paper prepared for Contemporary Theological Trends, Winnipeg Bible College, April 1991), 3.

27. Mercy Oduyoye, *Hearing and Knowing: Theological Reflections on Christianity in Africa* (Maryknoll, N.Y.: Orbis Books, 1986), 5.

28. Tienou, "The Uphill Road," 74.

29. Ibid.

30. John S. Mbiti, as quoted by Richard Henry Drummond, *Toward a New Age in Christian Theology* (Maryknoll, N.Y.: Orbis Books, 1985), 174.

31. Ibid., 175.

32. Ibid.

33. Ibid.

34. E. Bolaji Idowu, *African Traditional Religion: A Definition* (London: SCM Press, 1973), xi.

35. E. Bolaji Idowu, *Odulamare: God in Yoruba Belief* (London: Longmans, 1962), 31.

36. Byang H. Kato, *Theological Pitfalls in Africa* (Nairobi, Kenya: Evangel Publishing, 1987), 49.

37. Ibid., 99.

38. Cf. Paul Tillich, *Systematic Theology* (Chicago: Univ. of Chicago Press, 1951) 1:108ff; D.M. Baille, *God Was in Christ* (New York: Chas. Scribner's Sons, 1948), 108ff.

39. Idowu, *African Traditional Religion*, 56.

40. Ibid., 57.

41. Cf. Rudolph Otto, *The Idea of the Holy*, trans. John W. Harvey (London: Oxford Univ. Press, 1950), 54ff; Mircea Eliade, *The Sacred and the Profane*, trans. W.R. Trask (New York: Harcourt, Brace and World, 1959), 9ff.

42. Ibid., 104.

43. Ibid., 125.

44. Kato, *Theological Pitfalls*, 113.

45. Drummond, *Towards a New Age in Christian Theology,* 177-79.

46. Tienou, "The Uphill Road," 75.

General Index

A

Abyss, God as   *78, 79*
African National Congress   *216*
American Baptist Association   *16*
American Council of Christian
   Churches   *17–18, 59*
Anglican Church   *122*
Anti-evolution League   *11*
Amillennialism   *68, 267, 270*
Annihilationism   *68*
"Anonymous" Christianity   *93,
   94, 209, 220*
Anthropology   *32, 53–53, 67–68,
   79, 97–98, 111, 146–47, 160, 170,
   251–52, 284–85, 300-301*
Apostolic Church of
   Pentecost   *51*
Apostolic Faith Mission   *47*
Arminians, Arminianism   *14, 52,
   127*
Assemblies of God   *45, 49, 55*
Asuza Street Mission   *43–44, 46*
Atheism, "Christian"   *135*

B

Baha'i   *263*
Baptism   *1, 16, 51, 63, 97, 112*
Baptism, Spirit   *41–43, 44–49,
   51–52, 120, 121, 122, 123, 125,
   127, 129*
Baptists   *12–16, 18–19, 44, 52,
   117, 192*
Being-Itself   *78, 79*
Bible:
   Inerrancy of   *12, 18, 22–23,
      37, 62, 63–65, 73, 109, 127,
      321n., 327n.*

Inspiration of   *11, 39, 155, 259*
Bible Baptist Fellowship   *18–19*
Bible schools   *14–15*
Bible Crusaders of America   *12*
Black power   *212*
Brandon College   *14*
Buddhism   *100, 170, 263, 276, 277,
   307, 308*

C

Calvinism, Calvinists   *14, 65, 115,
   127, 182*
Catholicism, charismatic   *120,
   123–25, 126-27*
Chalcedon, Definition of   *92, 176*
Channelers   *281–82, 284*
Christ:
   Atonement of   *11, 22, 23–24,
      28–29, 34, 38, 82, 110–11,
      195–96, 224, 250, 285, 287,
      307–08*
   Death of   *18, 34, 38, 74, 82, 100,
      111, 145, 158, 159, 169, 285,
      299, 308*
   Deity of   *11, 22–23, 28, 32, 75,
      80, 95, 145, 170–71, 177, 310*
   Humanity of   *32, 157, 158, 172,
      177*
   Incarnation of   *31–32, 74, 75,
      110 145, 147–48, 157–58, 169,
      171, 174, 310*
   Resurrection of   *18, 22, 24, 30,
      34, 36, 38, 40, 77, 145–46,
      159–60, 299*
   Return of   *18, 22–23, 30, 32, 73,
      177*
   Virgin birth of   *11–12, 18,
      22–23, 30, 32, 73, 177*

O

Omega Point   *81, 276*
Orthodox Presbyterian
   Church   *12*
Other, God as   *28, 37, 78, 97, 157,
   171*

P

Pacific Apostolic Faith
   Movement   *43*
Panentheism   *75, 82, 154, 162,
   174, 224, 298, 302, 304*
Pantheism   *98, 157, 221, 254, 277,
   282, 284*
Penance   *112*
Pentecostal Assemblies of
   Canada   *45–46, 53*
Pentecostal Assemblies of the
   World   *51*
Pentecostal Free-Will
   Baptists   *44*
Positive Confession   *198–99*
Postmillennialism   *24, 54, 68, 260,
   264, 266–67, 270*
Premillennialism   *14, 17, 24, 25,
   54, 68, 267, 270*
Pride   *33–34, 38*
Presbyterian Church   *11–12, 60,
   125*

R

Radio, Christian   *17, 19*
Reformed Church   *180*
Regeneration   *20, 51, 80, 264–65*
Reincarnationalism   *277*
Relativism   *277, 278*
Revelation   *29, 31–32, 34, 36–37,
   51, 64, 88–89, 93, 100, 108–9,
   128, 139, 141, 144–45, 155, 268,*

281–82, 287, 314
Roman Catholic Church   *69, 104,
   117*

S

Satan   *285, 288*
Salvation   *30, 38, 51, 74, 90, 92–93,
   94, 96, 100, 110–13, 145–47,
   158–59, 184, 214, 217, 222, 224,
   250–51, 264–65, 284–85, 287–88,
   290*
Sanctification   *41, 51, 52, 80*
Scofield Reference Bible   *14*
Secondary separation   *20*
Security (of the believer)   *14*
Sin   *32, 33–34, 38, 52–53, 79, 112,
   146, 160, 182–83, 209, 284–85,
   287–88, 299–300*
Spiritual warfare   *54, 129, 233–34*

T

Theocracy   *265–66, 269, 271*
Theology:
   African   *215–18*
   Black   *213–15*
   Crisis   *27, 30–31*
   Dialectical   *27*
   God-is-dead   *78, 83, 135, 144,
      147, 151, 169–73*
   Minjung   *218–22*
   Missionary   *21*
   Natural   *28, 85*
   Post-liberal   *82–84*
   Prosperity   *188–200*
   Realistic   *33–35*
   Revisionist   *83–84*
   Secularization of   *167–69*
   Self-esteem   *179–88, 200–01*
   Waterbuffalo   *307–8, 311*
   Yin-yang   *308–10, 311*

Name Index

C

Caddy, Eileen 280
Caddy, Peter 280
Callahan, Daniel 178
Calvin, John 183, 238, 241, 269
Campbell, James 116
Campbell, Joseph 280
Capra, Fritjof 278
Carmichael, Stokely 212
Carnell, Edward J. 60, 66, 70
Carr, Burgess 316
Carradine, David 276
Cashwell, G.B. 44
Castro, Emilio 207
Castro, Fidel 206
Cayce, Edgar 275–76
Chawner, Charles 47
Chilton, David 262, 264, 267-68, 271
Chop, Paul Y. 49, 197
Christ, Carol 254, 257
Christenson, Larry 121–22, 131
Chrysostom, John 104, 111
Clark, Gordon 60
Cleage, Albert B. 212
Clouse, Robert 68
Cobb, John 151, 154, 163
Coe, Jack 117
Coffin, Henry S. 72
Coggins, James R. 240
Cole, Stewart G. 26
Coleman, Richard J. 70
Cole-Whittaker, Terry 280
Collins, A.P. 45
Collins, Phillip 235
Cone, James 212–15, 226
Conn, Charles W. 56
Conn, Harvie 7
Constantelon, Demetrios J. 116
Constantine 103
Copeland, Gloria 197, 202
Copeland, Kenneth 189, 193, 195, 198, 202
Cousins, Ewart 163
Cox, Harvey 165, 168–69, 174–76, 178
Crawford, Florence 43
Creme, Benjamin 280, 283, 286, 290
Cross, Lawrence 116
Cullis, Charles 189

D

Davis, Lola 281
Deckard, Barbara 245, 257
DeHaan, M.R. 17
DeMar, Gary 259, 262, 267, 271–72
Descartes, René 166
DeVries, John 277, 291
DeWolfe, Harold 86
Dixon, A.C. 26
Dixon, Jean 282
Dixon, Kwesi 317
Dowell, W.E. 18
Dowie, John 47, 189
Dowling, Eva 284
Dumas, Andre 40
du Plessis, David 47, 118–19, 122–23, 126
Durasoff, Steve 56
Durham, William 44

E

Eckhart, Meister 293, 295–96, 298
Eddy, Mary Baker 190, 200
Edwards, Jonathan 62, 238
Elwood, Douglas J. 317
Ellul, Jacques 63
Erhard, Werner 284

McDaniel, George *13*
McGavran, Donald *227*
McGee, Gary B. *56*
McIntire, Carl *17–18, 59*
McMahon, T.A. *194*
McPherson, Aimee S. *49, 54, 57, 190*
Maximus Confessor *112*
Mechtild of Megdeburg *295*
Mechta, Ved *178*
Meland, Bernard *151, 155, 163*
Merton, Thomas *292*
Metropolitan Platon *107*
Metz, Johannes Baptist *136, 142–44, 147–48*
Miguez-Bonino, Jose *207, 209–10, 226*
Mill, John Stuart *242*
Miller, Elliot *291*
Moberg, David O. *71*
Mohammed II *104*
Moltmann, Jurgen *136–40, 144–47, 149, 210*
Montgomery, Carrie *189*
Moody, Dwight L. *15*
Moon Hee-suk Cyris *222*
Moore, Basil *216, 226, 317*
Morgan, G. Campbell *11*
Morris, Henry *66*
Muller, Richard *280*
Mullins, Edgar Y. *11, 13*
Mwolaka, Christian *316*

N

Nash, Ronald H. *71*
Neuhaus, Richard J. *270*
Nichol, John T. *57*
Nicholas of Cusa *295*
Neibuhr, Reinhold *33–35, 40*
Nietzsche, Friedrich *169*
Newbiggin, Leslie *178*

Norris, J. Frank *12*
North, Gary *260–62, 267, 272*
Ntwase, Sabelo *216*
Nyerere, Julius *218*

O

Ockenga, Harold *58*
Oduyoye, Mercy *312, 317*
Ogden, Schubert *83, 86, 151, 155–57, 164*
Olga, Princess *104*
Opperman, Daniel *45*
Origen *103*
Orr, James *11*
Osborne, T.L. *117, 190*
Osteen, John *179, 193*
Otto, Rudolf *315*
Owen, John *62, 242*
Ozman, Agnes *41*

P

Paine, Stephen *58*
Pannenburg, Wolfhart *136, 139–42, 144–47, 149*
Pannikar, Raimundo *97, 99–100, 102*
Parham, Charles *41–43, 189*
Park, Chung-Kee *219*
Parrott, John *226*
Peale, Norman V. *180–81, 201*
Peter of Moghila *109*
Peter the Great *106*
Petrus, Lewi *52*
Photius *104, 113*
Pierard, Richard V. *71*
Pinnock, Clark *83, 234, 237*
Pinson, Mark *45*
Pittenger, Norman *151, 155, 164*
Plaskow, Judith *257*
Polman, Gerritt *46*